That All May Be One

Hierarchy and Participation in the Church

Terence L. Nichols

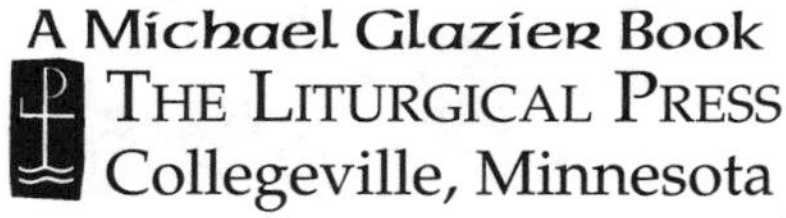

Cover design by David Manahan, O.S.B.

A Michael Glazier Book published by The Liturgical Press

1 2 3 4 5 6 7 8

Library of Congress Cataloging-in-Publication Data

Nichols, Terence L., 1941–
That all may be one : hierarchy and participation in the Church / Terence L. Nichols.
p. cm.
"A Michael Glazier book."
Includes bibliographical references and index.
ISBN 0-8146-5857-1
1. Catholic Church—Government—Controversial literature.
2. Laity—Catholic Church. I. Title.
BX1802.N47 1997
262'.02—dc21 97-21588
CIP

For Mabel

Contents

Abbreviations

ABD	*The Anchor Bible Dictionary.*
ACO	*Acta Conciliorum Oecumenicorum,* ed. by E. Schwartz (Berlin, 1928–1938).
ACW	*Ancient Christian Writers Series*
AG	Decree on the Church's Missionary Activity (Vatican Council II). ET from Walter Abbott, ed., *The Documents of Vatican II* (New York: Guild Press, 1966).
AMJ	John Meier, *A Marginal Jew: Rethinking the Historical Jesus* (New York: Doubleday, vol. 1: 1991, vol 2: 1994).
CD	Decree on the Bishops' Pastoral Office in the Church (Vatican Council II).
DS	*Enchiridion symbolorum,* ed. by H. Denzinger, Adolfus Schönmetzer, 36th ed.
DTC	*Dictionairre de théologie catholique,* ed. by A. Vacant, E. Mangenot, and É Amann, 15 vols. (Paris, 1930).
DV	*Dei Verbum,* Dogmatic Constitution on Divine Revelation (Vatican Council II).
ET	English Translation.
HE	Eusebius, Bishop of Caesurea, *The History of the Church (Historia Ecclesiae).* ET by George Williamson (Minneapolis: Augsburg, 1965).
HC:II	*The Imperial Church from Constantine to the Early Middle Ages,* ed. by Karl Baus, Hans-Georg Beck, Eugen Ewig, and Hermann Josef Vogt, vol. 2 of *History of the Church,* ed. by Hubert Jedin and John Dolan (New York: Crossroad, 1980).
HCH:IV	*Handbook of Church History,* vol. IV: *From the High Middle Ages to the Eve of the Reformation,* by Hans Georg Beck, Karl August Fink, et al. (Montreal: Palm Publishers, 1970).

HC:V — *History of the Church,* vol. V: *Reformation and Counter Reformation.* Erwin Iserloh, Joseph Glazik, and Hubert Jedin, eds. (New York: Crossroad, 1990).

L'Église — Yves Congar, *L'Église de Saint Augustin à l'époque moderne* (Paris: Cerf, 1970).

LG — *Lumen gentium,* the Dogmatic Constitution on the Church (Vatican Council II).

LW — *Luther's Works,* American Edition. J. Pelikan and H. Lehmann, eds. (Philadelphia and St. Louis, 1955–).

Mansi — G.D. Mansi, *Sacrorum Conciliorum Nova et Amplissima Collectio* (Florence, 1759–1763).

NCE — *New Catholic Encyclopedia* (New York: McGraw Hill, 1967).

NJBC — *New Jerome Biblical Commentary,* Raymond E. Brown, S.S., Joseph A. Fitzmyer, S.J., Roland E. Murphy, O. Carm., eds. (Englewood Cliffs, N.J.: Prentice Hall, 1990).

NPNF2 — *Nicene and Post Nicene Fathers, Second Series.* Philip Schaff and Henry Wace, eds. (New York: Charles Scribner's Sons, 1904–).

NRSV — *New Revised Standard Version,* 1990.

PPATUC — *Papal Primacy and the Universal Church.* ed. by Paul C. Empie and T. Austin Murphy, Lutherans and Catholics in Dialogue, vol. 5. (Minneapolis: Augsburg, 1974).

PL — J.P. Migne, ed., *Patrologiae latinae cursus completus* (Paris, 1844–1866).

RSV — *Revised Standard Version,* 1971.

SCG — Thomas Aquinas, *Summa Contra Gentiles.* Anton C. Pegis, trans. (Notre Dame, Ind.: University of Notre Dame Press, 1975, 1955).

ST — Thomas Aquinas, *Summa Theologiae* (New York: Blackfriars, McGraw Hill, 1964–).

Tanner — Norman Tanner, S.J., ed. *Decrees of the Ecumenical Councils,* 2 vols. (London: Sheed and Ward; Washington D.C.: Georgetown University Press, 1990).

UD — Decree on Ecumenism (Vatican Council II).

Chapter 1

Introduction

I ask not only on behalf of these, but also on behalf of those who will believe in me through their word, that they may all be one. As you, Father, are in me and I in you, may they also be in us, so that the world may believe that you have sent me. (John 17:20-21)

Christ is the light of all nations. . . . By her relationship with Christ, the Church is a kind of sacrament or sign of intimate unity with God, and of the unity of all mankind. She is also an instrument for the achievement of such union and unity. (*LG* #1)

In the opening lines of the Decree on Ecumenism, the bishops of Vatican Council II declare that the restoration of unity among Christians is one of the chief concerns of the Council. The discord among Christians, the document continues, "openly contradicts the will of Christ, provides a stumbling block (L. *scandalo*) to the world, and inflicts damage on the most holy cause of proclaiming the good news to every creature" (*UD* #1). The Vatican II documents also indicate, both in the Decree on Ecumenism and elsewhere, that the visible source of unity in the Church[1] is the sacramental hierarchy of bishops

[1] The term "Church" in the Vatican II documents means the whole Church of Christ. This Church "subsists" in the Roman Catholic Church (*LG* #8), but exists in other Christian denominations as well. The use of "Church" in this book means the whole Christian Church, which would include those who are baptized, accept the Nicene-Constantinopolitan creed, and the definitions of the first seven ecumenical councils.

and the pope. *Lumen gentium,* the Dogmatic Constitution on the Church, states that "The Roman Pontiff, as the successor of Peter, is the perpetual and visible source and foundation of unity of the bishops and of the multitude of the faithful. The individual bishop, however, is the visible principle and foundation of unity in his particular church" (*LG* #23). Since the council elsewhere states that the invisible cause of Christian unity is the Holy Spirit, it also claims that the office of bishop, including the pope, is a charism of the Spirit, whose purpose is to preserve unity.

Yet any careful reading of Christian history will show that disputes over the nature of ecclesial hierarchy have been one of the chief causes of the fragmentation of the Church, especially of the Orthodox and Protestant schisms. And this remains true: the Catholic doctrine of the infallibility of the pope, pronounced at Vatican I, remains a huge stumbling block to ecumenical unity. Pope Paul VI himself said "The Pope, as we well know, is undoubtedly the greatest obstacle in the path of ecumenism."[2] Catholics have claimed since the third century that the words of Jesus to Peter, (Matt 16:18) "And I tell you, you are Peter, and on this rock I will build my church . . ." apply also to the papacy as a rock of unity and preservation of doctrine. Yet only five verses later (Matt 16:23) Jesus rebukes Peter with the words: "Get behind me, Satan! You are a stumbling block (Greek: *skandalon*) to me; for you are setting your mind not on divine things but on human things." Though Catholics have never applied this verse to the papacy, the Orthodox have: since 1204 they have seen the monarchial and imperialist claims of the papacy as the *skandalon* which impedes the reunion of the churches.

The problem of hierarchy is also causing grave divisions within Catholicism itself. For many, "hierarchy" is tantamount to domination, and should be eliminated for a more democratic church. Others, especially in Rome, are moving towards a more centralized and command style of hierarchy. This division is causing severe polarization in the Catholic Church.

Finally, it is obvious to many that the Roman Catholic Church is in a period of severe crisis. Vocations to religious orders and the priesthood have plummeted in most countries except South Asia and

[2] Address to the Secretariat for Promoting Christian Unity, Rome, April 29, 1967; ET from Patrick Granfield, *The Limits of the Papacy* (New York: Crossroad, 1987) 169.

Africa. Priest shortages are already causing the closure of parishes in the United States and elsewhere, and the number of United States priests is expected to decline sharply over the next ten years.[3] Many Catholic religious orders may vanish within a generation because of a dearth of members.[4] The numbers of Catholic laity is declining in many countries, including traditionally Catholic bastions such as Ireland. Latin America is rapidly being converted to Protestantism—mostly to evangelical or Pentecostal groups. According to the Mexican bishops some forty million Latin Americans left Catholicism for Protestant denominations from 1990–1995.[5] The Catholic Church has suffered a dramatic loss of credibility for various reasons (secularism, its teaching on artificial birth control and women's ordination, recent scandals concerning pedophiliac priests). In the United States, only nine percent agree with the magisterial teaching on artificial birth control, a percentage unchanged since the seventies.[6] Only one third of baptized American Catholics attend weekly mass, and of those only thirty percent believe the Eucharist to be the body and blood of Christ.[7] United States Catholics are increasingly polarized. In the words of the late Cardinal Joseph Bernardin and the National Pastoral Life Center: "It is widely admitted that the Catholic Church

[3] Archbishop Rembert Weakland of Milwaukee, addressing the National Conference of Priests of England and Wales, September 5, 1995, stated: "According to our statistics, almost half of the 277 parishes will have lay directors within a period of 15 to 20 years." Reported in *National Catholic Reporter* (September 15, 1995) 13.

[4] "Currently [1994], 54 percent of all women's communities, 36 percent of the communities of non-ordained men, and 22 percent of clerical men's communities have no new members applying at all." Patricia Wittberg, *The Rise and Decline of Catholic Religious Orders* (Albany: SUNY Press, 1994) 1. She also documents similar trends in Canada, Ireland, Italy, France, and other Western countries. However, communities in sub-Saharan Africa and South Asia are growing.

[5] "Reports from the Mexican bishops' conference say that nearly twenty million Mexicans, or one fourth of the population, are now Protestant. The reports say that between 1990–1995, an estimated forty million Latin Americans left the Catholic church to join Protestant churches. . . . Jehovah's Witnesses, Mormons, and independent evangelical groups were named as drawing the most new members." *National Catholic Reporter* (May 24, 1996) 10.

[6] Thomas Sweetser, "The Parish: What has Changed, What Remains?" *America* (February 17, 1996) 6.

[7] R. Scott Appleby, "Crunch Time for American Catholicism," *The Christian Century* (April 3, 1996) 372.

in the United States has entered a time of peril."[8] Although many blame secular culture for this decline, evangelical and Pentecostal groups are growing explosively, even in secular environments like the United States. I believe instead that the most serious problem with modern Catholicism is a misunderstanding of the nature of ecclesial hierarchy. Hierarchy has been misunderstood as domination, both by those who defend it, and those who reject it. This same misunderstanding is at the root of the schisms of the past.

I will claim in this book that a misunderstanding of hierarchy as domination has (1) resulted in the fracturing of the Body of Christ into competing denominations, (2) led to a loss of credibility and to decline in modern Catholicism. But the solution to this problem does not lie in abolishing hierarchy for an egalitarian or democratic church, which would be unworkable. I agree with Vatican II that ecclesial hierarchy was instituted by Christ to preserve the apostolic teaching, and to preserve the unity of the Church. Rather, the solution to the problem is to understand that ecclesial hierarchy ought to be a *participatory hierarchy,* which does not seek to dominate, but to draw persons into participation in the life of Christ and the Spirit. To explain the notion of participatory hierarchy, to ground it in Scripture and Christian tradition, and to justify it theologically is the aim of this book. Only through a participatory notion of hierarchy can the Christian Church realize a unity that also preserves diversity. A recovery of participatory hierarchy, or, to use a roughly equivalent phrase, hierarchical communion, is thus essential for the further progress of the ecumenical movement. It is also crucial for the renewal of Catholicism. The present trend toward a more authoritarian and centralized mode of hierarchy is disastrous for the Roman Catholic Church. But it is also disastrous for ecumenism, for it will take Catholicism effectively out of the ecumenical movement. No one is going to be interested in reuniting with the Roman Church if it is perceived to be governed by a papal autocracy. This book, then, is addressed to three possibly overlapping audiences: (1) those who are concerned about the state of hierarchy in the Roman Catholic Church, (2) non-Catholics who are concerned about the state of hierarchy in their own churches, (3) those who are concerned about the ecumenical movement.

[8] "Called to be Catholic: Church in a Time of Peril" (New York: National Pastoral Life Center, 1996) 1.

The Problem of Hierarchy

Hierarchy today is widely under attack. For many authors it connotes a social structure that is authoritarian, dominative, patriarchal, and static. For example, Stephen D. Brookfield, a well-known educator, writes: ". . . societies in which inquiry, reflection, and exploration are the prerogative of a privileged minority are likely to be static, ossified, and hierarchical."[9] Anthropologist Riane Eisler's view is typical: "As used here, the term "hierarchy" refers to a system of human rankings based on force or the threat of force." Thus, in a representative sentence, she writes: "Hesiod's world was already male dominated, warlike, and hierarchic."[10] Many authors typically reject hierarchy altogether in favor of egalitarian social structures. According to Joann Wolski Conn: "Ideas and projects in the relational feminist tradition feature a non-hierarchical, egalitarian vision of social organization."[11]

A prominent target is the hierarchical church. Leonardo Boff writes: "Through the centuries, the church has acquired an organizational form with a heavily hierarchical framework and a juridical understanding of relationships among Christians, thus producing mechanical, reified inequalities and inequities."[12] M. Francis Mannion argues that: "Reconstructive Catholic feminism has as its agenda a thorough dismantling and restructuring of the church in order to recreate new religious communities that are radically egalitarian and non-hierarchical."[13] Elizabeth Schüssler Fiorenza, in her recent book *Jesus: Miriam's Child, Sophia's Prophet* argues that the decrees of the Council of Chalcedon (A.D. 451), which is normative for almost all Christians (except Monophysites), are based on and reinforce structures

[9] Stephen Brookfield, "Understanding and Adult Learning," *School Library Media Quarterly,* 16:2 (Winter, 1988) 99.

[10] Riane Eisler, *The Chalice and the Blade* (San Francisco: Harper & Row, 1988) 105–106. Eisler recognizes that this is not the only kind of hierarchy. She distinguishes what she calls domination hierarchies which are oppressive from actualization hierarchies which are not. Nonetheless, the bare word 'hierarchy' as used throughout her book means domination.

[11] Joann Wolski Conn, "New Vitality: the Challenge from Feminist Theology," *America* (October 5, 1991) 217.

[12] *Ecclesiogenesis: the Base Communities Reinvent the Church* (New York: Maryknoll, Orbis Books, 1986) 1.

[13] *America* (October 5, 1991) 216.

of domination and patriarchy.[14] Sallie McFague, in her influential *Models of God*, explains:

> The primary metaphors in the tradition are hierarchical, imperialistic, and dualistic, stressing the distance between God and the world and the total reliance of the world on God. Thus, the metaphors of God as king, ruler, lord, master, and governor, and the concepts that accompany them of God as absolute, complete, transcendent, and omnipotent permit no sense of mutuality, shared responsibility, reciprocity, and love (except in the sense of gratitude).[15]

Now it would be foolish to deny that hierarchies in the past have been oppressive, sexist, and static. Examples like slavery, the class system in European history, the Hindu caste system, and the subordination of women to men in nearly all cultures and religions, come to mind. But is hierarchy *necessarily* dominative, sexist, and static, or are these features abuses of hierarchy?

It seems obvious that any sizeable society needs some kind of hierarchical structure to preserve its identity and function as a unified whole. In such societies as a family, a high school or college class, a university, a team, an orchestra, a corporation, or a church, the alternative to hierarchy would seem to be disintegration and paralysis, as in a family without a parent, a class without a teacher, a university or a corporation without a head, a team without a coach, an orchestra without a conductor, or a church without a minister or pastor. In all of these instances a hierarchy of expertise and competence is recognized, and this is expressed in some kind of a hierarchy of organization.

I believe that a consistent egalitarianism, i.e., the denial of all hierarchy, is not workable, especially in large groups. To conduct a class, but allow the opinions of the most ignorant to count the same as those of the learned, would destroy teaching and learning. To govern a family by allowing children an equal vote on every issue would in all likelihood destroy the children and the family itself. Nor could an orchestra successfully perform if at least one person did not have the authority to unify the participants. The same principles could be applied to governments, corporations, fire and police units, universities, etc.; without

[14] Elizabeth Schüssler Fiorenza, *Jesus: Miriam's Child, Sophia's Prophet* (New York: Continuum, 1994) 3–31; see also the review by Dennis M. Doyle, *Commonweal* (March 10, 1995) 18–20.

[15] *Models of God* (Philadelphia: Fortress, 1987) 19.

some form of legitimate leadership and authority, i.e., hierarchy, social units such as this would disintegrate, and be incapable of concerted action. The alternative to hierarchy, then, is fragmentation and inability to act. It is no accident, in the present age when most authority is challenged, that fragmentation and factionalism are endemic. Egalitarians are right in stressing the basic equality of *persons* before God, and with respect to basic rights. They err, however, in extending this to mean that there cannot be hierarchical *roles* within a society.

In fact, all Christian denominations confess the Lordship of God and Christ, and almost all evince some kind of hierarchical ecclesial structure. This is especially true of episcopal churches (Orthodox, Roman Catholic, Anglican, some Lutheran), who have traditionally understood the episcopal hierarchy to flow from the authority of the apostolic college, itself rooted in the authority of Christ, but it is true in a lesser degree even of evangelical and independent Protestant groups.

Two Models of Hierarchy

The crucial question is not: should there be hierarchy? Rather, it is: what kind of hierarchy should there be, and how should it be structured? It is a mistake to equate hierarchy *tout court* with dominance, imperialism, patriarchy, authoritarianism and oppression. This is indeed one model of hierarchy. It might be called the *command* model. In this model power tends to be centralized, control is from the top down and is based on force or the threat of force. There is little allowance for feedback from the bottom up, for the independence of subordinate social units, or for internal development. Such hierarchy is found in many animal societies (the pecking order). It is perhaps appropriate in human society for emergency situations, such as a fire or a military threat, in which there is not time to develop a consensus, quick decisions must be made and acted upon, and it is imperative for survival that someone take command to insure order. The weakness of this kind of hierarchy is that it does not foster the participation of those lower in the scale; rather, over the long term it tends to provoke passivity, apathy, and rebellion (by either passive or active resistance). By depending too much on the decisions of the ruler at the top, it becomes closed to new ideas stemming from below. And, because persons and groups in power do not want to relinquish control, command hierarchies tend to become ossified, static, and impervious to change. Finally, the exclusive possession of power by a ruler or ruling elite often corrupts the rulers, who then use their office to exploit the governed. As a long-term provision for social structure this is a disastrous solution, recognized by thinkers since Plato as tyranny or autocracy, the worst form of social order. Examples in modern history have been the French monarchy, the rule of the czars in Russia, and the rule of the Communist despots who followed them. The collapse of all these regimes in revolutions is a testimony to the folly of government by command hierarchy.

But there is another model of hierarchy, based on participation, inclusion, integration, and subsidiarity, in which members are empowered by participation in a larger whole and in which influence flows both from the leadership to the members and from the members to the leadership. Such a model might be called a *participatory, integrative,* or *inclusive* model of hierarchy. Examples of this might be a religious master and his or her disciples, a teacher and her students, a master craftsman and his apprentices. The aim of these hierarchies is to allow the learners to appropriate what the teacher already is or knows—whether that be knowledge, practical expertise, or spiritual holiness. Whereas the aim of a command hierarchy is typically to accomplish a task external to the participants, such as winning a military victory, producing a product, or making a profit, a principal aim of a participatory hierarchy is fostering the good of the participants themselves. Whereas command hierarchies typically enforce an inequality of persons, in a participatory hierarchy there is an *equality of persons,* but a *hierarchy of function or office.* Whereas in a command hierarchy the supreme virtue is obedience, in a participatory hierarchy, the supreme virtue is learning and participation in the goal to be achieved. Whereas command hierarchies suppress discussion and dissent, participatory hierarchies allow dissent as necessary to the learning and growth process. Where power, in being shared, is attenuated, expertise, knowledge, or holiness are not attenuated by being shared, but can actually be increased (this is true with all spiritual goods as opposed to material goods, which are limited). Whereas a command hierarchy is governed by an *authority of force or domination,* a participatory hierarchy is governed by what might be called an *authority of virtue.* 'Virtue' is here used in its widest sense as excellence in any practice or activity. A master craftsman has authority of virtue due to his superior knowledge and experience in the craft. A wilderness guide has authority of virtue because she knows the lay of the land and survival techniques in the wilderness. A doctor of a discipline has an authority of virtue due to her expertise, knowledge, and mastery of that discipline. An authority of virtue does not depend on force, coercion, or fear; it depends rather on the recognition and respect accorded to virtue by those who wish to learn or grow in a practice, knowledge, or holiness.

Just as in a command hierarchy power is centralized, in a participatory hierarchy power tends to be decentralized. Furthermore, participatory hierarchies allow influence to flow from the bottom to the top, whereas command hierarchies do not. Typically, there are checks and balances on excessive concentration of power in a participatory hierarchy, and different groups share in the power, though power is not evenly distributed, as is the case with egalitarianism. Participatory hierarchy then, is a mean between two extremes: command hierarchy on the one hand, and egalitarianism on the other. But command hierarchy and participatory hierarchy are ideal types, rarely encountered in their pure form. Most examples of institutionalized hierarchy contain elements of both models and both types of authority. Most command hierarchies contain some vestige of participatory hierarchy, else they would disintegrate. Conversely, most institutionalized participatory hierarchies contain some element of command, if only to reject those things that would destroy the whole institution.

Corresponding to these two types of hierarchy are two types of obedience and two types of unity. The unity purchased by a command hierarchy—a command unity—is unstable, always liable to disintegration by schism or rebellion, or to vitiation by apathetic servitude. The unity of a participatory hierarchy—a consensual unity—is stronger because it is based on internal assent, consensus, and mutual interest. Similarly, obedience in a command hierarchy tends to be *servile obedience,* based on fear or love of power (lower members identify with the authoritarian head and his power). Typically such social structures demand a *sacrificium intellectus;* no questioning or challenging of the commander is allowed. Obedience in a participatory hierarchy, on the other hand, is based on recognition of an authority of virtue, on the value of participation itself, and on recognition of the common good of the community. Such obedience, which I call *filial obedience,*[16] does not entail the sacrifice of one's intelligence but its enhancement. But again,

[16] I borrow the distinction between servile and filial obedience from the sixteenth-century Anabaptist, Michael Sattler. See *The Legacy of Michael Sattler,* John H. Yoder, ed. and trans. (Scottsdale, Penn.: Herald Press, 1973) 121–126.

these two types of unity and obedience are ideal types, usually mixed in institutions.

Ontological Hierarchy

The foregoing paragraphs have described hierarchy as social. But like Christ, whose presence it continues in history, the Church has both a human and divine aspect. Its hierarchy, therefore, has a social aspect but also an ontological aspect, that is, it is grounded in a hierarchy of being (ontological hierarchy). A typical mistake in assessing ecclesial hierarchy is to assume that it is no more than a human construct, having its roots only in society, human custom, and history. But the Christian Church from the beginning has understood its hierarchy as grounded in the Lordship of Christ and the Trinity. Episcopal churches generally have claimed that the authority of the bishops derives from the apostles and ultimately from Christ. Thus some consideration of what kind of hierarchy the Trinity and Christ exercise over human beings, creation, and the Church is essential to an understanding of ecclesial hierarchy, though admittedly this consideration will make the argument of the book much more complex.

Ontological hierarchy impinges on questions of ecclesial hierarchy in several ways.[17] First, it is constitutive of the Church itself: the confession "Jesus is Lord" is foundational for believers, and submission to the will of Christ is essential for discipleship. This submission is not made because Christ is more powerful, or even more good, than we; it is made because of his divinity, i.e., his ontological status. Second, ecclesial hierarchy has consistently legitimized itself by an appeal to the authority of Christ. Third, distortions in conceptions of ontological hierarchy cause distortions in ecclesial hierarchy. If people think of God

[17] I use "social hierarchy" to refer to those aspects of hierarchy, whether within or without the Church, which can be described sociologically; "ontological hierarchy" to refer to the hierarchy of being, which is described metaphysically; and "ecclesial hierarchy" to refer to the sacramental hierarchy of the Church, which expresses both social and ontological hierarchy: a bishop or priest has a position of social hierarchy in the community, but in his sacramental role also acts as a mediator for the grace and authority of Christ. For example, when a Catholic priest forgives sins in the confessional, it is Christ acting through him who forgives the sin; when he offers Mass, it is Christ who transforms the bread and wine into his own body and blood.

as a commanding autocrat, they will likely create an ecclesial autocracy, and justify it by reference to God's authority. This has happened repeatedly in Christian history. Fourth, the *loss* of a credible conception of ontological hierarchy means an inability to believe in, conceive, or even experience transcendent or sacred reality. Being is leveled out so that only the physical and natural level exists. This might be called ontological egalitarianism: in modern Western society consciousness has been secularized.[18] Whereas ancient, medieval, renaissance, and early modern persons believed almost universally that an unseen, supernatural reality surrounded and penetrated the natural world, such an awareness is diminished in contemporary culture, especially among the media and intellectual elite who shape cultural opinion. This makes it difficult for persons to participate in a transcendent reality and whole greater than themselves. Persons are ontologically isolated, unable to escape the prison of the self, and seek release in surrogate wholes, like gangs, sporting crowds, etc. This is devastating for the Church, whose mission is to draw persons to participation in a transcendent reality: the life of God. Its sacramental system exists to mediate transcendent grace to persons. Its hope is in the resurrection, or at least a heavenly afterlife, states in which persons are raised to a transcendent level of reality. If that reality does not exist, this hope is empty, and the Church has no reason to exist, except as a psychological security blanket.

I will claim in the following chapters that distortions and misunderstandings of ontological hierarchy—either in the direction of dominance or of egalitarianism (i.e., the denial of any ontological hierarchy)—have been just as destructive for the Church as distortions in its ecclesial hierarchy. Indeed, the two have usually interconnected and legitimize each other. In particular, the loss of a sense of the transcendent in modern life is rooted in a loss of a conception of a participatory hierarchy of being. Both ancients and medievals had such a sense, and it was the basis for the sacramental system of the Church, through which God and sacred reality were made present to the world by the mediation of physical signs. But in the late Middle Ages, the hierarchical communion of being elaborated by Aquinas and other medieval thinkers, which understood created things participating by

[18] See Peter Berger, *A Rumor of Angels* (Garden City, N.Y.: Doubleday Anchor, 1969) 1–27.

degrees in God's being, gave way to the philosophy of William of Ockham. Ockhamism conceived of God as extrinsic to the world, ruling it as an external judge whose will was absolute, but whose grace was not immanent in creatures. This prepared the way for the absentee God of Deism, who created the world but thereafter did not become involved. Eventually this marginalized God, and with God the sacred, which became remote from everyday life and faded from consciousness like the Cheshire cat, leaving only the grin. This undermines the Church, its credibility, and its sacraments.

As with social hierarchy, one can discern two models of ontological hierarchy: a command model and a participatory model. A command model yields a conception of God as divine autocrat, who commands obedience and rules through coercion and fear. We find elements of this image in scripture (especially the Hebrew scriptures), and in the Christian tradition as well. At the other end of the spectrum is ontological egalitarianism, which is approximated in philosophical materialism and secularism (i.e., the cosmos is nothing but matter, organized in differing degrees of complexity), or in pantheism. A participatory model of God, however, while emphasizing ontological hierarchy—God is greater in being than any creature—also emphasizes that humans can participate in God's own life, to a degree impossible for other creatures (except angels). This is the principal understanding of God in Scripture. In the Old Testament idea of covenant, and in the New Testament idea of the indwelling of the Spirit, the emphasis is on fellowship and communion with God in love: "It is no longer I who live, but it is Christ who lives in me" declares St. Paul (Gal 2:20). This is participatory hierarchy, or hierarchical communion. Our relation with God and Christ is not a relation of equals, nor should it be one of fear and servile obedience. It ought to be one of surrender to the Lordship of God and Christ, through which we receive the indwelling of the Spirit and the love of God. As St. Paul declares: "God's love has been poured into our hearts through the Holy Spirit that has been given to us" (Rom 5:5). This participation in the divine life is the aim and completion of Christian life. "By an utterly free and mysterious decree of His own wisdom and goodness, the eternal Father created the whole world. His plan was to dignify persons with a participation in His own divine life" (*LG* #2). This means the restoration of harmony between God and humanity, God and creation, a harmony that was lost through sin, which led to alienation between God and humanity, and the fragmentation of humanity itself (cf. Gen 11:1-9).

Now in fact social and ontological hierarchy are interrelated, such that each affects the other. To an extent, a culture's view of ontological hierarchy is modeled after its social hierarchy. Thus cultures with strong social hierarchies, such as the medieval European and the traditional Hindu, also have strongly delineated ontological hierarchies. But, conversely, ontological hierarchy affects and legitimates social hierarchy. Thus the king in Israel was thought to be the representative of God, and his authority derived from God's authority—he was "God's son" or anointed ruler (Psalm 2). This was also true of other forms of Near Eastern kingship, and the medieval pope, who was styled Christ's sole Vicar on earth. On the other hand, in the modern age, following the scientific revolution, being tended to be reduced to atoms alone, and society was reduced to individuals alone, each of whom is equal, just as each atom is equal. Thus social and ontological hierarchy tend to go together. It is not clear which is primary; arguments could be given either way. Rather, there seems to be a reciprocal interaction: each influences the other.

Social and ontological hierarchy come together in the Church, a community whose source and rule is a sacred authority. By submitting to Jesus as Lord, one comes to participation in God's Spirit, which, in the language of the Orthodox Church, *deifies* the believer such that he or she shares in the very life of God and becomes an adoptive child of God. Thus the Church is meant to be a hierarchical communion of love, not of dominance and command. And if it is to be an effective sacrament and sign of God's love in the world (*LG* #1), its ecclesial hierarchy must express participation and love, not dominance. Nonetheless, some periods of Christian history have distorted both social and ontological hierarchy into dominance, with the result that many Christians today have difficulty with hierarchical images of God, especially kingship (cf. McFague, above, p. 6). But with Catherine LaCugna and others, I will maintain (chap. 10) that the development of a trinitarian understanding of God undercuts and opposes any attempt to understand God's reign autocratically, or to erect an autocratic ecclesial structure.[19] But I will disagree with Dr. LaCugna that a trinitarian understanding of God favors a non-hierarchical ecclesial structure; rather, I believe it favors a participatory hierarchy, in which there is a balance of power

[19] Catherine LaCugna, *God for Us* (San Francisco: Harper, 1991) 388–400.

and authority between bishops (including the pope), clergy, and laity, and between institutional and prophetic forms of authority. Historically this has been best expressed in ecumenical councils, such as Nicaea. But admittedly, genuine participatory hierarchy has been rare in Christian history. All too often, in both the West and the East, God's reign has been understood monarchially and ecclesial structures of domination have resulted. Ecclesial hierarchies of dominance, such as developed in the high Middle Ages and just prior to the Reformation, have historically resulted in rebellion and schisms in the Body of Christ.

Thus this book will argue against *two* distortions of hierarchy: dominance on the one hand, and on the other, egalitarianism, i.e., the denial of any form of hierarchy, social or ontological. These are in fact obverse faces of the same coin: both dominators and egalitarians have the *same* model of hierarchy: a command model. And this tends to be true for both social and ontological hierarchy. Both dominance and egalitarianism deform the Church, and result in disintegration, fragmentation, and a loss of communion, wholeness, and catholicity. If the Christian Church is to recover the wholeness, both ontological and social, with which it has been endowed by Christ and which it is meant to embody and manifest in the world, then a proper understanding of hierarchy is essential; if hierarchy is reduced to egalitarianism, or deformed into command and dominance, disintegration and fragmentation is inevitable.

A Participatory, Integrative Model of Hierarchy

As it happens, recent science has come to understand creation as composed of a hierarchy of levels, and this understanding of hierarchy can serve as a valuable analogy in our attempt to understand participatory hierarchy in the Church.

One of the principal marks of modern science has been a commitment to a reductionistic method that focused only on material and quantifiable causes. Recently, however, a number of scientists and philosophers have concluded that an atomistic, reductionistic method is inadequate to account for the *wholeness* and unity manifested by entities, particularly organisms. Thinkers as various as Michael Polanyi, Ludwig von Bertalanffy, Paul Weiss, Alfred Whitehead, Roger Sperry, Rupert Sheldrake, Charles Birch, and Ian Barbour have argued that in organisms there exists a holistic cause which influences the parts, just as the parts influence the whole.[20] The action of this cause is to organize the entity as an organism, and to guide its development. Thus these thinkers speak of a "top-down" causality as well as a "bottom up" causality. Organic entities are subject to what Polanyi calls "dual control": the parts exercise a control over the larger whole, but the whole also exercises control over the constituent parts. Yet the manner of this holistic control is such as to not interfere with the characteristic operations of the parts. In a cell, for instance, the chemical laws which govern the operation of the DNA proceed just as they would if the DNA was not incorporated into a cell, but in the cell these laws, and the operations of the DNA itself, are harnessed into the service of a larger whole.[21]

Incorporating such recent scientific opinion, Arthur Koestler has developed a general model of hierarchy from which the following figure is adapted.

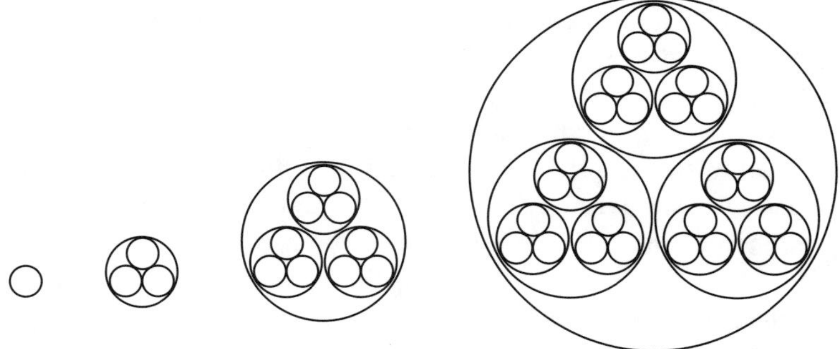

Successive levels in a nested hierarchy of morphic units, or holons. At each level, the holons are wholes containing parts, which are themselves wholes containing lower-level holons, and so on. This diagram could represent subatomic particles in atoms, in molecules, in crystals, for example; or cells in tissues, in organs, in organisms.[22]

[20] Cf. the following: Michael Polanyi, *Knowing and Being* (Chicago: University of Chicago Press, 1969) 225–239; Ludwig Bertalanffy, *Problems of Life* (New York: J. Wiley & Sons, 1952); Paul Weiss, "The Living System," *Beyond Reductionism,* Arthur Koestler and J.R. Smythies, eds. (Boston: Beacon Press, 1971) 3–55; Rupert Sheldrake, *A New Science of Life* (London: Anthony Blond, 1985); Charles Birch, *A Purpose for Everything* (Mystic, Conn.: Twenty Third Publications, 1990); Ian Barbour, *Religion in an Age of Science* (San Francisco, Harper, 1990) 165–171. See also Marjorie Grene, "Hierarchies in Biology," *American Scientist,* vol. 75 (1987) 505–510.

[21] See Polanyi, "Life's Irreducible Structure," ibid., 225–239.

[22] Figure and description taken from Rupert Sheldrake, *The Presence of the Past* (New York: Vintage, 1988) 95. For Koestler's argument, see Arthur Koestler, "Beyond Atomism and Holism—the Concept of the Holon," in Koestler and Smythies, 192–216.

Here, the medium-sized circles are wholes with respect to the circles which they enclose, but are parts with respect to the circles which enclose them. Such entities Koestler calls *holons;* the whole series is a *holarchy.* In the human heart, for example, many different muscles and cells are organized into a single whole functioning for a single purpose. It is a whole which can be kept alive outside the body, *in vitro,* and can be transplanted into another body. But within the body it is a part of a larger whole which regulates its activity. It is thus both a whole and a part—a holon. And this is true of every element of the body, which is composed of a hierarchy of levels or systems, each incorporating subsystems, and each a part of a larger system. Atoms are organized into molecules, which are organized into macro-molecules, such as DNA, which are organized into organelles and into cells, which form organs which are integrated into a unified functioning whole, the human body. In the body, the chemical parts affect the whole, but are themselves organized into a whole by an integrating, holistic cause. There is mutual or dual control: the parts affect the whole, and the whole the parts.

Now in this understanding of hierarchy, "higher" wholes do not dominate lower; they allow the "lower" wholes to function according to their own laws, while organizing and integrating them into larger systems. Unity here does not mean uniformity: it means integrated diversity. And "higher" in this conception means "more inclusive and more integrated, but also "more diverse." A living human body is an example of such integrated diversity; it includes highly complex cells and molecules that cannot remain intact outside the body. When the body dies, only simple molecules remain, and there is much less diversity and much less integration. Thus, in this conception, a lack of hierarchy means an absence of integration or unity. Without a more comprehensive holon, elementary units are not integrated, for there is no holistic cause to organize them. Without hierarchy, one has a heap or aggregate of fragments; with a hierarchy of holons, one can have an integrated and diverse system, such as a body, a society, an ecosystem, or a universe.

Koestler argues that this general model of hierarchy has a wide range of application, from organisms to language to social systems. Of course the nature of the whole/part relationship varies with each kind of system. An animal is a holon which is a part of a larger ecosystem, yet is has greater freedom than an organ which is part of a body. But both are holons situated in holarchies. In fact, as Ken Wilber argues, every created thing is a holon: every entity, from quarks to galaxies, is some kind of whole and is yet a part of a larger system or holarchy.[23] The human body is a series of holons—a holarchy; so is human society, so is the ecosphere, so is the universe. So widespread is the principle of holarchy that it would seem to be a universal structure of created being. I will maintain that holarchy, as universal in nature, reflects a divinely intended principle of order in creation, which is applicable to society and the Church. Of course there is a difference between organisms and societies, and so the application of this principle to social and ecclesial bodies must be understood as *analogous,* and in need of completion by other models. But there is good precedent for this use of analogy: in 1 Corinthians 12, St. Paul applies the analogy of the body to the Church, and envisions a structure very like a holarchy.

A number of parallels can be seen between the above model and the traditional understanding of the Body of Christ. But some new nuances can also be gained. First, the elements of an organism are integrated within a larger whole. But the pattern of that whole does not destroy the laws and processes by which the subsidiary units operate. Rather, each subsidiary unit becomes a part of a greater whole *without its individuality being suppressed.* In fact, to contribute to that whole, it must be true to its own nature. The same should be true of members of the Body of Christ (a point implied in 2 Corinthians 12). Further, since each part expresses a facet of the whole, the sense of the whole can only be found in the concurrence and consensus of the parts. A command hierarchy, which suppresses the activity of the parts, will deform the Church.

That which integrates the whole is a holistic cause; in the Body of Christ this is the Spirit (which parallels the function of the soul in the body, a comparison drawn by Augustine). But the experience of the Church has been that there must be an institution that is responsible for maintaining the teaching of Christ, preserving ecclesial unity, discerning the will of the Spirit, and settling disputes among members. Traditionally, this was the apostles (cf. Paul's insistence on his apostolic authority in Galatians; also Acts 15, especially 15:28: "It has seemed good to the Holy Spirit and to us . . .") and their successors, the bishops. This ecclesial hierarchy ideally should put into effect visibly what the

[23] *Sex, Ecology, and Spirituality* (Boston and London: Shambhala, 1995) 17–78.

Spirit wills invisibly. But the Spirit is given to the whole Church, not entirely to any individual. Therefore this hierarchy should be collegial and conciliar.[24] This does not rule out a single figure (a pope), whose mission is to unify the hierarchy and the Church, but it indicates that such a figure should not act independently from, but rather, act to facilitate and proclaim the consensus of the college and the Church, insofar as this is possible.[25] As for the idea that the head "rules" the body: this makes no sense in present thinking. The head does not rule the body, it is a part of the body, and in any case is not one organ, but composed of many. And since the parts influence the whole, even as the whole influences the parts, and since each part expresses only a facet of the whole, it is imperative that the ecclesial hierarchy consider the *sensus fidelium*—the mind of the faithful—in its decisions.[26] This appears to have been the practice in the early Church. For example, Cyprian writes: "I have made it a rule, ever since the beginning of my episcopate, to make no decision merely on the strength of my own personal opinion without consulting you (priests and deacons), without the approbation of the people."[27] This also is in accord with the ancient

[24] Cf. Yves Congar, "The Council as an Assembly and the Church as Essentially Conciliar," *One, Holy, Catholic, and Apostolic*, Herbert Vorgrimler, ed. (London: Sheed and Ward, 1968). Another way of arguing the same point is from the perspectival nature of knowledge. It is widely accepted that knowledge is conditioned and limited by the perspective of any single knower. This was accepted by St. Thomas, who frequently repeats the medieval adage "The thing known is in the mind of the knower according to the mode of the knower." Thus no single person has a comprehensive view of truth, rather only one perspective on it. But a group of persons—a college or council—could come much closer to a truly comprehensive view.

[25] This seems to contradict the sentence of Vatican I (repeated at Vatican II), that the pope's definitions are irreformable in themselves, and not from the consent of the Church. But *Lumen gentium* (#25) also says that the infallibility which the pope exercises in making an infallible definition is the infallibility *of the church itself*, and that to such a definition, "the assent of the church can never be wanting." Many noted theologians, such as Francis Sullivan, argue therefore that if the consent of the Church is found to be wanting, the definition was not infallible in the first place. See Francis Sullivan, *Magisterium* (Mahwah, N.J.: Paulist Press, 1983) 102–118.

[26] Both Pius IX and Pius XII, before they proclaimed infallibly the doctrines of the Immaculate Conception (1854), and the Assumption of Mary (1950), asked the bishops to consult their parishioners, to determine the mind of the Church.

[27] *Epistula* 14.4, cited in Yves Congar, *Power and Poverty in the Church* (Baltimore: Helicon Press, 1964) 43.

principle of Roman law: "Quod omnes tangit ab omnibus tractari et approbari debet" (What touches all, must be treated and approved by all).[28]

Again, the hierarchical model given above emphasizes the subsidiary structure of hierarchy: the whole affects the parts through subsidiary holons, which affect sub-holons, etc. In applying this concept to the Church, local churches might be understood as holons, along with religious orders, which have their own independent traditions and governing structures. In the event of ecumenical reconciliation, whole denominations might be recognized as holons, and accorded the greatest possible independence in their rites, governments, traditions, etc. The concept of the holon, which accents the semi-autonomy of the subsidiary unit, is thus a useful corrective to traditional (Catholic) interpretations of the mystical body, which tended to consider the local church as merely an arm of the whole, controlled by the head (the pope). In such an interpretation, there was always the danger that a subsidiary holon would be overridden by a command hierarchy.[29] Finally, the model emphasizes development: all organisms are teleological. They do not just grow quantitatively; they change their forms in the course of their maturation. The analogy here is obvious: the Body of Christ also develops, not just in terms of quantitative growth (the traditional interpretation), but also, as it responds to new historical situations, in its doctrines and structure. To insist that the Church never changes is a prescription for fossilization and extinction. Organic development implies both continuity (a core identity remains the same), and change. What is crucial in the development of the Church is the discernment of which elements are essential to the core identity, and which are not (this was the problem facing the apostles in Acts 15). This discernment is the responsibility of the whole Body of Christ, but has traditionally been expressed in ecumenical councils (e.g., Nicaea).

There are, of course, a number of objections that might be raised against the above model of participatory hierarchy. A standard criticism of organic social models is that they cannot deal well with conflicts that

[28] See Yves Congar, "Quod omnes tangit, ab omnibus tractari et approbari debet," in *Révue historique droit française et étranger* (1958) 210–259.

[29] See Thomas O'Meara, "The Raid on the Dominicans: the Repression of 1954," which tells of Pius XII's suppression of some Dominican institutions and traditions. In *America* (February 5, 1994) 8ff.

will inevitably arise between members of the body. The answer to this is to be found in the history of church councils. Every council (including the Council of Jerusalem in Acts 15) has had to deal with conflict. Their approach has been to allow extensive debate in which all views are argued, to deliberate, to attempt common discernment, perhaps to compromise, and to subject the matter to a vote by the bishops. Nicaea was an example of this, so was Vatican II (which was a good, though not perfect, example of participatory hierarchy in action). How any particular conflict is resolved cannot be specified in advance; resolution requires discernment, and hence an openness to the Spirit. Where this is lacking, resolution may fail, and schism may occur.

This model, then, can be useful as a way of understanding how hierarchy can be integrative and unified, but also allow for diversity and participation.

Thesis and Plan of Book

My thesis is that the Christian Church is by its nature a participatory hierarchy or hierarchical communion (cf. *LG*, #21), whose aim is to bring the believer into communion and participation in the life of God and Christ through the Spirit. This is expressed in many words and images in scripture, e.g., the Body of Christ (1 Corinthians 12), the indwelling of the Spirit (Rom 5:5), the vine and the branches (John 15). But if that is so, the Church also ought to be structured according to a participatory ecclesial hierarchy, so that its external, ecclesial structure expresses its inner structure. A reduction of either the ontological hierarchy or the ecclesial hierarchy of the Church into a command model deforms the very gospel which is its *raison d'être.* I will suggest that the misunderstanding and distortion of hierarchy into command has been largely responsible for crucial schisms in Christian history, and hence for the fragmentation of the catholicity of the Church. But I will also be critical of recent attempts to eliminate hierarchy from the Church. Both domination, which produces uniformity and so suppresses diversity, and egalitarianism, which produces diversity but loses unity, are untrue to the catholicity of the Church, and so betray its essential nature. Rather, I suggest full catholicity can only be preserved in a participatory hierarchy, which also has fruitful ecumenical possibilities.

This book is divided into four major sections. The first section is *chapter 1,* the Introduction. Second is a survey of hierarchy in the Christian scriptures. *Chapter 2* deals with hierarchy in the Old Testament. *Chapters 3 and 4* treat hierarchy in the New Testament and criticize the proposals of John Dominic Crossan and Elizabeth Schüssler Fiorenza that the original Jesus movement was egalitarian. The third section traces the history of ontological and ecclesial hierarchy in the Christian tradition. *Chapter 5* considers ecclesial hierarchy in the patristic period; *chapter 6,* hierarchy in the Middle Ages; *chapter 7,* Reformation notions of hierarchy; *chapter 8,* the Catholic Reformation and the Enlightenment rejection of hierarchy; and *chapter 9,* Vatican I and Vatican II. Naturally an historical survey of this scope must be compressed and can only consider selected historical evidence. The fourth section of the book treats the question of hierarchy from the perspective of systematic theology. *Chapter 10* develops a systematic treatment of hierarchy in creation (using scientific models), and ontological hierarchy, culminating in the Trinity and the Cosmic Christ. *Chapter 11* discusses models of hierarchy and authority in sociology, and considers hierarchy in light of Catholic social teaching. *Chapter 12* draws on all previous chapters, develops a model of the Church as Communion, and considers its implications for ecumenism and the catholicity of the Church.

This book has been written for a wide audience: both Catholic and non-Catholic, ordained and lay persons, scholars and non-specialists with only a moderate background in theology; all, in fact, who are interested in the problem of hierarchy in the Christian Church. I have therefore included extensive notes and documentation for scholars, but have also felt obliged to explain theological background which will be familiar to scholars but unfamiliar to non-specialists. This has made the book longer than it would have been if written only for scholars or only for a popular audience.

I wish to thank the following persons for reading all or parts of this book in manuscript: Fr. William McDonough, William Cavanaugh, Sr. Pauline Fritz, Fr. Norris Clarke, Sr. Susan Wood, Michael Hollerich, Catherine Cory, Sherry Jordan, and David Landry. My wife, Mabel, read multiple drafts of each chapter. I am grateful to the staff of The Liturgical Press for their patient editorial work and to the University of St. Thomas for the sabbatical year in which I completed most of the writing.

Chapter 2

Hierarchy in the Hebrew Scriptures

Methodological Note to Chapters 2–4

Anyone attempting to write on the theology of the Old or New Testaments today faces a problem. Modern biblical criticism has made it clear that there is not a single theology in either Testament; rather, there are multiple theologies and multiple voices, some of which seem to be contradictory. For example, there is not one, but two views of kingship in the Old Testament, which seemingly contradict each other: one view sees the king as chosen by God to unite the people; the other sees the king as oppressive and tyrannical. Further, many texts are multilayered: they represent an original text, modified by successive generations of editors, so that it is difficult or impossible to disentangle the original event from the text. Both the texts describing the Red Sea crossing (Exodus 14–15), and those describing the Sinai covenant (Exodus 19–34) are of this sort. Typically scholars disagree on what the layers are, which are early and which late, and so on. Thus one group argues that the texts describing the Sinai covenant contain an early historical core modified by a later editor or editors; others argue that there is no historical core, that there was no covenant at Sinai, but that covenant was invented by eighth-century prophets, and retrojected into the past. Scholars on each side view the theology of covenant differently.

The situation is similar in New Testament scholarship. Recently many scholars have reconstructed what they think is an historically accurate portrait of Jesus and his teachings. But these "historical Jesuses" differ markedly from one another. For example, Geza Vermes, a Jewish scholar, sees Jesus as a Jewish holy man, teaching the apocalyptic imminence of the kingdom of God, who was not resurrected, but whose disciples made him into a god.[1] John Dominic Crossan recreates a Jesus similar to a Greek cynic, and sees apocalyptic as the creation of the Gospel writers, who retrojected this teaching unto the historical Jesus.[2] Vermes' Jesus and Crossan's Jesus are strikingly different, but both assume that the canonical Gospel texts do not give an accurate picture of Jesus or his teaching, and that many of the texts were the fictitious creations of early Christian communities. In fact, it is extremely difficult to find a scholarly consensus on any aspect of Jesus' teaching.

And yet, as Vatican II says, and Joseph Fitzmyer reminds us, sacred scripture should be the "soul of theology."[3] My purpose here is to construct a theology of hierarchy in the Church, and for this the scriptures are of paramount importance. In attempting to ascertain the biblical theology or theologies of ecclesial hierarchy, it is essential to hold in balance both the results of the historical critical method, and the canonical text, which alone is inspired and hence normative for the Church. As Avery Dulles has written, "The deeds of God in salvation history are not Christian revelation except as taken up into the preaching and memory of the Church, which treasures Scripture as a privileged text."[4] Those, like Crossan, who think that the scriptural authors falsified the history of Jesus in fundamental ways, would seemingly have to hold that the Holy Spirit and the Risen Christ did not really guide the writing of scripture. My method here, in balancing the results of historical-critical exegesis with the meaning of the canonical text, is an attempt to approximate the approach recommended by Fitzmyer and Avery Dulles,[5] and also what is called "actualization" by the Pontifical

[1] See Geza Vermes, *Jesus and the World of Judaism* (Philadelphia: Fortress Press, 1983), and especially *The Religion of Jesus the Jew* (Minneapolis: Fortress, 1993).

[2] John Dominic Crossan, *The Historical Jesus: the Life of a Mediterranean Peasant* (San Francisco: Harper, 1991).

[3] "The sacred Scriptures contain the word of God and, since they are inspired, really are the word of God; and so the study of the sacred page is, as it were, the soul of sacred theology." *Dogmatic Constitution on Divine Revelation (Dei Verbum)* #24, in Walter Abbott, S.J., *The Documents of Vatican II* (New York: The America Press, 1966) 127. Joseph Fitzmyer, *Scripture, the Soul of Theology* (New York: Paulist Press, 1994) *passim.*

[4] *The Craft of Theology: From Symbol to System* (New York: Crossroad, 1992) 81.

[5] Dulles, "The Uses of Scripture in Theology," in *The Craft of Theology*, 69–85.

Biblical Commission, a process by which the meaning of a biblical text or texts is brought into the present.[6] I shall try to make the method clear as we proceed through the discussion of hierarchy in the Old and New Testaments.

Hierarchy in the Old Testament

The perduring source of hierarchy in the Old Testament is Israel's relation to God, which is always conceived in hierarchical terms. Deuteronomy 6:4, the Shema—Israel's basic confession of faith—expresses this: "Hear, O Israel, the LORD is our God, the LORD alone. You shall love the LORD your God with all your heart, and with all your soul, and with all your might." Likewise, the first commandment (Exod 20:2) reads "I am the LORD your God . . . you shall have no other gods before me." Similar statements are scattered through the various classes of Old Testament writings; e.g., Psalm 97, which begins "The LORD reigns; let the earth rejoice. . . ." Indeed, God's holiness and power was so great that no human being (except Moses) could look on God's face and live. God is everlasting and all powerful; humans are like the dust or grass of the earth (Psalm 90). Though the conception of God develops through Israel's history, the notion that God's relation with humanity and the earth is hierarchical does not change. Whether this was conceived of as a command or a participatory hierarchy, we shall consider below.

Israel's notion of God is multivalent, and is expressed in a wide variety of names and conceptions. God is a warrior (Exod 15:3), king (Ps 95:3), redeemer (Exod 20:2, Isa 63:16), Creator (Genesis 1), Lord (Exod 20:2), Holy One (Isa 40:25), shepherd (Isa 40:11, Psalm 23), father (Ps 68:5, Isa 63:16), husband (Hosea), judge (Gen 18:25). There is a development in Israel's conception of God, from a tribal god, who fights for Israel in her wars (Exodus 15), to the God who is the creator of all the earth and all peoples, a universal god, the God of all humankind (Isaiah 40). There are also occasional passages in which God is likened to a mother (Isa 49:15). God's wisdom, in Proverbs 8:1-21, is personified as a woman who gives instruction. But the principal characterization of God is simply the proper name, YHWH, which God reveals to Moses at the burning bush, a name related to an archaic form of the

[6] Pontifical Biblical Commission, "The Interpretation of the Bible in the Church," in *Origins* 23:29 (January 6, 1994) 520–521.

verb "to be." W.F. Albright argues that YHWH is from the causative form of this verb, and therefore means "he who causes to be."[7] YHWH comes to be thought of as the Creator, the source of all existence and life, on whom the whole creation is utterly dependent, and whose authority over creatures is therefore absolute (Isa 40:18-26).

The hierarchical relationship between God and Israel is expressed in the form of covenants, especially the covenant at Sinai. According to G.E. Mendenhall, ". . . 'covenant' in the Bible is the major metaphor used to describe the relation between God and Israel (the people of God). As such, covenant is the instrument constituting the rule (or kingdom) of God."[8]

A covenant is an agreement or contract between two parties; it could be made between equals (a parity covenant) or unequals, as between a vassal and lord (a vassal or suzerainty covenant). The covenant between YHWH and Israel is of the latter type. G.E. Mendenhall has argued persuasively that the form of the Israelite covenant was patterned after the ancient Near Eastern suzerainty treaties, in which an overlord imposed conditions on a vassal. Such treaties are known from Hittite treaties, and were widely used in the second millennium B.C.[9] In the Sinai covenant, Israel accepts YHWH as their God, and YHWH accepts Israel as his people.

> Now therefore, if you obey my voice and keep my covenant, you shall be my treasured possession out of all the peoples. Indeed, the whole earth is mine, but you shall be for me a priestly kingdom and a holy nation. . . . The people all answered as one: "Everything that the LORD has spoken we will do." Moses reported the words of the people to the LORD (Exod 19:5-8).

Note that the covenant is based on the principle of consent: all the people consent to YHWH's covenant. And Moses acts as their representative before YHWH.

[7] *NJBC*, 286, #12.

[8] G.E. Mendenhall, "Covenant," in David Noel Freedman, *ABD*, vol. 1, 1179.

[9] G.E. Mendenhall, "Covenant Forms in Israelite Tradition," *Biblical Archaeologist* 17 (1954) 49–76. See also his more recent statement in *The Anchor Bible Dictionary*, ibid. 1179–1202. Here Mendenhall strongly defends his thesis that the Sinai covenant was modeled on ancient suzerainty treaties, against those, like E.W. Nicholson, who argue that covenant was a late invention of the eighth-century prophets (see Ernest W. Nicholson, *God and His People* [Oxford: Clarendon Press, 1986]).

Keeping the covenant means obeying the many laws and commandments given by God, and thereby participating in God's holiness: "You shall be holy, for I the LORD your God am holy" (Lev 19:2). Those who keep the covenant shall be blessed by God; those who do not shall be cursed. This is graphically portrayed in Deuteronomy 28, which details the blessings and the curses (these were standard features of suzerainty treaties). Indeed, *it is acceptance of the (Sinai) covenant which constellates Israel as the people of God ('am YHWH'),* and gives them their communal identity.[10] This is expressed in the saying, "I will be your God, and you shall be my people" (Exod 6:7, Lev 26:12, Jer 11:4, Ps 95:7), which occurs in both early and late texts. Thus one who breaks the covenant, for example by profaning the sabbath, is cut off from the people, and in some instances is to be put to death (Exod 31:14-15). The condition of being a member of the People of God is submission to YHWH, by acceptance of the covenant, which means principally the rejection of any rival gods or idolatry, and the practice of justice to the other members of God's people (Amos). This message is sounded persistently in Exodus, Deuteronomy, the Psalms, and the writings of the prophets. "I will give them a heart to know that I am YHWH; and they shall be my people and I will be their God" (Jer 24:7).

There are a variety of covenants in the Old Testament, and more than one way of understanding covenant. God forms covenants with Noah (Gen 9:1-17), Abram (Genesis 17), Moses and the people Israel (Exodus 19ff.), and David and his dynasty (2 Sam 7:1-17, Psalm 89). Jeremiah foresees a "new covenant" written on the hearts of the people (Jer 31:31-34).[11] But central to covenant in all its forms is submission and obedience to YHWH. Moreover, there is a dispute between those, like G. Mendenhall, who think that covenant was an early institution in Israel, and those, like E.W. Nicholson, who think it was a late creation of the prophets. But even Nicholson thinks that "covenant is the central expression of the distinctive faith of Israel as 'the people of Yahweh', the children of God by adoption and free decision rather than by nature or necessity."[12]

[10] So argues John McKenzie, in "Aspects of Old Testament Thought," in Brown, et al, *NJBC* 1298:82. See also Brevard S. Childs, *Biblical Theology of the Old and New Testaments* (Minneapolis: Fortress, 1993) 421–425.

[11] Commentators see the Abrahamic and Davidic covenants as the creations of the Davidic monarchy; the Noachic covenant was probably the creation of the Priestly writer, hence is to be dated about the time of the Exile.

[12] Nicholson, *God and His People,* 216.

Now, is the hierarchy between YHWH and the people Israel, as understood in the Hebrew scriptures, a command hierarchy, a participatory hierarchy, or a mixture of both?

On the one hand, a case can be made that it is a command hierarchy. After all, YHWH expresses his will in commandments (Heb *mitzvoth*), couched in a series of absolute imperatives, and threatens Israel with curses and even destruction if the commandments are not obeyed (Deut 28:15ff.). But on the other hand, a case can be made for participatory hierarchy. The whole aim of the covenant is to allow Israel to enter into participation in God's holiness, justice, and blessing. Israel's earliest experience of YHWH is as savior (Exodus 1–15): and this is how YHWH consistently identifies himself: "I am the LORD your God who brought you out of the land of Egypt, out of the house of bondage" (Exod 20:2). Later conceptions (e.g., Jeremiah 31) portray YHWH as a God of love, who wishes to share this love with the people. Images of God as king, which strike modern readers as dictatorial or oppressive, according to John McKenzie "should not be conceived of in the patterns of ancient Egypt and Mesopotamia or of more recent royalty. Theoretically, the Israelite king could be approached by any of his subjects. . . . Where the title of king is given to Yahweh, it emphasizes his power and will to save."[13] The images of God as father, mother, and shepherd, protector, as in Psalm 23 or 91, convey YHWH's caring and nurturing side. The image of the covenant as a marriage in Hosea 2 brings out the partnership aspect of YHWH's relationship with Israel. Nicholson concludes his study of covenant as follows:

> [YHWH] himself was a partner to it [the covenant]. In no sense, therefore, did the covenant theology conceive of life as mere observance, upon penalty of disaster, of divinely decreed laws. Rather, life for Israel was understood as fellowship with Yahweh who had entered a covenant with his people, and the fulfillment of Yahweh's commandments was to be an expression of this fellowship. Hence keeping the commandments can be described as loving Yahweh (cf. Exod 20:6 = Deut 5:10; Deut 7:9; 10:12; 11:1,13,22; 13:3; 19:9; 30:16,20; Josh 22:5).[14]

Actually one finds elements of both command hierarchy and participatory hierarchy in Israel's conception of YHWH, but it seems that

[13] John McKenzie, *NJBC* 1297, #75.

[14] Nicholson, *God and His People,* 215.

the participation motif is the more fundamental. This can be seen clearly if Israel's conception of creation is compared with that of Babylonia, as expressed in the Babylonian creation epic, the *Enuma Elish.* In the Babylonian account, which preceded that of Israel, the god-hero Marduk, after defeating the chaos-monster Tiamet, creates the world out of her corpse, and decides to create man:

> Blood will I mass and cause bones to be.
> I will establish a savage, 'man' shall be his name.
> Verily, savage-man I will create.
> He shall be charged with the service of the gods
> That they might be at ease![15]

Marduk then creates humanity out of the blood of an evil god, Kingu, who was put to death for inciting Tiamet to rebel.

In the Genesis account, which was modeled on the *Enuma Elish,* the understanding of creation is transformed. The created world is good precisely because it participates in and reflects the goodness of YHWH, its creator. Humanity is not created to be slaves to the gods, as in the Babylonian account, but to be God's steward or representative, governing the creation as God would if God were actually present. This is one meaning of the metaphor that humans are made in God's "image" (Gen 1:26). Ancient kings, since they could not be present in all parts of their kingdoms simultaneously, erected statues of themselves, or appointed deputies, as their 'images' or representatives, to govern in their stead. Far from being a slave, humanity is honored as being God's representative, and is given the dignity of naming the animals, and of tending and caring for the creation. In the Israelite conception, hierarchy, in the sense of oppression, only enters the world as a consequence of the first sin, after which God punishes the humans, and the woman is placed under the rule of the man (Gen 3:16). Before this, humankind is in fellowship with God, who walks in the garden and speaks with them, and cares for their welfare (Genesis 2).

The contrast is clear. In the *Enuma Elish,* humans are made to be slaves; in Genesis, they are made to be in fellowship with God. This can also be seen in the structure of the Priestly creation account (Gen

[15] English translation from James Pritchard, ed., *The Ancient Near East: an Anthology of Texts and Pictures* (Princeton: Princeton University Press, 1958) 36.

1–2:4). The creation of the world and humanity culminates in the sabbath, a day set aside for communion with God. Michael Welker argues that the process of creation is only fulfilled with the Sinai covenant and the construction and consecration of the sanctuary (Exodus 25–40), which becomes YHWH's dwelling place among the Israelites. He cites the Midrash Genesis Rabba 3:9, which says "from the beginning of the creation of the world the Holy One, to whom be praise, longed to have communion with those below (= human beings/creatures)."[16] The aim, then, of the creation of the world is not the subjugation of humanity to God, but communion between God and humanity, the condition of which is humanity's submission and filial obedience to YHWH. The relationship with God is meant to be a participatory hierarchy. A command hierarchy enters after the fall. But the aim even of command is to restore the participatory relationship lost by sin.

In sum, the hierarchical relationship with YHWH is expressed in covenants, submission to which creates and integrates Israel as the "People of God," and is intended to bring them into the presence of YHWH, the source of all blessings: "In your presence there is fullness of joy" (Psalm 16).

Mediation of the Covenant

The covenant with YHWH is mediated by holy men and women called for that purpose: patriarchs, prophets, judges, kings, and priests. The whole people, it is true, ratify the covenant (Exod 19:8). But YHWH's presence and will is mediated to the people by holy persons, preeminently Moses. It is Moses who goes up on Sinai alone to receive the words of the covenant; the people must wait at the foot of the mountain (Exod 19:16-25). Similarly, it is Moses (or Moses and Aaron) who goes into the presence of YHWH in the tent of meeting; the people wait outside the tent (Lev 9:22-24).

During the course of Israelite history various classes of mediators develop. Sometimes, especially in the early periods of Israelite history, the boundaries between these types are not rigid. What is important to

[16] Michael Welker, "Creation: Big Bang or the Work of Seven Days," *Theology Today* 52:2 (July 1995) 183. Welker is citing from Bernd Janowski, "Temple und Schöpfung: Schöpfungstheologische Aspekte der priesterschriftlichen Heiligtumskonzeption," *Schöpfung und Neuschöpfung. Jahrbuch für Biblische Theologie,* 5 (Neukirchen: Neukirchener, 1990) 61.

note is that typically YHWH's presence is mediated to the people *through more than one person, and more than one class of mediators*. Both priests and kings become institutionalized mediators of the covenant, but if either of these misuse the power entrusted to them, they may be confronted by prophets who call them back to covenant fidelity.

Patriarchs. The patriarchs were mediators between YHWH and their people. The classic instance of this is Abram, through whom God makes a covenant with all of Abram's descendants (Genesis 15). As mediator, Abram conveys YHWH's promises to the people, but also represents the people before YHWH, as shown in the scene where he intercedes for those who may be just in Sodom and Gomorrah (Gen 18:16-33). But Abram is not, even in his own time, the only mediator of God. Another is Melchizedek, king of Salem (= Jerusalem), who blesses Abram in the name of El Elyon (God Most High), which deity Abram identifies as his own God (Gen 14:17-24).

Priests. Though Exodus names Moses' brother Aaron as the first priest of Israel, the origins of the priesthood are probably more complex. A priest in Israel was one made holy so as to be able to approach YHWH more closely than non-consecrated persons. Though in one sense, the whole people were priests (Exod 19:6), YHWH's holiness was such that only specially consecrated persons could approach his sanctuary.

Priests in Israel had several functions. Prominent in the early years was the function of oracular consultation, in which the priest would "ask" God a question on behalf of a petitioner, and for reply would consult the Urim and the Thummim, objects used (as lots?) to divine the will of YHWH (cf. Judg 18:5; 1 Sam 14:41, 22:10,13,15; Deut 33:7-11). A related function was teaching the law (Deut 33:10). But the predominant function was offering sacrifice to YHWH for the sins of the people. In the earlier periods, non-priests (e.g., Abram, Saul, David) offered sacrifice, but during the Second Temple period (ca. 515 B.C.E.–70 C.E.), offering sacrifice was characteristic of priests. In the Second Temple period, a hierarchy developed within the priesthood itself, corresponding to the degree of holiness of different places in the Temple. Thus the Israelite laity, a holy people, could enter the Temple courtyard, whereas pagans (by definition an unclean or unholy people) could not. But only priests and Levites could enter the Temple building, because they were holier than the laity; again, only priests, but not Levites or laity, could approach the most holy objects: the altars of holocaust and incense; lastly, only the High Priest could enter the Holy of Holies, the most holy place, where YHWH dwelt.[17]

According to W. Eichrodt, the priest in Israel was "the indispensable mediator for entrance into the sphere of the divine."[18] Fr. Roland de Vaux also argues that the priest was always an intermediary between the people and God.

> The priest was a mediator, like the king and the prophet. But kings and prophets were mediators by reason of a personal charisma, because they were personally chosen by God; the priest was *ipso facto* a mediator, for the priesthood is an institution of mediation.[19]

What required mediation was the holiness of YHWH, which ordinary people could not approach except through sanctified persons. Like Abram and Moses, the priests transmit YHWH's will to the people. But they also represent the people before YHWH, for example when they sacrifice on behalf of the people, or consult YHWH on behalf of a petitioner.

Kingship. Two views of the monarchy are apparent in the Hebrew scriptures. The anti-royalist view is given in 1 Samuel 8ff.: the king will take the sons of the people and press them into his military service; he will take their daughters as servants, and will take a tenth of their crops, flocks, and vintage as tax to provide for his court. In short, the king will oppress the Israelites, and place them under a command hierarchy. The positive view is given in 1 Samuel 10, and elsewhere. Here Saul is anointed king by Samuel to rule the people of YHWH, and to defend them against their enemies. The anointing signifies that the king is inspired by the Spirit of YHWH to carry out his duties, primarily duties of war and defense. But, as consecrated persons, the kings also offered sacrifice on behalf of the people in difficult times, as when David offered holocausts and communion sacrifices to YHWH to avert a plague (2 Sam 24:25). Solomon is also shown praying for a wise and understanding heart, so that he can dispense justice among the people (like modern Arab sheiks), who approach him with peti-

[17] *NJBC*, 1258, #22.

[18] Cited in John McKenzie, *Dictionary of the Bible* (New York: Macmillan, 1965) 691.

[19] Roland de Vaux, O.P. *Ancient Israel, Religious Institutions*, vol. 2 (New York: McGraw Hill, 1965) 357.

tions (e.g., the two prostitutes who both claim to be the mother of one child—1 Kings 3).

Some psalms speak of the human king as God's son or as God's elect (Psalms 2, 18, 20, 21, 89, 110). Many scholars think that the king in Israel may have functioned as YHWH's deputy or representative, mediating the blessings of YHWH to the whole nation. Helmer Ringgren writes:

> The king is considered Yahweh's son: he is enthroned at Yahweh's side. Since he was chosen and installed as king by Yahweh, he exercises dominion on Yahweh's behalf. . . . He is Yahweh's representative, so to speak.[20]

Lawrence Boadt notes:

> Thus the person of the king was sacred and above violation; he embodied blessing for the land (see Psalms 2, 110). He brought harmony to the state, and so all must pray for his well-being (Pss 20:1-5; 72:15). He was an adopted son of God (Ps 2:7), protector of his people (Ps 89:18), gave fertility to the land (Ps 72:3, 16) and established justice for all (Ps 72:1-4).[21]

But as Boadt also notes, in Israel YHWH alone was truly king. The Israelite king was always subject to YHWH, and at most claimed to be his deputy, ruling with the wisdom given him by YHWH's Spirit. The king in Israel was never considered to be a divine being, like the Egyptian kings. Though anointed by YHWH, the king was also acclaimed by all the people as their leader. The consent of the people was crucial. Saul was proclaimed king by the people at Gilgal (1 Sam 11:15). David was anointed king over Judah by the men of Judah (2 Sam 2:4), and king over Israel by the elders of Israel (2 Sam 5:3). Rehoboam is rejected as king of the Northern kingdom because he fails to receive the consensus of the people (1 Kings 12). These stories seem to conflict with, or at least complement, the passage where David is anointed king by Samuel in the presence of his brothers (1 Sam 16:13). But the

[20] Helmer Ringgren, *Israelite Religion* (Philadelphia: Fortress Press, 1966) 227. The view that the king was consecrated as YHWH's adopted son, perhaps in a New Year ceremony, has been championed by members of the so-called Scandinavian school, but has been subjected to criticism. See Brown, et al., *NJBC,* 1280–1281.

[21] Lawrence Boadt, *Reading the Old Testament* (Mahwah, N.J.: Paulist Press, 1984) 243. See also Keith Whitelam, "King and Kingship," *ABD,* IV, 40–48.

principle is clear: the king's authority derives *both* from YHWH and from popular consent.

The king, then, along with the priests, ideally mediated the blessings of YHWH to the people, particularly the blessing of political unity and stability, but also justice. But there was always the temptation for the king to misuse his power and oppress the people. For example, Solomon enslaved the descendants of the pre-Israelite population (1 Kgs 9:15-24), and laid heavy burdens on the Israelites themselves (1 Kgs 12:2-5). His son Rehoboam proclaimed to the people, "My father made your yoke heavy, but I will add to your yoke; my father disciplined you with whips, but I will discipline you with scorpions" (1 Kgs 12:14). The result of this speech was schism: the Northern kingdom separated from the "house of David" which continued to rule the Southern kingdom (1 Kgs 12:16-19). The negative view of kingship, which exists in the texts side by side with the positive view, reminds us of the tendency for participatory hierarchy to decay into command hierarchy, and the tendency of command hierarchy to promote rebellion and fragmentation.

Prophets. The word prophet means "one who speaks for another." Prophets in Israel thought of themselves as speaking the words that YHWH gave them to speak; they were mouthpieces of God. Hence the recurring phrase, "Thus says the Lord." Prophets might be inspired by dreams, visions, mystical experiences, or by hearing the word of the Lord; but in all cases they mediated the divine mind and will. Even in the Hebrew scriptures, prophets did not have to be Israelites; the oracles of Balaam (Numbers 22–24), an enemy of Israel, were regarded as true prophecies.

The greatest of those called prophets in the Old Testament was Moses, the mediator par excellence (Deut 34:10). It was to Moses that YHWH revealed the divine name (Exodus 3), Moses who led the Israelites out of Egypt, and who ascended the mountain to receive the words of the covenant at Sinai. Yet even in Moses' time, there were other mediators of God's mind and will: Moses' sister Miriam is said to be a prophetess (Exod 15:20), and his brother Aaron, a prophet (Exod 7:1, Num 12:2-8) and the first priest.

Prophecy was institutionalized at times in Israel. 'Court prophets' served the king, who consulted them on important matters. For example, Ahab consulted the court prophets before marching to war against Ramoth-gilead (1 Kgs 22:1-54). But often these prophets were not true prophets, as the incident with Ahab shows. There, Micaiah predicted defeat, while the court prophets predicted victory; Micaiah, however, proved to be right.

True prophets were those who spoke the authentic words of YHWH, as could be demonstrated by the way events turned out (Deut 18:21-22). They were, so to speak, free-lance mediators, called unpredictably by YHWH from amid the people to speak his words, usually to hostile hearers (e.g., Micaiah, Amos, Jeremiah). Often the prophets were called to challenge the king or people for violations of the covenant. A famous example is Nathan's rebuke of David for David's murder of Uriah the Hittite and his possession of Uriah's wife, Bathsheba (2 Sam 12:1-25). The saga of Elijah and Ahab is another extended example of this (1 Kings 17ff.). Amos was called to challenge the wealthy of the Northern kingdom for oppressing the poor, which was a covenant violation. And Isaiah condemns the people for injustice, which he sees as rebellion against Yahweh and the covenant (Isaiah 1).

Prophets also challenged the institutionalized priesthood. Amos writes (YHWH is speaking):

> I hate, I despise your festivals, and I take no delight in your solemn assemblies. Even though you offer me your burnt offerings and grain offerings, I will not accept them; and the offerings of well-being of your fatted animals I will not look upon. . . . But let justice roll down like waters, and righteousness like an ever-flowing stream (Amos 5:21-24).

Such strictures were not criticisms of the priesthood per se, but of its misuse.

The prophets also challenged the people to live righteously, so that they might be truly the Holy People of God. This is a common theme in the prophets. Isaiah sounds this theme in his great opening chapter: "I reared children and brought them up, but they have rebelled against me. The ox knows its owner, and the donkey its master's crib, but Israel does not know, my people do not understand" (Isa 1:2-3).

Thus the prophets were YHWH's gadflies, calling the institutional mediators of the covenant, the priests and kings, to covenant fidelity and the people to righteousness. In this connection it is important to note that YHWH's mind and will were mediated to Israel not by one person or by one class of persons, but by diverse persons and classes of persons, who often conflicted. There was a system of checks and balances, lest persons or groups misuse their status as mediators of the covenant for selfish or unholy purposes (as did David with Bathsheba).

Elders. Early in Israel's history a class of men known as elders (Hebrew: *zeqenim;* Greek: *presbyteroi*) appears, whose function is to give counsel, set community policy, and administer covenant law.[22] Yahweh charges them with the quotidian care of the people Israel:

> So the LORD said to Moses, "Gather for me seventy of the elders of Israel, whom you know to be elders of the people and officers over them; bring them to the tent of meeting, and have them take their place there with you. I will come down and talk with you there; and I will take some of the spirit that is on you and put it on them; and they shall bear the burden of the people along with you" (Num 11:16-17).

In the Second Temple period, Jewish communities appear to have been governed by councils or colleges of elders, many of whom were elected or were representatives of synagogue congregations. The synagogue building at Alexandria held seventy-one thrones for its elders and president.[23] John Meier notes that at Antioch, the elders "were the representatives of the various synagogues in the city . . . The council of elders *(gerousia)* would thus be the governing body for all Antiochene Jews."[24] The college of seventy elders at Jerusalem was the Sanhedrin. The college of elders in turn was often presided over by a chief officer or officers—a ruler, "archon," or community chief.[25] James Burtchaell argues persuasively that this community structure was imitated by the earliest Church, which structured itself on the pattern of the synagogue. The role of elders in the synagogue was taken by the presbyters in the Church, whose presiders eventually became known as *episcopoi,* bishops. This type of representative community structure would continue to be important in the early Church. Like the elders of the synagogue, Christian elders and bishops drew their authority both from a divine

[22] See James Burtchaell, *From Synagogue to Church* (Cambridge: Cambridge University Press, 1992) 228ff. For biblical examples of the administrative authority of the elders, see Deut 19:12; 21:2-6; 22:15-18; Judg 11:5-11; Ruth 4:2-11; etc. Many more citations are given by Burtchaell.

[23] Burtchaell, *From Synagogue to Church,* 230.

[24] Raymond E. Brown and John P. Meier, *Antioch and Rome: New Testament Cradles of Catholic Christianity* (New York: Paulist Press, 1983) 31.

[25] Ibid.; Burtchaell, *From Synagogue to Church,* 233–244.

anointing or consecration, and from the fact that they were representatives of their communities.

It seems that the hierarchical mediation of the covenant in Israel became too centralized, established, and exclusive towards the end of the Second Temple Period, when kingship had disappeared, prophets had mostly become Temple officials producing liturgical texts, the sanctuary and priesthood had been centralized at the Temple, somewhat remote from the life of the average Israelite.[26] The High Priests of the Temple had become an elite clerical caste, no longer representative of the people. In Jesus' time, pilgrimages were made to the Temple three times a year, for the feasts of Passover, Tents, and Pentecost. From Galilee, this meant a journey of some eighty miles, probably on foot. How often did the average Israelite make this journey? Three times a year? Less? We cannot be sure. But worship was held in local synagogues frequently (weekly or more often), as can be seen in the Gospel narratives, where Jesus preaches regularly in the synagogues, but travels to the Temple only infrequently (once in the synoptic Gospels, three or four times in John). Synagogue services were conducted by rabbis (teachers), not priests, and, if we can trust the Gospel accounts, any male Israelite could rise to read the scriptures, or to speak (Luke 4:16-30). In short, the structure was more participatory than the Temple structure, which was remote, and in which the male Israelite, and even more the women, had to view the sacrifices from afar (only the priests could approach the altar of sacrifice). It was only the synagogue structure which was to survive the war with the Romans (66–70 C.E.)

In sum, then, hierarchy in Israel was grounded in the hierarchy of the Creator YHWH, who called his people Israel to participate in his blessings by being faithful to the covenant. *It was submission to YHWH and his covenant that constituted Israel as the People of God.* Hierarchy, therefore, was essential to Israel's existence as a holy people. Violation

[26] John Dominic Crossan writes: "By John's [the Baptist] time the only place in the country where Jews could legally offer sacrifices was Jerusalem, and its services were expensive. To introduce into this situation a new, inexpensive, generally available, divinely authorized rite, effective for the remission of all sins, was John's great invention. His warning of the coming judgment was nothing new; prophets had been predicting that for the past eight centuries. The new thing was the assurance that there was something the average man could easily do to prepare himself for the catastrophic coming of the kingdom." *The Historical Jesus*, 231.

of the covenant meant that one was cut off from the people; violation of the covenant by the whole people meant destruction. The covenant was mediated by different groups: principally priests, kings, prophets, and elders, each having unique functions: the priests sacrificing for the sins of the people and mediating YHWH's presence and holiness; kings (ideally) mediating justice and political unity; prophets calling for moral righteousness and worship of YHWH alone, elders administering the day-to-day governance of the people. Mediation of the covenant was never exclusively given to just one individual or group; each group, but especially the prophets, provided checks and balances against misuse of covenantal responsibilities by other groups. The people held an essential role of consent and election; they elected the king, and elected the elders of the synagogues. When this privilege of acclamation and consent was bypassed, as in the case of the High Priests of the late Second Temple, an ingrown clerical caste developed.

The pattern of hierarchy in Israel continued on into the early Christian Church. There also the fundamental relationship with God was to be a participation in God's own life, through the mediation of Christ and the Spirit. The whole Christian people was regarded as a consecrated people, like ancient Israel (1 Pet 2:9-10). The New Covenant in Christ was mediated to the people through different groups: apostles, community elders, bishops, teachers, prophets. The people retained the right of election of bishops, and (probably) of community elders. This was grounded in the fact that the New Covenant, like the Old, was made with a whole people, not just with a clerical hierarchy, and so the whole people had the right to share in ecclesial decisions.

The following chapters will consider the emergence of hierarchy in the Jesus movement and the early Church.

Chapter 3

Hierarchy in the New Testament

And he sat down and called the twelve; and he said to them, "If any one would be first, he must be last of all and servant of all." (Mark 9:35)

Jesus and the Kingdom

The New Testament is composed of writings derived from traditions which span the period from the birth of Jesus to the formation of the early Church—the critical period in Christian history. In the later New Testament writings we can already see the emergence of a church hierarchy. Thus, in the letters to Timothy and Titus, the so-called pastoral epistles, the author instructs Timothy and Titus to appoint elders (Greek: *presbyteroi*) in the churches. The same process is apparent in Acts 20, where Paul instructs the elders (whom he had presumably appointed earlier) of the church at Ephesus.

The question is, how did this hierarchy emerge? The traditional Catholic answer has been that Jesus appointed apostles, who then appointed bishops to govern the Church in their absence. But modern scholarship has shown that this picture is oversimplified. Further, Protestant scholars have long argued that the early Jesus movement was non-hierarchical, and that the emergence of established bishops and church offices was a deformation of Jesus' more egalitarian intentions.[1]

[1] "Since the nineteenth century there has been a consensus among most historical scholars . . . According to that consensus a vitally new kind of community

Recently some Catholic scholars have argued the same. This is a critical point, for if we cannot establish any hierarchy, even a participatory hierarchy, in the time of Jesus himself, it would be difficult (though not impossible, from a Catholic point of view) to legitimatize a subsequent hierarchy. In this chapter, then, I shall take up several questions: was Jesus' own relationship with God hierarchical? Was the original Jesus movement hierarchical? Did Jesus vouchsafe hierarchical authority to his disciples?

The literature on these problems is immense. Due to space limitations, my treatment of this material must be brief and selective; endnotes will refer the reader to the larger discussion.

Jesus and the Father

It seems almost beyond dispute that Jesus' own relationship with the Father was not egalitarian (i.e., he did not claim to be the equal of the Father), but one of hierarchical communion. His use of the Aramaic *Abba,* a term still used by Palestinian children for their fathers, indicates as much. Children do not think of themselves as the equals of their fathers, least of all in Jesus' culture. Jesus is reported to have said "The Father and I are One" (John 10:30), and "the Father is greater than I" (John 14:28), but not "the Father and I are equal." His attitude throughout his ministry suggests profound obedience to the Father, most evidently in Gethsemane, where he prays, "not what I will, but what thou wilt" (Mark 14:36, RSV). His whole ministry is one of surrender to the will of the Father. His notion of the kingdom, or reign, of God, which was the core of his preaching, seems likewise to have been an affirmation of God's absolute sovereignty. Nevertheless, some modern scripture scholars now argue that Jesus' notion of the kingdom of God was not hierarchical, but egalitarian. Here I will consider two of the most prominent: John Dominic Crossan and Elizabeth Schüssler Fiorenza.

---

arose among the disciples of Jesus. It enjoyed two or perhaps three generations in which the Spirit was given free play, without formal structures of an official establishment. It was the threat of division within the community, and of perverse teaching, that persuaded the faithful to consolidate under the protection of a clerical regime with a hierarchy of officers. Christian life, so this story goes, has never been as animated since then." Burtchaell, *From Synagogue to Church,* xiii. Burtchaell sees the roots of this consensus as reaching back to the Reformation.

Was the Jesus Movement Egalitarian?

In two recent books, *The Historical Jesus: the Life of a Mediterranean Peasant* (1991) and *Jesus: a Revolutionary Biography* (1994),[2] Crossan has argued that the original Jesus movement was egalitarian, but that this died out shortly after Jesus' death and was replaced by a hierarchical Church. Crossan's books are widely read and directly contradict my contention that the original Jesus movement exemplified participatory hierarchy, so I will engage his argument at length.

The reconstruction of an historically accurate picture of Jesus—the so-called "historical Jesus"—from the New Testament writings is an exceedingly difficult and intricate task, fraught with scholarly controversy. This is true for several reasons. First, we do not have a direct record of Jesus' deeds or his teachings. The gospel accounts were first handed on orally for some forty years after his death before they were written down. When they were written down, the ancient authors used considerable editorial liberty in telling the stories, at times retrojecting comments of their own into the story, or even into the mouth of Jesus. Thus two gospel accounts of the same event may differ considerably (e.g., the two versions of the Lord's prayer: Matt 6:9-13 and Luke 11:2-4). Second, the New Testament accounts, while historical, are also faith-documents, concerned as much for the Christ of faith as with the Jesus of history. Third, the gospel accounts are extremely brief, and there are very few non-Christian references concerning the historical Jesus. The result is that the data on Jesus' life and teaching are so meager and ambiguous that they may be compatible with many different reconstructions, depending on the viewpoint, or prejudices, of the historian. Recent scholars have proposed a number of different "historical Jesuses," as Crossan himself notes: "There is Jesus as a political revolutionary by S.G.F. Brandon (1967), as a magician by Morton Smith (1978), as a Galilean charismatic by Geza Vermes (1981, 1984), as a Galilean rabbi by Bruce Chilton (1984), . . . as an Essene by Harvey Falk, and as an eschatological prophet by E.P. Sanders. . . . it seems we can have as many pictures as there are exegetes."[3] The very diversity and even incompatibility of these various portraits should make us suspicious of the 'objectivity' of the historical Jesus reconstructed by scholars.

[2] *The Historical Jesus: the Life of a Mediterranean Peasant* (San Francisco: Harper, 1991); *Jesus: a Revolutionary Biography* (San Francisco: Harper, 1994).

[3] *The Historical Jesus,* xxviii.

Most historians use a number of criteria to assess the historicity of a gospel saying or event.[4] Some of the most commonly used are the following. 1. *Multiple attestation.* If a saying or event is attested by more than one independent source, it is likely to go back to the historical Jesus. The key here is "independent." If Matthew and Luke both copy a pericope from Mark, there is only one independent attestation. 2. *Multiform attestation.* If a saying or theme is reflected in a number of different forms, such as sayings, parables, and narrative, it is more likely to be authentic. 3. *Discontinuity.* If a saying reflects a teaching which is not found in Jesus' Jewish context and is not found in the early Church, it must go back to Jesus. Classic examples of this are Jesus' use of "*Abba*" = "Daddy" to address God and his use of "Amen" to introduce an important saying, both forms of speech not found in the Judaism of Jesus' time nor in early Christian usage. Discontinuity, however, can only be used to ascertain a minimum of reliable data about Jesus, since used by itself it would yield an historical Jesus who was disconnected both from his contemporary Jewish environment and from the later Church. 4. *Embarrassment.* If an incident would have been embarrassing to the early Christian communities, it probably was not created by them and retrojected, but must go back to the historical Jesus. An example is Jesus' baptism by John, which would have been embarrassing for the early Church because it implied that Jesus needed to be baptized for sins. 5. *Coherence.* Whatever coheres with what can be established by multiple and multiform attestation, discontinuity, embarrassment, etc. is likely to be authentic. A special class of this is the coherence of sayings and events. For example, Jesus' sayings about the destruction of the Temple cohere with his action of cleansing the Temple (a symbolic destruction), and with the charges made against him at his trial.

Crossan's own method involves a reconstruction of Jesus' cultural, social, and political context using anthropology and history, and then an assessment of Jesus' deeds and sayings within that context. For example, he provides anthropological evidence that peasant movements

[4] See for example the discussion of criteria in John Meier, *A Marginal Jew: Rethinking the Historical Jesus,* vol. 1 (New York: Doubleday, 1991) 167–195. Also Marcus Borg, "The Teaching of Jesus," *ABD,* vol. 3, 805. The limitation of these criteria is that in practice they focus only on those aspects of Jesus' life and teachings that can be demonstrated with a high degree of historical probability. This yields a scanty or minimalist portrait of Jesus.

generally have opposed hierarchical structures of domination and exploitation. But Jesus was a peasant. Therefore anthropological evidence reinforces those sayings and deeds of Jesus which seem to be egalitarian, such as eating with outcasts and sinners.

But, as Crossan admits, "any study of the historical Jesus stands or falls on how one handles the literary level of the text itself."[5] How does he establish which of Jesus' sayings and deeds were authentic? His method, in effect, depends mainly on one criterion: multiple attestation in the earliest sources. First, he assigns dates to all the texts concerning Jesus, both those within the canon and extra-canonical or apocryphal texts (he gives no method for this, however, but expects the reader to trust his judgment). He elects to use only those texts written in the earliest stratum (i.e., those written between 30 and 60 C.E.) on the assumption that the earlier texts are more historically reliable than later texts. Then he excludes all those texts which have only one attestation in the first strata. His reasoning is that if a text appears in two independent sources, neither source could have invented the material, which must therefore go back to a period before the authorship of either text, presumably to the historical Jesus. This method excludes a great deal of material, including many of the parables in Luke (e.g., the good Samaritan).[6] Nonetheless, enough remains to allow Crossan to reconstruct an historical Jesus, especially because he dates many of the apocryphal texts, particularly the Gospel of Thomas, much earlier than most scholars, and assumes that they are independent sources.

Crossan begins *The Historical Jesus* with a long sociological and historical reconstruction of the Roman, Greek, and Jewish milieu into which Jesus was born. He details a hierarchical society deeply stratified into classes, organized according to patronage and slavery, honor and shame. Ruling the society was the governing class (one percent of the population), accompanied by the retainer class (scribes, bureaucrats, military personnel), the merchants, and the priests, all of whom served the governing class. At the bottom was the peasant class, the vast majority of the population who existed in a permanent state of oppression and exploitation. There were a number of revolts by Jews against Roman domination, culminating in the Roman Jewish war of

[5] *The Historical Jesus*, xxix.

[6] Crossan does not argue that such material is not authentic, only that it cannot be demonstrated to be so by his method.

66–70 C.E., when the Temple was destroyed by the Romans (70 C.E.). Apocalyptic leaders and movements also emerged, predicting that God would intervene miraculously to destroy the Romans, judge between the wicked and the righteous, and restore sovereignty and prosperity to Israel. Foremost among these was John the Baptist who preached the coming of the kingdom of God, in which God would appear as judge, destroying the wicked (both Jews and Gentiles) and vindicating the righteous. To prepare people for this coming judgment, John preached the necessity of repentance, and baptized those who repented in the Jordan river.

Within this milieu Crossan traces the career of the historical Jesus. Jesus was baptized by John, indicating an initial acceptance of John's message and apocalyptic outlook. But, according to Crossan, Jesus changed his mind after the death of John, and came to understand the kingdom as the present power of God rather than as a coming apocalypse. This Crossan terms a *sapiential* vision of the kingdom, because it requires wisdom (L. *sapientia*) "for discerning how, here and now in this world, one can so live that God's power, rule, and dominion are evidently present to all observers. One enters that kingdom by wisdom or goodness, by virtue, justice, or freedom. It is a style of life for now rather than a hope for life for the future."[7] Jesus welcomed all into this kingdom, especially the destitute, the outcasts, the marginalized—it was a radically egalitarian kingdom of "nuisances and nobodies," which "rendered sexual and social, political and religious distinctions completely irrelevant and anachronistic."[8] Jesus expressed by "open commensality": open table fellowship with those most despised by his society. This "brokerless kingdom" existed without any mediators: Jesus himself was not a mediator, nor were the disciples or apostles. Furthermore, Jesus did not settle in one place (and so did not end up creating a place-centered hierarchical mediation of the kingdom, as was the case with the Temple), but wandered about the Galilean countryside teaching the kingdom. Finally, Jesus opposed the patriarchal family, as indicated by some of his sayings: e.g., "they will be divided: father against son and son against father, mother against daughter and daughter against mother, mother-in-law against her daughter-in-law and daughter-in-law against mother-in-law" (Luke 12:53 = Matt 10:34-36).

[7] Crossan, *Jesus*, 56.

[8] Crossan, *The Historical Jesus*, 298.

Crossan writes: "But, for Jesus, the Kingdom of God is a community of radical or unbroken equality in which individuals are in direct contact with one another and with God, unmediated by any established brokers or fixed locations."[9] In his itinerant and impoverished lifestyle, and in his use of short, gnomic wisdom sayings, Jesus is likened by Crossan to the wandering Greek philosophers known as Cynics. But his egalitarianism was that of Mediterranean peasantry.

Jesus aroused the antipathy of those who controlled the Temple: the religious, social, and political hierarchy of Israel, by his egalitarian lifestyle, his "cleansing of the Temple" (which was actually a symbolic destruction of the Temple), and by his prophecies against the Temple. For this he was put to death. Because all the disciples ran away, they knew nothing of the details of his passion and crucifixion. Consequently the stories of Jesus' passion and death, as recounted in the four Gospels, have been invented by the evangelists in order to make the events of Jesus' death conform to Jewish prophecies. Much the same is true of the Last Supper accounts, which were also invented by the evangelists. Jesus was probably buried in a shallow unmarked grave by those who crucified him; his followers would not have known where he was buried. Crossan implies his body was dug up and eaten by wild dogs.[10] There was no resurrection; resurrection accounts were invented by Jesus' followers, emphasized by Paul (to legitimize his role as an apostle), and retrojected by the Gospel writers.[11] But Jesus did live on in the hearts and minds of his followers, as a kind of empowering presence. Nonetheless, his open commensality and brokerless kingdom was perverted by his followers into a hierarchical operation, in which Jesus became the mediator between God and humanity[12] and the disciples became the mediators of Jesus. From this came the Constantinian church, with all its emphasis on hierarchy and imperial authority.

[9] Ibid., 101.

[10] Crossan, *Jesus,* 154.

[11] Ibid., 163–170.

[12] Crossan insists that Jesus was "neither broker nor mediator" (*The Historical Jesus,* 422) but also writes that he sees no betrayal or contradiction in the Pastoral Letters' confession of Jesus as the "one mediator between God and humankind . . ." (1 Tim 2:5), because Jesus was "himself the unmediated presence of the divine to the human" (*The Historical Jesus,* 424). I think this latter statement makes no sense unless one denies that Jesus was human, and so could claim his divinity came to us "unmediated." In fact Crossan seems to contradict himself here: Jesus was not a mediator, yet he was one.

How reliable is Crossan's portrait of Jesus? The first thing to say is that his Jesus bears little resemblance to the Jesus preached by the Gospel writers, by Paul, or indeed by any New Testament writer. Crossan's Jesus welcomes all into fellowship *without demanding any repentance.* Unlike the Gospel Jesus, there is no emphasis on judgment (which would be hierarchical), no threats delivered to those who will not repent (e.g., Matt 11:20-24), no harsh words (except to the Temple authorities), no coming of the kingdom, as mentioned in the Lord's prayer, for the kingdom is already present. There is no Lord's Prayer, no Son of Man sayings (all retrojected), no second coming or Last Judgment, no Last Supper, no institution of the Eucharist. All the details of the passion and crucifixion were made up and retrojected, and there was no resurrection. Jesus did not appoint the twelve apostles in his lifetime (to do so would connote the establishment of a hierarchy). Furthermore Crossan's Jesus dissolved family ties, and was indifferent to and ignored the ritual laws of Judaism. He thus can scarcely be considered a Jew. Rather he is a Jesus who is discontinuous both with his Jewish milieu and with the memories of the early Church.

A second consideration is Crossan's method. Whereas virtually all scholars use many criteria of historicity simultaneously, Crossan uses mainly one: multiple attestation. The problem with relying too heavily on one criterion is that each criterion is limited and needs to be complemented by others. Excessive reliance on one criterion will likely result in a skewed picture of the historical Jesus. Sayings such as Jesus' promise to the Twelve that they would sit on thrones judging the twelve tribes of Israel (Matt 19:28), which are widely regarded as authentic because they would have been an embarrassment to the early Church, fail the criterion of multiple attestation, and so are not considered by Crossan.[13] Another problem with his method is his extremely early dating of apocryphal gospels and sources, especially the Gospel of Thomas, which many scholars regard as dependent on the canonical Gospels. This dating has been criticized by John Meier, Raymond Brown, and others.[14] A third criticism of Crossan's method is that he cites only scholars who agree with him and ignores those who do not. Nor does he inform readers that many of his positions are disputed by most New Testament scholars.

[13] See E.P. Sanders, *Jesus and Judaism* (Philadelphia: Fortress, 1985) 98ff.

[14] Meier, *A Marginal Jew,* vol. 1, 114–123, 142–152; Raymond Brown, *New Testament Studies* 33 (1987) 321–343.

Much of Crossan's method derives from the so-called Jesus Seminar, which he and Robert Funk have co-chaired. Typically those who support Crossan's reconstruction, such as Marcus Borg, are also members of this seminar. But, according to Richard B. Hays, professor of New Testament at Duke University, "most professional biblical scholars are profoundly skeptical of the methods and conclusions of this academic splinter group."[15] In particular, this group, like Crossan, sees Jesus as a Cynic philosopher who did *not* preach a coming apocalyptic judgment and kingdom. Hays has this to say: "The depiction of Jesus as a Cynic philosopher with no concern about Israel's destiny, no connection with the concerns and hopes that animated his Jewish contemporaries, no interest in the interpretation of scripture, and no message of God's coming eschatological judgment is—quite simply—an ahistorical fiction, achieved by the surgical removal of Jesus from his Jewish context."[16] In contrast with Crossan, Geza Vermes, the foremost Jewish scholar writing on the historical Jesus, argues that Jesus was an observant Jew who regularly attended synagogue and attended the pilgrimage feasts at the Temple.[17] Since the end of the nineteenth century, when Johannes Weiss and Albert Schweitzer argued that Jesus was an eschatological prophet, most scholars writing on the historical Jesus (except those connected with the Jesus Seminar) have argued that Jesus preached an eschatological judgment and restoration of Israel. John Meier, in *A Marginal Jew,* which Raymond Brown considers the best study of the historical Jesus in this century, writes:

> Across all these strands and forms of the Jesus tradition one point was constantly confirmed: Jesus did understand the central symbol of the kingdom of God in terms of the definitive coming of God in the near future to bring the present state of things to an end and to establish his full and unimpeded reign over the world in general and Israel in particular. . . . Any reconstruction of the historical Jesus that does not do justice to this eschatological future must be dismissed as hopelessly inadequate.[18]

[15] Richard B. Hays, "The Corrected Jesus," *First Things* (May, 1994) 47.

[16] Ibid., 47.

[17] Geza Vermes, *Jesus and the World of Judaism* (Philadelphia: Fortress, 1983), and *The Religion of Jesus the Jew* (Minneapolis: Fortress, 1993) 13ff.

[18] Meier, *A Marginal Jew,* vol. 2, 349–350. Raymond Brown's comment is as follows: "When John Meier's work (at least three volumes) is finished it will be the best historical Jesus study produced in the twentieth century—a necessary antidote

E.P. Sanders, in his highly regarded *Jesus and Judaism*, agrees: ". . . to pull Jesus entirely out of this [eschatological] framework would be an act of historical violence."[19]

The question of an eschatological reign of God, involving vindication for the righteous, and punishment for the wicked, is important, for it would be *ipso facto* an expression of hierarchy, and a denial of Crossan's ideology of an egalitarian kingdom.

What is it that leads Crossan to deny the eschatological and apocalyptic character of the kingdom Jesus preached? Does it follow as a result of his method? In fact it does not. In a pivotal chapter entitled "John and Jesus,"[20] Crossan discusses primary strata texts from *six* independent sources (indicating extremely high multiple attestation, and therefore highly probable authenticity) which describe Jesus' apocalyptic return. But he dismisses the historical accuracy of all these texts, apparently on the grounds that the title "Son of Man," which appears in one of them, could not have been used by or of the historical Jesus. But, as Meier notes, Jesus' apocalyptic return does not stand or fall with the historical accuracy of the Son of Man title; it is independent of that title.[21] Yet Crossan argues at the beginning of *The Historical Jesus* that "Something found in at least two independent sources from the primary stratum cannot have been created by either of them."[22] Therefore one would think that *six* independent attestations of Jesus' apocalyptic return would indicate a tradition probably originating with the historical Jesus. Nevertheless Crossan rejects it for a superficial reason: the problem with the "Son of Man" title.

This pattern recurs throughout *The Historical Jesus*. The most egregious example is Crossan's rejection of the historicity of the whole passion and crucifixion narratives, attested to in all Gospels and Paul (1 Cor 15:1-5). His reason is that the disciples ran away during the passion and crucifixion and therefore could not have wit-

---

to the unwarrantedly speculative (and historically minimizing) character of the work of 'The Jesus Seminar' . . . and of books like J.D. Crossan's *The Historical Jesus*." From Raymond E. Brown, *An Introduction to New Testament Christology* (New York: Paulist Press, 1994) 216.

[19] Sanders, *Jesus and Judaism*, 329–330.

[20] Crossan, *The Historical Jesus*, 227–264.

[21] Meier, *A Marginal Jew*, vol. 2, 350.

[22] Crossan, *The Historical Jesus*, xxxii–xxxiii.

nessed it![23] What shall we say to this? In the first place, the fourth Gospel places Mary, Mary's sister, Mary Magdalene, and the beloved disciple (who is not named), as eyewitnesses to the crucifixion. Yet Crossan ignores this testimony, not even bothering to refute it. But secondly, even if all the disciples had run away, they could have found out what happened by talking later to those who had been present.

For similarly insubstantial reasons Crossan rejects the historicity of the Last Supper, the institution of the Eucharist, and the appointment of the Twelve during Jesus' lifetime,[24] events which have multiple attestation from independent sources and which the majority of scholars accept as approximately historically accurate.[25] Not surprisingly, Crossan's Jesus turns out to be a modern egalitarian, quite like Crossan himself. Having swept away most of the historical evidence with specious assumptions, Crossan is free to reconstruct a Jesus in his own image.[26] This nicely illustrates the problem with historical reconstructions which sever the historical Jesus from the memory of the early Church. Luke T. Johnson writes:

> For all their self-conscious methodology and social-scientific sophistication, Crossan's efforts reveal themselves as an only slightly camouflaged exercise in theological revisionism rather than genuine historiography. Crossan pays virtually no attention to the light that might be shed on "the historical Jesus" by references, for example, in Paul. His accounts of Christian origins bypass completely those in canonical writings such as the Acts of the Apostles. To construct his portrayal of Jesus, he will draw on any apocryphal writing in preference to any canonical writing. The criteria that matter for determining authenticity are those that make up the predetermined portrait that Crossan wishes to emerge. His use of cross-cultural patterns reduces Jesus to a stereotyped cultural category, that of a member of

[23] Ibid., 375ff.; Crossan, *Jesus,* 145.

[24] Crossan, *The Historical Jesus,* 360–367; *Jesus,* 130 (The Last Supper and Eucharist). See John Meier's criticisms in his review of *The Historical Jesus,* in *America* (March 7, 1992) 198–199.

[25] John Meier, "Jesus," *NJBC,* ibid., Ben Meyer, "Jesus Christ," *ABD,* ibid.

[26] E.P. Sanders comments: "It is amazing that so many New Testament scholars write books about Jesus in which they discover that he agrees with their own version of Christianity. After [Albert] Schweitzer's devastating exposé of previous scholarship on just this point, one would think that people would be more sensitive to the issue. But it is seldom raised." *Jesus and Judaism,* 330.

"peasant culture." Into this *historical cipher* Crossan can pour his own vision of what "Christianity" ought to be.[27]

The strongest evidence Crossan provides for Jesus' egalitarianism is that he practiced "open commensality" with the marginalized and disregarded the social rankings of his time. Now this much is certainly historically true of Jesus. Does this make his movement egalitarian, as Crossan claims?

Actually, others before Crossan have also claimed this. Crossan stands in a long line of scholars who have used sociology to reconstruct the early Jesus movement. One of the first and most distinguished is Gerd Theissen, Professor of New Testament at the University of Heidelberg, whose sociological reconstruction is far more balanced than Crossan's. Theissen sees the early Jesus movement as composed of wandering charismatics, who had given up home (Matt 8:20), family (Luke 14:26), wealth and possessions (Mark 10:17ff.), and protection, and had entrusted themselves to God's care, though they also depended on sympathizers (e.g., Lazarus, Mary and Martha) in local communities.[28] Given this sociological setting, many of Jesus' radical ethical pronouncements make sense, for example the demands to "hate" father and mother, wife and children, brother and sister, and even one's own life (Luke 14:26), or the radical demand to give up wealth, and trust in God to provide (Matt 6:25-32). Jesus and his followers were outsiders, who, in Theissen's words "lived as those who expected the end of the world."[29] As well as preaching in synagogues, Jesus consorted and ate with the poor, the sick, prostitutes and tax collectors, the marginalized. Like Crossan, Theissen interprets this as meaning that the Jesus movement was egalitarian. Is this correct?

First, it is undeniable that Jesus flouted the social conventions of his time, including the social hierarchies, and associated with those whom the society rejected. Crossan is right to call attention to this. If Jesus' mission was to restore Israel, the People of God, then he had to regather *all* Israelites, including the marginalized (see below). Furthermore, for Jesus all persons were by nature children of the Father and

[27] *The Real Jesus: the Misguided Quest for the Historical Jesus and the Truth of the Traditional Gospels* (San Francisco: Harper, 1996) 50.

[28] Gerd Theissen, *Sociology of Early Palestinian Christianity* (Philadelphia: Fortress, 1978) 7–16.

[29] Ibid., 15.

equally valuable to God. There is no instance of his rejecting anyone, though he does give fierce prophetic warnings to those who oppose the message of the kingdom (e.g., Matt 11:21). But though he overturns the conventions of his society, that does not mean there was no hierarchy in the Jesus movement itself. First, Jesus himself functioned as a hierarchical authority in his own movement, much like other religious founders (e.g., Buddha, Moses, Muhammad), but his appears to have been an authority of teaching, example, virtue, and service, not dominance. Unlike the prophets, who saw themselves as merely mouthpieces for God ("The word of the Lord came to me"), Jesus gives dominical teachings in his *own* name, using the unique formulaic introduction, "Amen, I say to you" (synoptic Gospels) or "Amen, Amen, I say to you" (John).[30] This manner of speaking, utterly unlike that of the Jewish prophets, is found in all the Gospels, and would appear to go back to the historical Jesus by the criteria of discontinuity and multiple attestation. Second, Jesus saw himself as under the kingship or authority of God, as many sayings show (e.g., Luke 10:21-22, Mark 13:32). His use of "Abba," Father, indicates as much. Third, Jesus appointed the Twelve as an inner or elite group of disciples to carry on his message. This is especially apparent in their privileged place at the Last Supper, and their reception of the commission to "Do this in remembrance of me" (Luke 22:19, 1 Cor 11:24). The authority of the Twelve, especially Peter, is apparent immediately after Jesus' death (cf. Acts 1:15-26, the election of Matthias) and is acknowledged by Paul (Gal 1:18). Thus it would seem that, though there was equality of *persons* in Jesus' movement (though no person was the equal of Jesus himself), Jesus did institute a hierarchy of *roles* or functions, which was later developed and elaborated in the early Church. I will consider the role of the apostles and the Twelve in more detail below. First, however, let us consider briefly the work of another scholar, Elizabeth Schüssler Fiorenza.

Hierarchy, Oppression, and Ideology

Like Crossan, Schüssler Fiorenza sees hierarchy as equivalent to oppression, though her specific concern is with patriarchy, that is, male

[30] Cf. Matt 5:18, 26; 6:2, 5, 6; 10:15; 11:1; et al.; Mark 3:28; 6:11; 8:12; 9:1, 12, 41; et al.; Luke 4:24; 11:51; 12:37; et al.; John 1:51; 3:3, 11; 5:19, 24, 25; et al. This expression,

domination and oppression. Since the Christian scriptures were written by males, she sees them as embodying a patriarchal-oppressive perspective, and repeatedly refers to the scriptures as the "androcentric text." The history of women in the Jesus movement and early Church, she believes, has been systematically expunged from these texts due to androcentric bias. Faced with this, feminist critical hermeneutics must reject the patriarchy embodied in the texts and imaginatively reconstruct the history of women in the Jesus movement and early Church, following whatever clues still remain in the texts. Schüssler Fiorenza rejects the historical-critical ideal of historical objectivity as "theoretically impossible," and instead aligns feminist hermeneutics with liberation theology, which does not aim to be objective or value-neutral, but rather advocative and adversarial. "The basic insight of all liberation theologies, including feminist theology, is the recognition that all theology, willingly or not, is by definition always engaged for or against the oppressed."[31] Feminist theology, therefore, must take an advocacy stance for women, and an adversarial stance against patriarchy; this is determinative of its hermeneutics and perspective:

> A feminist theological hermeneutics having as its canon the liberation of women from oppressive patriarchal texts, structures, institutions, and values maintains that—if the Bible is not to continue as a tool for the patriarchal suppression of women—only those traditions and texts which critically break through patriarchal culture and "plausibility structures" have the theological authority of revelation. The "advocacy stance" of liberation theologies cannot accord revelatory authority to any oppressive and destructive biblical text or tradition. . . . Such a critical measure must be applied to *all* biblical texts, their historical contexts, and theological interpretations, not just to the texts on women.[32]

This subjects the revelatory text to a political and ideological criterion: whatever seems like patriarchy (i.e., hierarchy) to the feminist interpreter cannot be revelation—rather it must come from the androcentric bias of the New Testament authors; but whatever supports or magnifies

---

in Greek *Amēn lego hymin* (synoptics), or *Amēn, Amēn, lego hymin* (John) is translated variously: "Truly" or "very truly" or "truly, truly I say to you" (NRSV, RSV) "Verily" or "verily, verily, I say to you" (King James), etc.

[31] *In Memory of Her* (New York: Crossroad, 1985) 6.

[32] Ibid., 33; italics in original.

the role of women in the scriptures is revelatory. But since most of the evidence for the role of women has not been retained in the scriptures, feminist interpreters must reconstruct the events which have been left out: "In the attempt to make the past intelligible the historian must go beyond the events in an act of 'intellectual recreation.'"[33]

Schüssler Fiorenza's reading of the texts and reconstruction of the history, then, is ideologically driven, and does not even claim to be objective or value-neutral (in contrast to biblical scholars like Raymond Brown and John Meier). This seems to leave the door wide open for biased interpretations. Schüssler Fiorenza would perhaps reply that all readings are biased, but that her reading is to be preferred because it advocates the role of women. But then why not other advocacy readings: those which advocate the role of Jews, of Pharisees, of Samaritans, of Romans, etc.? In such a cacophony of advocacy stances, there is no way to separate truth from falsehood and distortion; one's reading becomes merely a matter of personal taste, or prejudice, and, typically, the most powerful group wins. Thus we find her maintaining that Mark 12:18-27, in which the Sadducees ask Jesus whose wife the woman who married seven brothers would be in the resurrection, is really a rejection of patriarchal marriage (since Jesus says those in heaven are not married). To maintain this, she has to dismiss the second part of the pericope as a "secondary insertion by the later community," since it concerns the resurrection, not marriage.[34] Jesus' saying in Mark 3:35 "Whoever does the will of God is my brother and sister and mother" means that "The discipleship community abolishes the claims of the patriarchal family and constitutes a new familial community, one that does not include fathers in its circle."[35] The God of Jesus is Sophia, i.e., Wisdom (feminine in the Hebrew and Greek languages). The language of "Father-Son" used by Jesus in all the Gospels, she argues, is a creation of the "Q" community, probably men, overlaid on a more pristine sophialogy. "The Q people (men?) who articulated this saying [Father-Son language] replaced the inclusive sophialogy of the earliest Jesus traditions with an exclusive understanding of revelation."[36] (This, despite the fact that almost all biblical

[33] Ibid., 69–70.

[34] Ibid., 143–144.

[35] Ibid., 147.

[36] Schüssler Fiorenza, *Jesus: Miriam's Child, Sophia's Prophet* (New York: Continuum, 1994) 144.

scholars since Joachim Jeremias, even the Jesus Seminar, have accepted Jesus' use of *Abba* ("Father") as authentic, confirmed by the criteria of multiple attestation and discontinuity.) Finally, her rejection of "kyriarchy" in the name of "sophialogy" seems to entail a rejection of the Lordship of God and of Jesus, as well as of the Chalcedonian doctrine of Christology.[37]

The strongest argument presented by Schüssler Fiorenza for the egalitarianism of the Jesus movement is based on two texts. Mark 9:35 reads: "And he sat down, called the twelve, and said to them, 'Whoever wants to be first, must be last of all and servant of all.'" Similarly, Matthew 23:8-12 reads: "But you are not to be called rabbi, for you have one teacher, and you are all students. And call no one your father on earth, for you have one Father—the one in heaven. Nor are you to be called instructors, for you have one instructor, the Messiah. The greatest among you will be your servant. All who exalt themselves will be humbled, and all who humble themselves will be exalted." These Schüssler Fiorenza interprets as indicating that the community of disciples was a discipleship of equals, which had no teacher or offices, and rejected all patriarchal structures, because all had only one God.[38] What shall we say to this?

First, as Schüssler Fiorenza herself notes, the prohibitions on calling one rabbi, father, master are "very difficult" to situate within the pre-Matthean tradition, since they are not found in Luke (or Mark).[39] Hence they are probably redactional additions of Matthew or his community, and we cannot be sure that they go back to the historical Jesus. The more original saying is Matthew 23:12: "All who exalt themselves will be humbled, and all who humble themselves will be exalted," which is also found in Luke (but not Mark), and therefore probably stems from Q. Both these sayings are independently supported by the Last Supper scene as portrayed by John (13:2-15). My own interpretation of this is not that the discipleship community was to be entirely egalitarian (especially after Jesus' death—see below), but that anyone holding authority in the community should do so in a way which serves and empowers the others, rather than lording it over them.

[37] Ibid., 157: "I find the early 'Jesus messenger of Sophia' traditions theologically significant because they assert the unique particularity of Jesus without having to resort to exclusivity and superiority." On Chalcedon, see p. 22.

[38] Ibid., 150.

[39] Ibid., 149.

Indeed, the teaching seems to be directed against *both* domination (command hierarchy) *and* egalitarianism—for the point is: those who would be first, i.e., be in positions of authority, should use their authority for service (not domination). This seems to be the point of the foot-washing text in John 13:12-15 (which probably recalls an actual historical incident, by the criteria of discontinuity and embarrassment) "After he had washed their feet . . . he said to them, 'Do you know what I have done to you? You call me Teacher and Lord—and you are right, for that is what I am. So if I, your Lord and Teacher, have washed your feet, you also ought to wash one another's feet. For I have set you an example, that you should do as I have done to you.'" During Jesus' lifetime the community was under his authority, which was an authority of service that aimed to allow the disciples to participate in the spiritual power Jesus himself possessed. The whole point of the foot-washing scene, so near to Jesus' death, is to give an example of the kind of authority that should be exercised in the community *after Jesus is gone:* an authority which is used to serve and empower the members. This was Jesus' own teaching on hierarchy: it is meant to be in service to the larger community. This seems to be the principal idea of hierarchy in the New Testament.[40]

In the end, even if one agrees (as I do) with the claim that women's contributions have been slighted in the scriptures and the later Christian tradition, it is difficult to avoid the conclusion that Schüssler Fiorenza interprets the texts to fit her own agenda, and that much of her reading is not exegesis, but eisegesis, i.e., reading her own opinions into the text.[41] This indeed would seem to follow from the advocacy method which she embraces. As Joseph Fitzmyer writes "This hermeneutical approach [the Feminist approach] tends to substitute for the revelation enshrined in the biblical text an imaginative reconstruction of historical reality—for instance, of the Jesus movement—as the norm for Christian belief and practice, which is unacceptable."[42] He specifically criticizes Fiorenza for making the "historical Jesus," which is no more than a scholarly reconstruction, changing from scholar to scholar

[40] See Yves Congar, "La hiearchie comme service, selon le Noveau Testament et les documents de la Tradition" in Yves Congar, O.P. and B.D. Dupuy, O.P., *L'Episcopat et L'Eglise Universelle* (Paris: Editions du Cerf, 1964) 67–99.

[41] See the review by Dennis Doyle, *Commonweal* (March 10, 1995) 18, 20.

[42] Joseph Fitzmyer, *Scripture the Soul of Theology* (New York: Paulist Press, 1994) 53.

and decade to decade, the norm for Christian faith and theology, a criticism which also applies to Crossan.[43]

It seems, then, that the Jesus movement itself was not socially egalitarian. But what kind of hierarchy did it entail?

The Kingdom of God

Mark summarizes Jesus' public proclamation as follows: "The time is fulfilled, and the kingdom of God has come near, repent and believe in the good news" (Mark 1:14). Scholars such as Rudolph Bultmann, Joachim Jeremias, Norman Perrin, Ben Meyer, and E.P. Sanders have seen the proclamation of the kingdom of God as the core of Jesus' message.[44] John Meier thinks it is a central, though not necessarily the central theme. "Kingdom" (Greek: *basilea*) of God in this usage means primarily God's kingly rule or reign over God's people; to the extent that that reign is actualized in Israel, "kingdom" may also imply a domain. The language of kingdom, rule, or reign is of course hierarchical. But, as Norman Perrin has insisted, the kingdom of God is a tensive symbol, combining multivalent meanings.[45] To understand those meanings, it is first necessary to review the notion of God's kingly reign in the Hebrew scriptures.

As mentioned in chapter 1, the relation between Israel and God was conceived as one of rule or kingly reign, and this was expressed in the notion of covenant. Nonetheless, the phrase "The kingdom of God" does not occur in the Hebrew Bible (though it is found in the apocryphal Wisdom of Solomon [10:10]). Rather, the notion of YHWH's kingly rule is conveyed by verbal statements such as *Yahweh mālak* ("Yahweh rules as king") or *Yahweh yimlōk* ("Yahweh will reign as

[43] Ibid., 89, note 64.

[44] Rudolph Bultmann, "The dominant concept of Jesus' message is the *Reign of God." Theology of the New Testament* (New York: Charles Scribners' Sons, 1951, 1955) 2; Joachim Jeremias: "The central theme of the public proclamation of Jesus was the kingly reign of God." *New Testament Theology* (London: SCM, 1971) 4; Norman Perrin, *Jesus and the Language of the Kingdom* (Philadelphia: Fortress, 1971); Ben F. Meyer, *The Aims of Jesus*, 135; E.P. Sanders, *Jesus and Judaism*, 222–241. The literature on the Kingdom of God is immense. See also: John Meier, *A Marginal Jew*, vol. 2, 237–506, and bibliography, 272–273; Dennis C. Duling, "Kingdom of God, Kingdom of Heaven," in *ABD*, vol. 4, 49–69; Benedict T. Viviano, *The Kingdom of God in History* (Wilmington: Michael Glazier, 1988).

[45] *Jesus and the Language of the Kingdom* (Philadelphia: Fortress, 1976) 29–30.

king"). To the Jews, YHWH's kingship connoted a reign of justice, equity, prosperity, and the vindication of Israel against her enemies: "The Lord is king! Let the earth rejoice. . . . righteousness and justice are the foundation of his throne. Fire goes before him and consumes his adversaries on every side. . . . All worshippers of images are put to shame. . . . The Lord loves those who hate evil; he guards the lives of his faithful; he rescues them from the hand of the wicked. Light dawns for the righteous, and joy for the upright in heart" (Ps 97:1-12).

During and after the Babylonian Exile, the hope for YHWH's kingly rule became associated with the defeat of Israel's enemies and the restoration of Israel, the regathering of the twelve tribes (dispersed in the Assyrian conquest of 722 B.C.E.), the redemption of Jerusalem, and the recognition by the Gentiles of the glory of Yahweh and Israel (cf. Isa 52:7-10; Zeph 3:14-20; Tobit 13). Deutero-Isaiah writes: "How beautiful upon the mountains are the feet of the messenger who announces peace, who brings good news, who announces salvation, who says to Zion 'Your God reigns'" (Isa 52:7). Through the prophet Zephaniah YHWH declares: "I will deal with all your oppressors at that time. And I will save the lame and gather the outcast, and I will change their shame into praise and renown in all the earth" (Zeph 3:19).

In some of the later prophets (e.g., Daniel, Zechariah), and especially some intertestamental literature (1 Enoch, the Psalms of Solomon, Testament of Moses), the idea develops that the return of YHWH and his rule will involve a devastating apocalyptic war, in which YHWH destroys Israel's foes, establishes an everlasting kingship over the whole earth, and the surviving Gentiles come to Jerusalem to worship YHWH (cf. Daniel 4; Zechariah 14). Daniel 7 recounts a prophetic vision in which "One like a Son of Man" is given everlasting kingship and dominion over all peoples. This figure came to be identified with the Messiah. Much of the intertestamental literature speaks of the return of YHWH as king, the restoration and regathering of Israel, a final war, the defeat of the Gentiles, and occasionally, the resurrection of the dead. The Psalms of Solomon (Psalms 17 and 18) see the reign of God manifested through the reign of the Messiah, the Son of David. This God-like figure leads the Jews back to a restored holy land and a purified Jerusalem, to which the Gentiles come in pilgrimage to see the glory of YHWH. Some passages imply the resurrection of the dead as well.[46]

[46] See Meier, *A Marginal Jew*, vol. 2, 257–260; Duling, "Kingdom of God," 51.

Finally, the Kaddish prayer used in Jewish synagogues at the time of Jesus speaks of the kingdom: "Magnified and sanctified be his great name in the world that he has created according to his will. May he establish his kingdom in your lifetime and in your days and in the lifetime of all the houses of Israel, even speedily and at a near time."[47] Norman Perrin thinks the central petitions of the Lord's prayer: "Hallowed be thy name, Thy Kingdom Come" were drawn from this Kaddish prayer.[48]

Even this brief survey shows that for the Jews, the notion of God's kingly rule meant joy and salvation—in a word, the participation of the people in YHWH's blessings, not domination by YHWH. (Yet YHWH's reign would mean domination of Israel's enemies and judgment of the wicked.)

Drawing from this background, Jesus made the kingdom of God the central theme of his preaching. To get an idea of its meaning, let us consider those sayings and actions which reveal Jesus' conception of the kingdom.[49]

The petition "Thy Kingdom Come" in the Lord's prayer is judged by Perrin, Meier, and others to go back to the historical Jesus.[50] Perrin thinks that this petition derives from the Kaddish prayer cited above: "The petition is to be considered a deliberate echo of the Kaddish prayer, revised in accordance with the language style of Jesus himself."[51] Meier thinks that the petition reflects the eschatological hope of Israel: "In short, when Jesus prays that God's kingdom come, he is simply expressing in a more abstract phrase the eschatological hope of the latter part of the OT [Old Testament] and the pseudepigraphia that God would come on the last day to save and restore his people Israel. . . . Jesus' message was focused on a future coming of God to rule as king, a time when he would manifest himself in all his tran-

[47] Cited in Perrin, *Jesus and the Language of the Kingdom,* 28.

[48] Ibid., 29.

[49] The exposition which follows draws principally from the following sources: John Meier, *A Marginal Jew,* vol. 2, 289–506; Norman Perrin, *Jesus and the Language of the Kingdom,* 32–56; Ben F. Meyer, *The Aims of Jesus,* 129–173 (particularly good on the relation between the gratuity of the kingdom and the condition of repentance); Sanders, *Jesus and Judaism,* 222–241; Duling, "Kingdom of God," 456–469; Brevard S. Childs, *Biblical Theology of the Old and New Testaments* (Minneapolis: Fortress, 1993) 636–657; Geza Vermes, *The Religion of Jesus the Jew,* 119–152.

[50] Meier, ibid., 291–294; Perrin, ibid., 47–48.

[51] Ibid., 47.

scendent glory and power to regather and save his sinful but repentant people Israel."[52]

That God's kingly rule would mean justice and happiness for the poor, the downtrodden, and the marginalized is revealed by the Q Beatitudes, which Meier along with most scholars judge to be authentic.[53] Meier reconstructs the original form of these as follows: "Happy are the poor, for theirs is the kingdom of heaven (= God). Happy are the mourners, for they shall be comforted. Happy are the hungry, for they shall be satisfied."[54] This aspect of the kingdom is strikingly conveyed in the image of the Messianic banquet, expressed in parables (e.g., the wedding feast: Matt 22:1-14; Luke 14:16-24), miracles (the multiplication of loaves and fishes, found in all four Gospels), and sayings: "I tell you, many will come from east and west and will eat with Abraham and Isaac and Jacob in the kingdom of heaven, while the heirs of the kingdom will be thrown into outer darkness" (Matt 8:11-12).[55] Such sayings cohere with and are supported by Jesus' actions. His eating with the poor and marginalized was a prophetic embodiment of the banquet of the kingdom. The Last Supper with the Twelve also symbolized the coming kingdom.[56] Norman Perrin writes: "The imagery of the Messianic banquet . . . teaches that it [the kingdom] will mean a perfect participation in the ultimate blessings of God; and the imagery of the New Temple . . . which . . . is a regular apocalyptic symbol for the final blessed state, describes the community of the redeemed as enjoying a perfect sacral relationship with God."[57]

The miracles and exorcisms of Jesus and his disciples (Matt 10:5-8) also embody the plenitude of the kingdom. As the poor, hungry, and wretched will be made happy, so will the sick and possessed be healed. This is apparent in Jesus' reply to John the Baptist, who had asked if he (Jesus) were the Messiah: "Go and tell John what you hear and see: the blind receive their sight, the lame walk, the lepers are cleansed, the

[52] *A Marginal Jew,* vol. 2, 299–300.

[53] Ibid., 319.

[54] Ibid., 323.

[55] Meier assigns this saying to Q, and argues strongly for its authenticity in the mouth of Jesus. *A Marginal Jew,* vol. 2, 309–317; the parallel passage in Luke is 13:28-29.

[56] Sanders, *Jesus and Judaism,* 340.

[57] *The Kingdom of God in the Teaching of Jesus* (Philadelphia: Fortress, 1963) 188ff., cited in Sanders, *Jesus and Judaism,* 148.

deaf hear, the dead are raised, and the poor have the good news brought to them" (Matt 11:4-5, cf. Luke 4:18-19). The exorcisms are themselves signs of the presence of the kingdom, and its mediation by Jesus himself: "But if it is by the Spirit of God that I cast out demons, then the kingdom of God has come to you" (Matt 12:28, par. Luke 4:18-20). The miracles were also signs of the presence of God's reign, for in that reign there would be no sickness or suffering. Thus Jesus' instructions to the Twelve, when he sent them out on mission, included preaching the good news of the kingdom and curing the sick, cleansing lepers, raising the dead, and casting out demons (Matt 10:5-8). Just as the kingdom meant liberation from political and social bondage, so also it meant liberation from physical bondage.[58] Jesus is, as Ben Meyer puts it, "the restorer of the paradisal communion with God shattered by the sin of Adam."[59]

Yet the coming of the kingdom also heralded the judgment of the wicked, and made repentance urgent; only the righteous would find their place in the kingdom. This is consistent with the Old Testament and pseudepigraphical notion of the kingdom. It is supported by many of the parables and sayings in the Gospels (e.g., Matt 8:11-12, above), by the stress placed on repentance in Acts and righteousness in Paul's epistles, and by Jesus' action of cleansing the Temple.[60]

There remains a final question concerning Jesus' notion of the kingdom. Geza Vermes claims that Jesus expected the kingdom to come in this world in his lifetime, and was wrong—he never therefore intended to found a church.[61] Meier, however, points out that the saying in Matthew 8:11-12 (which he regards as historically authentic): "Many will come from east and west and will eat with Abraham and Isaac and Jacob in the kingdom of heaven" points to an otherworldly conception of the kingdom. "With the affirmation that the Gentiles will join the long-dead patriarchs of Israel at the banquet, Jesus indicates

[58] On the gospel view of miracles, see Raymond Brown, "The Gospel Miracles," in *New Testament Essays* (Milwaukee: Bruce, 1965) 168–191. Also Rene Latourelle, *The Miracles of Jesus and the Theology of Miracles* (New York: Paulist Press, 1988).

[59] Meyer, *The Aims of Jesus,* 140.

[60] See Sanders, *Jesus and Judaism,* 61–76.

[61] "For let it be re-stated for a last time, if he meant and believed what he preached—and I for one am convinced that he did—namely that the eternal Kingdom of God was at hand, he simply could not have entertained the idea of founding and setting in motion an organized society intended to endure for ages to come." *The Religion of Jesus the Jew,* 214–215.

that this fully realized kingdom of God is not only future but also in some ways discontinuous with this present world. Whether Jesus is thinking in this logion more of the resurrection of the dead or of the souls saved in heaven is not clear."[62] This same idea is supported by the saying at the Last Supper, "Truly I tell you, I will never again drink of the fruit of the vine until that day when I drink it new in the kingdom of God" (Mark 14:25).[63] This also points to a transcendent aspect of the kingdom, perhaps including resurrection, for it indicates that Jesus, despite his impending death, expected to share in the Messianic banquet himself.

Thus I maintain that the Kingdom of God, as preached by Jesus, involved both hierarchical submission to YHWH as king, and participation and communion in God's kingdom for those who did submit (symbolized by the banquet). Those who did not submit were rejected—"thrown into outer darkness." This interpretation is supported by many sayings which are not multiply attested, but which cohere with this notion, for example, the parable of the sheep and the goats (Matt 25:31-46). This parable shows that the condition for inclusion in the kingdom is above all love and compassion for the poor and the victimized: the hungry, thirsty, naked, and imprisoned. And the reply of the King: "Truly I tell you, just as you did it to one of the least of these who are members of my family, you did it to me" (Matt 25:40) shows that this hierarchy of YHWH and Christ is not one of command, but of participation: the King shares the sufferings of the unfortunate, as they will share in his glory. Like Jesus' relation with the Father, the kingdom of God in its fullness is best described as hierarchical communion.

Some of Jesus' actions and sayings indicate what kind of hierarchical authority was appropriate for the kingdom. In his triumphal entry into Jerusalem, he rode an ass, not a horse (as victorious Roman generals did). Sanders comments: "He deliberately demonstrated, by riding on an ass, that the claim to a special role in God's kingdom was being made by one who was 'meek and lowly.' It is Matthew, of course, who has looked up the passage and quoted the words 'humble and riding on an ass' (Matt 21:5, quoting Zech 9:9), but the action speaks for itself. Jesus saw himself as one who was the servant of all (Matt

[62] *A Marginal Jew,* vol. 2, 317.

[63] Meier treats this logion at length (*A Marginal Jew,* vol. 2, 302–309). He thinks it is authentic in the mouth of Jesus (mainly by the criterion of discontinuity), as do "the vast majority of commentators" (303).

20:28a; Mark 10:45a), not their glorious leader in a triumphal march through parted waters."[64] This action, like the washing of the disciples' feet at the Last Supper (John 13:12-15), coheres with the several sayings in Mark 9:35, 10:45, and Matthew 20:28, and 23, discussed above, that the one who would be first must be last and servant of all.

The ontological aspect of this notion of authority is well expressed in the famous passage in Philippians. Jesus' Lordship is expressed as emptying (Greek: *kenosis*):

> Christ Jesus, who, though he was in the form of God, did not count equality with God as something to be exploited, but emptied himself, taking the form of a slave, being born in human likeness. And being found in human form, he humbled himself and became obedient to the point of death—even death on a cross. Therefore God also highly exalted him and gave him the name that is above every name so that at the name of Jesus . . . every tongue should confess that Jesus Christ is Lord . . . (Phil 2:6-11).

This, then, is the supreme model for all New Testament hierarchy, ontological and ecclesial: Jesus' Lordship expressed as *kenosis* and service.[65] Jesus is the mediator of the kingdom, and his mediation is hierarchical, but it is not a hierarchy of domination, nor is it egalitarianism, rather a hierarchy of inclusion and service, whose aim is to foster participation of as many as possible in the kingdom of God. Such participation requires filial obedience, like Jesus' own, rather than servile obedience.

Jesus and the Apostles

Did Jesus make any provision for authority among his followers after his death? The principal evidence here is his appointment of the Twelve. Most commentators see the Twelve as instituted in Jesus' own lifetime.[66] To them he made the following promise: "Truly I tell you, at

[64] *Jesus and Judaism*, 235.

[65] I wish to thank Sr. Susan Wood for pointing out to me the importance of *kenosis* to my model of hierarchy.

[66] See for example, Sanders, *Jesus and Judaism*, 98–103; Joseph Fitzmyer, *The Gospel according to Luke I–IX* (Garden City, N.Y.: Doubleday, 1981; the Anchor Bible Series) 253–254; John Meier, "Jesus," *NJBC*, 1322. Paul mentions the Twelve as receiving a resurrection appearance of the Lord, in 1 Corinthians 15:5, indicating that they were in existence at the time of Jesus' death.

the renewal of all things, when the Son of Man is seated on the throne of his glory, you who have followed me will also sit on twelve thrones, judging the twelve tribes of Israel" (Matt 19:28).[67] This reveals an expectation of the regathering of the twelve tribes of Israel, which, as we have seen, was a persistent theme in Jewish texts of the kingdom. The text is particularly striking because in Jesus' time there were only two tribes: the other ten tribes having disappeared into captivity during the Assyrian conquest of the Northern kingdom (c. 722 B.C.E.) But a restored Israel, to be whole, should include all twelve tribes, hence the symbolic number twelve.

The twelve were thus to be the nucleus of the new, restored Israel.[68] Finally, they shared in the cup of his blood at the Last Supper (indicating a sharing in his suffering, so as to share in his triumph) and received the instruction, "Do this in remembrance of me." These words are found only in Luke's version, but are attested also by Paul (1 Cor 11:23-26). This instruction, if it comes from the historical Jesus, would indicate that he had in mind for the Twelve some kind of role and ministry after his death.

It is possible that Jesus' conception of the role of the Twelve changed during his ministry. Perhaps in the early phases of his ministry he really did hope that Israel would be converted, and the eschatological Reign of God established. If so, the saying that the Twelve would judge the twelve tribes of Israel could be dated to that time.[69] But near the end of his ministry, when he realized that Israel would not convert, he envisaged instead a Messianic remnant which would be the nucleus of a restored Israel, but which would endure for a period of time after his death, until the *parousia* (the date of which not even he, but only the Father, knew—Mark 13:32). In that remnant, later called the Church, the Twelve were to have a role of authority, as can be seen from their role at the Last Supper.

[67] Sanders argues strongly for the authenticity of this passage, which most scholars think came from Q. See *Jesus and Judaism,* 98–102, 233–234. I would argue for its historical authenticity based on the criteria of embarrassment (Jesus made an unfulfilled prophecy) and discontinuity.

[68] Meier writes: "Rather, he sought to make his circle of disciples the exemplar, nucleus, and concrete realization of what he was calling all Israel to be: the restored people of God in the last days." "Jesus," *NJBC,* 1322.

[69] We cannot tell from the gospel accounts the chronology of the sayings of Jesus, since the gospel writers group them differently according to their redactional purposes.

But the authority of the Twelve, like the authority of Jesus himself, was to be not one of domination, but of service. This is brought out forcefully in a famous passage. James and John, sons of Zebedee, requested to sit at Jesus' right and left hand (the places of highest honor), when he came in glory (Mark 10:37). Jesus' reply indicated, (1) that to do so they must share in his suffering, his "cup," and (2) that he did not have the authority to decide who is to sit at his right hand and at his left, "but it is for those for whom it has been prepared" (Mark 10:40). Note that Jesus does *not* say, there are no such places, everyone is to be equal in the kingdom. On the contrary, his reply assumes some kind of hierarchy in the kingdom. This coheres with another saying concerning John the Baptist: "He who is least in the kingdom of heaven is greater than John." But the remaining ten were indignant with James and John, so Jesus called them together and gave them an instruction on authority: "You know that among the Gentiles those whom they recognize as their rulers lord it over them, and their great ones are tyrants over them. But it is not so among you; but whoever wishes to become great among you must be your servant, and whoever wishes to be the first among you must be slave of all" (Mark 10:42-44). Jesus enacts this conception of hierarchy when, at the Last Supper, according to John, he washes the feet of his disciples, with the following instruction: "You call me Teacher and Lord (Greek: *Kyrios*)—and you are right, for that is what I am. So if I, your Lord and Teacher, have washed your feet, you also ought to wash one another's feet. For I have set you an example . . . Very truly, I tell you, servants are not greater than their master, nor are messengers greater than the one who sent them" (John 13:13-16). Aside from the address "Lord," which is probably a retrojection here, I would see this pericope as historically authentic, by the criteria of discontinuity, embarrassment, and coherence. Notice that hierarchy is clearly implied in this passage (a servant is not greater than his/her master), but the lesson, like that of the previously cited saying, is that hierarchy is meant for service. This is not the same as saying that hierarchy does not exist. Rather it means that hierarchy is not dominance, but exists to facilitate the welfare of those within the hierarchy, empower them, and enfranchise them. *This is the hierarchy of the kingdom: as Jesus pours out his life for the sake of others, so must the disciples do likewise.* And the fact that Jesus passed this on to his apostles and disciples indicates that he intended this to be the structure of the Church as it would exist after his death.

The Role of Peter

Among the apostles, Peter is given a special role. In all the lists of the Twelve, he is named first (e.g., Matt 10:2). When Jesus asks his disciples "Who do people say that I am?" it is Peter who responds "You are the Messiah" (Mark 8:27-30). This passage is expanded by Matthew:

> He said to them, "But who do you say that I am?" Simon Peter answered, "You are the Messiah, the Son of the living God." And Jesus answered him, "Blessed are you, Simon son of Jonah! For flesh and blood has not revealed this to you, but my Father in heaven. And I tell you, you are Peter [Greek = *Petros;* Aramaic = *Kepha*], and on this rock [Greek = *Petra;* Aramaic = *Kepha*] I will build my church, and the gates of Hades will not prevail against it. I will give you the keys of the kingdom of heaven, and whatever you bind on earth will be bound in heaven, and whatever you loose on earth will be loosed in heaven" (Matt 16:15-19).

If the term "Peter" is put in the language of Jesus, Aramaic, the fourth sentence reads: "You are *Kepha* (rock), and on this *Kepha* I will build my church" (Greek: *ecclesia*). Now it is certain that Peter was known as Kephas (cf. Gal 2:9), and that that term was not used as a proper name before Jesus' time. Thus it is nearly certain that Jesus did, in fact, dub Peter *Kepha.* Did Jesus then say to Kepha that he would found the church on him? Or is this a Matthean creation?

Traditionally, Catholic commentators have argued for the authenticity of the passage in the mouth of Jesus, and Protestant commentators against it, since, from the third century, this passage has been used to underwrite the authority of the Roman Catholic papacy. Peter, it was argued, was made the cornerstone of the Church, and the bishop of Rome is Peter's successor. Vatican Council I in particular used this passage as the principal proof text upon which it based its definition of papal jurisdiction and infallibility.

A few points should be noted. First, the statement "what you bind on earth will be bound in heaven," is also made to the whole body of disciples in Matthew 18:18. But only to Peter is the power of the keys given (Matt 16:19). A problem for the authenticity of this passage, however, is that it does not appear in Mark, thought to be the first Gospel and used as a source by Matthew in composing his Gospel. If Matthew did use Mark, then he is clearly following Mark's account of Peter's confession at Caesarea Philipi here. But if that is so, why is the important commission to Peter omitted in the passage in Mark? It is easier to believe that Matthew added it than to believe that it was originally present in Mark's tradition, and Mark suppressed it.[70] Further, if the promise to Peter was present in Mark's tradition, why was it not included in Luke, who also used Mark as a source?

The question of the authenticity of this passage is difficult to disentangle from confessional biases. Yet almost the only scholars who argue that it goes back to the historical Jesus are Catholics. Some suggest that, although Peter is given a prominent role in Matthew's Gospel, Matthew 16:18-19 (Jesus' commission to Peter) does not go back to the earthly life of Jesus, but possibly derives from a post-resurrectional appearance of Jesus to Peter, as mentioned in 1 Corinthians 15:5.[71] My own view is that this passage reflects the view of the author of the Gospel of Matthew and his community about 85 A.D. (when the gospel was written), but we cannot be sure it goes back to the historical (or resurrected) Jesus.

Peter is said to be the "rock" on which the Church will be built.[72] But the meaning of the passage is problematical; one finds a wide range of interpretations among patristic commentators. For Origen, "every imitator of Christ is a rock . . . of Christ, who is the spiritual rock."[73] Cyprian held that Matthew 16:18 applied to all bishops, who shared equally in what was originally bestowed on Peter.[74] Augustine

[70] See, however, Peter F. Ellis, *Matthew: His Mind and His Message* (Collegeville: The Liturgical Press, 1974) 128–129. Ellis argues that Mark suppressed the pericope because of his redactional emphasis on the "obtuseness" of the apostles. Ellis therefore argues that the Matthean form is more original, and was actually said by Jesus. Ben Meyer also argues for the authenticity of this passage. See *The Aims of Jesus,* 185–197.

[71] Raymond E. Brown, Karl P. Donfried, and John Reumann, eds. *Peter in the New Testament* (Minneapolis: Augsburg, 1973) 92. The whole discussion of this pericope, 83–101, is most interesting, and important for Protestant-Catholic ecumenical dialogue.

[72] Many of the Fathers of the Church, for example, Augustine, had understood the rock to be not Peter himself, but the faith which he professed. But the authors of *Peter in the New Testament* conclude: "There can be no doubt that the rock on which the church was to be built was Peter" (92). Nonetheless, they do think that Augustine's interpretation remains a legitimate possibility (93).

[73] *Commentary on Matthew,* Book 12, *PG* 13, 997; ET from E. Giles, ed., *Documents Illustrating Papal Authority: A.D. 96–454* (London: SPCK, 1952) 46.

[74] *De unitate,* 4, cited in James McCue, "The Roman Primacy in the Patristic Era," in *PPATUC,* 62.

interpreted the "rock" as Peter's faith. We do not find the Church at Rome basing its authority on this text until the time of Damasus (c. 382).[75]

Other passages in which Peter is given prominence among the apostles are John 21:15-19, in which Jesus says three times to Peter "Feed my sheep," and Luke 22:31-34: "'Simon, Simon, listen! Satan has demanded to sift all of you like wheat, but I have prayed for you that your own faith may not fail; and you, when once you have turned back, strengthen your brothers' [Greek: *adelphoi*]. And he said to him, 'Lord, I am ready to go with you to prison and to death.' Jesus said, 'I tell you, Peter, the cock will not crow this day, until you have denied three times that you know me.'" John 21 is the last chapter of John, and is thought to have been added by the final editor of the Gospel, c. 90–100 C.E.[76] Thus this image of Peter in this passage comes from the sub-apostolic period, and not from the time of Jesus. The passage from Luke, which is found only in that gospel, probably dates from the time of the composition of that gospel, though it may combine elements from Jesus' lifetime with later elements. It points forward to Peter's role in Acts, when he functions both as missionary (Acts 10), and as spokesman for the apostles. But the "brothers" whom Peter will strengthen are not limited to the apostles, but probably include all the disciples in the Church (cf. Acts 1:15 where Peter stands up and speaks in the midst of the "believers" *[adelphoi]*—about 120 persons).[77]

Thus in Matthew, Luke, John, and Acts, Peter is given a role of primacy among the apostles and disciples. While we cannot be certain that this goes back to the historical Jesus, the combined testimony of different traditions in the early Church makes that seem likely. Yet Peter's role is not one of domination over the apostles, but of unifying leadership within their community. In Mark and Matthew especially, Peter is the spokesman for the disciples, the one who proclaims the consensus. This role is continued in Acts. In Acts 1, 6, and 15, Peter serves as the facilitator of and spokesman for the consensus of the Twelve, or the apostolic

[75] A Roman synod in 382 declared: "The holy Roman church has obtained primacy by the word of the Lord our Savior in the gospel: 'You are Peter.'" Cited in Arthur C. Piepkorn, "The Roman Primacy in the Patristic Era," in *PPATUC,* 82.

[76] See Raymond Brown, *The Gospel According to John I–XII* (Garden City, N.Y.: Doubleday, 1966) lxxxv; Pheme Perkins, *NJBC,* 984.

[77] See the commentary on this passage in Donfried and Reumann, eds. *Peter in the New Testament,* 119–125.

college. Only in Acts 5, the condemnation of Ananias and Sapphira, does he act unilaterally, but even there he seems to be acting as the representative of the community. I believe that Peter's role in Acts ought to serve as a normative interpretative lens for the more obscure gospel passages, such as Matthew 16:18 (the keys of the kingdom), John 21:17 ("feed my sheep"), and Luke 22:32 ("strengthen your brothers")—which became proof texts for later papal claims to absolute jurisdiction—for *Acts portrays the nature of the primacy given to Peter.* It is not a primacy of individual, separate jurisdiction or dominance *over* the other apostles, but a primacy within the apostolic college, ordained to fostering and proclaiming the consensus of the college.

But there is another side of Peter in the Gospels—the Peter who denies Jesus three times (Luke 22:34), the Peter who is reproached by Jesus: "Get behind me, Satan! You are a stumbling block [Greek: *skandalon*] to me; for you are setting your mind not on divine things but on human things" (Matt 16:23). This passage comes five verses after the passage in which Jesus says to Peter "You are Peter, and on this rock I will build my church." But here the "rock"—*petra,* has become a stumbling block, a scandal to Jesus. The authors of *Peter in the New Testament* surmise that: "when Peter 'thinks the things of men' he can become a stone of stumbling *[skandalon]* to Jesus."[78] I agree with this. We will see in later chapters that when not only Peter, but also those who are held to be the successors of Peter, the Roman pontiffs, "think as God thinks," i.e., act according to the will of God, they do indeed function as rocks of orthodoxy and integration for the whole Church. But when they "think the things of men," i.e., act from pride or lust for power, they become stumbling stones and scandals to Christ and the unity of his Church. I believe these two Petrine passages, Matthew 16:13-20 and 16:21-23, should be grouped together and read as a unit. The promise to Peter concerning the rock and the keys is in fact accompanied by a stern warning: the Petrine office of primacy, which is meant to be a foundation for the Church, can become a stumbling stone, a scandal, to the Church if it is abused. And the same dialectic is found in Luke 22:31-34. Directly after Jesus tells Peter to "strengthen your brothers" he predicts that Peter will deny him three times, again, indicating that Peter, or his successors, can fail in their primatial mission if they think as humans think and not as God thinks.

[78] Ibid., 93.

Summary and Conclusion

The Jesus movement does not seem to have been egalitarian. Both Jesus' own relation to the Father and the kingdom he preached were communions formed by submission to the Father. Jesus himself functioned as a clear authority and mediator in the movement. His authority was not one of domination, but of virtue: holiness, wisdom, and divine power (the miracles). Yet this divine power was kenotic, self-emptying, and self-giving, as can be seen in his death on the cross. Similarly, Jesus' authority was expressed in service and empowerment to the larger group (e.g., the footwashing scene in John). It was an authority which was not exclusive, but inclusive: the disciples were given the power to preach, heal, and exorcise as Jesus did, and functioned as his very representatives (Matt 10:40: "Whoever welcomes you welcomes me"). Jesus did institute a structure of authority to succeed him after his death. The appointment of the Twelve to be a nucleus of the restored Israel, the existence of a larger group of disciples, the fact that they were sent out by Jesus as his plenipotentiary representatives, to such an extent that rejection of them was rejection of Jesus himself, the instituting of the new Covenant, the sharing of the Twelve in the cup of the Last Supper, and the command "Do this in remembrance of me," all point to the fact that Jesus passed on hierarchical authority to some of his followers, especially the Twelve. The following chapter will consider the nature of the authority exercised by the apostles and their successors.

Chapter 4

The Apostles and Their Successors

And when they [Paul and Barnabas] had appointed elders for them in every church, with prayer and fasting they committed them to the Lord in whom they believed. (Acts 14:23)

The Twelve and Other Apostles

The authority of the Twelve was rooted in their appointment by Jesus, in their sharing of his ministry, in their role as witnesses to the resurrection, in their capacity to hand on what Jesus had said and done, and in their call to be the eschatological judges of a renewed Israel. The New Testament does not show any of the Twelve founding a church, or acting as the pastor of a church.[1] Rather, if we can trust Acts, they seem to have the care of the whole Church. This can be seen in the selection of the first deacons (Acts 6:1-7), an incident that is also illustrative of the exercise of apostolic authority.

In Acts 6, the Twelve summon "the whole body of the disciples" to consider a complaint by the Aramaic-speaking Jewish Christians (Hebraists) against the Greek-speaking, non-Palestinian Jewish Christians

[1] Though Peter has been called the first bishop of Rome, this may be an anachronism. Peter came to Rome in the 60s, after the Church was already in existence. D.W. O'Connor points out that "there is no mention of the Roman episcopacy of Peter in the New Testament, 1 Clement, or the epistles of Ignatius" *Peter in Rome* (New York: Columbia University, 1969) 207. On this question see Raymond

(Hellenists), that the widows of the Hellenists are not getting their fair share of the daily distribution of food. They ask the community to elect seven men to supervise the distribution of goods—these are the first deacons. The community agrees to this, selects seven candidates (all Hellenists), and the candidates are presented to the apostles, who lay hands on them, probably as a sign of commissioning. In this incident, the Twelve delegate the administrative processes of the local church to others, since their concern is for the whole Church. And the manner of the decision is participatory; as presented by Luke, it is a collegial and consensus decision, respecting the participation of all involved.

Others besides the Twelve were called apostles. "Apostle" (Greek: *Apostolos*) means "One who has been sent." Paul considered himself an apostle, but was not one of the Twelve. In his greetings at the end of Romans (c. 58 C.E.), he considers Andronicus and Junia (who may have been a female) to be "prominent among the apostles." James, the brother of the Lord, also may have been considered an apostle (Gal 1:19).

There were also more than the Twelve who were witnesses to the resurrection. According to John's Gospel, the risen Jesus appeared to Mary of Magdala (John 20:11-18). Paul says that the risen Christ appeared to Cephas, then to the Twelve, then to five hundred disciples at one time, then to James, "then to all the apostles," and finally, to Paul himself (1 Cor 15:5-8). Paul's own commission to be an apostle came from an appearance of the risen Lord to him on the road to Damascus (Acts 26:17-18; cf. Acts 9:1-19; Gal 1:12). As related in Acts 26, the risen Christ sent him to be an apostle to the Gentiles. Paul opens many of his letters by insisting that his call to be an apostle did not come from human origins, but from God (Gal 1:1; 1 Cor 1:1; 2 Cor 1:1; Rom 1:1).

Many of the post-resurrectional appearances, as narrated in the Gospels, involve commissionings. At the end of Matthew, Jesus appears to the eleven in Galilee, saying:

> All authority in heaven and on earth has been given to me. Go therefore and make disciples of all nations, baptizing them in the name of the Father and of the Son and of the Holy Spirit, and teaching them

---

Brown, *Priest and Bishop: Biblical Reflections* (New York: Paulist Press, 1970) 52–54, and idem., *The Critical Meaning of the Bible* (New York: Paulist Press, 1981) 126–129. Brown notes that the question of Peter's primacy is distinct from the question of whether he functioned as a bishop at Rome. Brown defends the Petrine primacy, as do I, on biblical grounds. See below.

> to obey everything that I have commanded you. And remember, I am with you always, to the end of the age (Matt 28:18-20).

Again, in an appearance (in Jerusalem) related by John, Jesus says "As the Father has sent me, so I send you" (John 20:21). Similar commissionings are found in John 21, Luke 24:48-49, and Acts 1:8. Some commissionings involve the apostles as a group, and some are directed towards individuals (e.g., Peter in John 21:15-18).

We may distinguish at least two classes of apostles commissioned by the Lord: the Twelve, whose ministry was largely confined to Palestine (except for Peter, who died in Rome), and missionary apostles, such as Paul and Barnabas, whose authority was over outlying areas and over particular missionary churches they had founded.[2] (The term "apostle" was also applied to those who were sent as delegates from particular churches; in such cases, they may or may not have been understood as having been also commissioned by the Lord.) Paul, a missionary apostle who had not known Jesus in his lifetime, is at pains in his letters to legitimize his apostolic authority. He insists that his apostolic authority comes from the risen Lord, to demonstrate that his authority is not inferior to that of other apostles (2 Cor 12:11). In addition, he appeals to the "signs and wonders and mighty works" (2 Cor 12:12) which the Spirit works through him, as testimony to his apostolic authority.

This points to another distinction. The authority of the Twelve, and James (if he is to be considered an apostle) depended to a great extent on their association with Jesus during his lifetime: as witnesses, they could hand on what Jesus had said or done. Hence their authority was grounded in *tradition* (as well as in resurrection commissionings and charismatic deeds, such as miracles): Peter's speeches as reported in Acts 2 and 3 are indications of this. Paul's authority was not and could not be so grounded; typically the authority of his statements derives from the Spirit or a saying of the [risen] Lord. Hence his authority is sometimes said to be "charismatic" as distinct from the more traditional or institutional authority of the Twelve and James. This distinction has been especially emphasized by Lutherans (e.g., Hans von Campenhausen). Certainly there is something to it; Paul seems to be much less bound by the traditions of the past than either Peter or James; he is willing to do away with the requirement of circumcision,

[2] See Brown, *Priest and Bishop,* 47–86.

whereas James' people are not (Gal 2:12), and to ignore traditional Jewish dietary restrictions, whereas Peter was not (Gal 2:12-13). Thus Paul is often typed as representing the Spirit-filled, prophetic drive for change, whereas the Twelve and James represent institutional conservatism. But this dichotomy must not be pressed too far. Peter also produces miracles, and his authority, like that of the Twelve, also derives from a charism of the Spirit (Acts 2).

The authority of the apostles,[3] then, derived first from their association with Jesus during his lifetime, as those who could reliably hand on accounts of Jesus' words and deeds. Their witness became foundational for the Church (cf. Eph 2:20).[4] In addition, their authority derived from having been witnesses to the resurrection and from having been commissioned by the risen Lord to proclaim his message. Paul also claimed apostolic authority on the basis of his commissioning by the resurrected Lord, though he had not known the Lord during his earthly life, but his case was probably exceptional, and it is noteworthy that he has to argue strenuously for his apostolic authority.

What was Paul's relation to the Twelve and to the mother Church in Jerusalem? First, there was obviously tension, as evidenced by Paul's account of the dispute with Peter over table fellowship in Galatians (2:11-14), and his defensive attitude towards those "reputed to be pillars" (Gal 2:6; cf. 2 Cor 12:11). Paul's ministry was more charismatic—open to the freedom of the Spirit, while that of James and the apostles in Jerusalem was more conservative, stressing continuity with Jewish law. Yet generally, the Church at Antioch and its emissaries seem to have submitted to the Church at Jerusalem. Thus, when questions arose concerning the legitimacy of baptizing Gentiles into the Church without circumcision, Antioch sent Paul and Barnabas as delegates to the Church at Jerusalem to seek approbation for their practice (Acts 15). Furthermore, when James later sent delegates to Antioch, the

[3] The term "apostle" could also mean one who was sent as an emissary of a church to other churches, as Paul and Barnabas were sent by the church at Antioch to Jerusalem, Acts 13:2-5. I will reserve the term apostle, however, for those who were sent by the Lord as witnesses. On this see Bengt Holmberg, *Paul and Power* (Philadelphia, Fortress, 1978) 52ff. Note that the "disciples" (Greek: *mathetes*) probably denotes a wider group than the apostles.

[4] On the foundational role of the apostles see Hans von Campenhausen, *Ecclesiastical Authority and Spiritual Power in the Church of the First Three Centuries* (London: Adam and Charles Black, 1969—German original: *Kirchliches amt und Geistliche Vollmacht*, 1953) 12–29.

Jewish Christians there (except Paul) began to eat separately from the Gentile Christians, since this (apparently) was the practice of the Jerusalem Church (Gal 2:11-14). Even during Paul's second and third journeys, when he had more freedom of action, he was concerned about collecting money for the "poor" at the Jerusalem Church (1 Cor 16:1-4; 2 Cor 8–9; Rom 15:27-29)—a collection which had been enjoined on him by the mother Church in Jerusalem (Gal 2:10a: "only they would have us remember the poor"). Bengt Holmberg, in his book *Paul and Power,* an exhaustive study of Pauline authority, argues that this collection was important to Paul because its acceptance by the Jerusalem Church would also be a validation of his apostolic authority and mission. Since Paul had not been a disciple of Jesus, nor known him personally, his apostolic message was to an extent dependent on those apostles who had. It was through these original apostles, such as the Twelve and James, that Paul was connected with the earthly Jesus, and his teaching.[5] Thus, although there was tension between Paul and his charismatic concept of the apostolate, and the Twelve and James, whose ministry was more conservative and institutional, nevertheless there was a mutual dependence. Paul depended on them for the validity of his message; they depended on him for the conversion of the Gentiles (Gal 2:9).

Besides the Twelve and the missionary apostles, there was another prominent figure, James, the brother of the Lord, who became the head of the Jerusalem Church. In Galatians 1:19 Paul seemed to consider James to be an apostle. Though not one of the Twelve, James had known Jesus, and had been favored with a resurrection appearance. According to Eusebius, he had "been elected by the apostles to the episcopal throne at Jerusalem."[6] James was not a missionary apostle, but a resident leader surrounded by elders; though never called a bishop, he was reckoned by Paul as a "pillar" of the Church (Gal 2:9). As the incident in Galatians 2:11-15 shows, his emphasis was on continuity with the Jewish law.

There are, then, several types of apostolic authority in the New Testament which complement each other. The authority of the Twelve was over the whole Church—a continuation of Jesus' authority. Their authority was exercised as a college, and hence demanded consensus,

[5] Holmberg, *Paul and Power,* 50–56.

[6] Eusebius, *The History of the Church,* G.A. Williamson, trans. (Minneapolis: Augsburg, 1965) 99.

as in Acts 6 and 15. Some of the Twelve may have exercised authority over individual churches, for example, Peter at Rome, but this is not shown in the New Testament. Missionary and charismatic apostles (e.g., Paul, perhaps Barnabas) had authority over churches they had founded, as evidenced in Paul's letters. James, if he is to be considered an apostle, had authority over a local church: the Mother Church in Jerusalem. Though there is tension between the "charismatic" wing of the apostolate (Paul and Barnabas) and the institutional wing (Peter, James), as evidenced in Paul's letter to the Galatians, these forms of apostolic authority balance and complement one another, and both are necessary for the full expression of hierarchical authority in the Church. This parallels the Old Testament, where the prophets check and balance the authority of kings and priests. Prophets clashed with kings—as Nathan with David or Elijah with Ahab, but they attacked only the abuse of office, not the office of kingship itself. Both the Old and New Testaments, then, witness to the principle that the Spirit acts through a plurality of authorities, not just one. Both "charismatic" authority and institutional authority (which is also a charism) come from the Spirit, and each checks the excesses of the other.

A paradigm example of this can be seen in Acts 15:1-34, the so-called "council of Jerusalem," where the Church had to decide whether to circumcise the Gentile converts before baptizing them. This decision was critical for the young Church's identity and its relation with Judaism, for its decision to admit uncircumcised Gentile converts would ultimately lead to an irreparable rift with Judaism and the establishment of a separate religion. In this decision, Paul and Barnabas came down from Antioch to describe to the Jerusalem apostles and elders what was happening in the mission churches: Gentiles were converting and being baptized. The question was: should they first be circumcised, and made subject to the law of Moses—that is, become Jews first before becoming Christians? The decision was made through extensive discussion, involving both apostles and elders (Acts 15:7), in which Peter, Paul, Barnabas, and James spoke. The final decision was delivered by James, but the consent of the whole Church is implied (Acts 15:22, 25, 28).

This passage is a model for the operation of participatory hierarchy. It was, in modern parlance, a collegial decision, reached after extensive participatory debate, in which the apostles and elders discerned and proclaimed the mind of the whole body. Furthermore, individuals representing different types of charisms came together in consensus—

Paul and Barnabas, representing the Spirit-filled wing of the apostolate, Peter, representing the Twelve, and James and the Jerusalem elders, representing the conservative and "institutional" wing, with its concern that continuity with Judaism be preserved. Consensus was understood to mean that the decision had been made in accordance with the will of the Spirit. Thus the letter written to communicate the decision says "it has seemed good to the Holy Spirit and to us" (Acts 15:28).

The account given in Acts is certainly simplified,[7] but, according to Raymond Brown, the Lucan picture of the Twelve convening the whole assembly for decision is historically plausible. He notes that this structure was paralleled by the Essene community at Qumran, where an assembly of the community, called the "Session of the Many" *(rabbim)* exercised judicial and legislative authority over sectarians. There was also a permanent community council of twelve men and three priests, which held authority within the "Session of the Many." Thus the early Christian community may have followed a pattern that already existed among other Jewish sectarians.[8]

The account in Acts is probably idealized: there appears to have been a dissenting "circumcision faction" (cf. Gal 2:12). But this is perhaps beside the point, for Acts is presented to us not only as history, but as a paradigm to be followed by the Church, a sort of narrative charter of decision making.[9] And in this instance, when the Church had to make a decision of critical importance, the decision is shown as being made not in an authoritarian manner and then imposed on the body, but in a manner respecting the participation of those involved. The fundamental task of the leaders at the Jerusalem Council was to discern how the Spirit was acting within the whole body of the faithful, and to proclaim this authoritatively, so as to preserve the Church in unity. The role of hierarchy in this episode was participatory and integrative, authoritative but not authoritarian.

[7] Acts 15 seems to combine two separate meetings into one. For the decision to require abstinence from blood, meat sacrificed to idols or killed by strangling was apparently unknown to Paul when he wrote Galatians, but was communicated to him later (Acts 21:25). See Brown, *Priest and Bishop* 57, n. 37.

[8] Brown, *Priest and Bishop,* 58–59.

[9] For a summary of the scholarly debate on Acts 15, see Luke T. Johnson, *Decision Making in the Church* (Philadelphia: Fortress, 1983) 46–58. Johnson argues that despite the apparent lack of historical accuracy in Acts 15, it remains relevant to the Church as a model of decision-making (56).

The question might be raised: if the Jerusalem Council decided against the pro-circumcisionists, in what way did it respect their participation? I will argue in a later chapter that even a participatory hierarchy must reject positions which would destroy the integrity of the body. Participation in such a context means that these positions are voiced, heard respectfully, and considered in deliberation, rather than suppressed, even though they are later decided against.

This incident is revealing in another respect. By leading the apostles and early missionaries to baptize uncircumcised Gentiles, the Spirit was acting creatively, breaking new ground. Had the apostles and elders felt that their hierarchical leadership entailed merely guarding a statically conceived tradition—a "deposit of faith"—they would have rejected this activity of the Spirit and insisted that believers be circumcised and follow the law of Moses. Thus the role of the apostolic hierarchy in this instance was to foster the developmental work of the Spirit. The result was an exercise of hierarchy that succeeded in solving problems while preserving unity and integration.

The Jerusalem Council set a very important biblical precedent for later councils of the Church, whose ideal was not to achieve decision by a democratic majority, nor by a single autocrat (e.g., the emperor), but by a consensus of the bishops present, for a consensus was thought to indicate the will of the Spirit.

The Successors to the Apostles

The traditional Catholic view, repeated at Vatican II (*LG* #20), has been that the successors to the apostles were the bishops (Greek: *episkopoi*), who inherited the authority of the apostles in matters of doctrine, discipline, and pastoral care. Evidence for this can be found in Acts (e.g., 14:23), which describes Paul and Barnabas appointing elders (Greek: *presbyteroi*), who are also called bishops (*episkopoi*—Acts 20:28); in the Pastoral epistles, which contain instructions to Timothy and Titus on appointing bishops; and especially in the first letter of Clement, c. 96 C.E., which states: "They [the apostles] preached in country and city, and appointed their first converts, after testing them by the Spirit, to be the bishops and deacons of future believers."[10]

[10] *1 Clement*, 42:4–5, Cyril Richardson, ed. and trans. *Early Christian Fathers* (New York: Macmillan, 1970) 62.

Protestant thinkers have challenged the Catholic view, chiefly on the basis of Paul's undisputedly genuine letters, which never mention presbyters or elders, and only once mention bishops (Phil 1:1).[11] The Protestant argument has been that in Paul's communities rule was by apostles and Spirit-inspired charismatics, such as prophets—a so-called charismatic or evangelical government. Paul's letters, they argue, are the best evidence for early church government. The Pastoral epistles were not written by Paul, but by one or more of his successors, and describe the situation of about 85 C.E., but not of the very early Church. The evidence in Acts cannot be trusted, since Acts does not agree with Paul's letters in some details. Therefore, the evidence is that the early Church was governed by charismatic and evangelical leaders, who were only much later supplanted by the rule of hierarchical bishops and "early Catholicism." Thus Adolph von Harnack, a famous Lutheran historian, wrote in 1900: "In the New Testament there was no early catholicism; rather such a theology and church organization were a second-century development distorting the pristine evangelical character of Christianity."[12] Recent biblical scholarship also has raised doubts about the traditional Catholic view that the apostles appointed the first bishops.

This debate has serious repercussions for any study of hierarchy in the Church. If the Protestant thesis is true, institutional and episcopal hierarchy is not, as Catholics have held, a divinely willed development in the early Church, but a deformation of an earlier, more egalitarian, Spirit-led community structure. Unfortunately, the biblical and historical evidence pertaining to this question is scanty, and can be interpreted in more than one way. Let us, however, consider it.

First it is necessary to introduce a distinction between *episkopos,* "bishop," and *episkopē,* "overseeing, supervising." As Raymond Brown points out, the function of *episkopē* is not always performed by bishops, especially in the very early Christian communities, when the office of bishop was not yet differentiated from other offices, such as *presbyteros* =

[11] The Pauline letters of which Paul is the uncontested author are 1 Thessalonians, Galatians, 1 and 2 Corinthians, Philippians, Romans, Philemon. On the authenticity of the Pastorals, Brown comments "Between 80% and 90% of scholarship today would regard the pastorals as Deutero-Pauline, written after Paul's death." Brown, *The Critical Meaning of the Bible,* 136, note 20. For the reasons most scholars think the Pastorals are Deutero-Pauline, see Robert A. Wild, S.J., "The Pastoral Letters," in *NJBC,* 892.

[12] Raymond E. Brown, "Canonicity," in *NJBC,* 1053.

"presbyter, elder."[13] In fact, different kinds of *episkopē* were exercised by different groups in the early churches.

As mentioned above, there is no biblical evidence that any of the Twelve ever served as the bishop or head of a church.[14] Peter most likely came to Rome in the 60s, sometime after the Church had been founded, but there is no evidence that he served as the first bishop of the Roman church. In their role as eschatological judges of Israel, the Twelve had no successors.[15] But did the Twelve, or the missionary apostles such as Paul, appoint bishops as their successors?

First, it is generally conceded that before the time of Clement and Ignatius, the terms bishop *(episkopos)* and presbyter or elder *(presbyteros)* are interchangeable. For instance, in Titus 1:5 the writer instructs Titus to "appoint elders in every town," but two verses later (1:7), the writer speaks of bishops. In Acts 20, Paul addresses the elders of Ephesus, who are called *presbyteroi* in Acts 20:17, and *episkopoi* in Acts 20:28. Thus, until the end of the first century, when the *episkopoi* are beginning to emerge as single overseers (e.g., the Letters of Ignatius), the terminology was fluid.

The Pastoral Letters show Paul giving instructions to Timothy and Titus (who seem to be apostolic delegates but not necessarily bishops) about appointing elders and bishops. "I left you behind in Crete for this reason, so that you should put in order what remained to be done, that you might amend what was defective, should appoint elders in every town as I directed you" (Titus 1:5). Both 1 Tim 3:1-7 and Titus 1:5-9 list the qualifications of bishops. But most scholars now think that the Pastoral Letters were not written by Paul, but by one of Paul's followers, about 80–85 C.E., and therefore portray the situation at that time, not in the time of Paul himself.[16]

[13] Brown, *The Critical Meaning of the Bible,* 125–126.

[14] Ibid., 129.

[15] Though Matthias was selected as a successor to Judas (Acts 1), no successor was elected when James the son of Zebedee was put to death by Agrippa I, in 43 or 44 C.E. (Acts 12:1). Apparently the thought was that the Twelve, as the eschatological judges of the twelve tribes, has to number twelve, and Judas had forfeited his role as judge by his defection. See Brown, *Priest and Bishop,* 52–55. I agree with Brown that the pope is the successor of the Petrine primacy, but that this succession does not depend on Peter's having functioned as bishop of Rome.

[16] For authorship and dates, see Jerome D. Quinn, *The Letter to Titus* (New York: Doubleday, Anchor Bible, 1988) 19. Also, Robert A. Wild, S.J., "The Pastoral Letters," in *NJBC,* 891–893.

Another portrait of a church late in the first century (or early in the second century) is provided by the *Didache,* a composition probably written in Syria.[17] The second part of this document concerns church order, and evinces a situation where rule by itinerant apostles, prophets, and teachers is being replaced by resident bishops and deacons.

> You must, then, elect for yourselves bishops and deacons who are a credit to the Lord, men who are gentle, generous, faithful, and well tried. For their ministry to you is identical with that of the prophets and teachers. You must not, therefore, despise them, for along with the prophets and teachers they enjoy a place of honor among you.[18]

John Meier notes the similarity of this situation to Acts 13:1-2: "Now in the church at Antioch there were prophets and teachers." He surmises that the *Didache* might come from a church in rural Syria, where a primitive church order would have been preserved longer than in the cities, such as Antioch (which by the time of the *Didache* probably had resident bishops).[19] Note that in the *Didache* the bishops are apparently *elected* by the community, rather than appointed, and they emerge as leaders from what was probably a more collegial and fluid form of ecclesial government—"prophets and teachers."

The Book of Acts, also written about 85 C.E., frequently mentions the presence of elders in the churches (Acts 11:30; 15:2, 6, 22, 23; 16:4; 21:18). In Acts 15:6, elders are shown gathering with the apostles to consider admitting Gentiles to the Church. Acts mentions in two places that Paul, or Paul and Barnabas, appointed elders *(presbyteroi)* in the churches they founded. Thus in Acts 14:23 we read: "And after they had appointed elders *(presbyteroi)* for them in each church, with prayer and fasting they entrusted them to the Lord." Acts 20:17ff. narrates Paul's farewell to the elders *(presbyteroi)* of the Church at Ephesus, a church which Paul had founded earlier, and whose elders therefore he had probably appointed. In this address, he enjoins them to be responsible "overseers," *episkopoi* (bishops). Raymond Brown calls these figures "presbyter-bishops," and considers that the bishop

[17] For the text of the *Didache,* see Richardson, ed., *Early Christian Fathers* (New York: Macmillan) 171–179; for a discussion of date, authorship, and provenance, see Raymond E. Brown and John P. Meier, *Antioch and Rome* (New York: Paulist Press, 1983) 81–84.

[18] *Didache,* 15:1-3; from Richardson, 178.

[19] Brown & Meier, *Antioch and Rome,* 81–84.

only gradually emersed as the overseer of his fellow presbyters.[20] Thus Acts does provide evidence that Paul and Barnabas appointed elders, sometimes referred to as bishops, to be leaders of the churches they founded. Other apostles may have done the same.

We cannot be certain, however, if Acts is describing the situation as it was in 85 C.E., when it was written, or whether it is describing the situation of Paul's first missionary journey, c. 45–49, almost forty years earlier. Many scholars doubt the historical veracity of Acts, since it conflicts in details with some of Paul's letters, which describe some of the same events. To ascertain the church-leadership situation before 70 C.E., we have to consider Paul's letters, the best primary sources for this period. These letters, however, were written to address specific concerns in particular churches; whatever information they give about the condition of the whole Church in this period is by way of *obiter dicta.*

A problem for the belief that Paul appointed elders in every church is that Paul's letters are not addressed to any elders, nor are elders *(presbyteroi)* even mentioned in the letters. It is noted that 1 and 2 Corinthians are addressed to "the Church of God at Corinth," and to the saints there: no elders or leaders are mentioned. And Paul writes in 1 Corinthians 12:28: "God has appointed in the church first apostles, second prophets, third teachers; then deed power, then gifts of healing, forms of assistance, forms of leadership, various kinds of tongues." There is no mention here of elders, bishops, or deacons. Thus some scholars have argued that the creation of elders, bishops, and deacons occurred much later than Paul's letters to the Corinthians (ca. 57 C.E.), and that Church government in Paul's time was in the hands of charismatically inspired apostles, prophets, and teachers, perhaps following the example of the Church at Antioch: "Now in the church at Antioch there were prophets and teachers" (Acts 13:1; cf. Eph 2:20 which says that the Church is "built upon the foundation of the apostles and prophets"). Because of the situation reflected in Paul's early letters, many scholars, especially Protestants, have concluded that an early period of charismatic church government was later replaced by a hierarchical and "early catholic" government of bishops, presbyters, and deacons, as seen in the Pastoral Letters, the Letter of Clement, and the Letters of Ignatius.[21]

[20] Brown, *Priest and Bishop,* 73.

[21] Burtchaell, *From Synagogue to Church,* provides an exhaustive survey of this thesis in Protestantism and in some recent Catholic authors.

This position, however, is an oversimplification. Paul's letter to the Philippians is addressed "to all the saints . . . at Philippi, with the bishops (plural: *episkopoi*) and deacons *(diakonoi).*" "Bishop" here probably does not indicate the "monarchial bishop" which will be found in the letters of Ignatius, but "presbyter-bishops" (note the plural), equivalent to elders. Again, in 1 Thessalonians 5:12, Paul writes "we appeal to you, brothers and sisters, to respect those who labor among you, and have charge of you in the Lord and admonish you." The verbs for "labor among" *(kopiao)* and "have charge" *(prostemi)* are used of elders in 1 Timothy 5:17. This indicates some sort of local leadership as early as c. 51 C.E., when this letter was written.

Many argue that the situation at Corinth (where no presbyter-bishops are evident) was the norm for Pauline churches; and that Philippi (which had local presbyter-bishops) was the exception. Brown, however, suggests that the reverse might be true: Philippi was the norm, and Corinth the exception.[22] Bengt Holmberg, who has written the most exhaustive study of authority in the Pauline churches, also argues this. He notes that the Corinthian situation was anomalous: apparently *nobody* exercised leadership there, thus forcing Paul to intervene. In other Pauline churches, leadership developed more harmoniously.[23] Thus the situation depicted in Acts, where Paul (and Barnabas) appoint leaders (i.e., elders, or presbyter-bishops) in the churches they found, does find some support in Paul's early and genuine letters. Even 1 Corinthians 12:28, which does not mention elders, does mention administrators, perhaps indicating some kind of nascent local leadership. But the offices of leadership appear to be much more fluid than they would be later. Acts speaks of elders, in the plural, as leaders in individual churches (cf. Acts 11:30; 15:2, 6, 22, 23; 16:4; 21:18), but also of "prophets and teachers" (13:1), and of the "apostles and elders" gathering for a decision in Acts 15:6. It appears likely, therefore, that there were a number of different types of leaders in various churches—apostles, prophets, teachers in some, perhaps the more Hellenistic churches, such as Antioch (cf. Acts 13:1) or Corinth, but also elders or presbyter-bishops, deacons, and administrators in others, especially the Jerusalem church and those churches close to it. Some churches may have had both types of leadership simultaneously. In

[22] Brown, *Priest and Bishop,* 69–72.

[23] Holmberg, *Paul and Power,* 114–115. Holmberg also notes that Romans 12:6-8 mentions administration as a gift operating in the churches.

others (e.g., the church of the *Didache*), institutional leadership may have gradually replaced a more charismatic leadership. That there was more than one type of supervision or *episkopē* in the early churches is argued by three quite different authors: James Burtchaell and Raymond Brown (both Catholics), and Bengt Holmberg, a Lutheran. I will summarize their arguments in the paragraphs below.

Burtchaell argues that the synagogue offices of elders and community chief (see chap. 2) continued in the nascent churches, who spontaneously organized themselves after the pattern of the synagogues which they had left. He notes that the evidence for the presence of elders in early Christian communities is pervasive:

> Acts repeatedly refers to elders in the Jerusalem community, and mentions them in Lystra, Iconium, Pisidian, Antioch (Paul's early foundations) and Ephesus. . . . Paul addresses elders in Philippi and describes them to the Thessalonians. Clement's entire letter concerns the elders in the Corinthian assembly; the *Shepherd of Hermas,* likely written in Rome, has much comment on elders; James, 1 Peter and 2 and 3 John all mention them; and Ignatius deals with elders in Ephesus, Magnesia, Tralles, Philadelphia and Smyrna.[24]

As in the Jewish tradition, the Christian election of elders and their community chief was the responsibility of local communities. Christian tradition records, however, that in the formation of new churches, the elders were appointed by an apostle or founder (e.g., Paul and Barnabas, Acts 14:23). But such elders would also have required designation by the local community, and after the passing of the apostolic founder, the election of elders would have reverted to the local community.[25] Thus:

> The officers of the local community carried a dual identity. They were the creatures of the community (unlike the charismatics, even the local ones), but the community itself was also their handiwork (as it was of the charismatics). This was embodied in the twofold manner of their mandate: elected by a show of hands within the community, they also required the laying-on of hands from someone in the charismatic discipleship/descent from the Lord.[26]

[24] Burtchaell, *From Synagogue to Church,* 293.
[25] Ibid., 295.
[26] Ibid., 343.

These local officers were not prominent in the early years of the communities because they were overshadowed by the presence of apostolic founders, like Paul, or apostolic deputies (like Timothy and Titus), and charismatics, both local and itinerant, such as prophets, healers, and perhaps teachers. But with the gradual passing of these charismatic apostles and leaders, the local elders emerged as the stable leaders. One of their group, the community chief, eventually became designated as the *episkopos,* bishop. The best example of such a community is probably the mother Church in Jerusalem, before 70 C.E. Here we find the Church headed by James, surrounded by elders; so that Paul and Barnabas, on coming to Jerusalem from Antioch, "were welcomed by the church and the apostles and elders" (Acts 15:4).

Against Burtchaell's thesis is Paul's comment in 1 Corinthians 12:28, (cited above, p. 82), which does not mention elders or bishops, though it does mention administrators. I think this can be explained by the peculiar situation at Corinth—a church which failed to develop stable local leadership, degenerated into factions, and so remained under Paul's tutelage, or as a situation prevailing in some of the more Hellenistic churches founded by Paul, which may have favored charismatic apostles, prophets, and teachers as leaders.[27] But I think the preponderance of evidence is on Burtchaell's side. What is important in his thesis is that there were several levels or forms of leadership and authority in the local churches, and that these had to be in balance. A church without stable local leadership, like Corinth, became a problem church, threatened by disintegration into factions.

For Burtchaell, then, the successors to the apostles were the central churches themselves, together with their local elders and community chief, who were both elected *and* commissioned by someone in charismatic descent from the Lord.[28] This pattern would remain true of early bishops, who were both elected by their communities and ordained by other bishops (chap. 5).

Bengt Holmberg also argues for a plurality of authority in the early Church, especially in the Pauline communities. His approach is

[27] Von Campenhausen and others have suggested that Jewish-Christian churches, such as that at Jerusalem, followed the synagogue pattern of elders, but that Paul followed the Antiochene practice of instituting charismatic prophets and teachers (cf. Acts 13:1), rather than elders, as authorities. See *Ecclesiastical Authority and Spiritual Power,* 70.

[28] Burtchaell, *From Synagogue to Church,* 330.

sociological. He notes the widespread influence in sociology of Max Weber's opposition between charismatic authority, and what Weber calls rational (bureaucratic), and traditional authority.[29] Holmberg thinks this opposition is overdrawn, and notes that "charisma . . . actively seeks institutionalization, albeit a radically new one in contrast to existing patterns of authority."[30] Thus, the communities founded by Paul were not completely governed by charismatic authority, as a superficial reading of 1 Corinthians 12:28 might indicate. Local leadership and offices did exist in the early Pauline communities, though on a rudimentary level. Holmberg notes that even in Corinth, Paul exhorts the congregation to put themselves "at the service of" Stephanas and his household (1 Cor 16:15-16). But local leadership was undeveloped in Paul's congregations because of the active role in governance taken by the apostle himself, as evidenced by his letters.[31] Yet for Paul, authority does not lie only with apostles, prophets, and teachers, but also with local administrators; and all such forms of leadership or instruction are charismatic, that is, inspired by the Spirit. There is no opposition, then, between charismatic and institutional authority for Paul.

Raymond Brown, in his essay "Are the Bishops Successors to the Apostles?" argues that a likely model for the *episkopos* or bishop was the "Supervisor of the Many," who presided over the community assembly at Qumran. Just as Christian communities adopted the institution of elders or presbyters from the synagogue, so they may have adopted the institution of supervisory bishop from Qumran.[32] Brown does not argue that all bishops were appointed by missionary apostles. Many probably were. Others may have emerged from the community

[29] "Since it is 'extraordinary,' charismatic authority is sharply opposed to rational, and particularly bureaucratic, authority, and to traditional authority." From Max Weber, *Economy and Society: An Outline of Interpretive Sociology,* 3 vols., Guenther Roth and Claus Wittich, eds. (New York: Bedminster, 1968) 244. Holmberg's analysis of Weber's concepts is given in *Paul and Power,* 137–176.

[30] Holmberg, *Paul and Power,* 165.

[31] Ibid., 116.

[32] Brown, *Priest and Bishop,* 66–69; idem, *The Churches the Apostles Left Behind* (New York: Paulist Press, 1984) 33: "I think it plausible that from the synagogue Christians borrowed a pattern of groups of presbyters for each church, while the pastoral-supervisor *(episkopos)* role given to all or many of these presbyters came from the organizational model of close-knit Jewish sectarian groups such as the Dead Sea Essenes."

without explicit apostolic appointment. Yet in nearly all cases bishops and presbyters succeeded to the governance of churches. Thus the bishops became the *functional* successors of the apostles, even if some were not explicitly ordained by apostles. Brown sees in this development the guidance of the Holy Spirit, and hence affirms that the bishops are by divine will the successors of the apostles.[33]

The process then by which bishops came to succeed the apostles as the principal authorities in the early Church was complex, and undoubtedly varied in different locations and at different times. Some early bishops may have been appointed by the apostles, as Acts, the Pastorals, and 1 Clement suggest. Others may have emerged by election, without apostolic appointment, as the *Didache* suggests. I think Burtchaell is right in arguing that even those receiving apostolic appointment would have been nominated and put forth by the community, and hence would have received their authority *both by election and by consecration;* they would be both representatives of the community and delegated successors of the apostles. By the time of the First Letter of Clement (96 C.E.), the complexity of this process had become simplified, so that Clement could state, without nuance, that the apostles appointed bishops as their successors. I agree with Raymond Brown that this whole process reflects the guidance of the Spirit, and hence was willed by God. Certainly this was the belief of the early Church, which universally accepted the bishops as legitimate authorities, and as the successors of the apostles (chap. 5).

Successors of the Twelve

As mentioned above, there is no evidence that any of the Twelve was the resident bishop of a local city; their care was rather for the whole Church. Who, then, succeeded to the Twelve in the custody of the whole Church? In chapter 5, I will argue that this function was taken over by the whole college of bishops, including regional patriarchs and the bishop of Rome. But this succession was complex: neither the bishops meeting in ecumenical councils, the eastern patriarchs, nor the papacy, exercised universal supervision over the whole Church. Rather, that supervision was exercised jointly, by the councils, patriarchs, the pope, and the emperor acting in concert. When that concert

[33] Brown, *Priest and Bishop*, 73.

was broken, as it has been since 1054 C.E., then each of these influenced only one region or branch of the Church.

Unity and Diversity in New Testament Hierarchy

Holmberg insists that Paul and the Pauline churches were subject to the authority of the Jerusalem Church. This is evidenced by the fact that the church at Antioch sent delegates to Jerusalem to obtain approval for its mission practice of baptizing Gentiles (Acts 15). Thus, he concludes, the authority structure of primitive Christianity was diverse, but united in an "'organic' system, where the different constituents are bound to one another in mutual but not symmetric dependence."[34]

Raymond Brown argues that there is a diversity of ecclesiologies in the New Testament, none of which is finished or comprehensive. This is also true of the New Testament understanding of authority and hierarchy. We have examined the diversity between Paul's notion of authority and that of James, and the tension between Paul and Peter. Brown discusses another interesting example: the Johannine community.[35] The Gospel of John places great emphasis on the believer's personal relation with Jesus, and on the indwelling of the Holy Spirit, or Paraclete. This is expressed in the image of Jesus as the vine and the disciples as the branches (John 15), and throughout Jesus' farewell discourses to the disciples (e.g., John 14:15-17, 23). But Brown notes that John does not emphasize the authority of apostles, or the Church's common descent from Israel, as do other New Testament ecclesiologies; the emphasis is on the individual disciple and his or her relation with Jesus and the Spirit. Thus John's community was probably egalitarian, the New Testament prototype of present day "Holiness," or Pentecostal churches, with their emphasis on the individual believer "born again" into a personal relation with Jesus, and their rejection of apostolic succession and any overarching hierarchical structures. Brown notes the strengths of this position: an egalitarian church in which all disciples have equal access to the Spirit, for "God is Spirit (John 4:24), and the Spirit of Truth dwells in every Christian everywhere."[36] But the weakness is that there is little sense of the Church as

[34] Ibid., 203.

[35] Brown, *Churches,* 84–123.

[36] Ibid., 109.

an organic community. Images of the Church as the People of God, the Body of Christ, or the "New Israel," images which emphasize corporate unity, are lacking in John. If every believer has the Paraclete dwelling within, there is no need for a collective authority: "The anointing you received . . . abides in you, and so you do not need anyone to teach you" (1 John 2:27). There is no provision for apostles, their delegates or successors, to reconcile the Church in case of division.

The result, according to Brown, was the development of a schism, evident in the Third Letter of John. There, a presbyter writes to one of the Johannine churches, but the leader of that church, Diotrephes, refuses to acknowledge the presbyter's authority or even to welcome members of the presbyter's church into his church (3 John 9-10). And the presbyter does not appeal to any apostolic authority to unify the church (as for example Paul does in 1 Corinthians), for the only authority acknowledged by these churches is the authority of the Spirit indwelling in each member. Thus the result was a schism in the Johannine church, in which the larger fragment seceded from the great Church, and moved towards gnosticism, Docetism, and Montanism. Brown surmises that the smaller fragment, recognizing the need for a unifying apostolic authority, eventually acknowledged "the authority of a human shepherd."[37] He sees evidence for this in the last chapter of John's Gospel, which most scholars understand as an epilogue, added by a final redactor.[38] In John 21 the authority of Peter is strongly recommended—the risen Jesus says three times to Peter (who symbolizes apostolic authority), "Feed my sheep." Brown suggests: "In the redactional chapter 21, we may have a more moderate voice persuading the Johannine Christians that the pastoral authority practiced by the apostolic churches and in 'the church catholic' was instituted by Jesus and could be accepted."[39] As in the Corinthian church, an excessive emphasis on freedom in the Spirit, apart from any unifying hierarchical authority, led to factionalism and fragmentation.

Though there was evident diversity in the New Testament churches, Brown notes that none of them (except for the schismatic part of the Johannine Church) ever broke *koinonia,* or community, with the others. This is apparent in the fact that churches sent delegates

[37] Ibid., 123. See the longer discussion of this issue in Brown's *The Community of the Beloved Disciple* (New York, Paulist Press, 1979) 145–164.

[38] Brown, *Community,* 161; *Churches,* 123.

[39] Brown, *Community,* 162.

(apostles) to one another, that they acknowledged the superior authority of the Mother Church in Jerusalem, in Paul's concern over the collection, and in the Council of Jerusalem. There, when the Church had to make one of its most momentous decisions, the charismatic, institutional, and traditional authorities, along with the elders and laity reached a consensus decision. This narrative is presented as an ideal or model of ecclesial unity which respects and incorporates diversity, rather than suppressing diversity, or allowing it to fragment the Church.

Brown presents other examples of New Testament ecclesiologies, each of which in its own way maintains unity with the larger "great church," yet exhibits its own uniqueness, especially in its view of hierarchy. I will mention several without much elaboration, and refer the interested reader to Brown's excellent book for further explanation.

The Gospel of Matthew[40] emphasizes continuity with Judaism, the Law, and apostolic authority, but balances this with an equal emphasis on the ongoing presence of Jesus to the disciples ("For where two or three are gathered in my name, I am there among them" Matt 18:20). Apostolic authority itself is clearly grounded in the risen Lord, who remains present with the disciples and the Church, as the last words of the gospel proclaim: "I am with you always, to the end of the age." John Meier argues that Matthew's church (probably Antioch in Syria) came to important decisions *jointly,* as a body.

> Of key importance here [in Matt 18:15-20] is the fact that no local leader or leaders are mentioned; the local church acts and decides as a whole. . . . perhaps no leaders are mentioned in 18:15-20 because Matthew is intent on making sure that all members of the church share in important decisions, especially disciplinary decisions involving excommunication. If the grave step of excluding someone from the brotherhood has to be taken all the members should be involved.[41]

Yet Meier also believes that

> Matthew exalts the figure of Peter as *the* human authority for the church as a whole. Matthew thus proclaims the Antiochene tradition of Peter as the bridge-builder [pontiff], the moderate center, to be the norm for the whole church, as opposed to those local churches, dissi-

[40] Ibid., 124–145; cf. also Brown and Meier, *Antioch and Rome,* 45–72.

[41] Brown and Meier, *Antioch and Rome,* 69.

> dent groups, or sects which would appeal to a one-sided interpretation of the Pauline or Jamesian tradition as normative for the whole church.[42]

But Meier emphasizes that Matthew is concerned with the problems of the Antiochene church circa 85 C.E., and "is certainly not concerned with the problem of whether a single-bishop in Rome is the successor of Simon Peter, especially since both Rome and Antioch around 85 do not seem to have known the single-bishop structure."[43] As we will see in the next chapter, however, a strong single-bishop came to authority in Antioch about 110 C.E., and the church in Rome claimed that the authority of Simon Peter devolved on the bishop of Rome, said to be Peter's successor.

The ecclesiology of Luke/Acts is centered on the presence and activity of the Holy Spirit.[44] The same Spirit which spoke through the Israelite prophets empowers Jesus after his baptism and the apostles after Pentecost (Acts 2). Authority itself flows from the Spirit (cf. Acts 15:28: "It has seemed good to the Holy Spirit and to us . . ."). But, as we have seen, the Spirit does not speak through just one voice, or work only through those who are apostles, but also through deacons, such as Stephen (Acts 7), prophets such as Agabus (Acts 11:28; 21:11-13), teachers (Acts 13:1), elders (Acts 15:22-29; 20:28), women (e.g., Lydia: Acts 16:14-15, Priscilla: Acts 18:2), and ordinary believers (Acts 19:7). The will of the Spirit is manifest when many diverse Spirit-led persons come together in consensus (Acts 15).

A different image of the Church is presented by the first Letter of Peter, probably written by a follower of the apostle from Rome in the 80s or 90s.[45] The First Letter of Peter, echoing the words of Exod 19:5-6, applies to the Christian community the Old Testament concept of the Holy People of God: "But you are a chosen race, a royal priesthood, a holy nation, God's own people" (1 Pet 2:9). This image, emphasizing the sanctification of the whole community by the Spirit, was the major image of the Church used by Vatican II. 1 Peter exhorts the elders of the community to "Tend the flock of God that is in your charge . . . Do not lord it over those in your charge but be examples to the flock"

[42] Ibid., 67.
[43] Ibid., 66.
[44] Brown, *Churches,* 61–74.
[45] Ibid., 75–83.

(5:2-3). Through trials, Christians will grow in sanctity, and come to participate in eternal glory in Christ (1:5-7; 5:10).

The Pastoral Letters, probably written by a Pauline disciple in the middle 80s, stress the importance of authority: elders are to be appointed in all the churches, and are to preserve sound doctrine. The Church is seen as the household of God (1 Tim 3:15), under the fatherly care of the presbyter-bishop.

Finally, let us consider the Pauline image of the Church as the Body of Christ (1 Cor 12:12-31; Rom 12:4-5, Eph 5:23; Col 1:18). In 1 Corinthians, the unifier of the body is the Spirit, and all members are part of the body, yet possessing different gifts and charisms. But Paul also writes that there is a hierarchical order among the charisms (1 Cor 12:28): "God has appointed in the church first apostles, second prophets, third teachers; then deeds of power, then gifts of healing, forms of assistance, forms of leadership, various kinds of tongues." Yet the highest of the charisms is the gift of love (1 Corinthians 13) which, coming from the Spirit (Rom 5:5), unifies the Body. (In a variant image in Ephesians and Colossians, Christ is said to be the head of the body.)

This image emphasizes the common participation of all members in the Spirit, and hence their unity, but also the diversity of their charisms, the value of each charism for the whole community, and a hierarchical order of charisms. Thus Paul can insist on his authority as an apostle in order to teach doctrine or reconcile factions (1 Corinthians 1). This metaphor emphasizes both the need for unity in diversity and the need for diversity in unity, lest it become uniformity, which would impoverish the whole Church. It is a model of what I am calling participatory hierarchy, in which the diverse participation of all is important for the health of the whole. Certainly it is an ideal, rarely attained in the history of the Church, but it remains nonetheless an image of what the Church should be. It resists both a unity imposed by authoritarian force and an egalitarian diversity which lacks any unifying center, and so succumbs to fragmentation (e.g., the Church described in 3 John). This metaphor of the Body of Christ became the major image of the Church in both Eastern and Western Christianity, and I will treat it at length in subsequent chapters.[46]

[46] Émile Mersch, S.J., devoted his life to the historical and theological study of the mystical body of Christ. See his *Le Corps Mystique du Christ* (Paris: Desclée de Brouwer, 1936) which traces this doctrine through scripture, the Greek and Latin

Thus the New Testament does not present a single image of the Church, or of authority and hierarchy, but a complex collage of images and models, each limited, each needing complementing by other images. If the Pastoral Epistles stress apostolic and presbyterial authority, John and the Johannine epistles, along with Luke/Acts, portray each disciple united with Jesus through the Spirit, Matthew sees the disciples as acting collegially as church (*ecclesia,* a word only used in Matthew), and 1 Peter sees the whole community as being sanctified by the Spirit. If the Body of Christ image appears too static, Luke emphasizes the dynamism of the Spirit. I would claim, however, that running through this diversity of images is a unity. All the churches accept apostolic authority and common descent from Israel, the original People of God.[47] All agree that believers participate in the Holy Spirit and are sanctified by it, and that their inclusion in the Church is not just juridical or due to bloodline but due to baptism, which brings them into the community with the risen Lord and the Spirit. All (except possibly the schismatic section of the Johannine church) accept the bishops as the successors of the apostles. No image of the church can be called egalitarian (again, excepting the putatively schismatic part of the Johannine community), nor is any autocratic; *each in different ways expresses participatory hierarchy.* Decisions concerning the universal Church (Acts 6, 15) were based on a consensus of all concerned, in a manner respecting *koinonia.* This pattern would be continued in the early Church, where universal decisions were made by the whole college of bishops in council.

Fathers, up into the twentieth century. English translation: *The Whole Christ* (Milwaukee: Bruce, 1938). Mersch's theological study of this doctrine appeared posthumously as *Theologie du Corps Mystique* (Brussels, 1944); in English as *The Theology of the Mystical Body* (St. Louis: Herder, 1951).

[47] See Raymond Brown, "Unity and Diversity in the New Testament Ecclesiology," in *New Testament Essays* (Milwaukee: Bruce, 1965) 41–47.

Chapter 5

The Early Church

Let whoever is to be set over all be elected by all.

(Pope Leo the Great)[1]

Just as I venerate and receive the four books of the holy evangelists, so also do I the four councils . . . since they have been decided by universal consensus.

(Pope Gregory the Great)[2]

The Emergence of the Episcopate

We have seen in the previous chapter that the *Didache* instructs the congregation to elect "bishops and deacons" whose "ministry is identical with that of the prophets and teachers."[3] Gradually during the second and third centuries, leadership in the Christian churches was consolidated in the hands of bishops, who were understood as inheriting the authority of the apostles to teach, discipline, and preserve the churches in unity. Over this period, independent charismatics such as prophets and teachers became less common. Instead, the work of the Holy Spirit was largely appropriated by the bishops,

[1] "Qui praefecturus est omnibus ab omnibus eligatur." *Epistula* X, 4; *PL* 54, 628.

[2] "Sicut sancti evangelii quattuor libros, sic quattuor concilia suscipere et venerari me fateor. . . . Quintum quoque concilium pariter veneror . . . quia dum universali sunt consensu constituta. . . ." *Epistula* I, 24; *PL* 77, 486, *MGH* 1:36.

[3] *Didache*, 15, 1-2, from Cyril Richardson, ed. *Early Christian Fathers* (New York: Macmillan, 1970) 178.

in their activity of forgiving sins (the power of the keys), teaching and guiding the Church, celebrating the Eucharist, and ordaining other bishops and presbyters. We can trace this process through several ancient writings: the Pastoral Letters, the first Letter of Clement, the Letters of Ignatius of Antioch, and Irenaeus' *Adversus Haeresis (Against the Heretics).*

As we have seen (chap. 4), the terms *presbyteros* (elder, presbyter, priest) and *episkopos* (overseer, bishop) were in the earliest literature interchangeable. The presbyter-bishop emerged as one of a group of presbyters who was given special authority, for example to represent his local church at regional synods. For centuries bishops continued to address their priests as "fellow presbyters."[4] In the Pastoral Letters, the emphasis is on the presbyter-bishop as the conservator and guardian of sound doctrine. A bishop, according to Titus 1:9 "must hold form to the sure word as taught, so that he may be able to give instruction in sound doctrine." First Timothy 6:20 exhorts Timothy to "guard what has been entrusted to you."

About 96 C.E. the First Letter of Clement was written from the church of Rome to the church at Corinth, probably by Clement, a presbyter-bishop at Rome.[5] The writer is concerned that a faction—possibly charismatics—at Corinth has ousted the legitimately elected leaders, apparently presbyter-bishops (1 Clement 44; 47, 6; presbyter and bishop are used interchangeably in the letter), and exhorts them to reinstate their legitimate leaders. In chapters 42–44 of his letter, Clement asserts that the first bishops were appointed by the apostles as their successors. The gravamen of 1 Clement is that the episcopal leaders of the community, who succeeded the apostles in authority, ought to be obeyed, lest the Church dissolve into factions.

About 110–115 C.E., Ignatius, bishop of Antioch in Syria, wrote letters to various sister churches as he was being taken in imperial custody to Rome, where he was martyred.[6] For Ignatius the bishop was to

[4] Henry Chadwick, *The Early Christian Church* (New York: Penguin, 1967) 50.

[5] See text and commentary in Richardson, *Early Christian Fathers,* 33–73. The attribution to Clement, who is listed as the third bishop of Rome in early bishop lists, is not in the letter, and is made later. Eusebius reports that Dionysius, bishop of Corinth, c. 170 C.E. attributed the letter to Clement (*The History of the Church,* translated by G.A. Williamson, hereafter abbreviated as *HE* [Minneapolis: Augsburg Publishing House, 1965] 185).

[6] More than seven letters are ascribed to Ignatius, but seven are usually considered authentic. These are the letters to the churches at Ephesus, Magnesia, Tralles,

be obeyed as one would obey Jesus Christ: "We should regard the bishop as the Lord himself" (*Eph* 6:2, cf. *Trallians* 2:1). In these letters we find a clearly defined hierarchy of bishop, presbyter, and deacon. Both the presbyters and the deacons are to be united under the authority of the bishop. Ignatius insists that only the bishop himself, or his deputies, can celebrate Eucharist or baptisms (*Smyrnaeans* 8:1-2), and that no ecclesial act should be performed without the bishop's approval (*Smyrnaeans* 8:1). It is the bishop who is the center of the Church: "Where the bishop is present, there let the congregation gather, just as where Jesus Christ is, there is the Catholic church" (*Smyrnaeans* 8:2).

Ignatius is reacting against schism, which he had experienced in his own church (*Smyrnaeans* 11). The churches he addresses are threatened by Docetism and Judaizers; hence his many diatribes against schismatics, whom he views as cut off from God's kingdom (*Philadelphians* 2 and 3). He is greatly concerned for unity: "Make unity your concern—there is nothing better than that" he wrote to Polycarp, bishop of Smyrna (*Polycarp* 1:2). It is obedience to the bishop that defeats schism and ensures unity in each church and among churches.

Though Ignatius stresses the threefold hierarchy of bishop, presbyter, and deacon (*Magnesians* 2), and the supremacy of the bishop, it seems likely that this was an ideal church order which he was exhorting other churches to follow, rather than a church order already in place. In fact, he addresses very few bishops by name in these letters—the letters are rather written to the individual churches. But towards the end of the second century, the order he describes had become general in the churches.

In these letters, God the Father and Jesus Christ are mentioned in almost every paragraph, but the Holy Spirit is referred to only five times, and never in the Pauline sense as producing various charisms in the members of the Church. Yet Ignatius himself apparently prophesied. But we do not hear in his letters of others in the churches prophesying, or of the charismatic gifts active among the members. And this is only some thirty years after Luke wrote in Acts 13:1, "In the church at Antioch there were prophets and teachers." Ignatius does write, to the Magnesians (14:1): "I realize you are full of God." But that is the extent of his recognition of the activity of the Spirit among the laity.

Rome, Philadelphia, Smyrna, and a letter to Polycarp, bishop of Smyrna. See text and commentary in *Early Christian Fathers*, 74–120.

Instead, in Ignatius' letters we seem to see the "capturing" of the activity of the Spirit by the bishop, and the equation of the bishop with Christ.

Around 185 C.E. Irenaeus, bishop of Lyons, wrote *Against the Heretics,* attacking the Gnostics,[7] who claimed that Jesus had passed esoteric oral traditions on to them, in addition to the public, exoteric traditions passed onto the apostles. Irenaeus countered this argument by insisting that the full teaching of Jesus had been passed onto the apostles, who had handed that teaching onto the bishops: "It is one and the same life-giving faith which has been preserved in the church from the apostles to the present and is handed on (Latin: *tradere*) in truth."[8] Thus it is through the bishops that the Church remains united with the true faith taught by Jesus and the apostles. The bishops, especially the bishops of sees founded by the apostles (e.g., Antioch, Rome), become the bearers and guarantors of the apostolic tradition.[9] When serious conflicts arise in the Church (e.g., Arianism), it is the bishops who meet in council to settle these conflicts.

A number of factors contributed to the emergence of an episcopal hierarchy.[10] First was the need of a center for unity and orthodoxy in the face of schism or heresy (this was Ignatius' emphasis). Second, the power to ordain was typically assigned to a senior presbyter, who would ordain other presbyters, and travel to sister churches to ordain new bishops. Third, correspondence with other churches was usually carried on by the presiding presbyter (e.g., 1 Clement). Fourth, the bishop was seen as a link back to the apostolic tradition, since through his consecration he was understood to participate in the Spirit which also had guided the apostles. It does seem that this "institutional" aspect of the Spirit became more prominent in the early Church, especially after the charismatic excesses of the Montanist heresy (c. 155–200), and that the charismatic aspect, such as prophecy, became less prominent. James L. Ash argues that "the charisma of prophecy

[7] Irenaeus wrote in Greek, but only a Latin translation of his book survives, hence the Latin title: *Adversus Haereses.* For an English translation of books 1 and 3, see *Early Christian Fathers,* 358–397.

[8] Ibid., 373.

[9] Compare this idea with Paul's statement in 1 Corinthians 15:3: "For I handed on to you as of first importance what I also received, that Christ died for our sins . . . ."

[10] *Early Christian Fathers,* 49.

was captured by the monarchial episcopate, used in its defense, and left to die an unnoticed death when true episcopal stability rendered it a superfluous tool."[11] However, the charismatic and prophetic gifts of the Spirit do not entirely disappear from the Church, (though they do diminish), but remain active among the people and the martyrs, and inspire independent theologians such as St. Justin the Martyr, Origen, and Gregory of Nazianzus, holy men and ascetics, as well as monastic thinkers, some of whom will, in the Middle Ages, issue prophetic denunciations of corruption in the Church (e.g., St. Bernard, Catherine of Siena, Martin Luther).

The Church as *Communio*

The Latin term *communio* translates the Greek *koinonia,* which means, approximately, "communion." For several decades writers in ecclesiology have emphasized that the early Church was a communion in which the bishops, the faithful, and various churches saw themselves as united with each other in a spiritual community.[12] The ancient notion of *communio* differs from modern notions of community because *communio* was a religious concept; the source of unity was participation in the Holy Spirit and the body of Christ, received at the Eucharist, and common recognition of a unifying center, the bishop. *Communio* described both the relation of the bishop to the laity in the local church and the communion between local churches throughout the world. These two aspects of *communio* will be discussed in that order.

The phrase "monarchial episcopate," often used to describe the episcopacy of Ignatius of Antioch, is a misnomer. For in the early Church the bishops did not rule the laity like kings. They were usually elected by the people (or sometimes by the presbyters), could be deposed by them, and customarily consulted both the presbyters and the people in making their decisions. They were ordained by other bishops of the same region. A fairly typical description is given by the *Apostolic Tradition,* an early third century (c. 215) Roman church order usually ascribed to Hippolytus of Rome.

[11] See James L. Ash, Jr., "The Decline of Ecstatic Prophecy in the Early Church," *TS* 37, #2 (June, 1976) 252.

[12] For a recent treatment of the church as a communion, with bibliography, see J.-M.R. Tillard, *Church of Churches: The Ecclesiology of Communion* (Collegeville: The Liturgical Press, 1992).

1. Let the bishop be ordained being in all things without fault chosen by all the people.
2. And when he has been proposed and found acceptable to all, the people assembled on the Lord's day together with the presbytery and such bishops as may attend, let the choice be generally approved;
3. Let the bishops lay hands on him and the presbytery stand by in silence,
4. And all shall keep silence praying in their heart for the descent of the Holy Spirit.[13]

Here we see all the elements described above: election and consent by the people, ordination by several bishops, and the idea that the same Spirit that guided the apostles comes upon the bishop at ordination.

Similarly, Cyprian, bishop of Carthage, in a letter written about 256 C.E., signed by thirty-seven bishops of North Africa, and sent to the bishops of Legio and Asturica (Spain), writes:

> Hence we should show sedulous care in observing a practice which is based on divine teaching and apostolic observance, a practice which is indeed faithfully followed among us and in practically every province. And it is this: when an episcopal appointment is to be duly solemnized, all the neighboring bishops in the same province convene for the purpose along with the people for whom the leader is to be appointed; the bishop is then selected in the presence of those people, for they are the ones who are acquainted most intimately with the way each man has lived his life and they have had the opportunity thoroughly to observe his conduct and behavior.
>
> And we note that this procedure was indeed followed in your own case when our colleague Sabinus [a Spanish bishop] was being appointed: the office of bishop was conferred upon him and hands were laid upon him in replacement of Basilides, *following the verdict of the whole congregation and in conformity with the judgment of the bishops. . . .*[14]

[13] *The Treatise on the Apostolic Tradition of St. Hippolytus of Rome,* ed. by Gregory Dix, reissued with corrections, preface and bibliography by Henry Chadwick (London: The Alban Press, 1992) 2–3. For a discussion of the problems of authorship see Paul F. Bradshaw, *The Search for the Origins of Christian Worship* (Oxford: Oxford University Press, 1992) 89–92.

[14] Cyprian, epistle 67, 5, from *The Letters of St. Cyprian of Carthage,* vol. IV (Letters 67–82), (*Ancient Christian Writers Series* #47), translated and annotated by G.W. Clarke (New York, Newman Press, 1989) 24. Emphasis added.

This letter indicates, then, that the practice of popular consent to episcopal elections was widespread in Africa and Spain in the third century. The *Apostolic Tradition* shows its presence in Rome at about the same time.[15]

In another letter of Cyprian, written to the priests and deacons of Carthage while he was in hiding from the persecution of Decius (250 C.E.), Cyprian confesses: "But as for that which our fellow priests . . . wrote to me, I have been able to reply nothing in writing alone because, from the beginning of my episcopate, I decided to do nothing of my own opinion privately without your [the priests and deacons] advice and the consent of the people."[16]

For Cyprian then, the local church is a *communio,* in which the bishop and the people are joined in a unity which derives from the unity of God and Christ: "God is one, and Christ is one, and His church is one; one is the faith, and one the people cemented together by harmony into the strong unity of a body."[17] But this is a *hierarchical* communion, for the bishop, as well as being elected, is also consecrated by God, acting through the ordination of other bishops, and hence is a divinely appointed center of unity for the church. Cyprian believes it is God who makes the bishop: *"Deus qui episcopos facit."*[18] Patrick Granfield comments that for Cyprian "the divine will and the community's will coincided."[19] Therefore the bishop is accountable both to the community, as its representative, and also to Christ for his governance

[15] See Patrick Granfield, "Episcopal Elections in Cyprian: Clerical and Lay, Participation" in *TS* 37, # 1 (March, 1976) 41–52. Granfield notes that lay participation in episcopal elections diminished with the centuries, and that in 1215 the Fourth Lateran Council decreed that the sole electorate should be the cathedral chapter [i.e., priests]. We cannot say exactly how widespread the custom of electing bishops was in the early Church. Henry Chadwick thinks that in the early period it was usual for the Church to choose the bishop. See Henry Chadwick, *The Role of the Christian Bishop in Ancient Society* (Berkeley: The Graduate Theological Union and University of California: Center for Hermeneutical Studies, Protocol of the Thirty-Fifth Colloquy, 1980) 14. Also cf. E. Roland, "Election des evêques," *DTC* 4:2256–81.

[16] Cyprian, epistle 14,4, from *Saint Cyprian: Letters,* Rose Bernard Donna, C.S.J., trans. (Washington D.C.: The Catholic University of America Press, 1964) 43.

[17] Cyprian, *De ecclesiae unitate,* ET: *The Unity of the Catholic Church,* Maurice Bévenot, S.J., trans. (Westminster, Md.: The Newman Press, Ancient Christian Writers Series, 1957) 65.

[18] Epistle 3,3 (CSEL 3,471).

[19] Granfield, "Episcopal Elections in Cyprian," 43.

of the Church: "So long as the bond of friendship is maintained and the sacred unity of the Catholic Church is preserved, each bishop is master of his own conduct, conscious that he must one day render an account of himself to the Lord."[20] The bishop is "responsible to God alone."[21] Cyprian, incidentally, though he had great respect for Roman authority, thought that *each* bishop was a successor of Peter. Thus the bishop of Rome held the chair and succession of Peter in Rome, the bishop of Carthage, the chair and succession of Peter in Carthage, etc.[22] Cyprian espoused an ecclesiology based on two dialectic principles: the primacy of the individual bishop, and the unity of the Church, held together by God and the Spirit. The prime organizational principle in such an ecclesiology was the synod or council; if the community's will and God's will coincided, it was important to hold councils to determine what the community's will was. And Cyprian did in fact frequently hold councils during his episcopate, to decide questions concerning the North African church. For Cyprian the bishop is not over the church, but within the church, as its elected representative and divinely consecrated leader. He operates by the principles of participation and consensus, not dominance. Cyprian's conciliar and episcopal ecclesiology was characteristic of the North African church, and was also maintained by St. Augustine, who, according to Robert Eno, "seems to have held to councils as the organs for the settling of disputed questions within the Church. He writes for example that 'the best opinion was established, to the removal of all doubts, by a general council of the whole world' (*De Bapt.* I.9)."[23] Cyprian's ecclesiology remains an important alternative to Roman ecclesiology in the West, which came to see the Church as stemming from the bishop of Rome, whose unity consisted in obedience to the bishop of Rome.

Henry Chadwick has commented on the position of the bishop in ancient (Christian) society. He notes that bishops were the protectors of the poor; their most frequent duty "was to intercede for members of

[20] Epistle 55, 21; English translation from Maurice Bévenot, "A Bishop is Responsible to God Alone," from *Recherches de Science Religieuse,* vol. 39 (1951) 401.

[21] See Bévenot, "A Bishop is Responsible to God Alone," 397–415.

[22] See Robert Eno, S.S., *The Rise of the Papacy* (Wilmington: Michael Glazier, 1990) 58.

[23] Ibid., 78–79. The famous saying attributed to Augustine "Roma locuta est; causa finita est" is a misquote. What he actually said (*Sermo* 131) was "Already two councils on this question have been sent to the apostolic see; and replies have come from there. The case is closed," ibid., 73.

their flock when they were in trouble with the courts or the fisc. . . . Otherwise the oppressed would never get justice at all."[24] This, plus the fact that they were elected, made them popular representatives. But they were also consecrated, and so enjoyed a holy aura.

> The bishop's power-base, so to speak, lay always in the allegiance of his flock to the ministry of word and sacrament and pastoral care of which he is the focus. To the faithful he represented not merely a properly constituted officer of the community, but an instrument of divine grace, inasmuch as his ordination is a sacramental act conferring a charismatic gift of grace appropriate to the office (1 Tim 4:14; 2 Tim 1:6).[25]

The bishop's authority was thus grounded both in popular consensus and representation, but also, through divine consecration, in a sacred source, a *hieros-archē*. His was an authority from below and an authority from above, since he was consecrated not as an individual but as a person who represented the local congregation before the larger Church at synods and councils. In later chapters I will hold that this ought to be the model for contemporary bishops as well.

In addition to the local bishop being in *communio* with his flock, he was also in *communio* with the bishops of other churches, thus uniting the local church with other local churches, to form the universal Church or "great Church." This communion was effected in a number of ways.

First, bishops customarily exchanged letters with other churches with whom they were in communion. Ignatius' letters are examples of this, as is Cyprian and the African bishops' letter to the Spanish bishops, quoted above. If a bishop was considered schismatic or heretical, his letters would not be accepted by other bishops. These letters were often conveyed by travelers from one church to another.[26] Second, bishops in the various local churches kept lists of those bishops with whom they were in communion, and when a bishop died and was replaced, sister churches were notified by letter. In the Byzantine Church, the names of bishops, metropolitans, and patriarchs were inscribed on the so-called diptych tablets, kept on the altar, and were recited at liturgy, indicating communion with those named. Third, when one bishop traveled to

[24] Chadwick, *The Role of the Christian Bishop in Ancient Society*, 8.

[25] Ibid., 5.

[26] See Ludwig Hertling, S.J.: *Communio: Church and Papacy in Early Christianity* (Chicago: Loyola University Press, 1972) 28–36.

another church, it was the custom for him to concelebrate the Eucharist with the bishop and presbyters of the host church, thus indicating that they stood together in communion.

Fourth, bishops were to be ordained by three or more bishops of the same region, indicating that their ordination was approved by the whole community of bishops. The fourth canon of Nicaea states: "It is by all means desirable that a bishop should be appointed by all the bishops of the province. But if this is difficult because of some pressing necessity or the length of the journey involved, let at least three come together and perform the ordination, but only after the absent bishops have taken part in the vote and given their written consent. But in each province the right of confirming the proceedings belongs to the metropolitan bishop."[27] Chadwick comments that "Episcopal consecrations by only two bishops were almost always partisan."[28]

Fifth, the bishops frequently met in regional synods or councils to discuss and decide problems facing the Church. Cyprian, for example, held many regional synods of bishops at Carthage to settle questions such as whether schismatics should be rebaptized. Major problems came to be considered at ecumenical or universal councils, to which all bishops were invited. In these councils the bishops taught with their highest authority, and the creeds, canons, and decrees of these councils became normative for the whole Christian Church. The following paragraphs will treat briefly one such council, Nicaea.

The Council of Nicaea was convened by the Emperor Constantine in 325 to settle the Arian dispute and bring about unity within the Church. It is the first council considered to be ecumenical; all bishops of the Church were invited (whereas in regional synods only bishops of a region attended). Not all bishops did attend, however; in particular, the bishop of Rome, Pope Sylvester, did not attend due to illness, but instead sent two priests to represent him. Largely under the guidance of the emperor, the council was successful in restoring unity concerning the Arian question. Both sides presented their views, and after disputes, a compromise formula was reached, which claimed the Son was *homoousios* ("of one substance"—a non-biblical term apparently suggested by Constantine himself) with the Father.[29]

[27] Tanner, vol. I, 7.

[28] *The Role of the Christian Bishop in Ancient Society*, 3.

[29] The acts of this council are not preserved, though the creed, synodal letter, and canons are. For an account of the council, see Baus et al., *The Imperial Church*

There was not complete unanimity, of course. Of the approximately two hundred and fifty to three hundred bishops present, two refused to sign the final creed, which contained an anathema of Arianism; some fifteen may have signed due to the threat of exile. Nevertheless, Constantine apparently did not interfere in the discussions of the bishops, or attempt to coerce their decision, though once taken he did enforce the decision as law. In his judgment, the work of the council was guided by the Holy Spirit. He wrote to the congregation at Alexandria: "What the three hundred bishops have decided is nothing else than the decree of God, for the Holy Spirit, present in these men, made known the will of God."[30]

The creed and canons generated by this council were not immediately recognized as ecumenical or universal. Over the next fifty-six years fierce controversies ensued between Nicaeans and Arians or neo-Arians. Nevertheless, the Creed of Nicaea in 381 was accepted by the Council of Constantinople and became the basis for the Nicene-Constantinopolitan creed, issued by that council. In 451 the Council of Chalcedon accepted Nicaea as the first ecumenical council, and all churches accepting the Council of Chalcedon adopted the Nicene-Constantinopolitan creed, usually called simply the Nicene Creed. William de Vries comments, "The creed of Nicaea became the absolute and uncontested norm of orthodoxy only when it had been received by the universal church."[31]

A close study of the Council of Nicaea, such as that of de Vries, reveals several important points. 1. Early synods saw themselves operating under the guidance of the Holy Spirit in making their decisions. Thus, the Council of Arles (314) used the formula, "It has pleased us, in the presence of the Holy Spirit and the angels . . ."[32] For the same reason, synods designated themselves as "Holy." The bishops at Nicaea, in their Synodal Letter, refer to the council as "the great and holy synod,"[33] a phrase not found in earlier synods, indicating a

from Constantine to the Middle Ages, 22–29; J.N.D. Kelly, *Early Christian Creeds* (London: Longman, 1972) 211–217; and the detailed study by William de Vries, *Orient et Occident: Les structures ecclésiales vues dans l'histoire des sept premiers conciles oecumeniques* (Paris: Cerf, 1974) 13–42.

[30] *HC:II,* 28.

[31] *Orient et Occident,* 41.

[32] Ibid., 16.

[33] See the text of the Synodal letter of Nicaea, Socrates, *Ecclesiastical History,* 1, 9, ET *NPNF2,* vol. II, 12–13.

consciousness of their ecumenical importance for all churches, as well as their conviction of being guided by the Spirit in their decisions. 2. This in turn is paralleled by the belief that it was the whole college of bishops that succeeded to the authority of the apostles. Karl Baus comments on the episcopate in the fourth century: "The *ordo episcoporum,* for its part, maintained its independence, which, since Irenaeus was based on the conviction that the bishops as a whole were the successors of the Apostles and continued their function within the Church."[34] Thus the bishops in their decisions at Nicaea were doing just what the apostles did at the Jerusalem Council: deciding the direction of the Church under the guidance of the Spirit. 3. De Vries comments that "in the consciousness of the fathers, the decision of the Fathers has a definitive and irrevocable character." This can be seen, for example, in the anathema at the end of the creed, in which the Arians are rejected in the name of "the Catholic and apostolic church."[35] The council, then, saw itself as speaking for the whole Church. 4. According to the histories of Eusebius and Socrates, at Nicaea "whatever could be fittingly advanced in support of any opinion was fully stated."[36] The decision of the bishops was not coerced, but taken freely; had coercion been present, it would be difficult to conclude that the decision was guided by the Spirit. 5. Though two legates of the pope were present, Constantine did not confer with the pope before convening the council, nor did the papal legates preside at the sessions. The hierarch who brought about unity at the council was the emperor, not the pope. 6. Insofar as one may speak of an ecclesiology implicit in the Council of Nicaea, that ecclesiology is participatory and conciliar. The council mandated in its fifth canon that all the bishops of every province should assemble in synods twice a year to discuss and settle problems affecting the churches of that province. And it saw its own pronouncements as having the highest authority in the Church. Canon six, however, acknowledged the authority of metropolitan bishops and patriarchal bishops: thus the bishop of Alexandria had jurisdiction over Egypt, and the

[34] *HC:II,* 287.

[35] De Vries, *Orient et Occident,* 18. The final anathema appended to the Nicene Creed reads: "But as for those who say, 'There was when he was not . . .' these the Catholic and apostolic church anathematizes." See Kelly, *Early Christian Creeds,* 215–216.

[36] Socrates, *Ecclesiastical History,* 1,9; *NPNF2,* vol. II, 14; Eusebius, *Life of Constantine,* 3,13; *NPNF2,* vol. I, 523.

bishop of Rome over the region centered on Rome. 7. But the council also demonstrates the necessity for a hierarchical center to bring about unity—in the case of the Council of Nicaea, the emperor himself; in the case of regions, the metropolitan or patriarchal bishops of those regions. Notably, it does not mention any universal jurisdiction or primacy of the Bishop of Rome. 8. Overall, the Council of Nicaea seems to have been as close to a functioning participatory hierarchy as one could expect. Bishops from every part of the Church were gathered together; the views of both sides were fully aired; the decision was close to a consensus—not quite unanimous, but based on more than a ninety percent majority. Bishops of all churches were immediately notified by the emperor. There remained strong Arian resistance, but after a period of controversy, the Nicene creed was received by the entire Church.[37] In this the decision taken at Nicaea parallels the decision of the Jerusalem Council.

I would claim then that the Council of Nicaea is a good, though not perfect, example of participatory hierarchy in action. Indeed, there probably can never be a major communal decision which is wholly free of coercion and achieves 100 percent consensus. But like the decision of the Council of Jerusalem, the Nicene decision has stood the test of time. It achieved unity in essentials while not stifling diversity. Constantine, and the bishops themselves, took the high degree of unanimity as a sign that the decisions of Nicaea were guided by the Spirit, and the subsequent reception of Nicaea by the universal Church confirms this belief. Yves Congar has written: "If there is one truth universally affirmed from antiquity until Vatican II, it is that the faith and Tradition are carried by the whole church; that the universal church, under the sovereignty of the Spirit who has been promised to it and abides in it, is alone the subject of 'Ecclesia universalis non potest errare'" (the universal church cannot err).[38] An Orthodox theologian, Georges Florovosky, writes: "The teaching *authority* of the ecumenical councils is grounded in the infallibility of the Church. The ultimate

[37] The Goths, evangelized by the Arian bishop Ulfilas, did not convert to Catholicism until the sixth century. Some modern groups, notably the Jehovah's witnesses and various Unitarian groups, would also not accept the Nicene Creed, but these are relatively recent splinter groups, which would not be accepted as Christians by any major Christian denomination.

[38] "La 'Réception' comme réalité ecclésiologique," *Revue des Sciences Philosophiques et Théologiques,* Tome 56:3 (July, 1972) 380.

"authority" is vested in the Church . . . . It is not primarily a *canonical* authority. . . . It is a *charismatic* authority, grounded in the assistance of the Spirit: *for it seemed good to the Holy Spirit and to us."*[39]

The ecumenical council, then, was the highest expression of the church as *communio,* in which the union and community of the local churches was expressed in the unanimity of the council of bishops, who themselves were collectively the successors of the apostolic college. But, as Hilaire Marot has emphasized, the ecumenical council did not stifle or override local diversity. Instead, the councils and the popes mandated that regional councils meet regularly. "It is certain that in the middle of the fifth century the individual character of every province found expression in the councils that were held more or less frequently."[40]

The Rise of the Papacy to the Council of Nicaea[41]

As we saw in chapter 3, Peter exercised a role of primacy among the apostles. After Jesus' resurrection, he became the spokesman for the apostles (Acts 1:15-22; 2:14-36; 3:11-26; 4:8-17). In the words of the Catholic and Protestant authors of *Peter in the New Testament:*

> Peter is portrayed even during Jesus' ministry as the one who gave voice to a solemn revelation granted him by God about who Jesus was: the Messiah and the Son of the living God (Matt 16:16-17). In the light of the Post-Easter events it becomes clear to the Christian community that with this faith Peter is the rock on whom Jesus has founded his church against which the gates of Hades shall not prevail.
>
> Not only is Peter presented as a confessor of the Christian faith: eventually he can be seen as a *guardian of the faith against false teaching.*[42]

[39] Georges Florovsky: "The Authority of the Ancient Councils," in *Bible, Church, Tradition: an Eastern Orthodox View* (Belmont, Mass.: Nordland Publishing, 1972) 103.

[40] Cited in Hilaire Marot, O.S.B., "The Primacy and the Decentralization of the Early Church," in *Concilium,* 7:1 (September, 1965) 11–12; cf. idem, "Unitē de l'Église et diversité géographique aux premiers siècles," *L'Épiscopat et L'Église Universelle,* ed. by Yves Congar and B.D. Dupuy (Paris: Cerf, 1964) 565–590.

[41] Because of space constraints, I can here only give some major texts and vignettes of the progress of papal authority in this period. For a history and bibliography see Eno, *The Rise of the Papacy.* Also, James F. McCue and Arthur Carl Piepkorn, "The Roman Primacy in the Patristic Era," in *PPATUC,* 43–97. For documents in English, see E. Giles, ed., *Documents Illustrating Papal Authority:* A.D. *96–454* (London: SPCK, 1952).

[42] *Peter in the New Testament,* 165–166, italics in original.

When was this Petrine authority passed on to the church at Rome and its bishop? In answering this question, we should not forget that the church at Jerusalem, at least until the destruction of the Temple in 70 C.E., carried the role of primacy among the churches.

An early instance of this Petrine authority is often claimed for the First Letter of Clement, discussed above. There are problems, however, in interpreting this as an exercise in Petrine authority by the bishop of Rome. First, the letter is written in the name of the church of Rome to the church at Corinth. It opens with these words: "The church of God, living in exile in Rome, to the church of God, exiled in Corinth."[43] Clement (putatively the third bishop of Rome) is not mentioned in the letter. The attribution to Clement comes from Eusebius' *History of the Church,* 4, 23, in which Dionysius, bishop of Corinth (c. 170 C.E.), mentions this letter as having been written by Clement. Secondly, it is not clear if 1 Clement is an exercise of papal authority or simply a letter of instruction from one church to another. Such letters were common in the ancient *communio:* Eusebius, in the passage just cited, mentions a number of epistles of Dionysius of Corinth written to sister churches, many containing instructions on orthodoxy, just as 1 Clement does.[44] What 1 Clement does show is that the church at Rome felt responsibility for the church at Corinth. It seems to be the Roman Church in this letter, not the Roman bishop, which exercises authority. Indeed, no mention of Petrine or episcopal authority is made in the letter.

A better indication of the status of Petrine and Roman primacy in the second century is given by a famous passage from Irenaeus' *Against the Heretics.* Irenaeus argues against the Gnostics, who claimed to have secret oral teachings from Jesus that were more authentic than the teaching of the apostles, which had been corrupted. Irenaeus responds as follows.

> The tradition of the apostles . . . can be clearly seen in every church by those who wish to behold the truth. We can enumerate those who were established by the apostles as bishops in the churches, and their successors down to our time, none of whom taught or thought anything like their [the Gnostics] mad ideas. Even

[43] ET of 1 Clement from *Early Christian Fathers,* 43.

[44] Eusebius, *HE* 4, 23; 183–185. For an analysis of 1 Clement, see James F. McCue, "The Roman Primacy in the Second Century and the Problem of the Development of Dogma," *TS,* vol. 25 (1964) 161–196.

> if the apostles had known of hidden mysteries . . . they would have handed them down especially to those to whom they were entrusting the churches themselves. . . . But since it would be very long in such a volume as this to enumerate the successions of all the churches, I can by pointing out the tradition which the very great, oldest, and well-known Church, founded and established at Rome by those two most glorious apostles Peter and Paul, received from the apostles, and its faith known among men, which comes down to us through the succession of bishops, put to shame all those who in any way . . . gather as they should not. For every church must be in harmony with this Church because of its outstanding preeminence, that is, the faithful from everywhere, since the apostolic tradition is preserved in it by those from everywhere.
>
> When the blessed apostles had founded and built up the Church, they handed over the ministry of the episcopate to Linus. . . . Anaclétus succeeded him. After him, Clement received the lot of the episcopate in third place from the apostles. He had seen the apostles and associated with them, and still had their preaching sounding in his ears and their tradition before his eyes. . . .[45]

Besides setting out the basis for the apostolic tradition, this passage is crucial for assessing the importance of the Roman church in the second century. For Irenaeus, it is the Roman church, not just the Roman bishop, that is the touchstone of orthodoxy, the church which has signally preserved the apostolic tradition. Thus to be in communion with the church at Rome is to be in communion with all the churches that preserve the apostolic tradition. The Roman Church, in this conception, is not the source of orthodoxy—other churches also preserve the apostolic tradition—but it is the standard, the touchstone, of orthodoxy. Irenaeus mentions the Roman bishop (Eleutherus) later in this same passage, but he clearly does not see apostolic orthodoxy as vested only in the *bishop* of Rome; it is also vested in the *church* at Rome.

About the same time as Irenaeus, Victor, the bishop of Rome (189–199), attempted to force the churches of Asia Minor, who celebrated Easter on 14 Nisan, the date of the Jewish Passover, to observe Easter on the same day as the Roman church (i.e., on a Sunday, which would only occasionally fall on 14 Nisan). This the Asian bishops refused to do, arguing that their custom had been inherited from the apostles who had founded their churches. Thereupon Victor attempted to excommunicate

[45] *Adversus Haereses*, III, 3, ET from Richardson, *Early Christian Fathers*, 371–372.

the churches of Asia. For this he was severely criticized by other bishops, among them Irenaeus, who wrote to Victor that in earlier times Bishop Polycarp of Smyrna had visited Anicetus, bishop of Rome, to discuss this matter, and the two had agreed to keep their separate customs, but not to break church unity because of it. This whole affair, called the Quartodeciman controversy, is reported in Eusebius,[46] and is noteworthy as the first recorded instance in which Rome attempted to impose its customs on other churches. It is also noteworthy because the Roman bishop was "sternly rebuked," in Eusebius' words, by other bishops, and apparently did not succeed in his attempt to force the Asian churches to comply with his wishes. In fact the Easter date was not made uniform until the Council of Nicaea.[47] Respect for the Roman church, then, did not automatically translate into obedience to the Roman bishop, nor mean that Roman jurisdiction was accepted in all geographical areas.

Another incident involving Roman jurisdiction arose in the time of Cyprian. Cyprian evinced great respect for the primacy of the Roman see. In his epistle 59, he even refers to "the chair of Peter . . . the primordial church, the very source of episcopal unity."[48]But in 256 Pope Stephen demanded that the churches of Africa and Asia Minor abandon their practice of rebaptizing schismatics who wished to join the Catholic Church. Both the churches of Asia and North Africa refused to change their custom. Cyprian, following African practice, summoned a council to discuss the matter (September 256). He addressed the bishops as follows:

> For neither does any of us set himself up as a bishop of bishops nor by a tyrannical terror force his colleagues to a necessity of obeying; inasmuch as every bishop, in the free use of his liberty and power, has the right of forming his own judgment, and can no more be judged by another than he himself can judge another.
>
> But we must all await the judgment of Our Lord Jesus Christ, who alone has the power both of setting us in the government of his church, and of judging our acts therein.[49]

[46] *HE* 5, 23–24, 229–234.

[47] Constantine claims in a letter that the Council of Nicaea determined that all churches would celebrate Easter on a Sunday. Socrates, *Ecclesiastical History, NPNF2*, II:15.

[48] *The Letters of Cyprian of Carthage*, vol. III, ACW (New York: Newman Press, 1986) 82.

[49] Cyprian, *Sententiae episcoporum*, ET from Eno, *The Rise of the Papacy*, 65.

The council supported the North African practice of rebaptism, and the North African church did not change its practice until much later, in the time of Augustine. As in the Quartodeciman controversy, respect for the preeminence of the Roman church did not translate into automatic obedience to the Roman bishop.

Finally, we have already seen that the Council of Nicaea did, indeed, recognize that the bishop of Rome had a regional jurisdiction, just as the bishops of Alexandria and Antioch had: "The ancient customs of Egypt and Libya and Pentapolis shall be maintained, according to which the bishop of Alexandria has authority over all these places, since a similar custom exists with reference to the bishop of Rome."[50] This recognition of regional jurisdiction would become the basis for the development of the patriarchates of Alexandria, Antioch, Jerusalem, and Rome. But Nicaea did not indicate any *universal* primacy or jurisdiction of the Roman bishop.

In sum, then, the church at Rome was accorded a preeminence in its conservation of the teaching of the apostles, and was regarded as a touchstone for orthodoxy. In this sense it had a primacy of honor even among apostolic churches. But the jurisdiction of the bishop of Rome was not accepted outside of the local region centered on Rome. The Roman view, however, appeared to be that other churches ought to conform to Roman customs, as normative. This was asserted by both Victor and Stephen. And indeed the Roman date of Easter and the Roman prohibition of rebaptism did eventually prevail in the universal Church. But the view of non-Roman churches was not identical with that of Rome; these churches insisted on the right to maintain their own traditions, some of which were themselves of apostolic origin. We will see a widening discrepancy between Roman and non-Roman views of Roman authority as the history of the Church unfolds.

Papal Authority from Nicaea to Chalcedon

In 380 Emperor Theodosius I issued a famous decree making Christianity the religion of the empire: "It is our pleasure that all the nations which are governed by our clemency and moderation should steadfastly adhere to the religion which was taught by St. Peter to the Romans, which faithful tradition has preserved, and which is now professed by

[50] Tanner, vol. I, 8–9.

the pontiff Damasus and by Peter, bishop of Alexandria. . . ."[51] This expresses clearly the belief that Rome was the touchstone of apostolic orthodoxy, but also indicated that Alexandria enjoyed that reputation.

From the time of Pope Damasus (366–384) on, we find the text "You are Peter, and on this rock I will build my church." (Matt 16:18) used to support Roman primacy. Pope Siricius (384–399) introduced the idea that Peter himself continued to preside in the Roman see, in the person of the Roman pontiff. "We—or rather, the blessed apostle Peter in us, who, as we trust, protects and keeps us in everything as the heirs of his government—bear the burden of all those who are burdened."[52] Siricius also seems to have introduced the idea, which would be enormously influential from medieval to modern times, that the see of Rome is the *head* of the body that is the Church.[53] Finally, with Siricius began the first papal decretals: papal responses to questions posed by bishops outside of Rome. In Siricius' decretals, according to Klaus Schatz: "we find . . . the commanding style of the imperial court. . . . Before this, only synods could create new law in the Church. Now papal writings were placed *de facto* on the same level as synodal law." [54]

Some years later, Pope Innocent I (402–417) wrote to Decentius, bishop of Gubbio: "All must preserve that which Peter the prince of the apostles delivered to the church at Rome and which it has watched over until now, and nothing may be added or introduced that lacks this authority or that derives its pattern from somewhere else."[55]

This letter admirably illustrates the conservative Roman attitude of watching over and guarding a static "deposit of faith" that was handed on from Peter to the church at Rome, to which nothing may be added, nor anything subtracted—an attitude that has remained characteristic of Rome right down to the present. This vigilance or guarding

[51] *Codex Theodosius* l. xvi. tit. i leg. 2. ET: Edward Gibbon, *The Decline and Fall of the Roman Empire,* vol. 2, chap. xxvii (New York: Modern Library, no date) 7–8.

[52] *Epistula* 1; *PL* 13, 1132. ET, Arthur C. Piepkorn, "Roman Primacy in the Patristic Era: From Nicaea to Leo the Great," *PPATUC,* 82.

[53] *Epistula* 1, cap. 15 (*PL* xiii, 1132), "Ad Romanam ecclesiam, utpote ad caput tui corporis" Cited in Walter Ullman, *The Growth of Papal Government in the Middle Ages* (London: Methuen, 1955) 7.

[54] Klaus Schatz, *Papal Primacy: From Its Origins to the Present* (Collegeville: The Liturgical Press, 1996) 29–30.

[55] *Epistula* 25, *PL* 20, 552. ET in Piepkorn, ibid., 84.

of the integrity of the deposit of faith is, in the Roman view, the task of the bishop of Rome, to whom the deposit has been entrusted. In the words of Pope Leo I: "If we do not intervene with the vigilance which is incumbent upon us, we could not excuse ourselves to him who wished that we should be the sentinel."[56] Certainly the faith needs to be conserved—this is the mission of the apostolic succession. But still, this traditionalism represents an important change from the attitude evident in Acts, in which the Spirit inspired the apostles to new and creative developments in Christian history, such as admitting uncircumcised Gentiles into the Church. Had these apostles, including Peter himself, followed the later maxim of adding nothing and subtracting nothing from what had been handed on, they would have demanded that Christians observe the Mosaic law in all its strictness—as did the "circumcision faction" in the Jerusalem church (Gal 2:12).

The attitude of Roman leadership in the universal Church found a prominent exponent in Pope Leo the Great (440–461). Leo saw the Roman church as the head of the whole Church, the body of Christ, because of the primacy of Peter which had been passed onto the bishop of Rome, who was Peter's vicar or representative. "When, therefore, we utter our exhortations in your ears, holy brethren, believe that he is speaking, whose representative we are *(cuius vice fungimur)."* [57] Leo may have derived this notion from the Roman law, in which an heir succeeded to all the legal rights and duties of the one whose heir he was; so the bishop of Rome had inherited the full power and authority of Peter the apostle.[58] Peter, he notes in a sermon, had been sent to Rome so that "the light of truth which was being displayed for the salvation of all nations, might spread more effectively throughout the body of the world from the head [i.e., Rome] itself."[59] In another sermon, he implies that the apostles received their strength and stability from Christ *through* Peter: "So then in Peter the strength of all is fortified, and the help of divine grace is so ordered that the stability which

[56] *Epistula* 4.1; *PL* 54, 610B, cited in J.-M.R. Tillard, *The Bishop of Rome* (Wilmington: Michael Glazier, 1983) 91. See also Eno, *The Rise of the Papacy,* 97–101.

[57] *Sermo* 3, 4.

[58] See W. Ullman, "Leo I and the Theme of Papal Primacy," *Journal of Theological Studies* 11 (1960) 25–51.

[59] *Sermo* 82, *PL* 54, 422; ET in Giles, *Documents,* 284. See also *Epistula* 78: "Ut ab ipso quodam capite dona sua velut in corpus omne diffunderet." Cited in Ullman, *The Growth of Papal Government,* 6.

through Christ is given to Peter, through Peter is conveyed to the apostles."[60] This expresses the papal claim, already made by Boniface I (pope 418–422), that Peter is not only the head, in the sense of leader, but the *source* of the Church.[61] (This notion would become central to the medieval Roman claim of universal jurisdiction.) Therefore, the solicitude and care of the whole Church has been given to Peter and his successors. Leo argues that the apostles were all equal in being chosen, but that one [Peter] was above the others, and that from this arrangement came the hierarchy of bishops, wherein some bishops [e.g., metropolitans] had greater authority than others. "And through them [metropolitan bishops] the care of the universal Church was to converge in the one see of Peter, and nothing was ever to be at odds with his leadership."[62] Thus, Leo's delegates to the Council of Chalcedon could assert that the bishop of Rome was the head of all the churches: "Bishop Paschasinus, guardian of the apostolic see, stood in the midst [of the assembled council] and said: 'we received directions at the hands of the most blessed and apostolic bishop of the Roman city, who is the head of all the churches'"[63]

But for Leo, as for most early popes, the idea of headship coexisted with the belief that the bishops shared an organic communion, like that of the body, through the Holy Spirit—a *communio*, of which the pope was the head. In his letters, Leo emphasized the unity of the bishops in the body of Christ, and recalled Christ's words (Matt 23:11): "The greatest among you will be your servant."[64] Thus with Leo the principle of primacy remained balanced by the principle of episcopal collegiality.[65] Leo also insisted that leaders be elected (see epigraph at beginning of chapter), and regularly consulted Roman synods in making his decisions. Unity was thus based on consensus as well as command.

The strongest statement of Roman hegemony in ancient times comes from Pope Gelasius (492–496):

[60] *Sermo* 4; *PL* 54, 149; ET in Giles, *Documents,* 280, where the full text is given.

[61] Boniface I: "Institutio universalis nascentis Ecclesiae de beati Petri sumpsit honore principium in quo regimen eius et summa consistit. Ex eius enim ecclesiastica disciplina per omnes, Ecclesias . . . fonte manavit." *PL* 20, 777.

[62] *Epistula* 14:11; ET in Eno, *The Rise of the Papacy,* 104.

[63] *ACO,* Tom. 2, vol. 1, 65. ET in Giles, *Documents,* 298.

[64] In *Epistula* 14, 12, written to Anastasius, bishop of Thessalonica, a vicar of the pope.

[65] See Yves Congar, "La collégialité de l'épiscopat et la Primauté de l'évêque de Rome dans l'Histoire," *Angelicum,* 47:4 (1970) 412.

> The see of blessed Peter the Apostle has the right to unbind what has been bound by sentences of any pontiffs whatsoever, in that it has the right of judging the whole church. Neither is it lawful for anyone to judge its judgment, seeing that canons have willed that it might be appealed to from any part of the world, but that no one may be allowed to appeal from it.[66]

Here and elsewhere, Gelasius formulated the claim that the Roman see is the judge of the whole Church, but can itself be judged by no one, a claim which would in the medieval period be expanded into the claim for Roman infallibility.[67] In claiming a primacy of jurisdiction, and not merely headship, over the whole Church, Gelasius prepared the way for the papal monarchy of the high Middle Ages.

Thus the earlier attitude that the Roman church was the touchstone of orthodoxy was incrementally expanded by the popes into the claim that the Roman see and bishop had the care for *(sollicitudo),* leadership, authority, and even jurisdiction over all the churches. Klaus Schatz writes: "The church of *tradition,* . . . became the church of the capital city that extends its laws to the whole world." [68] In this view it is the bishop of Rome who succeeds to the authority of Peter, who is interpreted as a lawgiver having authority over the whole church. (In the apse mosaic of Old St. Peter's in Rome, Peter was shown as receiving from Christ the tables of the law of the New Testament. [69] The fact that the Twelve acted as a college, with Peter as their spokesman but not their commander, is ignored in this view, a view which was never shared by the East. Later ecumenical councils exhibit a tension between this centralized Roman view of authority and the more conciliar view of the East.

[66] *Epistula* 26.5, cited in Eno, *The Rise of the Papacy,* 124. The canons referred to by Gelasius were the canons of the Council of Sardica (modern Sofia, Bulgaria) held in 342, whose canons 3, 4, and 5 gave bishops the right to appeal to Rome. The popes had the habit of unhistorically claiming that these canon were really from Nicaea, and so possessed universal authority, whereas in fact the canons were never accepted in the East. Cf. documents in Giles, *Documents,* 100.

[67] *Epistula* 10, c.5: "illam [sedem] de tota ecclesia iudicare, ipsam ad nullius commeare iudicium." Thiel, 344.

[68] Schatz, *Papal Primacy,* 31. Schatz thinks this happened because the old Roman aristocracy became Christianized in the fourth and fifth centuries and brought its ideas of order, law, and rulership into the Roman church (31).

[69] Ibid., 29.

The Balance between Papal and Conciliar Authority: The Ecumenical Councils of Chalcedon, II and III Constantinople[70]

The Council of Chalcedon was the last of the four ecumenical councils of the ancient Church which laid down the foundational doctrines of Christianity. It was convened by Emperor Marcian in 451, to reach accord between those who confessed both a human and divine nature in Jesus the Christ and those followers of Cyril of Alexandria and of Eutyches, an abbot of Constantinople, who held that Jesus had only one nature, a divine nature. The "one nature" people, later called *monophysites,* had held a synod at Ephesus in 449, chaired by Dioscursus, bishop of Alexandria, in which the papal legates had not been allowed to present their case, and in which threat of physical violence had been used to force those bishops present to condemn major figures of the Antiochene or "two-nature" school. When Pope Leo heard of this, he dubbed the council a "robber's synod," and worked strenuously to overturn it. One of the tasks of the Council of Chalcedon was to repudiate the "robber's synod of Ephesus," defend the teaching of two natures in Christ, and attempt to find a formula of union between the Alexandrian Monophysites and the Antiochenes, who held for two natures.

Pope Leo had opposed convening the council, but sent legates to it, bearing an earlier letter from him, called "Leo's Tome," to Flavian, archbishop of Constantinople. Leo wished the council to avoid any discussion of doctrines, and instead concentrate on rehabilitating those who had been deposed by the robber's synod. To this end he urged that the council simply read his "Tome," which he insisted was a complete and adequate statement of the apostolic faith. In Leo's view, the authority of Peter's vicar should have compelled assent to the "Tome" without the necessity of discussion. The emperor and the council, however, refused to abide by Leo's directives; for the emperor, it was necessary to produce a new statement of faith which would succeed in reuniting the Orthodox and the Alexandrians. Thus, when the papal legates insisted that Leo's Tome, along with the definitions of the Councils of Nicaea, Constantinople, and Ephesus, should simply be

[70] On Chalcedon, see C.J. Hefele and H. Leclerq, *Histoire des Conciles, d'apres les documents originaux* (Paris: Letouzey et Anē, 1908) Tome II, 659–857; R.V. Sellers, *The Council of Chalcedon* (London: SPCK, 1961); de Vries, *Orient et Occident,* 101–160. On II and III Constantinople, see de Vries, 161–220.

accepted as the doctrine acclaimed by the bishops at Chalcedon, the imperial commissioners countered that the Tome first be discussed in detail and approved by all the bishops. Eventually Leo's Tome was accepted by acclamation of the bishops: "This is the faith of the fathers! This is the faith of the apostles! Thus we believe! Peter has spoken through Leo. It is the teaching of the apostles . . . It is the teaching of Cyril."[71] But as William de Vries makes clear, it was accepted *because* it accorded with the apostolic and traditional faith, not because it was proclaimed authoritatively by Leo: "The Tome of Leo himself was only received by the council after a long and minute examination which permitted the conclusion that it agreed with the traditional faith."[72] The council, then, did not accept Leo's claim to jurisdiction over the whole Church. Another instance which illustrates this is that of canon 28, which repeated canon 3 of the Council of Constantinople in elevating the see of Constantinople to a place just after Rome in authority. This was passed by the bishops at Chalcedon over the protests of the Roman legates. Leo never accepted it (it still is not in Western canon law), but it was eventually accepted and put into practice in the East, by the authority of the emperor.

The events at Chalcedon show that the pope exercised a great deal of authority in the East. Leo's Tome was given a ranking in the council on par with the teachings of the three previous ecumenical councils. Rome was acknowledged as the center of orthodoxy, and the see with which it was necessary to be in communion if one were to be in communion with the universal Church. To some extent the pope could declare who was and was not in communion with the whole Church, even in the East—his repudiation of Dioscuros and his "Robber's synod" of Ephesus was accepted. The pope was recognized as having a primacy of apostolic authority, but *not* a primacy of jurisdiction.

Chalcedon is instructive in another respect. De Vries notes that, though the task of the council was to restore peace and unity to the church of the East, it only partly succeeded. The Monophysites of Egypt, Syria, Ethiopia, and Armenia rejected Leo's Tome, never accepted Chalcedon, and separated from the larger Church, which accepted the Chalcedonian definition of the two natures in Christ as orthodox. Why did the council fail to reconcile them? De Vries hazards an explanation:

[71] *ACO* II, I 2, 155; de Vries, *Orient et Occident*, 119.

[72] *Orient et Occident*, 119.

> In reality, there was not at Chalcedon any real explanation or true dialogue between the opposing parties . . . if we wish to be objective, it is certainly the lack of a true dialogue which explains the relative failure of the council. At Chalcedon, the opposition party was not truly convinced, but more or less constrained by imperial pressure to confess the doctrinal definition of the council. It is not in this manner that true and lasting peace can be realized in the Church. [73]

This deserves comparison to Nicaea, where the opposition was not coerced into agreement, and where, in consequence, a compromise formula was worked out which was acceptable to all, making the council acceptable to the whole Church, and hence an expression of the mind of the whole Church. Coercion, i.e., a hierarchy of command, does not produce real unity, but schism, a point which will be explored also in later chapters.

Two other councils, II and III Constantinople, accepted as ecumenical by both East and West, are pertinent to the question of the balance between conciliar and papal authority.

The Second Council of Constantinople was convened by Emperor Justinian in 553 to consider the question of the "Three Chapters."[74] Briefly, Justinian sought to condemn the person and writings of Theodore of Mopsuestia, the writings of Theodoret of Cyrus against Cyril of Alexandria, and a letter of Ibas of Edessa. His object in this was to placate the schismatic Monophysites by impugning three writers who had been their opponents. At first Justinian simply published an edict condemning the "Three Chapters" on imperial authority but met such opposition from bishops (for interfering with church affairs) that he called a council to decide the question. However, the council was from the first manipulated by Justinian, who invited bishops who would be subservient to his opinions. Pope Vigilius (537–555) in his *First Constitution,* refused to condemn the Three Chapters, demanded that the council follow his teaching, and refused invitations to appear at the council. The council responded that questions of faith must be decided by debate, and that no single person alone could decide questions of faith for the universal Church. They recalled that even the apostles had considered it necessary to come together in discussion to settle the issue of circumcision of the Gentiles. They continue:

[73] De Vries, *Orient et Occident*, 160 (my translation).

[74] See the account of this council in de Vries, *Orient et Occident*, 161–194.

> The holy fathers, who have gathered at intervals in the four holy councils, have followed the examples of antiquity [i.e., the apostles at the Council at Jerusalem]. They dealt with heresies and current problems by debate in common, since it was established as certain that when the disputed question is set out by each side in communal discussions, the light of truth drives out the shadow of lying. *The truth cannot be made clear in any other way when there are debates about questions of faith, since everyone requires the assistance of his neighbor.*[75]

It is curious that this important statement, from a council accepted as ecumenical by both East and West, remains almost forgotten in the tradition of the West. The meaning of course is that the pope cannot decide questions of faith and doctrine by himself, apart from dialogue and consultation with the larger Church, represented by the bishops in council. This text has important implications for how we understand papal authority and infallibility.

The council also declared that Vigilius had separated himself from the communion of the Church. They further anathematized anyone who would hold that the letter of Ibas was orthodox. This was targeted at Vigilius. Eventually, under pressure from the Emperor, Vigilius reversed his position and, in his *Constitution II,* agreed with the council's position. Subsequent popes, including Gregory the Great, insisted that the council be accepted as ecumenical.

As de Vries admits, this council raises difficult questions for the magisterial authority of the pope.[76] If the council was really ecumenical (as both East and West hold), then Vigilius was wrong and even heretical in initially opposing it; further, he only consented under duress, which argues that his final consent was not genuine. I will take the position that the council was ecumenical, since it was subsequently accepted by the whole Church, and that therefore Pope Vigilius was in error until he aligned himself with the council.

A similar tension between council and the pope emerged at the Third Council of Constantinople in 681. That council, presided over by Emperor Constantine IV, condemned as heretical the opinion, known as Monotheletism, that there was only one will, a divine will, in Jesus. Rather it asserted that Jesus had both a human will and a divine will. But a previous pope, Honorius (625–638) had apparently sided with

[75] Emphasis added. Latin text and English translation in Tanner, vol. I, 108.

[76] De Vries, *Orient et Occident*, 162ff.

Monotheletism, for in one of his letters to Sergius, the patriarch of Constantinople, he had written: "We confess a single will of our Lord Jesus Christ, because our nature has been truly assumed by the divinity."[77] The council listed a number of teachers excommunicated as being Monothelites, and went on to declare: "And with these we define that there shall be expelled from the Holy church of God and anathematized Honorius, who was at one time pope of Old Rome, because of what we found written by him to Sergius."[78] Pope Leo II, Honorius' successor, accepted III Constantinople as an ecumenical council, and also condemned Honorius, saying he had "consented to the pollution of the unpolluted rule of the apostolic tradition, which he had received from his predecessors."[79] Most Catholic commentators argue that Honorius was at most guilty of careless terminology, and so neglected to safeguard the apostolic faith.[80] Jaroslav Pelikan (a Lutheran), however, seems to think Honorius was actually a Monothelite.[81]

One lesson to be drawn from II and III Constantinople is that popes may err if they do not align themselves with the faith of the larger Church. Thus papal authority and the authority of ecumenical councils are complementary: each needs the other to be complete and therefore catholic (universal). A council cannot be ecumenical without the consent of the pope, as both the Eastern and Western church teach, but neither can the pope issue authoritative pronouncements which depart from the consensus of the episcopate. This seems to be the thrust of the decree of II Constantinople quoted above. In fact, councils can subsequently correct popes, as III Constantinople did with Honorius, but likewise popes can influence and correct councils.

The View of the East

The Eastern churches had acknowledged Petrine authority from early times, and continued to do so through the Byzantine period. But

[77] Honorius I, *Epistula* 4, *PL* 80:472, cited in Jaroslav Pelikan, *The Spirit of Eastern Christendom* (*The Christian Tradition* vol. 2) (Chicago: University of Chicago Press, 1974) 151.

[78] *Mansi*, 11: 554–556, ET from Jaroslav Pelikan, *The Spirit of Eastern Christendom*, 152.

[79] Leo II, *Epistula* 7, *PL* 96: 419, cited in Pelikan, ibid., 152.

[80] See for example the accounts in Baus, 457–463, and H.G.J. Beck, in *NCE* 7:123–125.

[81] Pelikan, 151.

in the Eastern view, Peter's authority was that of a spokesman for the apostles, not an authority of rulership. "For the fathers of the early Patristic period, Peter held the same position that he occupied in the New Testament. He is 'the mouth of the disciples, the leader of the band.' He is the first who confessed Jesus . . . 'the chief of the apostles and the bearer of the keys of the Kingdom of Heaven.'"[82] The Eastern fathers did not give Peter juridical authority over the Church. They interpreted Matthew 16:17-19 ("on this rock I will build my church") in different ways. For Origen, the "rock" was each individual Christian: "For a Rock is every disciple of Christ . . . and on every such Rock is built the whole message of the Church."[83] For John Chrysostom, the rock is the *faith* professed by Peter: "Thou art Peter, and upon this rock I will build my church, that is on the faith of his confession."[84] It did not necessarily follow, then, from Matthew 16:18 that the pope was the only rock on which the Church was built.

Moreover, the East pointed out that other bishops also could claim to be successors of Peter: the bishop of Jerusalem, where Peter had ministered, or the bishop of Antioch, where Peter had also stayed (Gal 2:11). But in fact it was not apostolic succession which was the criterion for rank in the East: there were many Eastern churches that claimed apostolic founders. In their view the churches were ranked according to the importance of their cities in the empire.[85] This is apparent in canon 6 of Nicaea, where Alexandria is given jurisdiction over the region of Egypt, and Antioch over its outlying region. Canon 28 of Chalcedon, moreover, had elevated Constantinople to the rank just behind Rome, based on its importance as the seat of the emperor, though Constantinople was not at that time recognized as an apostolic church (later legend claimed that the apostle Andrew had been the founder of the church at Constantinople).

Alexander Schmemann, a Russian Orthodox theologian, distinguishes three types of primacy: regional primacy, exercised by the metropolitan bishop; the primacy of a patriarch, such as the patriarch of

[82] Veselin Kesich, "The Problem of Peter's Primacy in the New Testament and the Early Church," *St. Vladimir's Seminary Quarterly,* IV:2–3 (1960) 17–18.

[83] On Matthew, XII, 9; cited in Kesich, ibid., 15.

[84] Homily 54, 3, On Matthew, cited in Kesich, ibid., 25.

[85] See Francis Dvornik, *Byzantium and the Roman Primacy* (New York: Fordham, 1966) 27–58; also, John Meyendorff, "St. Peter in Byzantine Theology," in John Meyendorff, et al.: *The Primacy of Peter* (Bedfordshire: The Faith Press, 1963) 8–9.

Alexandria or Antioch; and universal primacy, which is primacy over the whole Church.[86] But Schmemann argues that primacy is not a power "over" the Church (this he sees as the error of the Roman church), since all bishops are equal in sacramental authority; *it is a power for bringing about unity within the church.* And this primacy is best exercised by synods and universal councils: "It is in the Synod that *primacy* finds its first and most general expression."[87] This demands participation of all the bishops in a region, and a clearly expressed primacy of one bishop. This primacy is expressed in Apostolic Canon 34: "The bishops of every nation must acknowledge him who is first among them and account him as their head, and do nothing of consequence without his consent . . . but neither let him (who is the first) do anything without the consent of all, for so there will be unanimity."[88] Schmemann notes that primacy is not a power or jurisdiction over the Church, but "the expression of the unity and unanimity of all the bishops." In other words, it is a primacy based on *consent* and *participation.*[89] Similarly, Serge Verkhovskoy argues that the supreme authority in Orthodoxy belongs to Christ, the head of the Body the church, but that this is expressed by the consensus of the episcopate, which is expressed in an ecumenical council: "Of all ecclesiastical institutions the ecumenical council is the one possessing the highest authority. . . . The gift of infallibility is given to the Church in its unity and can be expressed only in unity."[90] Orthodox historian John Meyendorff also maintains: "There does not exist, therefore, any visible criterion of Truth, apart from the *consensus* of the Church, the normal organ of which is the ecumenical council."[91] For this reason, the Orthodox Church considers itself the church of the seven ecumenical councils, and appeals to them as the highest ecclesial authority.

For the ancient Eastern Church, an ecumenical council had to be accepted by the whole Church, represented by the five great patriarchs.

[86] "The Idea of Primacy in Orthodox Ecclesiology," in *The Primacy of Peter,* 30ff.

[87] Ibid., 45.

[88] Cited in Schmemann, ibid., 46. The 85 apostolic canons are found in chapter 8 of the *Apostolic Constitutions,* a collection of ecclesiastical laws written in Syria about 380. They are included in Orthodox canon law. See John Meyendorff, *Byzantine Theology* (New York: Fordham, 1974) 80. See "Apostolic Canons," *Encyclopedia of the Early Church* vol. I (New York: Oxford, 1992) 62–63.

[89] *The Primacy of Peter,* 46.

[90] Serge Verkhovskoy, "The Highest Authority in the Church," *St. Vladimir's Seminary Quarterly,* vol. IV (1960) 84, 87.

[91] *Orthodoxy,* 214.

John of Jerusalem wrote that a council was not ecumenical unless "the five patriarchs proclaim a single faith and a single interpretation; and if only one of them is absent or does not accept the council, it will be no council but a futile and deceiving confabulation."[92] Councils whose decrees have been accepted as canon law in the East, but not accepted by the Roman bishop—such as the Second Trullan or *Quinsext* Council (692)—are not considered ecumenical by the Eastern churches. Some councils, notably I Constantinople (381), were not accepted by the whole Church as ecumenical until some time after they were held. I Constantinople was a synod of the churches in the East—no Western representatives were present—and it was not until Chalcedon that it was received by the universal Church as an ecumenical council. Conversely, some councils called themselves ecumenical, but were not subsequently received by the five patriarchs and the larger Church; an example of this was the "robber's synod" of Ephesus, which was never received by the Roman bishop.

Lastly, it is important to note the role of the emperor in the ecumenical councils. All seven of the councils recognized as ecumenical by both the East and the West were convened by the emperor, and at some of them (Nicaea, Chalcedon) he or his representatives presided. Further, it was the emperor who enforced the conciliar decrees as law. I would argue, then, that the emperor exercised a kind of primacy in the early Church in bringing the bishops together, and in bringing unity to the Church. Without the authority of the emperor, the ecumenical councils probably could not have succeeded in unifying the Church. It is thus naïve to assume (as Orthodox theologians sometimes do) that ecumenical councils by themselves, apart from an authority who could convene and direct them, could unify the Church. Though the East rejected the juridical claims of the Roman pope, they were subject to the juridical claims of the emperor. But it is also historically naive to argue, as modern popes have, that ecumenical councils can only be convened by the pope. In point of historical fact, none of the first seven ecumenical councils were convened by the popes.

In sum, by the fifth century, at the end of the patristic period, differing notions of hierarchy and authority were becoming apparent in Rome and in the East. Robert Eno comments:

[92] *PG* 100, 597 C; cited in J.-M.R. Tillard, *The Bishop of Rome*, 185.

> Thus we find two divergent tendencies, the one, especially in the East, that looked to consensus and reception as the ultimate criteria in doctrinal questions. Here the general council would be the supreme expression of this consensus with the emperor enforcing its decisions. The Roman see came to view itself as superior to councils, that its tradition was apostolic without taint, and therefore normative for the Church as a whole. It sought less to conform itself to a general consensus, even one formed at a council, as to impose its views on the Church as a whole, to impose a consensus more or less from above.[93]

This divergence would become more pronounced in the Middle Ages. But it is important to note that the Roman view, not accepted in the East, was also not accepted by all parties in the West. In fact a strong conciliar movement emerged in the Middle Ages, which drew on the conciliar tradition of North Africa.

Consensus and Reception

At the risk of possible repetition, it is worth clarifying the importance of consensus and reception in the ancient Church. As noted above, the Council of Nicaea was not accepted as ecumenical until it had been received by the whole Church, including subsequent councils, a process that took many years. This was in fact true of all the ecumenical councils. What is it that caused some councils to be accepted as ecumenical, and others not accepted? This is critical for understanding hierarchy in the ancient Church, for the ecumenical councils were seen as the highest teaching authority. Edward Kilmartin, in an article on ecclesiological reception, follows Hermann Sieben in arguing as follows: "Sieben found that a consistent view emerged from Nicaea I to Nicaea II (787). It was determined by the notions of *consentio antiquitatis et universitatis* and the function of the Spirit who grounded the horizontal and vertical consensus."[94] The council's claim to be ecumenical or universal had to be secured by a horizontal consensus—that is, the consent of the bishops (and the people) of the whole Church, and a vertical consensus, that is, its teachings had to

[93] Robert Eno, *Teaching Authority in the Early Church* (Wilmington: Michael Glazier, 1984) 29.

[94] Edward Kilmartin, "Reception in History: an Ecclesiological Phenomenon and its Significance," *Journal of Ecumenical Studies,* 21:1 (Winter, 1984) 48. Kilmartin is referring to H.J. Sieben, *Die Konzilsidee der Alten Kirche* (Paderborn: Schöningh, 1979).

concur with the teachings of scripture and tradition, including previous councils. Both of these conditions could only be satisfied by reception: that is, the bishops of the universal Church had to agree that the teachings of a council were in accordance with scripture and tradition and were accepted by all the bishops. If these conditions were satisfied, the council came to be received as ecumenical. Nicaea, for many fathers, such as Athanasius, was a model of what an ecumenical council should be.

Kilmartin gives a striking example of the process of reception. After the Third Council of Constantinople, Pope Leo II, who had accepted the council, asked the North African and Spanish bishops to review the council and declare if they accepted its decisions. They did so, and at the Council of Toledo XIV (684) they declared: "And so the *acta concilii* are venerated by us and stand received insofar as they do not disagree with previous councils, indeed, insofar as they seem to agree with them."[95]

Congar instances many patristic texts that support the idea of horizontal and vertical consensus.[96] Pope Gelasius, writing in 495, laid out the criteria for good and bad councils. A good council, he said, was assented to by the universal Church and approved by the Premier See (i.e., Rome); bad councils spoke against the scriptures, against the doctrine of the fathers, against the rules of the Church, were not accepted by the Church, and especially were not approved by the apostolic sees. Gregory the Great claimed to honor the first four councils because they had been decided by universal consensus ("quia . . . universali sunt consensu constituta").[97] A famous expression of this ideal was given by Vincent of Lerins in 434:

> Also in the Catholic Church we take great care that we hold that which has been believed everywhere, always, and by all. For that is truly and properly "Catholic," . . . which comprehends everything almost universally. We shall hold to this rule if we follow universality, antiquity, and consensus. We shall follow universality if we acknowledge that one faith to be true which the whole Church throughout the world confesses; antiquity if we in no way depart from those interpretations which our ancestors and fathers manifestly proclaimed;

[95] Ibid., 49, note 42.

[96] "La Réception . . . ," 375ff.

[97] *PL* 77, 478; texts in Congar, "La Réception . . . ," 376.

> consensus if in antiquity itself we keep following the definitions and opinions of all, or surely almost all, bishops and teachers.[98]

Vincent recognized that universality might be insufficient, if the whole Church were to be infected by heresy, and antiquity might also be insufficient, for there were ancient heresies; thus only the consensus of the fathers was decisive: "And whatever [the Christian] finds to have been held, approved, and taught, not by one or two, but by all equally and with one consensus . . . he may consider tenable without any reservations."[99]

The *Sensus Fidelium* and Development

This account of hierarchy in the ancient Church so far has focused only on bishops. What was the role of the people in the ancient Church? Did they have any authority? I shall treat this question here under the rubric of *sensus fidelium.* [100]

The expression *sensus fidelium* means the sense or opinion of the faithful, both clergy and laity, concerning church teachings and practice. The *sensus fidelium* was important in validating a doctrine or practice

[98] *Commonitorium II; PL* 50, 638; ET in Karl F. Morrison, *Tradition and Authority in the Western Church: 300–1140* (Princeton, N.J.: Princeton University Press, 1969) 4. For a commentary on Vincent's definition of tradition, see Jaroslav Pelikan, *The Emergence of the Christian Tradition (100–600)* (Chicago: University of Chicago Press, 1971) 333–339.

[99] *Commonitorium II;* ET in B.J. Kidd, *Documents Illustrative of the History of the Church,* vol. II (London: SPCK, 1941) 272. Vincent did, however, realize that development may occur in the Church: "But perhaps someone is saying: 'Will there be, therefore, no development in the Church of Christ?' Obviously there may be even very great development; for what man is so hateful to men, so odious to God as to strive to deny it? But, to be sure, it must truly be development, and not a transformation, of the faith. The quality of development is the elaboration of anything, preserving its own character; that of transformation, the change of something from one thing into another. With the passage of years and the ages of individual men and of everyone, of each man and of the whole Church, understanding, knowledge, and wisdom must grow and develop greatly and powerfully, but [each must grow] only in its own kind, in the same dogma, the same sense, the same meaning." This nuanced understanding of development, rare in antiquity, would not reemerge in the Catholic church until modern times.

[100] On *sensus fidelium* in the Fathers, see Yves Congar, *Lay People in the Church* (Westminster, Md.: Newman Press, 1957) 441-443. For recent ideas and a bibliography

as orthodox. One area in which this was manifested was in the selection of bishops, which involved the consent of the faithful. Again, we may presume that the assent of the faithful was a part of the reception of councils or teachings discussed above. Yet another area is expressed in the adage "lex orandi, lex credendi": "the rule of prayer (or worship) is the rule of belief." Loosely, this is the idea that the belief of the faithful as expressed in worship, ought to be normative for doctrine. There are many examples of this in the ancient Church.

To begin with, there are examples in scripture itself. The prologue to the Gospel of John (John 1:1-18) was a foundational text for the Church's affirmation that Jesus was the incarnation of the eternal Logos. This prologue, written in verse structure, is now thought to be a hymn coming from the Johannine community, which was incorporated into the Gospel (with interpolations) by one of the later redactors.[101] But if this was originally a hymn, its provenance was the worship and prayer of a community. Eventually what was expressed in worship came to be incorporated into the Gospel, and later expressed in the doctrine of Nicaea that the Logos is of one substance with God and preexisted with God eternally. A similar example is Phil 2:6-11, thought to have been a pre-existing hymn interpolated by Paul into his letter; like the Johannine prologue, this is also an important text for the doctrine of the incarnation.[102]

Another example is the formation of the canon of scripture. There were several criteria for acceptance of a book into the canon: apostolic authorship, antiquity, orthodoxy, and use in the liturgy of the churches. Books that were widely read in the churches—indicating acceptance by the *sensus fidelium*—were usually accepted as canonical. Indeed, this was often a condition for the books surviving at all. Those of Paul's letters which have survived did so because they were read in various churches, and so copied, preserved, and handed on. Liturgical use was not the only criterion for the acceptance of writings as scripture, but it was an important one.[103]

---

concerning *sensus fidelium* see Richard Gaillardetz, *Teaching with Authority: A Theology of the Magisterium of the Church.* Collegeville: The Liturgical Press, 1997, 230–235.

[101] See commentary in Raymond Brown, *The Gospel according to John I–XII* (Garden City, N.Y.: Doubleday, 1966) 18–23.

[102] *NJBC*, 794.

[103] See Joseph T. Lienhard, *The Bible, the Church, and Authority* (Collegeville: The Liturgical Press, 1995) 24–41.

In the fifth century we find both Augustine and Prosper of Aquitane appealing to the principle that the rule of worship and prayer is normative for belief. Both argued against the semi-Pelagians that God's grace must precede conversion (the semi-Pelagians denied this, and said that the initial turning to God was effected by human freedom alone). Both appealed to the liturgical prayers of the Church offered for the conversion of infidels, schismatics, heretics, and Jews. These prayers assume that the grace of Christ would be capable of effecting such conversions. On this basis Augustine and Prosper argued that the semi-Pelagian position opposed the teaching of the Church, since, according to Prosper "legem credendi lex statuat supplicandi" (the law of supplication establishes the law of belief).[104]

Thus the *sensus fidelium* is important not only passively, in consent, but actively, in shaping belief which later comes to be proclaimed by the hierarchy. It was Pope Gelasius I who formulated the distinction between *ecclesia docens* and *ecclesia discens,* the teaching church (the bishops and the pope) and the learning church (the laity)—a distinction which endured until Vatican II. But the principle "lex orandi, lex credendi" stands as an important corrective to this one-sided notion that all teaching proceeds from the hierarchy and flows down to the laity, whose sole task is obedience. In fact, teaching flows both from the bishops to the laity, and from the laity to the bishops; there is reciprocal influence.

The *sensus fidelium* was important in the development of belief and doctrine in the early Church. Typically, the bishops of the Church were traditionalist in their mentality: nothing was to be added and nothing subtracted from the consensus of the fathers. Yet there was a gradual development of practice, belief, and doctrine, which was largely unnoticed by the bishops (and most theologians) because of their traditionalist bias. The most obvious development was the acceptance of Gentiles into the Church without circumcision (Acts 15). But the institutions of the episcopate and the papacy developed over time also, though their roots can be found in the New Testament. Prayer to the saints was a development, not found in the scriptures, and was accepted by the whole Church until the Protestant Reform. Again, devotion to Mary seems to

[104] See Augustine, epistle 217, 2; *PL* 33,766; Prosper's letter in *DS* 246; *PL* 51, 209–210; Latin originals and French translations given in Paul Declerck, "'Lex orandi, lex credendi', sens originel et avatars historiques d'un adage équivoque," in *Questions liturgiques* 4 (1978) 193–212.

have developed; we do not find it in the New Testament, but it became a prominent feature of Christian life about the time of the Council of Ephesus (431), which, partly as a result of popular pressure, proclaimed Mary as *theotokos* (Mother of God). The development of prayer to the saints and devotion to Mary were clearly led by the *sensus fidelium;* they were in no way orchestrated from above, but developed within popular practice and belief and were eventually incorporated into the official teachings of the Church.

Conclusion

From this very compressed survey of hierarchy and authority in the early Church, we can distill some salient points. 1. Emerging from a college of presbyters, the bishops became the leaders of the individual churches during the second century. In the first few centuries these bishops were usually elected, and often consulted the presbyters and the laity in their decisions, as can be seen in the case of Cyprian, and Apostolic Canon 34, which stipulates that the head must do nothing without "the consent of all, for so there will be unanimity." The story of Ambrose, who was acclaimed by the people of Milan as their bishop while he was still only a catechumen, is well known. The authority of the bishop was based both on his being a representative of a particular church, and on his consecration: he was consecrated as the head of a local church standing in continuity with the authority of the apostles. He represented his church at episcopal synods, and so bound it to the *communio* of the universal Church. The bishops as a college were seen as the successors of the apostles. Hence major decisions were made in synods and in consultation with other bishops. The charismatic authority of the Holy Spirit tended to be absorbed and institutionalized in the authority of the bishops, and independent prophets mostly disappeared. But the will of Christ and the Spirit was most clearly manifest when all the bishops and the people were in unanimity as expressed in councils. Thus the early Church preserved the idea expressed at the Council of Jerusalem, that the will of the Spirit is most clearly expressed in the consensus of a plurality of agents, rather than through just one agent.

2. The most authoritative doctrinal statements in the early Church were made by ecumenical councils, which, having been received by the whole Church, were thought to represent the mind of the whole Church and hence the will of the Spirit. In this they were similar to the Council of Jerusalem, in which the apostles and the whole Church reached a con-

sensus and wrote "it seems good to the Holy Spirit and to us" (Acts 15). The first four ecumenical councils—Nicaea (235), Constantinople (381), Ephesus (431), and Chalcedon (451) came to be seen as definitive expressions of the faith in both East and West.[105] Gregory the Great compared the authority of the first four ecumenical councils to the authority of the four Gospels (see epigraph at head of chapter).

3. The mindset of the early Church was traditionalist. The ideal was to pass on the teaching of the fathers and of earlier councils, neither adding nor subtracting anything. The bishop of Rome considered his task to "watch over" the deposit of faith received from the fathers, so that it is passed on in its integrity. Yet there was some development of practice and doctrine in the early Church, led by the *sensus fidelium.*

4. The church at Rome early acquired a reputation as the touchstone of orthodox doctrine. The popes attempted to attach this reputation to the bishop of Rome himself, and the papacy, which was not prominent in the second century, gradually claimed greater and greater authority over the Church. The East acknowledged the primacy of the Roman church and bishop, but not their universal jurisdiction. Thus we begin to see a divergence between the Eastern and the Roman view of authority in the Church. The Second Council of Constantinople excommunicated Pope Vigilius, and III Constantinople anathematized the deceased Pope Honorius. This indicates that, just as a council cannot be ecumenical and hence authoritative without the consent of the bishop of Rome, so also a pope cannot make an authoritative declaration apart from the consensus of the Church, which is represented by an ecumenical council.

5. The principle of unity in the early Church was collegial and conciliar, though councils required a primate (emperor or pope) to achieve unity. As Hubert Jedin has written: "Almost every page of the history of the early Church tells of a synod; the whole discipline of the ancient Church rested on synodal canons."[106] This contrasts with the principle that unity is obtained by obedience to one common head, a theory which came to prominence during the papal monarchy of the Middle Ages, to which we now turn.

[105] Three later councils (II Constantinople, 553; III Constantinople, 680–681; and II Nicaea 787) would later come to be accepted as ecumenical by both East and West.

[106] *A History of the Council of Trent,* vol. 1 (London: Thomas Nelson and Sons, 1957, German original, 1949) 163–164.

Chapter 6

Hierarchy and Participation in the Middle Ages

The Pope is the meeting point between God and man . . . who can judge all things and be judged by no one.

Pope Innocent III[1]

During the long medieval period, stretching from the end of the patristic period to the beginnings of the modern—almost nine hundred years, the Western and Eastern Churches gradually became estranged, and papal claims became more monarchial and imperial. But at the same time, a counterpoint current of conciliar thought also ran all through medieval times, culminating in the conciliar movement of the 1400s. Thus no simple picture of hierarchy in the Middle Ages is possible; like the patristic period, it is a time of great diversity which defeats generalizations. Many different movements contributed to medieval notions of hierarchy: the monastic movement, the role of kings and emperors, feudalism, the papacy, conciliar thought, and a strongly articulated ontological hierarchy deriving from Neoplatonism, especially Pseudo-Dionysius. This chapter will lay out some of the principal developments and positions, and at the end draw some conclusions about hierarchy and participation in this period.

[1] *Sermo* 2, *PL* 217:658, cited in Patrick Granfield, *The Limits of the Papacy* (New York: Crossroad, 1987) 32.

Monasticism

A monastic community may be regarded as a church in miniature, whose aim is the sanctification of its members through prayer, poverty, chastity, fasting, obedience, and community life. Monasticism was important in the development of hierarchy because both in the East and West it stressed obedience to superiors, and centralization of authority in a single abbot, and because, in the West, many clerics, bishops, popes, and theologians, were monks or friars.

The most influential type of monasticism in the West was that of St. Benedict (480–537), whose Rule became the basis of most Western monastic rules. Benedictine monks took vows of obedience and stability (to stay at one monastery), and to live as a monk. Obedience to the abbot was strongly emphasized, for Benedict saw the abbot as Christ's representative, so that in obeying the abbot (or any superior) the monk was obeying Christ and God. According to the Rule monks should "hasten to obey any command of a superior as if it were a command of God," and "obedience shown to superiors is, through them, shown to God."[2] Obedience was the master virtue according to Benedict, through which monks learned humility and surrender to Christ and God.

Thus the quality of a Benedictine monastery depended largely on the abbot. The abbot was under the same discipline as his monks, including taking his turn at common tasks like cooking, and was to teach holiness by example. As the Rule says: "He should show them by deeds, more than by words, what is good and holy."[3] Furthermore, though the abbot's word was law, he was instructed by the Rule to consult the whole community on all important matters, since "the Lord often reveals the best course to a younger monk."[4] Abbots were to be elected, according to the Rule, by the whole community; if a bad abbot was chosen, that choice could be annulled by the local bishop or even by the local Christian community.[5] It became common practice in Benedictine monasteries to hold chapter meetings daily, at which all monks attended, heard a sermon by the abbot, and discussed commu-

[2] *The Rule of St. Benedict* (Garden City, N.Y.: Doubleday, Image Books, 1975) chap. 2, 48; chap. 5, 55.

[3] Ibid., 48.

[4] Ibid., 51.

[5] Ibid., 99–100.

nity business. Most Benedictine monasteries had a special chapter room for these meetings. The practice of chapter meetings was carried on by later monastic orders also, such as the Franciscans and Dominicans. The latter instituted the practice of a general chapter, in which representatives of all the individual monastic houses would gather to discuss the governance of the whole order. Some authors have even suggested that this practice influenced the development of parliamentary democracy in England.[6]

Thus Benedict preserved the principle of consent found in the patristic Church and in Roman law: "Quod omnes tangit, ab omnibus tractari et approbari debet" (what touches all, must be treated and approved by all).[7] We have seen this principle at work in the election of the Hebrew king, who was acclaimed by all the people (1 Sam 11:15; 2 Sam 5:3), in the people's consent to the Mosaic covenant (Exod 24:7); in the consent of the whole Church to the pivotal decisions taken by the apostles in Acts (Acts 15:22); and in the election of bishops.

Yet the Benedictine emphasis on absolute obedience to superiors, and the idea that the abbot represented Christ, seems to have been an important influence in the shaping of Western medieval notions of hierarchy, with its strong emphasis on obedience. Pope Gregory the Great (590–604) and his successors used the Benedictines as missionaries to convert the barbarian tribes of Europe: both England and northern Germany were evangelized by Benedictine missionaries, who set up bishoprics and monasteries that were devoted to the supremacy of the bishop of Rome. Many bishops and popes came from Benedictine monasteries. Popes Stephen IX, Gregory VII, Victor II, Urban II, Paschal II, and Gelasius II were all Benedictines, and were active in the reform of the papacy, whose aim was to eliminate simony and lay investiture, and concentrate authority in the hands of the popes. This policy was largely successful. But, as we shall see, the reforming popes ended by claiming that they alone were the vicars (representatives) of Christ on earth, and were owed absolute obedience, like the Benedictine abbots. What worked well in a decentralized monastic setting, where the abbot lived among the monks as their spiritual father, and was himself meant to be an example of holiness, did not work so well when transplanted to a larger institutional setting,

[6] See Yves Congar, "Quod omnes tangit, ab omnibus tractari et approbari debet," in *Révue historique droit française et étranger* (1958) 229–231.

[7] Ibid., 210–259.

where the principle of consent could not operate so easily, authority came to be based more on force than on holiness and virtue, and obedience became more servile than filial.

Church and State

During the medieval period conflicts arose between the Church and what might be loosely called the state, whether in the person of lay lords, kings, or emperors. These conflicts, whose roots go back to the time of Constantine, continued into Reformation and modern times.

Early Christians, while they honored and prayed for those in political power,[8] refused to offer sacrifice before busts of the emperor. Rather, the true king was Christ, as Polycarp confessed during his martyrdom: "Eighty-six years I have served him, and he never did me any wrong. How can I blaspheme my King who saved me?"[9] But during the reign of Constantine, Hellenistic concepts of divine monarchy came to be applied to the emperor. As Francis Dvornik shows, such ideas go back to Mesopotamian and Persian ideas of kingship, where the king was seen as the vicar of God on earth, and the source of God's law, responsible for enforcing the law in his kingdom.[10] These ideas were taken up by Alexander the Great, who, in imitation of Persian kings, accepted divine honors. Thereafter the ruler cult became established in the East and eventually in the West: Roman emperors after Julius Caesar were given divine honors, sometimes even in their lifetime.[11] This thinking was applied to Emperor Constantine by Eusebius of Caesarea, whose thought was strongly marked by Neoplatonism:

> From him and through him [Christ] the king who is dear to God receives an image of the kingdom that is above and so in imitation of that greater king himself guides and directs the course of everything on earth . . . he . . . emulating the divine example, removes every stain of godless error from his earthly kingdom . . . Monarchy is su-

[8] "We Christians . . . we are all and ever at prayer for all rulers" Tertullian, *Apologeticus*, chap. 30, *PL* 1, 502, cited in Francis Dvornik, *Early Christian and Byzantine Political Philosophy* (Washington, D.C.: Dumbarton Oaks Center for Byzantine studies, 1966) 581.

[9] *The Martyrdom of St. Polycarp*, 9, 3, in Richardson, *Early Christian Fathers*, 152.

[10] Dvornik, *Political Philosophy*, 21–131.

[11] Ibid., 453–557.

> perior to every other constitution and form of government. For polyarchy, where everyone competes on equal terms, is really anarchy and discord. That is why there is one God, not two or three. . . . There is one king, and his Word and royal law are one . . . he is the author of kingship itself and of all rule and authority.[12]

Here we find formulated what might be called the monarchial ideal of heavenly and earthly unity: the unity of a social body is found in obedience to a single head rather than in consensus.

Yet Constantine, though he considered himself responsible for the governance and regulation of the Christian faith in his realm, was careful to leave the formulation of doctrine to the bishops and their councils. This became the pattern to be followed by emperors after him. Justinian, in a famous decree, distinguished between the authority of bishops and the authority of the emperor. "The greatest gifts of God's heavenly *philanthropia* bestowed upon men are the *sacerdotium* and the *basilea,* of which the former serves divine matters, the latter presides and watches over human affairs, and both proceed from one and the same principle and regulate human life."[13] In this vision, both the ecclesial and the imperial power derive equally from God. Harmony results when each rules its own domain justly. Bishops were to decide matters of doctrine, the emperors, being responsible for civil and ecclesial law, were to enforce their decisions. In practice, however, the emperors of the Eastern church had a great deal of authority in ecclesial matters. They appointed the patriarch of Constantinople, and often other bishops as well; they legislated on matters of church discipline, and were instrumental in suppressing heresy and maintaining orthodoxy in the empire. Occasionally they attempted to dictate church doctrine, as during the iconoclastic controversy (726–843), when Leo III and other emperors attempted to impose iconoclastic views on the Church. But generally such attempts were unsuccessful: iconoclasm was condemned by the second council of Nicaea (787), convened by Empress Irene and strongly supported by the pope.[14]

[12] Eusebius, "Oration in Honor of Constantine on the Thirtieth Anniversary of His Reign," ET in Maurice Wiles and Mark Santer, eds. *Documents in Early Christian Thought* (Cambridge: Harvard University Press, 1975) 231–232.

[13] Cited in Dvornik, *Political Philosophy,* 816.

[14] On iconoclasm, see J.M. Hussey, *The Orthodox Church in the Byzantine Empire* (Oxford: Clarendon Press, 1986) 30–68; on the role of the emperor, ibid., 297–304; also Meyendorff, *Imperial Unity and Christian Divisions,* 28–38.

The theology underlying the role of the emperor was monarchial and imperial. The emperor was thought to be the viceregent or vicar of Christ, who was the viceroy of God. Just as God was one, and Christ one, so there should be one emperor; just as God's will was one, so there should be only one religion in the empire: heretics and dissenters were banished. Just as God and Christ were the source of all law, so was the emperor the source of law, the *nomos empsychos* (living law). As Justinian stated: "The imperial station . . . shall not be subject to the rules which we have just formulated, for to the emperor God has subjected the laws themselves by sending him to men as the incarnate law."[15] This is the very essence of command hierarchy. This conception (which is closely associated with Neoplatonism) had more in common with Arianism—which held that the *Logos,* the second person of the Trinity, was not consubstantial with God the Father, but subordinate to him, and the Spirit subordinate to both—than with orthodox trinitarianism. Many of the strongest proponents of this monarchial theology, such as Eusebius of Caesarea and the emperor Constantius, were sympathetic to Arianism. Francis Dvornik surmises "It is possible that this monarchic plea contributed a good deal to the wide acceptance of Arianism in the Roman Empire."[16] Notably this theology minimized the role of the Holy Spirit, which "blows where it will," is difficult to confine within the forms of an institution, and tends to raise up prophets against those who abuse institutional authority. In the East, this understanding of the emperor was balanced and kept in check by the Orthodox notion that doctrinal authority resided in the pentarchy—the college of patriarchs. But monarchial theology was to have a very long life: first in the Byzantine emperor, then in the Russian conception of the czar. It also appeared in the West, both in Western conceptions of the emperor and of kings, and in the theocratic conception of the papacy, embodied by Innocent III and Boniface VIII.

One of the themes of this book is that a trinitarian conception of divinity should be reflected in a participatory ecclesial structure, such as the episcopal councils, since the Spirit speaks through not one but many agents, clerical and lay, priests, prophets, and kings, and the will of the Spirit can only be discerned in a consensus of the agents through whom it speaks. Yet it is a constant temptation in the life of the Church

[15] Cited in Dvornik, *Political Philosophy,* 722.

[16] Ibid., 728.

to reduce a trinitarian understanding of God to a monarchic or imperial conception, and to reduce participatory and collegial ecclesial hierarchy to a monarchy. This has happened repeatedly in church history and continues even now. To a large extent the Eastern system or emperor/pentarchy preserved a balance of power between the emperor, the bishops, and the pope, whose authority was important in the East until the break in 1054. But there was always the danger in the East of the emperor controlling the patriarch of Constantinople and the other patriarchs as well, especially after the Eastern Church separated from the West and hence the papacy. In the West, this same danger took the form of a monarchial papacy, which, once separated from the East, was no longer balanced by other patriarchs or Eastern bishops, nor by the Eastern emperor.

What became the orthodox theory of the relation between Church and state in the West was the doctrine of the "two swords," first enunciated by Pope Gelasius (492–496): "There are indeed . . . two powers by which this world is chiefly ruled, the sacred authority of the popes *(auctoritas sacrata pontificum)* and the royal power. Of these, the priestly power is much more important, because it has to render an account for the kings of men themselves at the divine tribunal."[17] In the West, the Eastern emperor ceased to be a major influence by the time of Gregory the Great (c. 600), who had to organize the administration and defense of the city of Rome because imperial government was ineffective. By 754 the papacy was allied with the Frankish kings for protection against the Lombards, and on Christmas Day, 800, Charlemagne was crowned emperor by Pope Leo III (the justification given was that the Eastern imperial throne was vacant, since it was at that time occupied by a woman, Irene). Until his death in 814, Charlemagne ruled the Church, appointing bishops, and delivering laws which remained in force for centuries. But his predominance was not carried on by his sons, and with the death of Charles the Fat (888), Charlemagne's empire disintegrated. Imperial power would not be revived until the tenth century, under Otto I.

What took the place of imperial jurisdiction in the West was the system of national and proprietary churches. National churches had their origin in the conversion of whole Germanic tribes, which formed a territorial people under the governance of a Christian king and his

[17] *Epistula* 12:2; Thiel, 350.

territorial bishops. This type of ethnic or national church prevailed in France and Spain from the sixth and seventh centuries.[18] In this conception, the Church, which was the whole ethnic group, was a Christian society ruled by both the king and the bishops, who convened in regional councils. It involved the idea that the regional or national kings were appointed by God to govern the people, and thus had their authority directly from God, not from the emperor or the pope (this became the basis for the later Renaissance doctrine of the divine right of kings). This type of ecclesial system was rooted in Germanic law, in which the lord of the land (usually the king) also owned the church, and the bishop was to a large extent responsible to the king, whereas in Roman law the bishop was responsible to the pope. National churches had a long history in Europe: they created conflicts in the late Middle Ages between popes and national kings, and surfaced in the Reformation with the formation of national and territorial churches, ruled by kings or princes, in England, Scotland, and Germany. The notion remained influential in France in the form of Gallicanism until Vatican Council I (1870).

Alongside the national church structure existed the regime of the proprietary church *(Eigenkirche),* which became ubiquitous by the ninth century. In this system the church was owned by a lord—on whose land and for whose use the church was built. Such a lord might be a lay noble, a monastery, a king, or even a bishop. The lord might own more than one church, was entitled to its tithes, could appoint its priest, could sell or trade the church, divide it among heirs, and so on. Often the priest was a serf who owed feudal allegiance to the lord, and his office was regarded as a gift or benefice from the lord. Usually the priest was married, and often passed the benefice and priesthood onto a son. Thus the church was drawn into the feudal hierarchical system, and the bishop gradually became dependent on seignorial power. Indeed, bishops were usually members of the feudal nobility themselves, were often married, and usually obtained their office by simony. Thus developed the "church in the hands of laymen," an intolerable system in which the churches and their resources were used mostly for the private gains of their owners. It was against this debilitated ecclesial system that Gregory VII and the popes of the eleventh century launched their great reform.

[18] See Congar, *L'Église,* 51–55.

The Medieval Papacy

The foundation for the medieval papacy was set by Pope Gregory the Great (590–604). In his administration Gregory evinced a strongly hierarchical outlook, probably derived from his Benedictine training, which emphasized strict obedience to superiors. Thus he saw the bishop as the *pater familias* of his diocese, over which he exercised a sacred rulership *(sacrum regimen).*[19] Gregory himself corresponded extensively with the bishops of the West, advising them on matters of administration and discipline, and saw these bishops as subject to Rome. As he said: "I know of no bishop who is not subject to the Apostolic See when fault has been committed."[20] Yet, like a good abbot, he also emphasized that authority was service, to be exercised with humility, and habitually styled himself "servant of the servants of God" *(servus servorum Dei).* This phrase later became a papal title, but Gregory seems to have embodied it more than most subsequent popes. He refused the title "universal pope" with which the emperor had addressed him in a letter, replying: "My honor is the honor of the universal Church. My honor is the strength of my brothers [the bishops]. Then am I truly honored, when honor is not denied to each one to whom it is due . . . your Holiness calls me universal pope . . . Let it not be so."[21]

Gregory is often said to be a transitional figure between the ancient and the medieval Church. What is significant about him with respect to hierarchy is that, by his firm leadership at a chaotic time when imperial power was declining, he succeeded in greatly enhancing the prestige of the papacy, and so in centralizing authority in papal hands, whereas in the ancient church authority had rested more with regional patriarchs and ecumenical councils.

Papal power, however, declined in the centuries after Gregory. Although Charlemagne had been crowned emperor by the pope (800), real power was exercised by Charlemagne, not the pope. After the breakup of the Carolingian empire (888), there was no effective centralized power in Europe until the emergence of Otto I, who was crowned emperor in 962. The papacy became controlled by powerful Roman

[19] Walter Ullman, *The Growth of Papal Government in the Middle Ages* (London: Methuen, 1955) 40.

[20] Cited in Thomas Bokenkotter, *A Concise History of the Catholic Church,* revised ed. (New York: Doubleday, 1977) 111.

[21] *PL* 77, 933.

families for their own gain, and later by Emperor Henry III (1039–1056), a champion of royal authority over the Church, who installed men of his choice as popes. Meanwhile, under the proprietary church system, bishops were usually appointed and installed in office by kings or nobles (a system known as lay investiture), to whom the bishop would render homage and fealty, after having paid a fee for the office.

It was against this system that the papal reform movement of 1046–1122 reacted.[22] Led by a series of powerful popes including Leo IX (1049–1054) and Gregory VII (1073–1085), the reformers attacked the system of lay investiture, simony, clerical marriage, and attempted to wrest control of the Church from local lords and kings and assert a monarchial papacy. To this end, they made the cardinals, rather than the clergy and people of Rome, the principal electors of the pope, and the clergy the electors of the bishops.[23] This aimed at removing papal elections from control by Roman families and the emperor, and episcopal elections from control by lay lords. There followed a long struggle between the popes and the German emperors over the investiture and control of bishops. Gregory VII, in 1075, tried to prohibit the king and all lay persons from bestowing bishoprics. In 1076 Gregory excommunicated the German emperor, Henry IV. Conservatives were outraged that the pope would dare excommunicate an anointed king, whose authority, putatively, came from God alone, not from the pope.[24] Eventually the whole problem of investiture was settled by a compromise at the Concordat of Worms (1122), which stipulated that bishops were to be elected, though in the presence of the king, and that their insignia of office, the ring and staff, would not be given them by lay rulers.

Thus the Gregorian reform was successful in its endeavor to regain control of the Church from lay nobility. Yet this success was ambiguous, for the price paid for *Libertas ecclesiae* was the beginning of a papal monarchy. This was not however due only to a will to power on the part of the papacy, but more to the collapse of any independent episcopal synodal power, since control of bishops had fallen into the hands of the nobility. [25]

[22] See Colin Morris, *The Papal Monarchy: the Western Church from 1050 to 1250* (Oxford: Clarendon, 1989) 79–133.

[23] Ibid., 92.

[24] For the royalist case, see Ernst H. Kantorowicz, *The King's Two Bodies: a Study in Medieval Political Theology* (Princeton: Princeton University Press, 1957) 42–86; Morris, *The Papal Monarchy*, 131.

[25] See Schatz, *Papal Primacy*, 95–96.

The result of the investiture struggle and the Gregorian reform was therefore an absolutist, monarchial conception of the papacy. Pope Alexander III addressed the Third Lateran Council (1179): "Is not the chief pontiff the king? The nobles or magnates are his brothers and flanks, the lord cardinals; the archbishops are the consuls; and we find other bishops and abbots are not ashamed in so noble a city to take the place of the people."[26] From about 1075 popes were crowned, like kings or emperors, and at the coronation wore an imperial robe and crown or tiara.[27] In Gregory VII's *Dictatus Papae,* the papal claims became absolutist. Some of the claims were that:

1. The Roman Church was founded by God alone [whereas all other churches had human founders].
2. The Roman pontiff alone is rightly to be called universal.
3. He alone can depose or reinstate bishops.
7. For him alone it is lawful to enact new laws according to the needs of the time.
9. The pope is the only one whose feet are to be kissed by all princes.
12. He may depose emperors.
16. No synod may be called General [i.e., ecumenical] without his order.
19. He himself may be judged by no one.
21. To this see the more important cases of every church should be submitted.
22. The Roman Church has never erred, nor ever, by the witness of scripture, shall ever err to all eternity.
26. He should not be considered as Catholic who is not in conformity with the Roman Church.[28]

The ideology behind this is monarchial, even imperial.[29] Gregory conceives of the Church as the Body of Christ, to which belong all the

[26] Cited in Morris, *The Papal Monarchy,* 205.

[27] Ibid., 130.

[28] *PL* 148, 407–408; ET in *Church and State through the Centuries,* ed. by Sidney Ehler and John B. Morrall (Westminster, Md.: The Newman Press, 1954) 43–44.

[29] The following is taken from Ullman, *Papal Government,* 262–309. On the Gregorian Reform, see also Karl F. Morrison, "The Gregorian Reform," in *Christian Spirituality: Origins to the Twelfth Century,* Bernard McGinn, John Meyendorff, and Jean Leclercq, eds. (New York: Crossroad, 1989) 177–193; Congar, *L'Église,* 89–124.

faithful. As such it is a Christian society that is unified by a hierarchy of command, at the summit of which stands the Roman pontiff. Since the spiritual power is superior to the temporal power, all temporal rulers, including kings and the emperor, are under the authority of the papacy. The pope can depose emperors, and Gregory VII did in fact depose the emperor, Henry IV, an unprecedented act. Bishops, too, are under the authority of the pope, indicating that they are on a fundamentally inferior level: the pope, in Gregory's thinking, is not just first among bishops; he is over all bishops, and he or his legates can intervene in local episcopal affairs and override local authority. Papal commands are issued *ex parte omnipotentis Dei* and have the authority of divine commands.[30] Obedience is the prime virtue in any Christian and any Christian prince; disobedience is due to pride *(superbia)* and whoever is disobedient to papal authority has no right to exercise governmental power. These demands of obedience extend also to the Eastern Church.

If the clergy were to be under Roman control, then any authority by laymen, including kings and emperors, over the bishops or clergy must be rejected. For this reason, the Reformers insisted that bishops be elected and installed only by the Church. By 1171, both rulers and people had been excluded from episcopal (and papal) elections; bishops were thereafter elected by the cathedral chapters, and popes by the cardinals.[31] For similar reasons they opposed simony: church offices could not be bought or sold. Again, they opposed a married clergy, and insisted on clerical celibacy. Gregory said: "The church is not able to be freed from servitude to laymen unless clergy are liberated from wives."[32] This "purification of the priesthood" had the effect of creating a clerical caste which was superior to and separate from the laity. The demand for universal celibacy, like the demand for universal obedience, shows the attempt to impose monastic ideals on the whole clergy (Gregory was a Benedictine monk).

Though the germs of some of the Reformers' ideas can be found in the popes of antiquity, for example Gelasius, the use of these ideas, and many of the ideas themselves, are revolutionary. The statement that the pope cannot be judged by anyone—item 19 in the *Dictatus Papae*—

[30] Ullman, *Papal Government*, 279.

[31] Ibid., 298–299.

[32] "Non liberare potest ecclesia a servitute laicorum, nisi liberantur clerici ab uxoribus." Cited in ibid., 297.

comes from a document forged in the sixth century.[33] (We have seen that the sixth ecumenical council not only judged but anathematized Pope Honorius.) Other claims can be traced to the so-called "false decretals (also called the 'Pseudo-Isidorian decretals')," ninth-century forgeries that placed exaggerated claims of papal power in the mouths of ancient popes, thus lending legitimacy to the claims. Among these claims were: only a pope can declare a council ecumenical, and other bishops were only the executors of the pope's power. In particular, these decretals saw the Roman Church as the head or source of all other churches, and claimed that Rome had the right to intervene in other churches.[34] It was an innovation that a pope would depose an emperor, that other bishops would be relegated to the level of papal deputies, or that the pope would wear imperial insignia and have his feet kissed by other bishops. The core of the reformers' argument was that Rome was supreme over other churches. This is expressed succinctly in Gratian's *Decretum,* a collection of canon law made about 1140: "The holy Roman church imparts right and authority to the sacred canons, but is not bound by them. For it has the right of establishing canons, since it is the head and hinge *(cardo)* of all churches, from whose ruling no one may dissent. It therefore gives authority to the canons without subjecting itself to them."[35] This conception, that the Church issues from Rome, as its head and source, could be found in germ in Leo the Great, but its translation into practice and law was a major break with previous church tradition. The idea itself is historically indefensible: the Mother church was Jerusalem, not Rome, and there is no indication in Acts that Peter was the source of authority for other apostles. The idea that Rome has not just a primacy, but absolute jurisdiction over other churches, including the ancient apostolic churches of the East, was also new, and became a major stumbling block—a *skandalon*—in relations with the East.

Many of these ideas of the reformers found their way into Gratian's *Decretum,* which, along with genuine papal decretals (papal rulings on specific questions) and conciliar canons, incorporated also

[33] Aristeides Papadakis, *The Christian East and the Rise of the Papacy* (Crestwood, N.Y.: St. Vladimir's Seminary Press, 1994) 47; Francis Oakley, *Council Over Pope* (New York: Herder and Herder, 1969) 81.

[34] See Congar, *L'Église,* 62–63; Congar, *L'Ecclésiologie du Haut Moyen-Age* (Paris, Cerf, 1968) 226–232; Morris, *The Papal Monarchy,* 207.

[35] Cited in Morris, *The Papal Monarchy,* 207–208.

the texts of the false decretals. The *Decretum* became the basis for the development of canon law after c. 1140. And, although Gratian preserved ancient texts which did not support papal monarchy, many monarchial principles were also incorporated into the *Decretum.* Among these were: that the pope could legislate for the whole Church; the pope was the supreme judge, who could be judged by no one; the pope was the head of the whole Church, and that other bishops were executors of the pope's power.[36] Congar writes "In the West, the popes from the time of Alexander III considered the council as an orchestration of their decision (the Council of 1179: the pope is the legislator *'sacri concilii approbatione')."*[37] Many later popes, such as Innocent III and Innocent IV, were trained as canon lawyers, and imbibed their ideas of papal monarchy from the study of Gratian and his commentators, whose ideas also influenced Aquinas' conception of papal monarchy.

By the reign of Pope Innocent III (1198–1215), the title Vicar of Christ had been reserved to the pope alone, whereas earlier it had been used for both kings and bishops. The notion was that the pope alone represented Christ, whereas the other bishops were simply vicars of the apostles.[38] The ancient more modest idea that the pope was the vicar of Peter was displaced: according to Innocent the popes were not "the vicars of some apostle or of some man but the vicars of Christ Jesus himself . . . truly vicar[s] of the true God."[39] The pope alone, in this view, possessed the "plenitude of power" *(plenitudo potestatis);* bishops and kings did not, and could be deposed by the pope. Innocent viewed the pope as above the Church and even above the law, *supra jus,*[40] and went so far as to say that the pope "stands midway between God and man . . . less than God but more than man"; the pope was the "Vicar of God."[41] Innocent, however, did not explicitly claim authority over secular rulers. But his successors, Innocent IV

[36] On Gratian and his influence, see Brian Tierney, *Foundations of the Conciliar Theory* (Cambridge: Harvard University Press, 1955) 23–84.

[37] "La collégialité de l'épiscopat et la Primauté de l'évêque de Rome dans l'Histoire," in *Angelicum,* vol. 47 (October–December 1970) 412.

[38] Morris, *The Papal Monarchy,* 206.

[39] *PL* 214, 292A; cited in J.-M. R. Tillard, *Church of Churches,* 263.

[40] Tierney, *Foundations of the Conciliar Theory,* 147.

[41] Cited in Tillard, *The Bishop of Rome,* 59, and Patrick Granfield, *The Limits of the Papacy,* 35.

(1243–1254) and Boniface VIII (1294–1303), did. Innocent IV asserted that he possessed power over temporal rulers and even over infidels,[42] and that "*De jure* the Pope possessed all the powers of Christ on earth."[43] The famous Bull *Unam Sanctam* (1302), issued by Boniface VIII as a result of his struggle with King Philip of France, asserted that both spiritual power and temporal power were controlled by the Church, which delegated temporal power to kings and emperors, who derived their authority not directly from God, but from the pope. The Church itself, according to Boniface, had as its head Christ, and Christ's vicar, the pope. Whoever was not in communion with the pope, was not in the Church: "If therefore the Greeks and others say that they were not committed to Peter and his successors, they necessarily confess that they are not of the sheep of Christ" (*DS* 872). Boniface goes on to say: "We declare, state, define, and pronounce that it is altogether necessary to human salvation for every human creature to be subject to the Roman pontiff" (*DS* 875).[44]

As Otto Gierke has argued, in his classic study of medieval political theory, the controlling idea behind the papal monarchy was the idea of unity.[45] God is one, Christ is one, and his Church is one. As there is one ruler in heaven, so there must be one ruler, Christ's vicar, on earth. Underlying this ideology is the notion that just as the whole Church derives from its head, Christ, the visible Church on earth derives from Christ's vicar, the pope. Therefore, whoever has separated from obedience to the pope (the supreme legislator), is not in the Church. Kings and emperors had claimed that their power was directly from God, and so independent of papal power. But, as Boniface put it, this would create a monster, a body with two heads (*DS* 872). Rather, the spiritual authority was higher than the temporal, which was therefore subject to the spiritual authority, which derived from God, and could be judged only by God, not by man (*DS* 873). Like heaven, where all the angels and saints obeyed the will of God, there should also be no division in the Church, ruled by Christ's vicar. It followed that heretics were criminals who broke the perfect unity of the Body of Christ. During the high and late Middle Ages many heretical

[42] Tierney, *Foundations of the Conciliar Theory,* 147.

[43] Ibid., 88.

[44] ET in *Church and State through the Centuries,* 91, 92.

[45] *Political Theories of the Middle Ages,* Frederic W. Maitland, trans. (Cambridge: Cambridge University Press, 1900, reprint: Boston: Beacon Press, 1958) 1–37.

groups—the Cathari, the Waldensians, and others—proliferated throughout Europe.[46] At first the popes sought to control them by sending missionaries, such as the Dominicans, to convert them. But this failing, the Church turned to the use of systematic persecution, embodied in the Inquisition. From 1184, bishops were directed by the popes to seek out heretics in their dioceses, and prosecute them without waiting for formal accusation. The Fourth Lateran Council (1215) made this the law of the universal Church.[47]

The extreme assertion of papal authority is the result of the papacy assuming the monarchial or imperial theology that derived from the emperors of the East. This was passed on to the West through Charlemagne, and appropriated by the popes in their struggle to regain control over the Church from secular lords. In this struggle they were largely successful. But in the process, the patristic principle that the authority of the emperor was balanced by the authority of the bishops and patriarchs, was largely lost. The popes attempted to combine in their persons the authority of both emperor and patriarch. Indeed, Greek ambassadors visiting Monte Cassino in 1137 declared to their hosts that the Roman bishop was acting like an emperor, not like a bishop.[48] Councils continued to be held in the West, but they were controlled by the popes.

Yves Congar sees in the Gregorian reform "the greatest turning which Catholic ecclesiology has known."[49] Ecclesiology moved from the ancient, conciliar mode, in which the pope, as vicar of Peter, had a primacy among the bishops, to an imperial mode, in which the whole Church derives from the pope, as its head, who alone represents Christ on earth, who is "king" (while other bishops are "people," that is to say, subjects), and who has not only primacy, but jurisdiction over all other churches.[50] The ancient idea that the unity of the body of Christ was to be found in the principle of consensus—which all ancient councils sought, though not always achieved—was replaced with the idea that the unity of the body of Christ is based on monarchial papal authority and absolute obedience. This idea was to be carried on by subsequent popes down to modern times.

[46] Hans Wolter, "Heresy and Inquisition in the Thirteenth Century," in *HCH:IV*, 208–216.

[47] Ibid., 211.

[48] Hussey, *The Orthodox Church in the Byzantine Empire*, 181.

[49] *L'Église*, 103.

[50] Ibid., 96.

And yet it must be noted that medieval popes were only partially successful in imposing a papal monarchy on the Church. In practice, lay lords, kings, and the emperor retained considerable ecclesial authority over certain regions, such as France and England. Furthermore, it was recognized in canon law that a heretical pope can be deposed, as could a pope whose election was judged illegitimate.[51] What medieval popes and theologians did succeed in creating was an *ideology* of a papal monarchy, in which the source of ecclesial unity was understood as obedience to one's superiors and especially to the pope. This ideology reached its culmination at and after Vatican Council I.

These criticisms, however, should not blind us to the legitimate achievements of the medieval papacy. The reforming popes did to a large extent regain control of the Church from lay lords and kings, who had reduced both bishops and popes to pawns in feudal politics. But in this process, the reformers went too far, and adopted imperial claims that exceeded even those of Christian emperors (whose power was limited by the bishops), and ignored the ancient principles of consensus and conciliarity, which nevertheless resurfaced in the conciliar movement. Such autocratic papal claims were to be a major factor in the Eastern schism and the Protestant separation.

The Eastern Schism

The schism between the Eastern and Western Churches is usually dated to 1054, but this is an oversimplification.[52] Tensions and misunderstandings, partly due to language differences, had been building between Latins and Greeks for centuries. Temporary schisms had occurred before. The insertion of the term *filioque* ("and the Son,") into the Western Creed to describe the procession of the Spirit ("from the Father *and the Son*") beginning from the seventh century, became a major cause of division. But the principal cause was probably the development of

[51] See Hans Küng, *Structures of the Church* (New York: Thomas A. Nelson & Sons, 1964) 249–268.

[52] For accounts, see Steven Runciman, *The Eastern Schism* (Oxford: Clarendon, 1955); Papadakis, *The Christian East and the Rise of the Papacy,* passim; and J.M. Hussey, *The Orthodox Church in the Byzantine Empire,* 69–101, 124–286. For a shorter account, see Francis Dvornik, "The Eastern Schism," *NCE* 5:21-25, or *The Church in the Age of Feudalism,* ed. by Friedrich Kempf et al. (New York: Herder & Herder, 1969) 409–425.

papal claims to absolute jurisdiction over all other bishops, including the Eastern patriarch. This claim was repeatedly made by the Gregorian reformers and subsequent popes. Byzantinist Aristeides Papadakis writes:

> But the decisive change in the Roman church was the unprecedented transformation of its legitimate primacy into monarchy. The theoreticians of the Gregorian movement were to devise a new ecclesiological model in which Rome was conceived legalistically and juridically as the head and mother of the Churches . . . Indeed, the autocratic basis of the new ecclesiology, in contrast with Eastern Christendom's traditional collegial and synodal structure, left little room for accommodation or compromise. The shrill demand of the Roman Church for submission was to become an invariable feature governing its relations with Byzantium . . . Historically, the mounting hostility which gives the period 1071–1453 a certain recognizable unity . . . has its origins in the eleventh century, in the highly centralized papacy and its novel claims.[53]

It is important to recognize that the Eastern Christians before and after 1054 acknowledged the primacy among bishops of the pope, based not so much on his being the successor of Peter as on Old Rome's status as the seat of the empire. What they denied was a universal jurisdiction of the pope over other bishops, except in the region traditionally given to the Roman patriarch.[54] The incident of 1054, in which Cardinal Humbert, a papal envoy, laid a Bull of excommunication on the high altar of Hagia Sophia, and the Greeks responded by excommunicating the papal envoys, was due to disagreements over the *filioque* and minor matters of liturgical usage. (Humbert, with an appalling ignorance of history, actually accused the Greeks of removing the *filioque* from the Creed.) Yet attempts at *rapprochement* continued after 1054. What really cemented the schism was the sacking and looting of Constantinople—including the burning of libraries and desecration of churches—by the Franks and Venetians during the fourth crusade (1204). Subsequently, Innocent III imposed a Latin patriarch on the city.

[53] Ibid., 14–15.

[54] See John Meyendorff, "St. Peter in Byzantine Theology," and Alexander Schmemann, "The Idea of Primacy in Orthodox Ecclesiology," in *The Primacy of Peter,* ed. by J. Meyendorff et al. (Leighton Buzzard, Bedfordshire: The Faith Press, 1963) 7–56.

To the Greeks, this act indicated that Innocent saw the patriarch of Constantinople as no more than a junior bishop, subject to the pope. In the opinion of Francis Dvornik, the noted Catholic Byzantinist: "The appointment of a Latin patriarch in Constantinople was regarded by the Greeks as the culmination of the schism."[55] Steven Runciman, the distinguished British historian, agrees:

> But when the papal demands were backed by the aggressive public opinion of the West insisting on the subjection of the East, and when the public opinion in the Orthodox East, remembering the Crusades and the Latin Empire, saw in papal supremacy a savage form of alien domination, then no amount of compromise over the Procession of the Holy Spirit or the bread of the sacrament would be of avail. The East had no wish to submit to the West and the West would accept nothing less than submission.[56]

Donald M. Nicol has recorded the Greek complaint, culled from dozens of almost inaccessible medieval documents. An interesting exchange of letters took place between Innocent III and the patriarch of Constantinople, John Kamateros, in 1199–1200. "'Where in the Gospels' asks the patriarch 'does Christ say that the church of the Romans is the head and mother of all the churches?'" He argues that the true head of the Church is Christ, that the church is governed by the pentarchy of bishops, among whom the pope has a primacy of honor, that there is a strong case for counting the Jerusalem church first in time and rank, and Antioch second, and that in Orthodoxy, each church possesses the fullness of grace and catholicity, and that no church can monopolize the title "catholic" for the whole.[57] As Nicol notes, the whole issue of papal jurisdiction came to be called by the Greeks the "papal scandal," referring to Matthew 16:23, where Jesus says to Peter, "you are a *skandalon,*" a stumbling block. Thus in the case

[55] *NCE* 5:25. In fact, however, Innocent was under pressure by the conquering Venetians, who had elected their own patriarch and had attempted to install him as the patriarch of the city. Innocent responded by insisting that he be allowed to appoint the patriarch. But both Steven Runciman (*The Eastern Schism* [Oxford: Clarendon, 1955] 154–156) and Donald Nicol note that even requests by the Greek citizens of Constantinople to elect their own patriarch were ignored by Innocent. ("The Papal Scandal," in *The Orthodox Churches and the West* [Oxford: Basil Blackwell, 1976] 148–149.

[56] Runciman, *The Eastern Schism,* 168.

[57] Nicol, "The Papal Scandal," 146–147.

of the Eastern schism, the vicar of Peter, rather than being a rock of unity for the Church, became a rock of scandal and stumbling. And this happened because of excessive papal claims to power, and the reduction of the Church to a command hierarchy, rather than a participatory hierarchy (the conquered Byzantines were allowed virtually no participation, not even being allowed to elect their own patriarch).

Later efforts to heal the schism took place, especially at the Councils of Lyons (1274) and Florence (1439). The Byzantine emperor, Michael VIII, anxious to secure unity with the West, in 1266 had proposed an ecumenical council to settle the differences between the Eastern and Western Churches. But Pope Clement IV (1264–1268) had rejected this request, arguing that Roman doctrine was "pure" and that "the purity of the true faith" could not be doubted.[58] Nonetheless, the Byzantines attended the Second Council of Lyons. However, there was no discussion of positions; the Byzantines merely read prepared statements of submission to Rome. This politically motivated submission was later rejected by the patriarch and people of Constantinople. The failure of this attempt at union was that there was no discussion and no equality among participants, indeed, no real participation by the Greeks at all. Instead, as Papadakis notes: the papal demand that "made all patriarchal rights and privileges stem from Rome was to be swallowed whole."[59] A century and a half later, with the Byzantine Empire in desperate straits, Western and Eastern bishops as well as the pope and the Eastern emperor agreed to a formula of union at the Council of Florence (1439). But this formula was not accepted in the East, largely because of the hostility of the populace in Constantinople, who remembered all too well Frankish cruelties during the Fourth Crusade.[60] Another reason appears to be that the Roman delegates to the council insisted on a strong statement of papal authority, which proved unacceptable to some of the Greek delegates.

The Eastern schism was a tragedy for both the Eastern and Western Church. The West lost contact with Eastern churches whose claim to apostolic foundation was as ancient as that of Rome, so that Rome remained the only apostolic see in the West. This meant that the imperial claims of the Roman Church were unchecked by the claims of

[58] Hussey, *The Orthodox Church*, 233.

[59] Papadakis, *The Christian East*, 222.

[60] See Hussey, *The Orthodox Church*, 267–286.

other churches, and the ancient tradition of episcopal conciliarism was minimized in the West, which gradually moved towards a papal absolutism unlike the church government of either the New Testament churches or the patristic church. The East, on the other hand, lost the support of the West, which might have saved it from the Turkish conquest of 1453. It also lost living contact with the primacy of the bishop of Rome, a primacy which it never ceased to recognize, and which could have been vital in preserving it from disintegration. After the death of the emperor, fighting on the walls of Constantinople in May, 1453, there was no effective unifying center in the East, with the consequence that the Eastern Orthodox churches gradually became national and nationalistic churches. The weakness of this system can be seen in the recent Bosnian wars, when the Serbian Orthodox Church never addressed any criticism against Serbian military practices, which in many instances were genocidal.

There are numerous reasons for the Eastern schism, but most commentators consider the monarchic papacy to have been a major factor in the schism, and an obstacle which continues to this day. This supports one of the themes of this book, which is that a command hierarchy provokes opposition and schism rather than a true unity. The Eastern schism is a cardinal example of this.

Ontological and Ecclesial Hierarchy

The late antique and medieval periods elaborated a complex hierarchy of being drawing from the works of St. Augustine and Pseudo-Dionysius, both of whom were strongly influenced by Neoplatonism.[61] In its developed, medieval form, this conception of ontological hierarchy paralleled and legitimized the monarchial understanding of the papacy. I will consider here four key thinkers: Augustine, Pseudo-Dionysius, Bonaventure, and Aquinas.

Following Plato, the Neoplatonists developed an ontology in which the fullness of reality, goodness, unity, and beauty were located in the transcendent, changeless, One, from which emanated Mind and

[61] The classic study of this is Arthur Lovejoy, *The Great Chain of Being* (Cambridge: Harvard University Press, 1936, 1964); see also C.A. Patrides "Hierarchy and Order," *Dictionary of the History of Ideas*, ed. by Philip Wiener vol. II (New York: Charles Scribner's Sons, 1973) 434–449.

the World Soul, and thence all lower levels of being in a descending hierarchy. This is expressed in a famous passage by Macrobius, in the fifth century:

> Since, from the Supreme God Mind arises, and from Mind, Soul, and since this in turn creates all subsequent things and fills them all with life, and since this single radiance illumines all and is reflected in each, as a single face might be reflected in many mirrors placed in a series; and since all things follow in continuous succession, degenerating in sequence to the very bottom of the series, the attentive observer will discover a connection of parts, from the Supreme God down to the last dregs of things, mutually linked together and without a break.[62]

What is significant in this ontology is that all unity, goodness, power, and reality flows from the top of the chain of being down. Lower beings exemplify or reflect some of the fullness of being, the One, but in themselves contribute nothing to it; rather their function is primarily symbolic: in reflecting the transcendent One from which they emanated, they point back to their source.

The intent of Neoplatonic spirituality was to achieve detachment from earthly things, which were fragmented, transitory, perishing, and disappointing, and by degrees ascend in contemplation to the vision of the One, whose changeless unity, light, beauty, and perfection brought fulfillment and peace. This method of ascent is found in Plotinus and in Augustine, who expressed it in a famous passage in his *Confessions:*

> And so step by step I ascended from bodies to the soul . . . and from there to its inward force . . . From there again I ascended to the power of reasoning . . . This power, which in myself I found to be mutable . . . withdrew itself from the contradictory swarms of imaginative fantasies, so as to discover the light by which it was flooded. At that point it had no hesitation in declaring that the unchangeable is preferable to the changeable . . . So in the flash of a trembling glance it attained to that which is.[63]

For Augustine, the things of the external world are interesting not so much in themselves, but as tokens and symbols of God: "Wherever

[62] *Comment. in Somnium Scipionis,* I, 14, 15; translation from Lovejoy, *The Great Chain of Being,* 63.

[63] *Confessions,* VII, 17; Henry Chadwick, trans. (Oxford: Oxford University Press, 1992) 127.

you turn you encounter the footprints of God made upon his work. It is by them that God speaks to you, and if you lean to the exterior, God uses the very forms of these exterior things to bring you back within."[64] The aim of life is to be free from the distraction of things without—being lost in multiplicity—as Augustine puts it, and to come to know the Truth within. Again, a famous passage from the *Confessions* proclaims this: "[I gathered] myself together from the scattered fragments into which I was broken and dissipated during all that time when, being turned away from you, the One, I lost myself in the distractions of the Many."[65]

Central to Neoplatonism is the idea that the multiplicity and fragmentation characteristic of lower levels of being are unified in higher levels of being, and fully unified in the One, the highest level of being. Participation in the One brings unity; alienation from the One brings fragmentation. This lent a strong otherworldly cast to Neoplatonism: Plotinus, it was said, "blushed to think that he had a body." In Christianity the unity of the One was modified by the idea of the Trinity, and Neoplatonic otherworldliness was modified by the Incarnation: God, in becoming human, also sanctified the physical world. Nonetheless, the Neoplatonic emphasis on unity through hierarchy and ontological ascent greatly influenced Augustine and Pseudo-Dionysius, and through them Bonaventure, Aquinas, and other medieval thinkers, and carried into the Renaissance, only to be lost during the Reformation and Enlightenment, when attention shifted from transcendent unity towards individuality and separateness.

Pseudo-Dionysius (hereafter Dionysius) was probably a sixth-century Syrian monk, who wrote under the name of Dionysius the Elder, whom medievals took to be Dionysius the Areopagite, a companion and disciple of Paul.[66] In his work the hierarchical system so prominent in medieval thought is fully articulated. At the top of the hierarchy of being is the One, which is ineffable, beyond all predicates and categories of being, but which nevertheless is known by many

[64] *De Libero Arbitrio,* XVI, 41; ET in M.C. D'Arcy, S.J., "The Philosophy of St. Augustine," in idem.: *St. Augustine: His Age, Life, and Thought* (New York: Meridian, 1957) 166.

[65] *Confessions,* II, 1, ET by Rex Warner (New York: New American Library, 1963) 40.

[66] See "The Odyssey of Dionysian Spirituality," by Jaroslav Pelikan, in *Pseudo-Dionysius: the Complete Works* (New York: Paulist Press, Classics of Western Spirituality, 1987) 11–24.

names. The author discusses, but minimizes, the triune nature of the One (God): "In the divine realm unities hold a higher place than differentiations."[67] The One communicates with all lesser beings through an elaborate hierarchy of angels: the celestial hierarchy. Dionysius was the first, in fact, to coin the term "hierarchy" defined as "a sacred order, a state of understanding and an activity approximating as closely as possible to the divine."[68] Higher beings in the hierarchy are more like God, lower beings less; higher beings have all the powers of those below them, but additional powers besides. The goal of this hierarchy "is to enable beings to be as like as possible to God and to be at one with him . . . the task of every hierarchy is to receive and to pass on undiluted purification, the divine light, and the understanding which brings perfection."[69] God, the One, is utterly dissimilar to humans, and so can be approached only through hierarchal mediators: Jesus and the angels in heaven, and ecclesiastical superiors on earth. Higher echelons of the hierarchy mediate God, light, and being to lower echelons: "each being is somehow superior to the one to whom he passes on the divine light . . . it is this latter order [of angels] which mediates the divine enlightenment to all other beings, including ourselves . . . secondary beings share in these holy properties through the mediation of the primary beings."[70] In this scheme the supreme hierarch is Jesus, "who is the transcendent mind, utterly divine mind, who is the source and the being underlying all hierarchy . . . who is the ultimate divine power."[71] He is the source of perfection and deification in all lower human hierarchs (this extremely high christology, and commensurate deemphasis on the human Jesus, is characteristic of Neoplatonism).

In Dionysius' view, the celestial hierarchy of Jesus and the angels is paralleled by the ecclesiastical hierarchy on earth, which brings initiates to perfection through the mediation of the sacraments. "The holy sacraments bring about purification, illumination, and perfection. The deacons form the order which purifies. The priests constitute the order which gives illumination. And the hierarchs . . . make up the order which perfects."[72] As in the celestial hierarchy, divine enlightenment is

[67] *Pseudo-Dionysius*, 67.
[68] Ibid., 153.
[69] Ibid., 154, 162.
[70] Ibid., 178, 179.
[71] Ibid., 195–196.
[72] Ibid., 248.

mediated to inferiors through their superiors in the ecclesiastical hierarchy. It would seem that the hierarchs, the order who perfect, would be the bishops, since they have the power of consecrating priests; but Dionysius also claims that "The order of those made perfect is that of the monks who live a single-minded life."[73]

Dionysius' theology is strongly Neoplatonic and Monarchic. God is the "One" of the Neoplatonic hierarchy, and Dionysius minimizes any relationality or differentiation within the One. Jesus, the Mind of God, is like the Mind emanated from the One; he derives his being and light from the Father above, and passes it on to those below. The pseudo-Areopagite scarcely ever speaks of the Spirit and never in the biblical sense that the Spirit "moves where it will" and may inspire prophets and people outside the ecclesiastical hierarchy. Rather, all spiritual authority is mediated in a vertical chain through the celestial and ecclesiastical hierarchy. This seems to be a vision much influenced by monasticism, for in both the Pachomian and Benedictine monastic systems the abbot was the representative of Christ to the monks, and the supreme spiritual authority.

The hierarchical ontology of Dionysius had extensive influence in the Middle Ages, especially among the monks and friars. Together with the work of Augustine, it formed the basis for the medieval emphasis on ascent from created things to the mystical vision of the uncreated light, which found expression in the Gothic cathedrals, and in works such as Bonaventure's *Journey of the Mind to God.* His notion that divine enlightenment and grace is mediated to lower members of a hierarchical order through higher members became crucially important in medieval ecclesiology. Thomas Aquinas, who quotes Dionysius some seventeen hundred times, argued that the bishops derived their jurisdictional (though not their sacramental) authority *through the pope,* their ecclesiastical superior, not directly from Christ, as the patristic Church thought and Vatican II reaffirmed.[74] This, indeed, was the prevailing opinion in the thirteenth century. Jean Leclerq notes that Dionysius' ideas were used in the Middle Ages to justify papal theocracy, and as well became keys to interpreting canon law.[75] Boniface VIII, in *Unam Sanctam,* argues that the temporal power is subject to the

[73] Ibid.

[74] Avery Dulles: *A Church to Believe In* (New York: Crossroad, 1982) 149–169.

[75] "Influence and Noninfluence of Dionysius in the Western Middle Ages," in *Pseudo-Dionysius: The Complete Works*, 31.

spiritual power because, according to Dionysius, the divine law is that inferiors are subjected to superiors through intermediaries.[76]

Dionysius' work was influential on St. Bonaventure and St. Thomas, both of whom defended papal theocracy. According to Bonaventure, the Church derives its life of grace only through Christ, and in its canonical and social order, from the pope, Christ's vicar on earth. Following Innocent III, he held that Peter had received the plenitude of power from Christ, and the other apostles only a portion of that power *(in partem sollicitudinis)*.[77] Aquinas, following Dionysius (but also Aristotle) elaborated a hierarchical ontology, which was reflected in his ecclesiology.

Aquinas sees all species, from simple elements to angels, arrayed in a hierarchy of being. Higher creatures contain all the powers that lower creatures do, but more besides. Thus plants have the power of nutrition, animals have this plus the power of sensation, humans have these, plus the power of intellection. Even higher than humans are the angels (each of whom is its own species). All species then are arranged hierarchically according to degrees of perfection and of being (*ST* I, q. 47, a. 2).

The purpose of this arrangement is to manifest the goodness of God. Goodness, which in God is unified, in lower levels of being can only be expressed through a multiplicity of creatures. Thomas argues that a universe which contains many diverse grades of beings more perfectly expresses God's goodness than a universe which contains only one grade of being (*ST* I, q. 47, a. 1). Thus a universe with angels, humans, animals, plants, and minerals is better than a universe made up only of angels. Creatures, in their being and their activity, express aspects of God's being and goodness, and contribute to the final good and order of the universe—the expression of God's goodness.

An important part of the order of the universe for Aquinas is the Dionysian idea that lower creatures are ordered to God through the mediation of higher creatures.[78] The highest earthly creature is humanity, whose fulfillment is the vision of God, in which end the whole corporeal creation is also fulfilled. Thus Thomas can say that "In a certain sense . . . the whole of the corporeal creation exists for man, inas-

[76] Congar, *L'Eglise*, 229–230.

[77] Ibid., 222–223.

[78] On the order of the universe in Aquinas, see John H. Wright, S.J., *The Order of the Universe in the Theology of St. Thomas Aquinas* (Rome: Gregorian University, 1957) passim.

much as he is a rational animal."[79] Thomas uses the example of an army, in which the actions of all the subordinate units are directed to the goal of victory, which is the end intended by the commander.[80] In the same way the activities of corporeal beings are directed to the goodness of God, but mediated through the activities of higher beings. In this scheme, then, the good of lower beings, to a large extent, comes to them through the agency of beings higher in the hierarchy. Disorder in the universe comes about if lower creatures are not submitted to higher: thus human rebellion against God is the major cause of evil. The state of original justice (the unfallen state of humanity) was a state of perfect order: "this rectitude consisted in his [humanity's] reason being subject to God, the lower powers to reason, and the body to the soul; the first subjection was the cause of both the second and the third."[81] The perfection of the universe, then, consists in creatures submitted to the proper hierarchy, and acting towards the ends given them by God, and so expressing God's goodness.

Now this view of hierarchy is to a large extent based on participation. All beings except God (whose essence *[essentia]* is "To Be" *[esse]*) have their being and goodness by participation in God's being and goodness: "all beings apart from God are not their own being, but are beings by participation. Therefore it must be that all things which are diversified by the diverse participation of being, so as to be more or less perfect, are caused by one First Being, Who possesses being most perfectly."[82] Human beings are unique because they can participate in the very light of God, the Holy Spirit, and so come to a share in God's own life, which is beatitude. To make this possible is the mission of the Church. Thus Aquinas' hierarchy is a participatory hierarchy, which points upwards, like a Gothic cathedral, to participation in the divine unity and life. But it is, so to speak, a vertical participation. As with Dionysius, all being and goodness comes from above, mediated to lower creatures by those higher in the hierarchy. Creatures, however, contribute nothing to God, who is unchanging and does not empathize with the suffering of creatures (something like the One of Plotinus or Aristotle's Unmoved Mover).

[79] *Compendium of Theology*, 148, Cyril Vollert, S.J., trans., ET *Light of Faith* (Manchester, N.H.: Sophia Institute Press, 1994) 167.

[80] *Compendium of Theology*, 103; ibid., 113–114; *SCG* I, 78, 4.

[81] *ST* 1, q. 95, a. 1.

[82] *ST* 1, q. 44, 1. ET by the Dominican Fathers vol. 1 (New York: Benziger, 1947) 229.

Aquinas' idea of ontological hierarchy will be discussed further in chapter 10. Here I note three critiques. First, Norris Clarke argues that Thomas' treatment of being focuses heavily on being as substance, but does not adequately treat the complementary theme of being as relationality.[83] Aquinas does develop relationality in his explanation of the Trinity, but in his treatment of creatures he focuses so strongly on the idea of being as substance—the "in itself" aspect of being—that he fails to fully explore the relation of beings, including persons, to one another—the "for others" aspect of being, which might be called the horizontal element in participation. These aspects of being are complementary. Clarke therefore proposes a "creative completion" of Aquinas' thought in this area.

A second area of incompletion lies in Aquinas' view of the relation of parts to wholes.[84] Aquinas argued that in any entity it was the substantial form that conferred specific identity and intelligibility; matter merely served to individuate one individual of a species from another. Thus it is the form "dogness" which makes a dog a dog; the matter of any particular dog's body only individuates the dog, making it *this* dog, not *that* dog. And what is known by the intellect is the form of the dog, not the individual dog. Further, Aquinas argued (against most of his contemporaries) that there was only one substantial form in a given entity; all subsidiary forms were merged into the single substantial form which determined the character of the whole. Thus, to take the example of a dog, there would be no separate substantial forms in the dog, such as "water" or "bone" or "hemoglobin"; these exist, as Thomas says, only "virtually." The effect of all this is that the nature of any entity is entirely determined by its substantial form, not by the parts of which it is composed. (In this Thomas' thought is the exact reverse of modern science, which seeks to understand complex wholes by analyzing their constituent parts.) The parts, in effect, and even the matter, have very little influence on the nature of the whole; indeed, in an organism, the parts cease to exist as substantial entities in their own right; their form, and hence their substantial identity, is swallowed up

[83] See Norris Clarke, S.J., "To Be Is to Be Substance in Relation," in *Explorations in Metaphysics* (Notre Dame, Ind.: Notre Dame Press, 1944) 102–122; also *Person and Being* (Milwaukee: Marquette University Press, 1993) 1–24.

[84] For a detailed discussion of the following argument, see my article, "Aquinas' Concept of Substantial Form and Modern Science," *International Philosophical Quarterly* (Fall, 1996).

by the whole of which they are a part. This, I maintain, represents an incompletion in Thomas' thought. Modern research has made it very clear that parts, for example, water or hemoglobin molecules, or genes, do retain their substantial identity within an organism, though their activity is modified by the whole in which they are included. Wholes influence parts, as Aquinas held, but parts also influence wholes, a point he developed insufficiently. This affects Thomas' ontology and his ecclesiology, biasing them towards monarchy: higher beings affect lower, but lower do not commensurately affect the higher.

A third criticism comes from the Orthodox. They argue that the addition of the *filioque* to the creed distorted the balance of the Trinity.[85] The Western belief that the Spirit proceeds from the Father *and the Son (filioque)* has two results. First, it tends to subordinate the Holy Spirit to the Son, Christ. Second, the unity of God cannot be grounded in the *arche* (source) of the Father who, (according to the Orthodox) is alone the source of both the Son and the Spirit, therefore the unity is located by Western thinkers in a unity of essence or substance. And this results in an overemphasis on the unity of God, at the expense of God's triplicity, and especially at the expense of the independent action of the Spirit. This in turn affects Western ecclesiology. Timothy Ware (now Orthodox Bishop Kallistos Ware) writes: "And just as in the western doctrine of God unity was stressed at the expense of diversity, so in the western conception of the church unity has triumphed over diversity, and the result has been too great a centralization and too great an emphasis on papal authority."[86] I agree with this point, and will discuss it at greater length in chapter 12.

Aquinas' ontology heavily influenced his view of the Church.[87] The Church for him is the *congregatio fidelium*, the congregation of all the faithful, who participate in the Holy Spirit, which unites and sanctifies them, bringing them into the very life of God. Thus the Holy Spirit, for Aquinas, is the soul or the heart of the Church.[88] Its grace is

[85] My account here comes from Timothy Ware, *The Orthodox Church* (New York: Penguin, 1963, 1980) 218–223.

[86] Ibid., 223.

[87] Aquinas did not write any separate text on the Church; his ecclesiology is scattered throughout the whole of his work. See Avery Dulles, "The Church according to Thomas Aquinas," chap. 10 in *A Church to Believe In*, 149–169; Yves Congar, "The Idea of the Church in Thomas Aquinas," chap. III in *The Mystery of the Church* (Baltimore: Helicon Press, 1960) 97–117; idem, *L'Église*, 232–241.

[88] *ST* II, II, q. 183, a. 3, ad 3.; Dulles, *A Church to Believe In*, 153–154.

the New Law, the law of love: "The New Law consists principally in the grace of the Holy Spirit, given to Christians."[89] The unity of the Church is primarily through the Spirit, which is interior. But Aquinas also argues that the Spirit comes to the Church through its head, Christ, and that just as there is one head of the Church in heaven, Christ, so there must be one head on earth, the pope (*SCG* 4:76). Institutional unity in the Church thus comes from submission to the pope and schism is caused by separation from the pope (*ST* 2-2, 39, 1). The bishops derive their jurisdictional authority from the pope, not from Christ. The whole unity of the Church, then, consists in submission of inferiors to superiors. Aquinas does not develop the idea of a horizontal interrelationship among the bishops, or consider that unity might come from the consensus of the bishops; indeed, he has no notion of collegiality among the bishops.[90] Since parts exist for the welfare of the whole, Aquinas concludes that individual citizens are subordinate to the community of which they are a part, and heretics ought to be executed for the good of the whole Church (*ST* 2-2, 11, 3). Since the whole determines the nature of the parts (not vice versa), Aquinas sees the Church deriving from Christ through his vicar the pope, rather than being built up from the communion of local churches (the patristic view). The local church is then an arm of the universal Church, rather than a semi-autonomous holon. In this, Aquinas was simply repeating what his scholastic contemporaries, St. Albert, St. Bonaventure, and others, held.

One can see here that the limitations of Aquinas' ontology affect his ecclesiology. His emphasis is on what constitutes the essence and substance of the church; the aspect of relationality is comparatively underdeveloped. There is little room for parts influencing wholes in Aquinas' ontology; similarly, there is little allowance for the universal Church being built up of local and particular churches, or for lower members in the ecclesial hierarchy to teach or influence higher clerical members. Finally, his ecclesiology is Christocentric, and open to the criticism of the Orthodox, given above.

And yet Aquinas' ecclesiology, like his ontology, emphasizes participation in and sanctification by the Spirit, which comes through the sacraments. Congar sees his treatise on the "new law" of the gospel as

[89] *ST* I, II, q. 106, a. 1; ET from Dulles, *A Church to Believe In*, 154–155.
[90] Congar, *L'Église*, 237.

profoundly ecumenical, it is "the most extraordinary charter of evangelical theology."[91] Here, Aquinas is at his most insightful. But because of the influence of Dionysius, Gratian, and his contemporaries, he understood the jurisdictional authority of the Church as flowing from Christ through the pope to the bishops, thus providing the source of institutional unity. One cannot help thinking that these two aspects of Aquinas' thought are in tension. Orthodox Christians, after all, participated in the Spirit through the sacraments, but were separated from the pope, hence were, in Aquinas' view, schismatics, who ought to be cut off from the Spirit. Aquinas' insight that the unity of the Church is drawn from the indwelling of the Spirit was also that of the patristic church, which drew from it the conclusion that the Spirit, operating variously through local congregations and bishops, could only be fully discerned in the consensus of a whole council. But Aquinas does not draw this conclusion, though his metaphysical system would have allowed it. It was Aquinas' papalism—the area in which he was least original and largely reproduced the thought of his contemporaries—which tended to be emphasized by the Dominican and Jesuit orders and later theologians such as Juan de Torquemada, Cajetan, and Robert Bellarmine. They in turn stressed more than Thomas the institutional and juridical elements of the Church, with less attention to the interior sanctification of the Spirit.

Conciliarism

The papal theocracy of Gregory VII, Innocent III and IV, and Boniface VIII, was not the only stream of opinion in the high Middle Ages. Paralleling it was the belief, called conciliarism, that ultimate authority in the Church was vested in ecumenical councils, and that an ecumenical council had a higher authority than the pope.

The roots of conciliar thought go back to the commentaries on canon law which developed after Gratian. This tradition, according to medievalist Brian Tierney, contained two different theories of Church unity. The major theory was that Church unity was produced by subordination to a single head—the Vicar of Christ on earth, the pope. But a second theory treated the Church as a corporation, "a theory which

[91] "Saint Thomas and the Spirit of Ecumenism," *New Blackfriars,* 55 (1974) 196–209, cited in Dulles, *A Church to Believe In,* 167.

stressed the corporate association of the members of the Church as a principle of ecclesiastical unity, and which envisaged an exercise of corporate authority by the members of the church even in the absence of an effective head."[92] This medieval law of corporations developed out of consideration of the relation between a bishop and the body who elected him, usually the cathedral chapter. Together the bishop and elective body formed a single corporation. Canon lawyers had established that the consent of the members (the body) was necessary for any action of the head (the bishop) which affected the whole corporation. Authority was seen to reside, not just in the bishop, but in the whole corporation, head and members together, and to revert to the members if the head were absent, as in the case of an episcopal vacancy. Later such theories, applied to the whole Church, became the basis for conciliarism. Foundational to this outlook was the belief that authority did not reside in the pope alone, but in the whole Church and the pope, which together formed a corporation. In the event of a papal vacancy (or a heretical pope) authority reverted to the members of the Church, to be exercised by the cardinals (as representatives of the Church), or by a general council. Thus it was generally held in this period, even by ardent papalists like canon lawyer Huguccio, that the pope in himself was not infallible, but that it was the whole body of the faithful which was divinely preserved from error.[93] Therefore it was widely accepted that an ecumenical council could depose a heretical pope, and that appeal could be made to an ecumenical council against a heretical pope. King Philip the Fair of France did just that against Boniface VIII.

Those, like Innocent IV, who held that the *plenitudo potestatis* exercised by the pope resided in the pope alone, had to argue that this power reverted to Christ in the event of a papal vacancy (e.g., on the death of a pope). But the pope was elected by the cardinals. What would happen, the canonists asked, if the pope and the whole college of cardinals became extinct? It would seem that God could only reestablish the papacy by a divine intervention.[94] Much more reasonable was the theory that the pope, cardinals, and faithful together formed a corporation, just like the bishop and his cathedral chapter,

[92] Tierney, *Foundations of the Conciliar Theory*, 240. The following account of conciliar theory follows Tierney, ibid., 87–153.

[93] Ibid., 43.

[94] Ibid., 149–153.

and that in the event of a papal vacancy, the *plenitudo potestatis* reverted to the whole Church, which could then elect a new pope either through the cardinals, as representatives of the Church, or through an ecumenical council. All sides admitted that the pope's *plenitudo potestatis* was a divinely granted power, but moderate conciliarists argued that this power was vested, not in the pope alone, but in the whole Church. The pope, said the great canonist Franciscus Zabarella, possessed plenitude or power not alone but as the head of a corporation, formed of the pope, the cardinals, and the whole body of the faithful.[95]

This theory remained academic until the papal election of 1378, when the cardinals elected first Urban VI as pope, then, some months later, claimed that this election had been made under duress and elected another pope, Clement VII. Thus began the Great Schism. Efforts to get one or another of the popes to resign were futile, and eventually it became clear that the split could only be resolved by a general council, which would depose both popes, and elect a new pope. This of course presented a problem, for canon law since Gratian had stated that only the pope could convene an ecumenical council. An attempt to solve the schism at the Council of Pisa (1409) led to the election of a third pope. Eventually, one of the three rival popes, John XXIII (of the Pisan line), was pressured by Emperor Sigismund into convening the Council of Constance in November 1414.

This council, the greatest representative assembly of the Middle Ages, comprised of clerics and laity, bishops, abbots, princes, and doctors of theology and canon law, lasted until April, 1418.[96] It did succeed in healing the schism by deposing all three rival popes and electing a new pope, Martin V. In its fifth general session, April 6, 1415, it enacted the decree *Haec Sancta,* which began:

> This holy synod of Constance, constituting a general Council and lawfully assembled to root out the present schism and bring about the reform of the church in head and members . . . declares that, being lawfully assembled in the Holy Spirit, constituting a General Council and representing the Catholic Church militant, it holds power immediately from Christ and that anyone of whatsoever state or dignity, even the papal, is bound to obey it in matters which pertain to the

[95] Ibid., 143, 220–237.

[96] On the Council of Constance, and succeeding events, see Karl August Fink, "The Council of Constance," in *HCH:IV,* 448–488.

> faith, the rooting out of said schism, and the general reform of the church in head and members.[97]

This statement, which seems to place the authority of a council over that of the pope, is regarded as the classic statement of conciliarism.

The reform measures of the council were promulgated in 1417, the most important of which was the decree *Frequens*, which stipulated that councils should continue to meet every ten years. The reform measures of the council, however, were not carried out, and the mandate to hold councils every ten years was soon abandoned. With the papacy of Eugene IV (1431–1447), papal hegemony was regained, and the strong statement of papal absolutism issued by the Council of Florence ended the conciliar movement. In 1460 Pius II condemned those who would appeal from a papal ruling to a future council (*DS* 1375). (This, however, did not prevent Luther from appealing to an ecumenical council against Leo X in 1518 and 1520.)

The decree *Haec Sancta* was not accepted by later popes, especially Eugene IV, and so is not considered binding on the Church.[98] It is not contained in any editions of Denzinger. Some historians and theologians, such as Francis Oakley and Hans Küng, however, consider it to be a still valid decree of an ecumenical council.[99] Karl A. Fink, a German Catholic historian, writes: "From the viewpoint of the contemporary political and intellectual situation, the Council of Constance in its entirety must be regarded as ecumenical and its decrees as universally binding."[100]

The reform measures promulgated by Constance were not implemented largely due to papal resistance, especially by Pope Eugene IV. The consequence was that the Church was not reformed in head and members. Fink writes that "the failure of reform is also his [Eugene IV] responsibility, for it had become all too clear that without a council there could be no reform. From the viewpoint of church history the decisive turning from the Middle Ages to modern times occurs around the middle of the fifteenth century. Rome had prevented reform and in

[97] Tanner, vol. I, 409–410; ET from B. Tierney, "Constance, Council of," *NCE* 4:221.

[98] See the discussion of the ecumenical character of Constance in Tierney, *NCE* 4:222–223, August Franzen, "Council of Constance: Present State of the Problem," *Concilium*, 7 (September 1965) 17–37, and Oakley, *Council over Pope*, passim.

[99] Oakley, *Council over Pope*, passim; Kung, *Structures of the Church*, 268–319.

[100] In *HCH:IV*, 467–468.

return soon received the Reformation."[101] Brian Tierney concurs: "The failure of the medieval Church to achieve a juridical structure consistent with the insights of its greatest thinkers was the supreme tragedy of the later Middle Ages. The downfall of a Catholic conciliarism, rooted in sound medieval ecclesiology, made inevitable the rise of a Protestant individualism alien to the traditional conception of the Church."[102]

Conclusion

In the Middle Ages a very different conception of hierarchy emerged from that of the patristic church. In spite of the emperor's authority, and the regional authority of metropolitan bishops and patriarchs, the primary idea of church in the patristic period was that of a communion, brought about by the consensus of local churches, each under the authority of a bishop who was usually elected. Congar writes: "Collegiality was seen as deriving from the local churches. Also the general council. Concord was sought in consensus *(concertation)*, not by the union and submission to a superior unique *caput* [head], which dominated the faithful and the pastors."[103] The highest doctrinal authority was the consensus of the bishops, expressed in ecumenical councils.

But in the medieval period, a pyramidal hierarchy developed, with the Church seen as deriving from its head, Christ's vicar, the pope, who possessed the plenitude of power. Unity came from obedience to this head. This claim to monarchial authority went far beyond the primacy which had always been granted by the Eastern and North African Churches. The patristic model of hierarchy, which was largely participatory, was displaced by a model-based command. This model was an ideology, pressed by the Roman popes and the Curia; in fact, the popes were not able to exercise the absolute control they claimed. But nonetheless this ideology became dominant in the Western church after the failure of conciliarism. What are the reasons for the shift from the patristic model, and how legitimate was it?

A major reason was the split of the West from the East, and the loss of the North African Church to the Muslims. The loss of contact with

[101] Ibid., 487.

[102] "Collegiality in the Middle Ages," in *Concilium*, 7 (September, 1965) 8.

[103] *"La Collégialité de l'épiscopat . . . ,"* 413.

the East left Rome as the only apostolic see in the West, with no counterbalance to its imperial claims. A related factor was the loss of knowledge of history in the West during the early Middle Ages. Only an ignorance of ecclesial history could have allowed Gregory VII to claim that the pope alone can convene an ecumenical council, or that the Roman see had never erred, or that the first see could be judged by no one. A third factor was the ubiquity of Benedictine monasticism in the West, with its obediential authority structure. As translated into papal authority, this structure became more command centered than it was in the monasteries, which discussed major decisions with all the monks in chapter meetings. A fourth factor was the influence of Pseudo-Dionysius, who argued that divine enlightenment and power flows to inferiors through the mediation of ecclesiastical superiors. Certainly the struggle to free the Church from control by lay nobles and kings was a major factor, as were later struggles between the popes and the emperors; in the course of these struggles, the popes ended by claiming powers which exceeded that of their opponents.

Another related reason is the papal decretals, which came to be the basis of canon law. Donald Nicol remarks that "the fiercer the battle between the emperors and the popes the more ambitious grew the claims made for the papacy by the commentators on the canon law, the decretalists. There was a vicious circle in operation: the decretalists attributing ever greater power to the institution from which they sought promotion, and the papacy using the decretalists' teaching to justify its claims."[104] Again, I would note the ideology, stated in the *Dictatus Papae*, that the Roman see has never erred, nor ever can err. This, a precursor of the later belief in papal infallibility, prevented the popes from ever admitting that an earlier papal claim might be false (even if it was historically dubious), or that their opponents might have a case. This ideology, plus papal greed for power, contributed to the failure of conciliarism, and to the Protestant Reformation. Finally, there is the Orthodox claim that the Western interpolation of the *filioque* was a factor leading to an excessively monarchial view of God and of the Church. It is moot whether this was in fact a cause, or merely a symptom; what does seem to be true is that the medieval view of God tended to be monarchist, and that this was paralleled by a monarchist conception of the Church.

104 From the Introduction to Dante's *Monarchy* (London: Weidenfeld and Nicolson, 1954) x. Nicol cites as a source for this view Walter Ullman, *Medieval Papalism* (London, 1949) passim.

How legitimate was this shift in the understanding of hierarchy? In judging this, one is of course limited by one's historical perspective. Given the anarchic world of medieval feudalism, and the pressing need to save the Church from monopolization by lay lords, some centralization of power and authority was necessary. Thomas Bokenkotter, in evaluating the papal monarchy, has this to say: "In all the disorder of the times it represented a stable element and stood for ideas of order and righteousness. By its proclamation of the Truce of God and its ban on tournaments it worked against feudal lawlessness, 'while the example it presented of a spiritual monarchy uniting the nations under its dominion was the very opposite of that anarchy which unrestrained feudalism produced in temporal affairs.'"[105] Against this should be noted the role of the papal monarchy in the Eastern schism, the Inquisition, the Crusades, and the Protestant split (next chapter). Based on the scriptural evidence—the role of Peter in the New Testament—and the evidence of the first centuries of the Church, the claim to the primacy of the bishop of Rome among all the bishops is certainly justified. But the claim to monarchial jurisdiction over all the bishops and the Church is not. Peter, as portrayed in Acts, never exercises a command hierarchy over the other apostles, nor did the East ever grant the bishop of Rome universal jurisdiction. Some claims made by the medieval papacy seem to derive from forged documents (e.g., the False decretals); specifically, the claim that the first see is judged by no one, which is still in canon law (1983 code: Canon 1404), goes back to a sixth-century forgery.[106] Some of the claims—such as that the pope alone can convene an ecumenical council (1983 code: Canon 338), or that the Roman see has never erred, are historically false. The claim made by Boniface VIII in *Unam Sanctam* that all humans had to be subject to the authority of the papacy for salvation, is, if interpreted according to its apparent meaning, probably blasphemous, since it arrogates to the pope a prerogative which can only belong to Christ.

At the same time, the hierarchical ontology of the medievals was more successful, though it led to a too-monarchial image of God. The main point of this ontology, monastic in its roots, was that a person can

[105] *A Concise History of the Catholic Church,* 141–142. Bokenkotter is quoting *The Cambridge Medieval History,* vol. IV (New York: Cambridge University Press, 1936) 643.

[106] See Küng, *Structures of the Church,* 251–264.

be elevated through grace to a participation in the very life of God. This produced a flowering of mysticism, and wonderful architecture that are treasured legacies to this day. A very similar ontology developed in the East, which, following Maximus the Confessor, emphasized the *theosis* or divinization of the contemplative through participation in God.[107] Furthermore, this hierarchical ontology did not represent a break with the patristic past; it is a legitimate development of the thought of Augustine in the West, and of the fathers of the East.

However, medieval ontology had limitations. The emphasis on transcendent unity and form led to an undervaluation of the material world and the individual and to the action of the Spirit among the laity. These would be reemphasized by Ockhamism, Protestantism, by modern science, and by the Enlightenment. I will argue, however, in chapter 10 that these movements are also incomplete, since they lost the ancient and medieval insight that unity is made possible by participation in higher levels of being.

In the final analysis, the medieval period was only partly successful in integrating diversity in unity, participation, and hierarchy. Unity was favored at the expense of diversity, and command hierarchy at the expense of participation. But a unity based on command rather than on consensus or moral authority was unstable, and eventually the suppressed urge for a more participatory Church issued in the Protestant reformation.

[107] See *Maximus Confessor, Selected Writings* (New York: Paulist Press, 1985), especially the Introduction by Jaroslav Pelikan, 1–14.

Chapter 7

The Reformation

"If God spoke through an ass against a prophet [Balaam], why should he not even now be able to speak through a righteous man against the pope?"
(Martin Luther)[1]

Many changes took place in conceptions of both ontological and ecclesial hierarchy during the Reformation period. Due to space limitations, this chapter will focus primarily on the shift in ontological hierarchy, the conditions in the Church leading up to the Reformation, and Luther's reform.

Ontological Hierarchy: Ockham and Ockhamism

A revolutionary conception of ontological hierarchy is expressed in the work of William of Ockham (c. 1285–1347). Ockham's philosophical tradition has in the past been categorized as "Nominalism," but some recent scholars have argued that neither Ockham, nor many of his followers were in fact Nominalists.[2] I shall describe this tradition, therefore, as "Ockhamism."

[1] *To the Christian Nobility of the German Nation,* in *LW* 44:136.

[2] See William J. Courtenay, "Nominalism and Late Medieval Religion," in *The Pursuit of Holiness in Late Medieval and Renaissance Religion,* C. Trinkhaus and Heiko Oberman, eds. (Leiden: E.J. Brill, 1974) 26–59. On Ockham and Ockhamism see Marilyn McCord Adams, *William Ockham* (Notre Dame: University of Notre Dame

Against Aquinas, Duns Scotus, and most medieval (and ancient) philosophers, Ockham argued that universal essences or natures did not exist outside the human mind or in God. The mind can form a universal concept such as "human" or "human nature," but this is just a concept; there exists no universal "human nature," which individual humans share. Only individual entities exist in reality: "No universal really exists outside the mind in individual substances, nor is any universal a part of the substance or being of individual things."[3] Thus at a stroke Ockham swept away the structure of substantial forms, essences, and natures upon which medieval metaphysics, especially Thomism, was erected. There was no universal being, nor any universal forms or qualities such as goodness, love, wisdom, etc., which creatures and God shared. "Being," "goodness," and the like were merely concepts formed by the mind to classify similar characteristics in individuals. Thus Ockham's philosophical position is best described as conceptualism. This belief had a number of consequences.

Aquinas, like most medieval theologians, argued that creatures and God are linked in a hierarchy of being. God is being by essence, but creatures have being by participation: their being is as it were a sharing in and reflection of God's being. God is infinite being, being without limitation, whereas the being of creatures is a limited participation in being. Because there is a commonality of being in God and creatures, qualities like goodness or wisdom, which can be predicated to a limited degree of human creatures can also be predicated in an unlimited degree of God. As Norris Clarke has argued, this "analogy of being" represents St. Thomas' Neoplatonic heritage, for Neoplatonism held that creatures could participate to a limited degree in real qualities or perfections (goodness, being, unity, etc.) which existed infinitely in God.[4] Thus in St. Thomas and in other ancient and medieval

---

Press, 1987); Gordon Leff, *William of Ockham* (Manchester: Manchester University Press) 1975; Idem., *The Dissolution of the Medieval Outlook* (New York: Harper, 1976); F.C. Copleston, *A History of Philosophy,* vol. 3 (Garden City, N.Y.: Doubleday, Image, 1963), 56–164; "William of Ockham," *NCE* 14:932–935; "Ockhamism," *NCE* 10:630–632.

[3] From the introduction to the *Expositio Aurea,* cited in Stephen Ozment, *The Age of Reform* (New Haven: Yale, 1980) 58.

[4] See "The Limitation of Act by Potency in St. Thomas: Aristotelianism of Neoplatonism?" and "The Meaning of Participation in St. Thomas," both reprinted in *Explorations in Metaphysics* (Notre Dame: University of Notre Dame Press, 1994) 65–101.

thinkers influenced by Platonism or Neoplatonism, creatures exist on a continuity of being that culminates in God. This is the basis for Thomas' doctrine of analogy: we can have real knowledge of God, and make true positive statements about God (God is good, wise, loving, etc.) precisely because our being and God's being are not totally dissimilar. In this view, God is not the "wholly other," because if God were, no real knowledge of God would be possible. Similarly, Aquinas and other medieval theologians, both Orthodox and Catholic, held that persons can really participate in God's grace, which dwells in them: this amounts to a real sharing in the very life of God.

The Catholic theology of the sacraments depends on a notion of ontological participation. Sacraments are visible signs, instituted by Christ, which mediate the grace they signify. For a sacrament to mediate grace, in some sense it must be able to participate in that grace. The eucharistic bread, for example, mediates the presence of Christ precisely because it participates, in a mysterious fashion, in the very being of Christ's risen body. Similarly, the priest granting absolution in the sacrament of penance participates and mediates the forgiveness of Christ himself, who acts through the priest.

Ockham and Ockhamism severed the ontological commonality between God and creatures, and hence destroyed the analogy of being. One consequence was that humans could know very little about God by natural reason or natural theology. One cannot argue that God is wise, using the analogy of human wisdom or the analogy of wisdom (or design) as manifested in creation, for there is no universal quality "wisdom" in which humans and creation share to a limited degree and which is unlimited in God. Wisdom is simply a concept, which can be applied to God, but which does not necessarily correspond to any quality in God. Thus the only way God can be known is through revelation, not by extrapolating qualities from the world to God, as is done in the Thomistic method of analogy. The continuity of faith and reason, so dear to Thomas and Thomists and to the subsequent Catholic tradition, was largely severed by Ockham. Gordon Leff writes: "There was a virtual abandonment of a systematic attempt at a natural theology in the thirteenth-century sense of finding natural reasons for revealed truths. . . . Reason's role was thus restricted to elucidating the meaning and implications of revealed truth."[5] The result is that for Ockham

[5] Leff, *The Dissolution of the Medieval Outlook,* 16.

and Ockhamism, one relates to God by faith alone, and faith in this understanding is not real knowledge (as it is for Thomas) nor mystical participation; it is trust in God's promises. Here we see the ultimate root of Luther's notion of justification by faith, and also his rejection of Aristotelian and Scholastic reasoning and the hierarchy of being.

Another consequence was the loss of real participation by human creatures in the being or qualities of God, especially grace. For Aquinas, sanctifying grace was an indwelling accidental form, a *habitus,* which truly sanctified persons, by allowing the charity of God to dwell in them (cf. Rom 5:5). This was similar to the Eastern idea of *theosis* (deification) except that Aquinas used Aristotelian categories to explain it and the East did not. But both traditions understood grace to be a real participation in the Spirit and charity of God. Such an understanding of grace does not exist in Ockham's system. Ockham insists that God can accept or reject any creature regardless of the created habit or form which indwells in them. "For Ockham grace is not a power which is communicated to man, renews him, and qualifies him for meritorious actions, but God's indulgence, whereby he accepts man or not, as he pleases."[6] Thus God could save a sinner without supplying indwelling grace, or damn a person who possessed indwelling grace.[7] For Aquinas, this would not be possible, because in damning a saint, God would be acting against God's own justice and wisdom, and hence against God's own nature. But for Ockham, we cannot know God's nature, nor is God bound by any "essential" qualities like justice or wisdom; whatever God wills is just, simply because God wills it. Most Ockhamists argued that God could justly command someone to hate God. The gift of eternal life is entirely due to God's inscrutable will and choice: God is not bound by human ideas of justice, goodness, fairness, etc. Here we see the roots of Calvin's doctrine of double predestination, that is, the belief that God predestines some persons to heaven and some to hell, irrespective of any merits or actions on their part.

A third consequence of Ockhamism was an attenuating of the sacramental principle. For neither humans nor things can participate in God's being; rather, they relate to God through God's will. It seems that the weakening of the sacramental principle in Protestantism derives in part from Ockham's ontology.

[6] Erwin Iserloh, in *HC:IV,* 350.

[7] See Leff, *William of Ockham,* 470–475.

The effect of Ockham's theology was to exaggerate the role of God's will at the expense of God's being. A characteristic of his theology is the distinction between God's absolute and ordained power. By God's absolute power Ockham meant the power God had before creating the universe; this power was limited only by the law of contradiction—not by God's nature, including God's justice, wisdom, etc. Once God had actually created the universe, however, God was bound to act according to its structures—this is God's "ordained power," that is, the power which God has voluntarily limited according to what God ordained in creation. Ockham delighted in speculating on the possibilities of God's absolute power; for instance, he argued that God, because of absolute power, could have chosen to become incarnate in an ass or a stone.[8] But in *this* creation, God could not do this; God's ordained power was limited by the created order God had already ordained and was bound to. By this distinction Ockham emphasized the absolute contingency of the present created order—it could have been otherwise—and stressed the absolute freedom and omnipotence of God. This carried over into Protestantism; both Luther and Calvin stressed the absolute sovereignty and omnipotence of God.

For Ockham, then, salvation depended on God's will alone, not on any intrinsic merit of creatures or on their participation in God's being or grace. Grace, for Ockham, is not the indwelling love and life of God; it is God's freely given acceptance of the person for eternal life. Ockhamists did argue that God would probably save those who did their best, but God was not bound to do so: God could damn them. Here is the root of Luther's later insistence that salvation depends only on faith, not on merit. What is eliminated in Ockhamism is any intrinsic mediation—for example, of an infused habit of grace—between the naked decision of God and the creature. There is no longer any intrinsic ontological connection between God (or Christ) and creature, only an extrinsic connection. The tendency in this line of thought is to conceive God (and Christ) as extrinsic, inscrutable judges whom we trust to be faithful to their promise, but who need not be. The conception of God as a wrathful, inscrutable judge was powerfully reinforced by the experience of the Black Death, which between 1347 and 1351 carried off one-third of the population of Europe, including, ironically,

[8] Heiko Oberman, *The Harvest of Medieval Theology* (Cambridge: Harvard University Press, 1963) 255.

Ockham himself. Luther witnesses to this conception of God: "From childhood I was so trained that I could not but turn pale and become terrified if I merely heard the name of Christ mentioned, for I was taught only to regard him as a stern angry judge."[9]

Ockhamism had at least three major influences on European thought. First, it laid the groundwork for naturalism and the emergence of modern science. Ockham had argued that the intellect knows individual entities directly, against Aquinas and others who held that what the intellect knows is the universal form of the species. Thus Ockhamists turned their attention to the understanding of concrete empirical facts rather than abstract metaphysical forms and essences. By emphasizing the contingency of creation rather than necessary metaphysical structures (form/matter, etc.) which could be discovered by reason alone, it prepared the way for empirical investigation, for one can only discover the laws of a contingent universe by experimental investigation, not by abstract reasoning. Frederick Copleston writes: "Ockhamism helped to create an intellectual climate which facilitated and tended to promote scientific research. For by directing men's minds to the facts or empirical data in the acquisition of knowledge, it at the same time directed them away from the passive acceptance of the opinions of illustrious thinkers of the past."[10]

Second, Ockhamism prepared the way for the Protestant Reformation. Luther was trained by Gabriel Biel, a fifteenth-century Ockhamist, and Luther's thought, while rejecting Nominalist semi-Pelagianism (God will reward those who do their best), follows Ockhamism in its rejection of Aristotelian categories of being and ontological hierarchy. Both Luther's and Calvin's view of God and salvation followed Ockhamism, which stressed God's absolute omnipotence and freedom, and that persons are saved by faith alone. Commensurate with this went a weakening of the sacramental principle. Luther and Calvin retained some sacraments, but the center of their theology was the preached word of God, whereas the center of Catholicism and Orthodoxy is sacraments.

Third, Ockhamism emphasized that only individual beings are real, and that the individual is what is known by the intellect, in contrast to the medieval view that the individual was a part of a larger

[9] *WA* 40, I, 298; cited in *HC:V*, 13.

[10] *A History of Philosophy*, 3:166.

whole. Ockhamism thus led to the development of modern individualism, which was a reaction against medieval emphasis on the corporate, organic unity of the whole people (and the Church). Further, Ockham marginalized the salvific role of the medieval, sacramental Church. By eliminating the Dionysian notion that God's power is mediated to humans through the agency of intermediates, such as bishops and priests, Ockham prepared the way for the Protestant notion that the individual is judged alone before God.

Thus the three movements that most shaped the modern worldview, science, Protestantism, and individualism, all flowed from Ockhamism, which must therefore be accounted the decisive intellectual change from medieval to modern times. By driving a wedge between the being of God and the being of creatures, and exalting God's will over God's being, Ockhamism led to the modern conception of God as external to creation and creatures; a God not bound by any intrinsic justice or goodness, whose will is absolute and inscrutable—a God who could damn a saint, who governs more by command rather than by inviting creatures to participate in grace. This in turn led to the authoritarian God of Calvin, and eventually to the detached, extrinsic God of Deism.

The Background of the Reformation

In addition to philosophical factors, social and ecclesial factors contributed to the Reformation. These are extensive and complex, and here only some of the most important can be mentioned. Among the principal social causes were the development of nationalism and the increasing autonomy of secular rulers: kings, princes, dukes, and free cities. Along with this went the development of a propertied urban class, especially wealthy merchants, who wanted more active participation in the Church. Among the principal ecclesial causes were the centralization of power in the papacy and the Curia, the growing wealth and materialism of the clergy, simony, and the use of episcopal offices for gain by nobility, especially in Germany. No one has more thoroughly documented the corruption of the late medieval Church than the conservative Catholic historian Joseph Lortz, whose *The Reformation in Germany* (1939) ranks as a classic history of the German Reformation.

Many of the roots of the Reformation reach back to the high Middle Ages. The movement begun under Gregory VII, to free the Church from secular control, also led eventually to a clericalization of the Church and "an exclusion of the laity from active participation in the government of the Church (strained relations with the ruling priestly caste arose and then changed to enmity)."[11] The centralization of papal and curial power also undermined the authority of the bishops in their dioceses. Popes could control friars and preachers, appoint clergy to benefices (clerical offices to which income was attached, usually from tithes or endowments), and take over a portion of the revenues attached to the benefice. Many of those appointed were absentee bishops or clergy. Subordinates could appeal from their bishop to the pope, and suffragan bishops could appeal from their archbishop to the pope. Lortz writes:

> Thus the papal system, as the prelates complained, subverted the natural order of the church. Because all roads led to Rome no initiative remained with the local prelates, and the diocese—formerly the basic unit of church government—became an empty shell. Constantly harried by the Roman curia, deprived of initiative, weakened in the face of their subordinates, the bishops became apathetic, lost heart or turned their energies in other directions. . . . The result was that the necessary reforms were not carried out; and for that result, without doubt, extreme and ill-calculated centralization was primarily responsible.[12]

During and after the Avignon papacy (1309–1378), the popes and the Curia garnered revenues from selling ecclesial offices (simony), taxes on the income of benefices, and annates (usually half the first year's income from a benefice), due as a payment for the popes "installing" the officer (e.g., a bishop) of the benefice. Nor was the Curia alone in expropriating the income from benefices:

> Princes, humanist critics of the church, town councils, all condoned this blatant exploitation of holy things, so long as proceeds flowed into their own pockets. Maximilian's chaplain was provost of Nurenburg, of Mainz, and a prebendary of Trent and Bamberg. He is but one of countless examples. In this way princes rewarded their servants out of the benefices of the church. . . . Everything had its price. . . . Even a cardinal's hat could be bought.[13]

[11] Joseph Lortz, *The Reformation in Germany,* vol. I (New York: Herder and Herder, 1968, German original, 1939) 15; cf. also Geoffrey Barraclough, *The Medieval Papacy* (New York: Norton, 1968) 127.

[12] Barraclough, *The Medieval Papacy,* 126.

[13] Lortz, *The Reformation in Germany,* vol. 1, 89.

Curial members typically lived off the income from many benefices outside Rome. "As late as 1556 Cardinal Alessandro Farnese, grandson of Paul III, possessed ten episcopal sees, twenty-six monasteries, and 133 other benefices—canonries, parishes, and chaplaincies."[14] Naturally, such absentee clergy could not attend to the pastoral needs of their benefices. The whole system of papal taxes aroused resentment against the papacy and the Curia. One of Luther's complaints, which resonated with all Germans, was that Rome was extorting German money for its own avaricious purposes.

Another means for raising income was the sale of indulgences. An indulgence is the remission "of the debt of temporal punishment after the guilt of sin has been forgiven."[15] The practice was based on the theory that the Church had acquired a "Treasury of Merits" stored up by the good works of Jesus, Mary, and the saints, and that the pope could apply this to the forgiveness of temporal punishment if a person sincerely repented and performed some holy work, such as going on a crusade, doing a work of charity, or contributing money to the Church. The construction of many medieval churches was financed by the sale of indulgences. In 1476 Pope Sixtus IV applied indulgences to souls in purgatory. Thereafter, people could purchase indulgences to remit the sufferings of their loved ones in purgatory. Obviously this system was open to abuse. By Luther's time, it had become a lucrative source of income for the Church.

The use of ecclesial office for material gain and power also extended to many bishops and other clergy. Especially in Germany the offices of bishop, cathedral canon, or abbot were often assumed by nobles, whose interest was in appropriating the income and power attached to benefices. Wealthy nobles reserved such benefices for their children, who were often appointed as minors, after a fee had been paid to the Curia for the appointment. The famous case of Albrecht of Brandenburg, on the eve of the Reformation, illustrates the problem. Albrecht, a scion of the Brandenburg nobility, was made bishop of Halberstadt and archbishop of Magdeburg in 1513, when he was twenty-three (an archbishop was supposed to be thirty). In 1514 the archbishopric of Mainz became vacant and Albrecht put forth his candidacy. To receive this office he had to pay the Curia fourteen thousand ducats for the installation fee and 10,000

[14] *HC:V*, 8.
[15] *NCE*, 7:482.

ducats for the dispensation to hold several sees. He borrowed the money from Jacob Fugger (at usurious interest rates), to be repaid by the selling of an indulgence in Mainz. Half the proceeds of the indulgence were to go to the building of St. Peter's Basilica in Rome—this was the ostensible purpose of the indulgence—and the other half (unknown to the purchasers), to repay the Fugger loan. It was the preaching of this indulgence which incited Luther to write his *95 Theses.*

Another unsavory incident involving episcopal exploitation of the laity was the affair of Richard Hunne in 1514. Hunne, a London merchant with Lollard sympathies, refused to pay the customary mortuary tax to the local priest for the burial of his deceased infant. The parish priest took him to ecclesial court, but Hunne countersued. Eventually, the case reached the bishop of London, who pressed full heresy proceedings. Hunne was charged with possessing a Lollard bible, and sent to the bishop's prison, where he was found hanged two days later, apparently by the bishop's guards, who claimed he had committed suicide.[16] Two weeks later the Church burned his corpse as a heretic. This incident aroused mass anticlerical demonstrations by the citizens of London and attacks in parliament on clerical benefits.[17]

The situation of the parish clergy was also debased in the late Middle Ages. The hoarding of many benefices by wealthy nobles who neglected their pastoral duties meant that the parish sacramental duties were farmed out to a clerical proletariat, a large mass of badly paid, ignorant, socially inferior, "Mass priests," whose function was to say daily Mass, and who in some cities numbered one-twentieth of the population.[18]

The religious orders also shared in the decline. In many orders, regular prayer had been abandoned, members had gotten permission to live outside the monastery, had taken up private property, and were living secular lives. Members of the mendicant orders were despised as indolent beggars and satirized by Erasmus and others.[19] Anticlericalism was fueled by the fact that large proportions of land and estates were held by the Church, especially the monasteries. In Germany,

[16] See the account in Ozment, *The Age of Reform*, 213.

[17] A.G. Dickens, *The Counter Reformation* (New York: Norton, 1968) 15. See, however, Eamon Duffy, *The Stripping of the Altars: Traditional Religion in England 1400–1580* (New Haven: Yale University Press, 1992). Duffy contends that traditional Catholicism in late Medieval England was vigorous, popular, and held the loyalty of the people.

[18] Lortz, *The Reformation in Germany*, vol. 1, 97–99.

[19] Ibid., 99–102.

in 1500, the Church owned approximately one-third of the land.[20] The situation was similar in England.

All this provoked passionate cries by contemporaries for reform of the Church in head and members. For example, at the Council of Vienne (1311), Bishop William Durand of Mende, among others, assailed the papal system, criticizing the sales of offices and the system of papal taxes. He claimed that the pope was undermining the rights of bishops and prelates, for example their right to hear suits in their own dioceses and provide for their clergy. The clerks of the papal chancery, he averred, had precedence even over archbishops. He defended papal primacy, but denied *plenitudo potestatis* to the pope, and demanded a restoration of the authority of bishops and their synods, as in the ancient Church.[21] For this he was imprisoned for seven years and his teachings suppressed. Dietrich of Niem, for years a curial official, in his *Avisamenta* to the Council of Constance (1414) argued that papal power must be limited against misuse, simony done away with, councils held regularly, and that "the evils that have befallen the Church are due to the Curia and to the absolutism of papal administration."[22] On the eve of the Fifth Lateran Council (1511), two Venetian monks presented the pope with an extensive program for Church reform, in which they blamed the state of the Church on the papacy's preoccupation with secular politics, and recommended councils every five years.[23] In 1518 the German princes presented the grievances *(gravamina)* of the German nation to the papal legate, Cajetan. These express German anger against the Curia, and help explain Luther's success in Germany:

> These sons of Nimrod [Curial officials] grab cloisters, abbeys, prebends, canonates, and parish churches, and they leave these churches without pastors, the people without shepherds. Annates and indulgences increase. In cases before the ecclesiastical courts, the Roman Church smiles on both sides for a little palm grease. German money in violation of nature flies over the Alps. The pastors given to us are shepherds only in name. They care for nothing but fleece[,] and batten on the sins of the people. Endowed masses are neglected, the

[20] Ibid., 95.

[21] Barraclough, *The Medieval Papacy*, 138–139.

[22] Ibid., 14.

[23] The details are given in Ozment, *The Age of Reform*, 400–401.

pious founders cry for vengeance. Let the Holy Pope Leo stop these abuses.[24]

Finally, the *Consilium de emendanda ecclesia,* drawn up by a reform commission of cardinals appointed by Pope Paul III in 1536, reiterated many of the same complaints against the curial system.

> It particularly assailed the venality and simony involved in papal appointments and benefice-holding and attributed these evils to an exaggerated concept of papal authority. "From this source," it boldly declared, "as from a Trojan horse," so many abuses and such grave diseases have rushed in upon the Church of God that we now see her afflicted almost to the point of despair.[25]

Joseph Lortz summed up the situation on the eve of the Reformation starkly: "The clergy have become the exploiters of the Church."[26] The corruption of the Church was not the only reason for the Reformation, but was the one most commented on by contemporaries. "Everyone knows," said a preacher at the Council of Constance in 1417, "that the reform of the church Militant is necessary—it is known to the clergy, it is known to the whole Christian people. The heavens, the elements . . . even the very stones cry out for reform."[27]

Another factor contributing to the Reformation was the growth of national consciousness and the power of secular rulers. By the Concordat of Bologna (1516), the French king won the right to nominate all candidates for bishop and abbot. These so-called "Gallican liberties" remained in force in the French church until Vatican I. In England, the statutes of Provisor (1351 and 1390) gave the king control over ecclesiastical appointments.[28] These provided the precedent for Henry VIII's declaration in 1534 that the king, not the pope, was the head of the English church. The Hussite movement resulted in a strong national church in Bohemia which endured for centuries. The Spanish

[24] Cited in Roland Bainton, *Here I Stand* (New York: Abingdon Press, 1950) 92.

[25] Cited in John C. Olin, *Catholic Reform from Cardinal Ximenes to the Council of Trent, 1495–1563* (New York: Fordham University Press, 1990) 20–21. An English translation of the *Consilium* is given in pages 65–79.

[26] *The Reformation in Germany,* vol. 1, 84.

[27] Francis Oakley, *The Western Church in the Later Middle Ages* (Ithaca, N.Y.: Cornell University Press, 1979) 213.

[28] The information on France and England is from Ozment, *The Age of Reform,* 187–189.

church was largely under the control of the Spanish monarchs. The pope's authority was less limited by national rulers in Germany and Italy than in other European countries. But the papal engagement in secular politics, their concern to maintain their political power at all costs, their engagement in war to defend the papal states (Julius II, [1503–1513] personally led his armies into battle), was ultimately destructive to their spiritual authority. In 1527 Charles V's unpaid and insubordinate troops attacked and pillaged Rome—the *sacco di Roma*—an event that was widely regarded as the just judgment of God on Rome and the papacy.[29]

A final factor that should be considered is whether the late medieval Church was adequate to the religious needs of most of the people. Since benefices were often controlled by absentee bishops, who left the spiritual ministrations to uneducated "Mass priests," there was a neglect of spiritual life in the late medieval Church. Yet there was a real, widespread demand for genuine spiritual reform. People wanted to be able to read the scriptures in their own language (a demand of the Lollards), to receive the Eucharist under both species (a demand of the Hussites), to be freed from burdensome legalism, to participate more in the life and governance of the Church. Stephen Ozment writes: "What the Reformation did have in common with late medieval reform movements was the conviction that traditional Church authority and piety no longer served the religious needs of large numbers of people and had become psychologically and financially oppressive."[30] Much of the appeal of Lutheranism and other Protestant denominations was that it freed people from the burdens of clerical taxation, an excessive legalism, gave them access to the Bible in their own language, a closer relation to Jesus through faith, and more participation in the local church. These had been the ongoing concerns of reform movements for two centuries before Luther.

Attempts at Reform

Two early reformers who indirectly influenced Luther were John Wycliffe and John Huss. Wycliffe (1330–1384), an Oxford scholar, rejected transubstantiation, arguing that the bread and wine remained in

[29] *HC:V*, 239–240.
[30] *The Age of Reform*, 222.

the consecrated elements, a position close to Luther's. He further taught that only those in a state of grace rightfully held authority in the Church or the state, a position which undermined the authority of the whole of medieval society. He encouraged the translation of scripture into English, and held that the Bible was the ultimate norm by which the hierarchical Church should be judged. His followers, called "Lollards," including priests as well as artisans and tradesmen, carried on his beliefs, arguing that the vernacular Bible should be available to all, and preaching a life of apostolic, evangelical simplicity.[31]

Wycliffe's doctrines strongly influenced the Czech John Huss (1369–1415) and his followers, the Hussites. Huss was condemned by the Council of Constance for allegedly teaching Wycliffism, though the degree to which he held the beliefs for which he was condemned is disputed.[32] The Hussites taught four points: the word of God should be preached freely by priests, both the bread and the wine should be given to Christians, the clergy should renounce worldly goods and live like the apostles, those committing mortal sins should be punished, including priests.[33] Hussitism continued in Czechoslovakia, influenced both Czech Protestantism and Catholicism, and continues to this day in some Czech sects.

Thus many of the themes that later surfaced in the Protestant Reformation were anticipated by late medieval reform groups: the demand for a vernacular Bible available to all, scripture as the norm of the Church, the belief that only the morally and spiritually pure should be ministers (a belief of the Anabaptists), and the insistence on apostolic poverty and an evangelical lifestyle for both clergy and laity. Running through all these groups was an insistence on greater participation of the laity in the Church, for example that the laity should have the Bible in their own language, be able to preach, and receive communion in both kinds. Along with this went a rejection of the clericalism, wealth, and materialism of the late medieval Church. John Huss was condemned by both the papalists and the conciliarists for appealing directly to Christ as the Head of the Church, and therefore marginalizing both popes and councils.[34] Luther would do the same.

[31] See Oakley, *The Western Church,* 189–195; *HC:IV,* 443–447.

[32] See *NCE* 7:271–272.

[33] *NCE* 7:273–275; Oakley, *The Western Church,* 201–203.

[34] Heiko Oberman, *Forerunners of the Reformation* (New York: Holt, Rinehart, and Winston, 1966) 212.

From the fourteenth century on there were repeated appeals to a general council to reform the Church. John of Ragusa (1395–1443) wrote: "I cry out, and publicly affirm . . . that of all the evils, divisions, schisms, errors, deformities and so on pertaining to and following from matters I have been touching upon, the cause and origin, and indeed the root, has been and remains today the neglect and disregard of general councils."[35] Councils were held at Vienne (1311–1312), Constance (1414–1418), Basel and Ferrara-Florence (1431–1445), and Rome (Lateran Council V, 1512–1517), all with the intent of reforming the Church. Giles of Viterbo, superior general of the Augustinian order and a renowned scholar and preacher, addressed the opening assembly of the fifth Lateran Council as follows: "Therefore, she [the Church] wishes nothing for herself except that the Holy Spirit's light *which is extinguished without Councils* . . . be again kindled and recovered in the Councils . . . without Councils faith cannot stand firm. Without Councils, therefore, we cannot be saved."[36]

Yet all these reforming councils, including V Lateran on the very eve of the Reformation, failed to reform the Church, largely because the popes did not cooperate with the councils. Luther himself appealed over the head of the pope to a general council twice. Cardinal Jerome Aleander, papal emissary to Germany, reported to the pope in February, 1521: "All Germany is in an uproar. For nine-tenths 'Luther' is the war-cry; for the rest, if they are indifferent to Luther, it is at least 'Death to the Roman Curia,' and everyone demands and shouts for a council."[37] Even John Eck, a papal emissary and Luther's great opponent, "called for the restoration of the conciliar system, whose decay was responsible for both the abuses in the Church and the [Lutheran] revolt."[38] The Imperial Diet of Worms in 1521, where Luther was tried before Emperor Charles V, also called for a council. In the 1520s, a critical period when reunification of the Church may still have been possible, great pressure was put on Pope Clement VII by Emperor Charles V and by the Diet of Speyer (1529) to summon a general council to reunite the Church. In 1530 the princes and free cities who presented the Augsburg Confession to Charles V called for a general council: "We offer in full obedience, even beyond what is required, to participate in such a general, free, and Christian council as the

[35] Ibid.

[36] Ibid., 50, italics added.

[37] Cited in *HC:V*, 76.

[38] Ibid., 111.

electors, princes, and estates have . . . requested in all the diets of the empire which have been held during your Imperial Majesty's reign."[39] But Clement stalled, fearful that a council would strengthen the emperor's authority and question his legitimacy as pope.[40] He never did call a council, and Charles V did not feel he, as emperor, could summon a council without the consent of the pope. By the time the Council of Trent convened (1545), it was too late for reconciliation. Hubert Jedin, himself a strong opponent of conciliarism, concludes:

> The fact remains that a Council did not come off betimes because Rome regarded it as a dangerous venture the issue of which was questionable; for that reason it refused to promote it energetically. Yet as things stood, only a Council could issue a decision on the controversy which all concerned would regard as undoubtedly binding in conscience . . . Futile negotiations for a Council dragged on for years . . . With despair in their hearts those who remained loyal to the Church were forced to look on while a whole generation was growing up estranged from the Catholic faith.[41]

Individual popes, such as Nicholas V (1447–55) and Adrian VI (1522–1523) attempted reform, but their reigns were too short and their efforts ineffective against the inertia of the system, especially the Curia. But popes like Adrian VI were the exception. Generally, the Renaissance popes (e.g., Alexander VI, Julius II, Leo X) used the papacy to further their dynastic ambitions, and they neglected the universal Church. Though prophetic voices were raised in abundance calling for reform, and though parts of the Church were reformed, the Church as a whole was not. Geoffrey Barraclough notes that "the failure [of the papacy] to lead and take command of the swelling religious currents—as Innocent III, for example, had taken command of the Franciscan movement at a similar turning point in the history of the Church . . . left the way open for Luther, who succeeded precisely because he gave the deep piety of the age an objective outside of itself, which was lacking."[42] Barraclough concludes:

[39] Preface to *The Augsburg Confession,* in Theodore G. Tappert, ed., *The Book of Concord: The Confessions of the Evangelical Lutheran Church* (Philadelphia: Fortress, 1959) 26–27.

[40] *HC:V,* 238–245.

[41] *A History of the Council of Trent,* vol. 1 (London: Thomas Nelson & Sons, 1957) 196.

[42] *The Medieval Church,* 172.

> But the reformers, no longer hoping for effective support from the papacy, looked more and more to kings and secular rulers for backing . . . It was characteristic that the great reformers of France and Spain, the cardinal of Amboise and Cardinal Ximenes, both worked hand in glove with the monarchy . . . [Reform] was a spontaneous revival which occurred in many centres simultaneously . . . but it was not a single great movement, spreading through the whole church . . . Individual churches and congregations were reformed; but the church was not reformed. For this the papacy without doubt, must be held to account. It abdicated its responsibility, and so it left the way open for Luther, who did not shirk responsibility.[43]

This conclusion is echoed by Protestant (e.g., Ozment), Catholic (e.g., Lortz, Fink), and non-confessional historians. The Church needed reform, but the members could not reform it without the leadership of the head. Had the popes been willing to share power with a council, they probably could have succeeded in reforming the Church and retaining the allegiance of the whole Western Church. Their failure was due to their clinging to a hierarchy of command, which set them at odds with secular rulers, laity, and religious, especially in Germany, whereas what was required was a hierarchy that fostered discussion, reform, and participation.

Luther's Reform

The details of Luther's early career are well known, and need not be repeated here. As an Augustinian monk he wore himself out with fasting, penances, vigils, and frequent confessions, in a fruitless attempt to find peace with God through the performance of monastic works. In this he was following late Ockhamist theology, which held that to those who did their best, God would not withhold grace ("Facienti quod est in se, deus non denegat gratiam")—a semi-Pelagianist position. As a lecturer in Old and New Testament at the new University of Wittenberg, he came to a theological insight that revolutionized his life, and changed his vision of God. Hitherto he had conceived of "the justice of God" (Rom 1:17) as that justice by which God condemns sinful humanity. His new understanding he explained in a famous passage:

[43] Ibid., 194.

> I had conceived a hatred of this phrase "justice of God," because . . . I had been taught to understand it philosophically as formal or active justice whereby God is just and punishes sinners and the unjust.
>
> Though as a friar I had led a blameless life, I felt myself to be a sinner before God . . . and I could not be confident that I had reconciled God by my satisfactions. Hence I did not love, but rather I hated the just God who punishes sinners . . . After days and nights of meditation God finally took pity on me and I noted the inner connection between the two passages: "the justice of God is revealed in the Gospel, as it is written, 'The just man lives by faith.'" Then I began to understand the justice of God as that by which the just man lives, thanks to the gift of God, that is, by faith; that the justice of God, which is revealed in the Gospel, is to be understood in the passive sense; that God in his mercy justifies us by faith, as it is written "the just man lives by faith." At once I felt myself to be reborn and as though I had entered paradise through opened gates.[44]

Thus the central doctrine of Luther's theology was that persons are saved by faith, not by any works they do; works should flow from the justified person, but there is no merit attached to the works nor do they count towards salvation; only faith in God and Jesus can save.

This explains Luther's attack on indulgences. For Luther, the practice of indulgences represented salvation by works, the antithesis of his theology, and was a dangerous deception of the faithful, who were being gulled into thinking they could purchase salvation. Accordingly, he challenged the practice and theology of indulgences in his *95 Theses* (1517), which also challenged the authority of the pope.[45] Printers soon distributed these all over Germany, and Archbishop Albrecht sent a copy to Rome.

Rome's first response was to order the head of the Augustinian order to silence Luther, but the Augustinian chapter meeting in April 1518 turned into a pro-Luther demonstration.[46] The pope then directed a Dominican, Sylvester Prierias, Master of the Sacred Palace in Rome, to reply to Luther's *95 Theses.* Prierias' argument rested squarely on papal infallibility. Neither the Roman Church, a true council, nor the pope, is able to err, he wrote. Therefore whoever contradicts the doc-

[44] Cited in *HC:V,* 35.

[45] On Luther's reaction to indulgences, and the *95 Theses,* see Scott Hendrix, *Luther and the Papacy: Stages in a Reformation Conflict* (Philadelphia: Fortress, 1981) 22–34.

[46] *HC:V,* 53.

trines *or practices* of the Church, is a heretic: ("Qui circa indulgentis dicit, Ecclesiam Romanam non posse facere id, quod de facto facit, haereticus est").[47] Luther challenged Prierias' identification of the Church with the Roman pope and the Church's practice with papal practice, noting that Prierias cited no scriptural texts or Church fathers, but simply appealed to papal authority.[48]

On August 7, 1518, Luther was summoned to Rome on charges of heresy (the penalty for which was burning at the stake). Through the intervention of Frederick the Wise, prince and elector of Saxony, the case was transferred to Germany. Before his trial, Luther was to appear before Cardinal Cajetan privately, who had instructions from Pope Leo not to debate with Luther but to influence him to recant his teachings, and if he would not, to arrest him and bring him to Rome.

Cajetan was one of the foremost Thomist theologians of the sixteenth century, author of a magisterial commentary on the *Summa Theologiae* which was regarded as authoritative through the nineteenth century. In his ecclesiology he argued that the pope, as head of the body the Church, represented Christ.[49] The pope possessed the whole power of the Church, others only participated in that power; the bishops received their jurisdiction through the pope. The whole power of the Church flowed from Peter and from Peter's vicar, who alone was the vicar of Christ. In the opening sermon at the second session of the Fifth Lateran Council (1512), he had argued for the symmetry of the heavenly and earthly churches. As Christ was the only head of the Church in heaven, so the pope was the only prince of the Church Militant on earth, whom all citizens of the Church must obey.[50] This ecclesiology was also that later expressed by Lateran Council V, and published in the Bull *Pastor Aeternus* in 1516. The Bull declares: "the person who abandons the teaching of the Roman pontiff cannot be within the church, for . . . obedience alone is the mother and protector of all virtues, it alone possessing the reward of faith" and "subjection to the Roman pontiff is necessary for salvation for all Christ's faithful."[51] In this view the juridical power of the Church was concentrated in the pope, and flowed from the pope to the rest of the Church.

[47] Cited in *HC:V,* 54; see also Hendrix, *Luther and the Papacy,* 46–52.

[48] Ibid., 46–52.

[49] Congar, *L'Église,* 349–352.

[50] Hendrix, *Luther and the Papacy,* 57–58.

[51] The Latin and English text of this Bull is given in Tanner, vol. 1, 640–645.

The unity of the Church came from obedience to the pope, and whoever disobeyed the pope was a schismatic or heretic, subject to civil penalties including death.

In his interview with Luther, Cajetan pointed out that Luther's Thesis fifty-eight contradicted *Unigenitus,* the papal decree of Clement VI (1343), which stated that the merits of Christ were a treasure that could be dispensed by the pope in indulgences (*DS* 1025–1027). Cajetan's appeal here was to the power of the pope alone, above that of scripture, the Fathers of the Church, councils, or reason. Luther had argued in Thesis 58 that the papal claim that Christ's merits formed a treasury for indulgences could not be proved by scripture or reason, and was therefore a debatable point. Unlike Cajetan, Luther relied on a consensus of authorities, including scripture, the Church fathers, councils, and clear reason; these did not support the pope in this matter, which therefore was open to debate.[52]

Thus here were two different conceptions of the Church opposing each other, one Roman and papalist, a command hierarchy depending on clerical obedience for its unity, the other, more conciliarist, depending on agreement among a plurality of authorities (including the pope) for unity. At this time Luther did not reject the authority of the pope, as he later confessed: "If the cardinal had acted more modestly in Augsburg and had accepted me as a suppliant, things would never have gone so far, for at that time I still knew little of the errors of the pope!"[53]

In July, 1519, Luther met John Eck in debate at Leipzig. In debating the authority of the papacy, Eck got Luther to admit that he no longer held the authority of councils or popes as primary, for both councils and popes had contradicted themselves in the past. Rather, Luther said, the authority of scripture was superior to that of popes and councils. This, along with salvation by faith alone, became the second great pillar of Lutheran theology. Eck lost no time in condemning this as Hussitism.

By 1520 Leo X published the Bull *Exsurge Domine,* condemning forty-one propositions taken from Luther's writings. Luther responded by appealing to the emperor, and to a future council. But by 1520 Luther had completed three of his most important writings: *To the*

[52] Hendrix, *Luther and the Papacy,* 56–61.

[53] Ibid., 44.

Christian Nobility of the German Nation, The Babylonian Captivity of the Church, and *The Freedom of a Christian.* These writings lay out the heart of his reform, and signal a decisive break with the medieval Church. Luther argued that the "Romanists" had erected three walls which prevented reform. They argued that (1) the spiritual power is above the temporal, (2) only the pope could interpret scripture, (3) only the pope could summon a council. Luther countered by claiming that all Christians are priests by virtue of baptism; this is the doctrine of the priesthood of all believers (based on 1 Pet 2:9 "But you are a chosen race, a royal priesthood, a holy nation, God's own people"). Therefore all Christians are members of the spiritual estate; the pope has no authority over lay rulers, who, as Christians, have an obligation to take control of the Church in their regions of jurisdiction and reform it. Any Christian can reprove the pope on the basis of scripture. As Luther wrote: "If God spoke through an ass against a prophet [Balaam], why should he not even now be able to speak through a righteous man against the pope?"[54]

Similarly, any Christian, particularly temporal rulers, can summon a council (Luther was thinking of Constantine who had summoned the Council of Nicaea). Luther denied that ordination is a sacrament, and limits the sacraments to three: baptism, the Lord's Supper, and penance, since, he says, only these were instituted by Jesus in the scriptures. In the Lord's Supper, the clergy has denied the chalice of wine, the blood of Christ, to the laity, without their consent, thus erecting a clerical tyranny over the laity. The papacy burdened Christians with intolerable rules, laws, taxes, and exactions, whereas every Christian is free from the necessity of works and the law, since salvation is freely given to all by grace through faith in Christ: "Anyone can clearly see how a Christian is free from all things and over all things so that he needs no works to make him righteous and save him, since faith alone abundantly confers all these things."[55] Again and again in these writings Luther accused the papacy and the Curia of tyranny, and of corrupting the Church (as well as stealing money from the Germans). His primary concern however was religious: Rome had misled the people into thinking that salvation can be gained by works like indulgences, pilgrimages, and the like, when it can only be gained by faith in Christ.

[54] *To the Christian Nobility of the German Nation,* in *LW* 44:136.
[55] *The Freedom of a Christian,* in *LW* 31:356.

The pope he identifies as the Antichrist, and the captivity of the German church by the Roman church as the captivity of the Jews by the Babylonians.

The Lutheran View of Hierarchy

The Lutheran tenets of justification by faith alone, the primacy of scripture as the norm for Christian belief, and the priesthood of all believers, effected a radical break from the medieval view of hierarchy and the Church. In that view, Christ's grace and salvation are mediated through the sacraments, which are administered by ordained clergy, so that one who rejected the Catholic, sacramental Church could not be saved. This was proclaimed by the Council of Florence in 1442.[56] The Roman and papal view, though not the view of conciliarists, was that one who was not subject to the Roman pontiff was outside the Church and hence outside salvation (Boniface VIII, *Unam sanctam,* 1302, *DS* 875). Luther and early Lutherans accepted the idea that the Church was necessary for salvation, but not that Christ's grace was mediated only through ordained clergy. Thus, for example, traditional Catholicism held that in the sacrament of penance Christ forgave sins through the priest, functioning as an ordained minister of the Church. But for Luther no clerical intermediary is necessary: "Christ has given to every one of his believers the power to absolve even open sins."[57] For Luther, every Christian, by virtue of baptism, was a priest and therefore could preach and baptize; the official, institutional, and above all the Roman Church was therefore rendered unnecessary for salvation. In its place stood the individual believer, armed with the word of God, alone before Christ, saved by faith, rather than by the intercession or mediation of the clerical Church.

This effected a radically different notion of the Church. According to the Augsburg Confession, the classic formulation of Lutheran belief: "[The Church] is the assembly of all believers among whom the Gospel is preached in its purity and the holy sacraments are administered according to the Gospel."[58] Thus it is the people, the Gospel, and the people's response in faith which constitute the Church, which is the Holy

[56] Bull of Union with the Copts, in Tanner, vol. 1, 578.

[57] *The Babylonian Captivity,* in *LW* 36:88.

[58] Article VII, in *The Book of Concord,* 32.

People of God (1 Pet 2:9). The decisive norm for the Church is the Gospel. What counts as a sacrament is similarly determined by scripture.

The power of ordination in this ecclesiology resides not with bishops ordained in the apostolic succession, but in the community itself (since all believers are already priests) which can ordain bishops and ministers as needed. Luther wrote: "It should be the custom for every town to choose from among the congregation a learned and pious citizen, entrust to him the office of ministry, and support him at the expense of the congregation. He should be free to marry or not. He should have several [priests or deacons] . . . to help him minister to the congregation and the community with word and sacrament."[59] As Philip Melanchthon explained in his *Treatise on the Power and Primacy of the Pope,* the churches by divine right can elect and ordain pastors and ministers.[60] Bishops, priests, and pastors, then, are officeholders whose office is to preach and administer the sacraments. There is no special privilege given to those who have been ordained by bishops standing in the apostolic succession.

Jesus Christ, not the pope, is the head of Christendom and the churches. The pope is primarily the bishop of Rome, and the head of any churches who have voluntarily attached themselves to him. As such, his authority is only of human institution, not divine right.[61] Luther himself did not concede that the pope had any superiority over other bishops, even by human right. But Philip Melanchthon appended this note to his signature of the Smalcald articles: "However, concerning the pope I hold that, if he would allow the Gospel, we too may concede to him that superiority over the bishops which he possesses by human right, making this concession for the sake of peace and general unity among the Christians who are now under him."[62] Melanchthon was more concerned about ecumenical unity than was Luther, and more sensitive to the consequences of rejecting the ancient Roman Church. In his *Treatise on the Power and Primacy of the Pope,* he does not reject the primacy of the bishop of Rome, as the first among equals, the way it was understood by the Orthodox. What he rejects is the papal claim to be lord of all bishops, the claim to have authority over secular kingdoms, the claim that it is necessary for salvation to be

[59] *To the Nobility of the Christian Nation,* in *LW* 44:175.

[60] In *The Book of Concord,* 332.

[61] *The Smalcald Articles,* article IV, in *The Book of Concord,* 298.

[62] *The Book of Concord,* 316–317.

obedient to the pope, the claim that the pope cannot be examined or judged by the Church ("the first see is judged by no one"), the cruelty with which the pope defends his power (e.g., by burning heretics at the stake), and the failure to teach that faith in Christ, rather than works, brings remission of sins and salvation.[63] What is rejected, in other words, is a command hierarchy with the pope *over* the Church; a participatory hierarchy might have been acceptable, though of course Melanchthon does not use such language.

Luther and the Lutherans, then, reasserted the prophetic task of correcting abuses of authority. Indeed, "Luther understood himself as a God-called prophet and his reformation as the execution of a God-given task."[64] Luther also reemphasized the participation of the laity in the Church, and the representative function of bishops and ministers. Theirs was an ecclesiology from the bottom up. In Lutheranism, the laity were encouraged to read the scripture in their own language (Luther translated the Bible into German); they were given Communion under both species, could elect their own ministers, participated in the services by singing hymns, and so on. The clergy were allowed to marry, and so were closer in lifestyle to the parishioners, rather than being a separated, quasi-monastic, clerical caste. The clergy, as elected, was representative of the community, especially as compared to the absentee Catholic bishops so common in Germany. In all this, Luther restored the ancient elements of community consent and representation which had fallen into desuetude in late medieval clericalism.

On the other hand, the whole sacramental principle, on which Catholicism is based, was weakened; God's word and promise became primary. Luther retained three sacraments, and the real presence, but most Protestant followers, including later Lutherans, retained only two: baptism and the Lord's Supper, and argued, like Zwingli, that the latter was a sign or memorial, which did not participate in the real risen body of Jesus, which was in heaven. The Catholic notion that visible things can partake in and mediate the holy came to be seen as superstition. Thus devotion to saints, Mary, pilgrimages, relics, and so forth were branded as idolatry or superstition and done away with. In

[63] Ibid., 320–334.

[64] Oberman, *Forerunners of the Reformation*, 18.

Calvinism even the use of images was banned, provoking an iconoclasm reminiscent of that opposed by the Orthodox Church at the Second Council of Nicaea in 800. All this, I believe, follows from a loss of a participatory hierarchy of being. Rather, for Luther and Calvin, God is exterior to us and justifies us by a free act of God's will, more than by a participation in God's grace and being. Though the latter is not denied by Luther, salvation is fundamentally a matter of God's will, and the human response in faith.

Particularly crucial was Luther's denial of the sacrament of ordination. In this he was followed by all other Protestants. In earlier chapters we have seen that the ancient bishop drew his authority both from representation—he was elected by the community, and represented that community in councils—*and* from consecration by one who stood in the apostolic succession. This latter consecration Melanchthon sees as merely a confirmation of the community's election.[65] But in the ancient Church, and in Catholicism, it is more; it communicates a grace and Spirit which unites the bishop with the apostles and with Christ, and confers a charism of discernment that helps the bishop maintain the Church in the truth bestowed by the apostles and in unity. Thus the bishop's power comes both from above and from below.

In reducing ordination to a power of the local community, Luther severed the ordinand from the apostolic succession, which is not just a physical or official succession conferred by laying on of hands; it is a succession in grace. Effectively, this left Lutheranism with no sacrament of unity, no principle of authority through which the disparate local churches could be unified. Luther seemed to think that the principle of *sola scriptura*—the assertion of scripture as the foundation of belief and the Church, would suffice for ecclesial unity. If the churches were devoted to scripture, they would persevere in the same truth. But the history of the Church both before and after the Reformation prove this belief wrong. Lutheran and Protestant churches found no way to preserve unity in the face of divisions and fissiparous sects, and were therefore forced to turn to the secular rulers to preserve the churches in unity. From this came the settlement of Augsburg in 1555, when the principle was laid down that whatever the religion of the prince, that would be the religion of his dominion: "cuius regio, eius religio." This led to the state churches which became characteristic of Protestantism. These in

[65] *Treatise on the Power and Primacy of the Pope*, in *The Book of Concord*, 332.

turn erected command hierarchies, and persecuted dissidents, such as the Anabaptists. As with the Orthodox, the rejection of episcopal authority and papal primacy led to nationalistic and regional churches. The tragedy here is that Luther, in rejecting the papacy, was actually rejecting a deformed caricature of the papacy, the Renaissance papacy in which the pope had become one secular lord among many. This point has been made by E. Gordon Rupp, in a commentary on Luther's *Against the Roman Papacy, the Institution of the Devil:* "What Luther here attacked so fiercely and cruelly was . . . not so much the modern papacy but 'popery,' the Renaissance papacy in its highly secularized, politically aggressive form, hopelessly entangled in the world and bringing souls into fear and bondage by a legalistic religion which set the traditions of men above the word of God."[66]

But neither Luther nor Melanchthon, in his *Treatise on the Power and Primacy of the Pope,* seems to seriously have considered the possibility of a papal primacy in which the bishop of Rome was first among equals, as the Orthodox had always held, a bishop exercising primacy within a college and council of bishops, whose task it was collectively to exercise authority over the universal Church. This understanding of the papacy, which I am defending here, was close to that of Luther before 1519 or 1520, when he thought of the Church as governed by a plurality of authorities: scripture, councils, the papacy, Church fathers, and right reason.

Other Protestant Denominations

Luther was more traditional than subsequent reformers, many of whom carried his own principles farther than he did. Luther argued for the principle of *sola scriptura,* for example, but retained those beliefs and practices which were traditional but were not contradicted by scripture, like infant baptism. But the radical reformers, such as the Anabaptists, argued that if a practice was not actually endorsed by scripture, it should be dropped, and so rejected infant baptism. Similarly, they carried the rejection of the medieval sacramental system farther than Luther, denying the real presence in the Eucharist and degrading it to a mere memorial.

This same pattern obtained in the radicals' attitude toward Church hierarchy and government. Luther, though a passionate foe of a tyran-

[66] In *LW,* vol. 41, xv.

nical papacy, was no social radical. When the German peasants, in 1525, misread Luther's *Freedom of a Christian* as a license to revolt against their overlords, Luther savagely opposed them. In his *Against the Robbing and Murdering Peasants* he encouraged the princes to strike the peasants down with the sword, which the princes did.[67] Though Luther recovered the ancient practice of laity electing their ministers, he did not endorse congregationalism, and turned to the German princes to impose unity and order on the churches. The result was German territorial and state Lutheran churches. More radical groups, such as the Congregationalists, the Baptists, and the Anabaptists, understood the individual local assembly as a sovereign unit, which could elect its own ministers. These groups practiced ecclesiastical democracy. In some groups, notably the Quakers, the consensus of the group was regarded as indicating the will of the Spirit, and decisions were made by group consensus. These structures were close to what I am calling participatory hierarchies, though on the scale of small congregations, not the universal Church.

Finally, the radical groups continued the prophetic element in the Church. Many of the stands for which they were persecuted eventually came to be universally accepted. These groups, especially the Quakers, were the first to denounce slavery, cruelty to animals, and coercion in matters of religion. Their courageous stand led to the modern acceptance of freedom of conscience in areas of religion. They also held that all are called to holiness, and that this holiness can be achieved in the practices of everyday life, a position endorsed also by Vatican Council II.

Conclusion

Many factors, some sketched above, led to the Reformation. But in the eyes of Luther and others the worst fault of the papal system was clerical oppression and tyranny. This is also Joseph Lortz's opinion: "Legalism in the chair of Peter was not in itself the worst evil. The worst evil was despotism, which dominated the curia."[68] The misuse of the papacy flowed from a system in which there were no checks on papal power within the ecclesial system itself, and from a Roman ecclesiology

[67] See the account in Ozment, *The Age of Reform*, 272–289.

[68] *The Reformation in Germany*, vol. 1, 86.

which held that the unity of the Church and even civil society flowed from obedience to the pope, that the papacy had never and could never err, that councils were subordinate to the pope, and that those disobedient to the pope were outside the Church. We find this affirmed by Boniface VIII in *Unam sanctam,* by Lateran Council V on the eve of the Reformation, and by Prierias and Cajetan in their colloquies with Luther. At any time before 1520 or 1530 a free ecumenical council could probably have healed the incipient schism. But a truly ecumenical council could not have been simply controlled by the papacy, as Lateran V was. At that council, few bishops were present, especially from outside Italy. Its decrees were not even given out in the name of the council itself, but were Bulls given in the name of the pope, "with the approval of the sacred council." Any council, to be effective, would have had to deal with the reformation of the papacy and the Curia, and hence with the unresolved theological tension between Roman ecclesiology and moderate conciliarism. At bottom, this was a matter of power: is ultimate authority in the Church held by the pope alone, or by the pope in conjunction with a council? This question lies at the heart of the problem of hierarchy in the [Catholic] Church, and is unresolved even now. Here we recall the words of Brian Tierney:

> The failure of the medieval Church to achieve a juridical structure consistent with the insights of its greatest thinkers was the supreme tragedy of the later Middle Ages. The downfall of a Catholic conciliarism, rooted in sound medieval ecclesiology, made inevitable the rise of a Protestant individualism alien to the traditional conception of the Church.[69]

The history of the Reformation confirms a major thesis of this book, that an excessive emphasis on command produces rebellion and schism. Conversely, unity can only be procured through the exercise of participatory hierarchy, in this case, through an ecumenical council, which, as even Jedin admits, was the only authority which all sides would have recognized as compelling. Often it is said that the primary reform of Luther was his emphasis on salvation by faith alone. But his shift in understanding of hierarchy and the Church is equally important. In the ancient Church, the bishop possessed an authority both from below, as a representative of his community, and from above, as

[69] "Collegiality in the Middle Ages," *Concilium,* 7 (September, 1965) 8.

consecrated as a successor of the apostles. Further, the community itself possessed the right of consent. Both Cyprian and Leo the Great emphasize this, as did Roman law. By the high Middle Ages, however, the community was mostly passive—it did not elect its pastors or bishops, who were appointed by the Curia, which also taxed the community without its consent. The representative function of bishops had become submerged, and the episcopacy itself, especially in Germany, had been taken over by lords eager to exploit its revenues. This was a deformation of the ancient Church's theory and practice. Luther was reacting against a Church and hierarchical system that had become corrupted by power and money, and deformed by a command hierarchy, a fact emphasized by both Catholic and Protestant historians. But in his reaction Luther went too far. Before 1519 he accepted the authority of councils, and appealed to a consensus of authorities. After 1520 scripture became the primary norm of the Church, and the role of bishops as interpreters of scripture was minimized. While recovering the legitimate role of the bishop as elected by and as representative of the community, he discarded the ancient belief that the bishop is consecrated into the apostolic succession, so as to preserve the truth flowing from Christ and the apostles and preserve the Church in unity.

Similarly, in his extreme and obstinate reaction against the papacy, Luther, with considerable justification, came to see the pope as a tyrant, the Antichrist, who had usurped power from the Church and set himself up as a god, declaring that he can be judged by no one. He failed to adequately consider the possibility of the pope as a unifying center within the college of bishops. But the loss of a primatial center meant that "things fall apart, the center cannot hold." Protestantism shivered into numerous denominations and sects, and the unity of the Western Church was lost.

As for ontological hierarchy, Luther and Calvin did not really break free of Ockhamism, which postulated a hierarchy based on will and power, but severed any continuous hierarchy of being, a break that also affected the Protestant view of sacraments. Between the God of Luther and Calvin and unredeemed humanity yawns an ontological chasm. Humans can contribute nothing to their own salvation; they have no ontological continuity with God, but are saved extrinsically by an act of God's grace. Calvin's God, who predestines some to heaven and some to hell apart from any decision on their part, seems more like an omnipotent tyrant than a God of love. But this conception of God came to infect both Catholicism and Protestantism. The optimism of

St. Thomas, who saw humans linked to God by a continuity in being, seemed to have been forgotten. After the mid-sixteenth century, both Protestantism and Catholicism became excessively authoritarian, Protestantism under state churches, and Catholicism under the post-Tridentine papacy.

Chapter 8

Catholic Reformation and the Post-Tridentine Church

The Jesuits

Reforming movements in the Catholic Church had been underway before Luther's reform. In particular, new or reformed religious orders, such as the Oratory of Divine love, the Theatines, and the Capuchins, were initiated, especially in Italy. The most influential of new religious orders, however, was the Society of Jesus, founded by Ignatius of Loyola (1491–1556).[1] Ignatius was trained in the ideals of medieval chivalry and aspired to heroic knightly deeds. He was seriously wounded in 1521, however, and during his long convalescence, he determined to become a knight for Christ. The core of his spiritual vision, based on his own mystical experiences, is found in his manual, The *Spiritual Exercises,* which became the core of Jesuit spirituality, and greatly influenced the post-Tridentine Church.

Ignatian spirituality[2] is profoundly Christ-centered. The aim of the *Spiritual Exercises* is to bring the seeker into an intimacy with Christ in order to serve him and carry out his work of establishing the Kingdom.

[1] On Ignatius' life, see *The Autobiography of St. Ignatius Loyola,* John C. Olin, ed. (New York: Harper Torchbooks, 1974); also William Bangert, S.J., *A History of the Society of Jesus* (St. Louis: Institute of Jesuit Sources, 1972) 3–46.

[2] See J. Lewis, "Ignatian Spirituality," *NCE* 7, 349–351; George Lane, S.J., *Christian Spirituality—an Historical Sketch* (Chicago: Loyola University Press, 1984) 45–68.

In contrast to earlier spiritualities, which centered on prayer and contemplation, and tended to be individualistic, Ignatian spirituality focuses on an active working with Christ in the service of the Church. "In activity and study . . . when we direct everything to the service of God, everything is prayer."[3] The principle here is not so much faith as active, outgoing love: the love of Christ and the Holy Spirit working through the companion of Christ to transform the world into the kingdom. It is one's duty to "seek God in all things," and to "love him in all his creatures."[4] Such a spirituality demands total obedience to Christ, the discernment of the will of Christ, an elimination of self-interest, the infusion of the soul with the charity of the Spirit, and the will to love and serve the divine majesty in all things.

Ignatius also placed great emphasis on hierarchy and on obedience to Christ, and to Christ's vicars: one's superior and the pope. Thus the original articles of association presented by Ignatius and his companions to Pope Paul II in 1539, read:

> Whoever desires, as a member of our society . . . to become a soldier of God under the banner of the Cross and to serve His Vicar, the Roman Pontiff, must vow himself to perpetual chastity . . . [and] abandoning each his own will [to] consider ourselves bound by a special vow to the present pope and his successors to go, without demur, to any country whither they may send us . . . subject only to the will of the pope and the General.[5]

Thus Jesuits, in addition to the usual three monastic vows of poverty, chastity, and obedience, take a fourth vow of obedience to the pope. One enters the Society of Jesus to "fight under the standard of the Cross and to serve the one Lord as well as the church, His Spouse, under the guidance of the Roman pontiff, who takes the place of Christ on earth."[6] In his "Letter on Obedience," Ignatius stresses that obedience does not only consist in doing the will of one's superior, but in willing and thinking in line with one's superior. "He who aims at an entire and perfect oblation of himself, in addition to his will, must offer his understanding, which is the highest degree of obedience. He must not only will,

[3] *Epistola Ignatiana,* VI, 91, cited in George Lane, S.J., *Christian Spirituality,* 48.

[4] *Constitutions* 3.1, 26, cited in *NCE* 7:351.

[5] Cited in B.J. Kidd, *The Counter Reformation: 1550–1600* (London: Society for Promoting Christian Knowledge, 1933) 28.

[6] *Formula Instituti* 1, cited in *NCE* 7:350.

but also think the same as the superior, submitting his own judgment to the superior so far as a devout will can bend the understanding."[7] Similarly, the thirteenth rule of "Rules for thinking with the Church," in the *Spiritual Exercises,* states: "If we wish to be sure we are right in all things, we should always be ready to accept this principle: I will believe that the white that I see is black, if the hierarchical church so defines it."[8] Coupled with this emphasis on absolute obedience, however, Ignatius allowed the Jesuits an extreme degree of apostolic freedom in their mission activities, sending them out by twos to the far corners of the world where they carried on their evangelizations apart from any centralized authority, except such directions as they received by letter.

Thus we find in Ignatius and the Jesuits an unusual mix of authority and freedom, hierarchy and participation.[9] The great success of the Jesuits, whose influence, especially on the European upper classes, was enormous, was due largely to the *Spiritual Exercises,* which proved very effective in bringing young men into an intimate relationship with Christ and consolidating them into a community with great *esprit de corps.* This is a participatory hierarchy. What is missing is any prophetic element, any possibility of criticism of the misuse of institutional or papal power, any intellectual freedom from the dictates of the papacy, the very aspect which is pronounced in Luther and Protestantism. Until the latter half of this century, the Society of Jesus tended to be strongly, even militantly pro-papal, and little inclined to ecumenical dialogue. And the Jesuit notion of obedience became that of the post-Tridentine papacy and Church. Yves Congar has pointed out that the post-Tridentine Church, under Jesuit influence, has subscribed to a kind of authoritarian "mysticism" which completely identifies the will of God with the will of institutional authority.[10] This provided a strong

[7] *Letters of St. Ignatius of Loyola,* William J. Young, S.J., ed. and trans. (Chicago, 1959) 290, cited in Ozment, *Age of Reform,* 416.

[8] *The Spiritual Exercises of St. Ignatius,* Anthony Mottola, trans. (New York: Doubleday, Image Book, 1964) 141.

[9] Avery Dulles writes: "The Ignatian charism . . . consists in the ability to combine the two tendencies without detriment to either. A purely mechanical obedience without regard for the movements of the Spirit and a purely individualistic reliance on the Spirit without regard for ecclesiastical authority would be equally foreign to the [Jesuit] heritage. . . ." "The Ignatian Charism and Contemporary Theology" in *America* (April 26, 1997) 22.

[10] "The Historical Development of Authority in the Church," *Problems of Authority,* J.M. Todd, ed. (London: Darton Longman & Todd, 1962) 145.

Catholic identity and contributed to the success of the Catholic Reformation, but also bred strong opposition, and deepened the divisions between Protestant and Catholic Christians.

The Council of Trent

After many delays, occasioned partly by the reluctance of the papacy to convene a council, partly by the hostility between the French king, Francis I, and the emperor Charles V, Pope Paul III was able to convene the Council of Trent in 1545. The Council met from 1545–1548, 1551–1552, and 1562–1563 under three different popes. Although some Protestant observers were present at the second session of the council, generally Protestants refused to attend, since Trent was not, in their eyes, a "free, Christian council on German soil." Rather they saw the council as dominated by the Italians and papal legates. In fact, the great majority of bishops and theologians present were Italians, though Jedin argues that they did not vote as a block, and some of the Italian bishops did oppose the positions of the papal legates.[11] Particularly noteworthy was the scarcity of bishops from Germany and France, precisely the bishops who were most strongly conciliar. A.G. Dickens observes: "Of the 270 bishops attending at one time or another, 187 were Italians, 31 Spaniards, 26 French and 2 German. Of the 255 ecclesiastics to sign the final Acts no fewer than 189 were Italians."[12] Though Dickens notes that not all the Italians were papalist, he nevertheless judges that "in our modern sense of the term its spirit can hardly be called ecumenical . . . Judged by any regional and mathematical criteria, it could not be pronounced representative of Western Christendom."[13] And in fact, though Trent invigorated Catholic reform, the Church which issued from Trent was firmly papalist rather than conciliar. No ecumenical council was held after Trent for over three hundred years.

Because it did not represent Protestant factions, there was no question of the Council of Trent unifying the Western Church. Rather, it opposed the Protestants on every important position. The Vulgate was declared to be the official Bible of the Church. No provision was made for clerical marriage. The question of communion in both kinds was de-

[11] Jedin, *A History of the Council of Trent,* vol. II, 482–495.

[12] A.G. Dickens, *The Counter Reformation* (New York: W.W. Norton, 1968) 109.

[13] Ibid.

ferred to the pope, who authorized it only for certain ecclesiastical provinces in Germany and in Hapsburg territory. Some of the fathers argued strongly that clerical education should focus on the Bible in the light of the critical and historical advances made by the Humanists. But in the end the council decided the traditional method of clerical education, which centered on the scholastic doctors, especially St. Thomas, should prevail. Dickens comments: "In no field did the fear of Protestantism leave deeper marks upon the developments of Catholic religion."[14] The critical study of the Bible was not to be encouraged until 1943, when Pius XII urged it in his encyclical *De Divinu afflante.*

Because of the presence of conciliarists and Gallicans, especially among the French, Trent made no pronouncement on papal primacy. A fierce debate took place in 1563 with the Spaniards and French arguing that the office of bishop existed by divine right *(Jus Divinum)*—a proposal which would have ensured greater autonomy for the bishops. But opposition to this on the part of the Italians ensured that no declaration on this topic would be forthcoming from the council. Even so modest a proposal as that of Seripando, general of the Augustinian order, that "the bishops had been established in the church by Christ," but received their jurisdiction from the pope, was defeated by the Italians and Rome.[15]

Trent did, however, enact an important reforming decree which strengthened the authority of the bishops in their own sees. Appeals to the Roman Curia over the head of the bishops were limited, and bishops were given authority over previously exempt chapters, orders, institutions, and individuals. But, as Hubert Jedin notes in a telling phrase, this authority was given to them "in their quality as delegates of the Holy See."[16] The bishops did not receive their authority from Christ and the apostolic succession; they received it from the pope, in effect making them papal deputies.

Though Trent made no statement on papal primacy, it did leave a great deal of unfinished business to be resolved by the pope. And it did, in the last of its decrees, request that all of its decrees be confirmed by the pope.[17] It further stipulated that at all provincial synods, each prelate must "promise and profess true obedience to the supreme

[14] Ibid., 115.

[15] *NCE* 14:275.

[16] Ibid., 276.

[17] *The Canons and Decrees of the Council of Trent,* H.J. Schroeder, ed. (Rockford, Ill.: TAN Books, 1941, 1978) 267–268.

Roman pontiff."[18] Effectively Trent greatly enhanced papal power and authority, and virtually ended conciliarism in the Catholic Church, though a kind of conciliarism survived in France in the form of Gallicanism, and in Germany in the form of Episcopalism, both of which were quashed at Vatican I.

Trent also provided for seminaries in every diocese, and virtually ended the host of abuses which had corrupted the late medieval Church, such as clerical absenteeism, the selling of benefices, simony, and so on. It set a model of ecclesiology which was to survive virtually unchanged until Vatican Council II. This model consisted of a monarchial pope, surrounded by deputy bishops, each a monarch in his own diocese. In one sense this was an advance towards participation over the late medieval Church. For in delegating genuine power to the bishops it ended the destructive centralization of power in the papacy, whereby suffragan bishops and individuals could appeal directly to Rome for exemptions from the local bishop. This system had paralyzed the local bishops, and crippled the medieval Church. In restoring power to the bishops, Trent restored the integrity of the Church. But in treating the bishops as merely deputies of the pope, it continued the papal monarchy while stifling the conciliarism which had continued through the Middle Ages alongside the papal model. The ecclesiology emerging from Trent was a pyramid: the pope ruling the bishops, who ruled the priests, who ruled the laity, who were "born to obey, not to command."[19] The unity of the Church consisted in obedience, not in conciliar consensus. And the laity were frozen out of an administrative influence in the Church. The post-Tridentine Church was highly clericalized, with the gap between the clergy and laity symbolized by dress, celibacy, language (the clergy used Latin, the laity the vernacular), and communion: the clergy received the wine, the laity only the bread. The old distinction between the "teaching church" (the clergy), and the "learning church"—*ecclesia docens* and *ecclesia discens,* received new prominence. Even the liturgy became more clericalized: "The gap between liturgy and believers, existing since the Middle Ages, was not overcome but deepened instead. The liturgy had become a liturgy for the clergy, touching the people only inasmuch as it could serve as a spectacle. The holy Mass was no longer a participatory event; the ser-

[18] Ibid., 234.

[19] The phrase is Cajetan's, but it reflects the ecclesiology enacted at Trent. Cited in Patrick Granfield, *The Papacy in Transition* (Garden City, N.Y.: Doubleday, 1980) 55.

mon had been removed from it and the Communion had become isolated from it as a separate devotion."[20]

Because of divisions among the bishops, Trent did not make any formal statement on ecclesiology. Yet it did leave a clericalized, centrally controlled, Church. But its impact was limited because of the continuing ecclesial authority exercised by kings and princes in such areas as France, Spain, and Germany.

Robert Bellarmine's Concept of Visible Church

The most important statement of ecclesial hierarchy made in the post-Tridentine period was that of Robert Bellarmine (1542–1621), whose conception of the Church became the standard Catholic response to Protestantism, and was foundational for most treatments of ecclesiology down to Vatican II.[21] Bellarmine opposed the separation of the Church into a visible and an invisible Church (e.g., by Calvin). "According to our doctrine, there is only one church, not two. And this one and true church is the assembly of men, bound together by profession of the same Christian faith, and by communion of the same sacraments, under the rule of legitimate pastors, and in particular of the one Vicar of Christ on earth, the Roman Pontiff."[22] Thus those who did not profess Christianity were excluded from the true Church, those not partaking of the sacraments (catechumens and those excommunicated) were also not full members, as were schismatics, who did not submit to the pope. Against Protestants who held that faith or internal virtues sufficed for ecclesial membership, thus making the Church invisible, Bellarmine insisted that the Church was a visible society, and hence required external profession of faith.

> We also believe that in the Church are found all the virtues: faith, hope, and charity, and all the rest. However, for anyone to be called in some sense a part of the true Church of which the scriptures speak, we do not think that any internal virtue is required, but only an external

[20] *HC:VI,* 548.

[21] See John A. Hardon, S.J., "Robert Bellarmine's Conception of the Church," *Studies in Medieval Culture,* John Sommerfeldt, ed. (Kalamazoo: The Medieval Institute, Western Michigan University, 1966) 120–127; Congar, *L'Église,* 370–375.

[22] *De Ecclesia Militante,* cap. 2 (*Opera Omnia;* Milano, 1857ff) II, cited in Hardon, ibid., 120.

> profession of faith and communication of the sacraments, which can be perceived by the senses themselves. For the Church is an assembly of men, as visible and palpable as the assembly of the Roman people or the Venetians.[23]

Though Bellarmine was influenced by St. Thomas, the emphasis here is not on the Holy Spirit as the soul and principle of unity in the Church, as with Thomas; it is on external, juridical profession. Bellarmine held that in some sense even secret heretics who professed the faith externally, remained members of the Church: they were members of its body, but not its soul. (Conversely, those who had faith and charity, but not external profession, were members of the soul of the Church, but not its body.) Like Cajetan, he held that the pope was the only vicar of Christ, as head of the Church represented Christ in relation to the body of the Church, and held the fullness of power, so that universal jurisdiction was transmitted by the pope to the bishops. He devalued the role of ecumenical councils.[24]

> The Pope simply and absolutely is above the universal Church, in that he is the Head of the whole Church on earth; and so he is above a General council, and can recognize no judge upon the earth above himself. He cannot be judged, punished, or deposed by a General council, or by any human authority. But should a Pope become a formal heretic he would by the very fact cease to be Pope, and could be judged and declared deposed by the Church.[25]

But Bellarmine did not think that councils were superfluous:

> For even though infallibility be in the Pope, for all that he ought not to neglect the human and ordinary means of arriving at true knowledge of the matter in question: but the ordinary means is a Council, greater or smaller, according to the relative magnitude of the matter in question. Besides, definitions *de Fide* depend principally on the apostolic tradition and the consent of the churches [*ex consensu ecclesiarum*]. But in order that, when a question arises, it may be known what is in the mind of the whole Church, there is no better way than that the bishops should come together for all provinces, and each one state the custom of his own Church.[26]

[23] Ibid., 121.

[24] Congar, *L'Église,* 372–374.

[25] Cited in C. Butler, *The Vatican Council,* vol. 1 (London: Longmans, Green, & Co., 1930) 37.

[26] Ibid., 37–38.

The role of councils here seems to be primarily advisory, though Bellarmine does recognize their importance in discerning the mind of the whole Church. But doctrinal and juridical authority seems to flow mainly from Christ to the pope, from the pope to the bishops, from the bishops to the priests and people. There is no indication of the bishops deriving doctrinal authority from their consecration as successors of the apostles. "The unity of the church is one of subordination of inferiors to superiors and the dispensation of grace is determined by the sincerity of this subordination."[27]

Bellarmine's ecclesiology became largely normative from the seventeenth century on. It is a pyramidical, top-down, juridical ecclesiology, based on a command hierarchy. The authority of the pope was of divine right, *Jus divinum,* like the divine right of kings. Schismatics, such as the Orthodox and Protestants, were not members of the visible Church, because they rejected the authority of the pope, though they could be members of the soul of the Church if they had faith and charity, and therefore could be saved. Bellarmine also taught the infallibility of the pope, though he admitted that this was not a defined doctrine, and was not therefore binding on the faithful. Implicit in this ecclesiology is the idea that the Church derives from the pope, who alone is the Vicar of Christ, and who transmits authority to all other members of the Church. Absent or minimized are the ancient ideas that the bishops derive their authority from Christ, that they are representatives of their congregations, that the Spirit speaks through a plurality of agents instead of just one, that prophets may be necessary to correct those in authority.

The Roman Inquisition

The medieval Inquisition (chapter 6) which flourished under Popes Innocent III (1198–1216), Gregory IX (1227–1241), and Innocent IV (1243–1254), had declined in the fifteenth and sixteenth centuries, except in Spain. There, it was directed by the state and used first against converted Jews, then against Moslems, then against Protestants and Spanish mystics (the so-called *alumbrados*). Both Ignatius Loyola and Therese of Avila came under its suspicion; indeed, Ignatius left the University of Salamanca for the University of Paris to avoid the Inquisition. The

[27] Hardon, 121.

Inquisition was ruthlessly effective in purifying the Spanish realm of heresy, diversity, and foreigners—both Jews and Moslems were expelled after 1492. The Roman nuncio to Spain, Cardinal Caraffa, was very impressed with the efficiency of the Spanish Inquisition in combatting heresy, and convinced Pope Paul III to reestablish the Inquisition in Rome in 1542.[28] Paul appointed six cardinals as Inquisitors-general, under Caraffa's direction. Their authority was almost total; only the pope could override it. Even bishops and cardinals were attacked by the Roman Inquisition. Indeed, Paul III, troubled by the *Consilium . . . de emenda ecclesia* (above, p. 182), turned the Inquisition against the liberal cardinals such as Contarini who had been its authors, thus destroying any vestige of sympathy for Protestant positions in Rome.

From 1542 through the 1570s, the Inquisition, under six different popes, succeeded in eliminating heretics and Protestants from Italy. Most fled, many were imprisoned, some were burnt at the stake. From 1555–1559, Caraffa himself, as Pope Paul IV, ruled Rome with an iron hand, so much so that at his death the populace sacked the buildings of the Inquisition, burned its records, and defaced his statue. His successor, the more moderate Pius IV (1559–1565) nonetheless had his inquisitors and the Jesuits assist Ascanio Colonna in massacring some two thousand Waldensians in Calabria. And Pius personally rebuked the Duke of Savoy for refusing to attack the main body of the Waldensians in Piedmont in 1561. Pius' successor, Pius V, sainted because of his irreproachable life, his suppression of simony and reform of the Curia, like Caraffa, had been an austere Inquisitor himself, and used the Inquisition or Holy Office to suppress the last remnants of Protestantism and religious diversity in Italy. He sent troops to aid Charles IX of France in extirpating the Huguenots, and ordered his commander to take no prisoners, but to slay every Huguenot falling into his hands.[29]

The Roman Inquisition after 1542 is an embarrassment that Catholic historians prefer to pass over quickly. It is barely discussed in the massive *History of the Church*,[30] and it is not mentioned in Y. Dossat's article on "Inquisition" in the *New Catholic Encyclopedia*.[31] Yet

[28] The following account of the Roman Inquisition derives in part from Kidd, *The Counter Reformation*, 39–52.

[29] Dickens, *The Counter Reformation*, 135.

[30] See *HC:V*, 486, 500.

[31] *NCE* 7:541.

it was important in setting the character of post-Tridentine Catholicism, especially in Italy and Spain (significantly, the Inquisition only prevailed in areas governed by Roman law, and never flourished in England, Germany, or Scandanavia).[32] In its rigorism, it suppressed not only Protestantism, but any sort of religious diversity, and made any attempt to meet Protestant concerns half-way impossible. It stamped post-Tridentine Catholicism with an authoritarian character from which it never recovered. It eliminated those, like Cardinal Contarini or Cardinal Moroni, who were in any way inclined to a moderate conciliarism, or to tolerance of religious diversity. This made post-Tridentine Catholicism very different from medieval Catholicism, which harbored great diversity and a strong conciliar movement. The Inquisition in Spain can be partly excused because it was a work of political coercion by the state.[33] But no such excuse can be summoned for the Roman Inquisition after 1542, which was controlled directly by the popes. It was a centralized command hierarchy of the worst kind, which overrode all intermediate and local authorities—bishops, religious orders, political rulers, and cardinals—and was subject to no checks except that of the pope.

The Holy Office of the Inquisition was also responsible for the condemnation of Galileo (1633) as "vehemently suspected of heresy" for arguing that the Copernican system was true.[34] In fact, Nicholas of Cusa had maintained a doctrine similar to that of Copernicus in his *Of Learned Ignorance* in 1440, and had not been accused of heresy.[35] What was different in Galileo's time was the polemics between Catholicism and Protestantism, and the activity of the Inquisition. In arguing that traditional interpretations of scripture might be wrong, Galileo was challenging the authority of the Church and the pope as the supreme

[32] Ibid.

[33] See the massive account of Benzion Netanyahu, *The Origins of the Inquisition in Fifteenth Century Spain* (New York: Random House, 1995). Netanyahu argues that the Inquisition against the converted Jews, the *conversos,* was not in fact religiously motivated. These Jewish converts, he argues, were really Christians, not secretly practicing Jews. The real motives of the Inquisition's attack on the *conversos* were economic envy—they had attained high positions in society and the court, and racial, the *Limpieza de la sangre* (cleansing of the blood).

[34] For an account of the Galileo case, see J.J. Langford, *Galileo, Science, and the Church* (Ann Arbor: University of Michigan, 1971, 1992).

[35] See Arthur Koestler, *The Sleepwalkers* (New York: Macmillan, 1959) 206–207.

interpreters of scripture, the very point that Luther and the Protestants had challenged. This could not go unpunished. The Galileo condemnation did not retard European science, but it did cripple Catholic natural science for over two hundred years. The Jesuits, who at the time of Galileo had a thriving interest in the new science, were ordered by their superior general in 1611 and 1613 to defend Aristotle against the newly emerging view of nature espoused by Galileo.[36] The result was the sacrifice of Jesuit science in the name of obedience: "With the notable exception of some isolated Jesuit scientists of the first rank . . . Jesuit science in general was never to regain the promise it exhibited in the period from Clavius to Scheiner. It was one of the casualties of the condemnation of Copernicanism."[37] And this was true of Catholic science generally; from the seventeenth century on, very few scientists of rank have been Catholics. As late as 1820 a book espousing Newton's theory of gravitation was placed on the *Index* in Rome.[38]

The great strengths of the post-Tridentine Church were the flowering of spiritual and mystical movements and devotions, new religious orders, a strong sacramental sense, and a glorious religious art, the baroque, expressing the transcendent dynamism of the soul for God. It fostered a strong and distinct sense of Catholic identity, precisely because it defined itself over and against Protestantism. But for this reason it was blind to any value in Protestant teaching or practice, and was anti-ecumenical. After the Galileo case, the Church was largely sequestered from modern currents of thought. Many of the ideas of the Enlightenment and Liberalism, such as the separation of Church and state, freedom of religious belief, religious toleration, freedom of the press, and freedom of conscience originated outside the Church and were opposed by it. For example, Pope Pius IX, in his *Syllabus of Errors,* condemned the separation of Church and state, freedom of religion and freedom of conscience. The Church remained an authoritarian, closed-in structure for three centuries, during which time no ecumenical council was called. To an unhealthy degree it identified the authority of the pope and bishops with that of God. The major exception to this was Gallicanism.

[36] Ibid., 196–197.

[37] Richard Blackwell, *Galileo, Bellarmine, and the Bible* (Notre Dame: University of Notre Dame Press, 1991) 164.

[38] Bokenkotter, *A Concise History of the Catholic Church,* 320.

Gallicanism

Gallicanism was a complex theological and political movement associated with French Catholicism, which from early times proclaimed certain liberties and prerogatives peculiar to the French Church. Some of these were: the independence of the French king in the temporal order, the superiority of general councils over the pope, or at least the assertion that the pope was not infallible apart from the consent of the episcopate, the rights of the episcopate vis-a-vis the papacy, and the right of the king and clergy to limit papal power in France.[39] Gallicanism can be traced back to Charlemagne's hegemony over the Church in his empire, and to Hincmar of Rheims' defense of the rights of metropolitan bishops to judge cases in their sees rather than ceding jurisdiction to the popes.[40] King Philip the Fair resisted the attempts of Pope Boniface VIII to subject the French king to papal control. During the medieval period, the University of Paris was a center for conciliar thought. The Pragmatic Sanction of Bourges (1438) made into law the conciliar thought of the Councils of Constance and Basel in France and deprived the pope of the majority of his powers and revenues in France. The concordat of 1516 between Francis I and Pope Leo X gave the French king the right to nominate candidates for bishoprics and abbeys.[41]

The classic statement of Gallicanism is the Declaration of the Gallican Clergy (1682), drafted by Jacques Bousset, bishop of Meaux, and accepted by Louis XIV, who made its teaching obligatory in France.[42] The declaration consists of four articles. Article 1 states that kings and princes are not subject to any ecclesiastical authority in temporal affairs and cannot be deposed by the pope. Article 2 admitted the authority of the pope in spiritual matters, but insisted that the decrees of Constance concerning the supremacy of ecumenical councils over popes were valid. Article 3 stipulated that papal authority was limited by the rules, customs, and institutions of the French kingdom and church. Article 4 stated that the judgment of the pope was not irreformable

[39] See C. Berthelot du Chesnay, "Gallicanism," in *NCE* 6:263.

[40] Congar, *L'Église,* 64.

[41] ET of the Pragmatic Sanction is given in *Church and State through the Centuries,* Sidney Ehler and John Morrall, eds. (Westminster, Md.: Newman Press, 1954) 112–121; ET of the Concordat of 1515, ibid., 134–144.

[42] ET of the declaration, ibid., 207–208; the Latin text is in *DS* 2281–2284.

unless it received the consensus of the Church ("nec tamen irreformabile esse judicium nisi Ecclesiae consensus accesserit"). Though these articles were later declared null and void by Pope Alexander VIII (*DS* 2285), and the king later withdrew his support, they remained influential in the French Church throughout the eighteenth century and in the early nineteenth century had the force of law. The fourth article was the target of Vatican I's famous declaration on papal infallibility (chap. 9).

Article 3 of the declaration refers to what were called the traditional Liberties of the Gallican church. Some of these were the following: The French king had the right to convene ecclesial councils in his dominion and to make laws concerning ecclesiastical matters. Papal legates could not operate in France without the king's consent. Bishops could not go out of the kingdom without the king's consent. The pope's Bulls or letters could not be exercised within the kingdom without the king's consent.[43]

Gallicanism was therefore a complex mix of conciliarism and episcopalism, and royal or parliamentary control over the French church—so called "Royal or Political Gallicanism." It is necessary to distinguish episcopal Gallicanism, which asserted the traditional rights of bishops and held that bishops drew their authority directly from God rather than from the pope, and political Gallicanism, which amounted to partial state control over the Church. Both these forms of Gallicanism were opposed to unilateral papal control of the Church. Episcopal Gallicanism was well expressed in the work of the great bishop, Jacques Bossuet (1627–1704), the "eagle of Meaux."[44]

Bossuet accepted the primacy of the pope but also insisted that individual popes have erred. He thus distinguished between the papal seat—*sedes*—which was infallible, and the occupant of that seat, the *sedens*, who was not. The inerrant faith of the Church, and the supreme authority of the Church was to be found in the consensus of the Roman see with the council of bishops. The Roman pontiff was not infallible by himself, apart from the consensus of the Church (which for Bossuet meant the consensus of the bishops). Bossuet makes the point that on

[43] A. Degert, "Gallicanism," *The Catholic Encyclopedia* (1910) 6:352.

[44] See Congar, *L'Église,* 397–400; Richard F. Costigan, S.J., "Bossuet and the Consensus of the Church," in *TS* 56 (December, 1995) 652–672; Aimé-Georges Martimort, *Le Gallicanisme de Bossuet* (Paris: Cerf, Unam Sanctam #24, 1953). The following paragraph is drawn largely from Costigan's article.

occasion the Roman church has been saved or corrected by the universal Church. Thus, during the tenth century, when the see of Peter was occupied by corrupt and unworthy popes, it was the German emperors who finally forced it to reform, and thereby saved the authority of the Roman bishop. Again, during the Great Schism, when the Roman pope himself could do nothing to reconstitute a unified, authoritative papacy, it was an ecumenical council, Constance, which reconstituted the papacy. Bossuet affirms that even during the reign of a false pope, or no pope, the Church retains its unity and authority. Individual popes, such as Liberius (352–366), have erred and been corrected by the universal Church. Bossuet notes the example of Pope John XXII (1316–1334), who taught that the just do not receive the beatific vision until the Last Judgment, a teaching at variance with that of the universal Church. But as a result of criticisms by theologians, he changed his position just before his death. Bossuet sees in this incident a pope being brought to true and certain faith by the consensus of the Church.[45] Bossuet opposed the idea that the pope had the power to judge and depose kings and emperors. He held this to be a new idea, first enunciated by Gregory VII (1073–1085), which had never been thought of in the preceding centuries.

Bossuet was not sympathetic to ecclesiastical democracy, and resisted granting ecclesiastical power to priests, deacons, or laymen.[46] For him the "church" was the bishops and their councils, and the models for all councils was the Council of Jerusalem (Acts 15). His was an episcopal Gallicanism, which sought to preserve the ancient authority of bishops and councils in the Church without denying papal primacy. This was the ecclesiology of most of the French seminaries (and Sulpician seminaries in the United States) until 1853.[47] Episcopal Gallicanism represented the most important survival of medieval conciliar theory in the West, and the most important alternative to the ultramontane ecclesiology which was to triumph at Vatican I. The Gallican emphasis on councils and the episcopate is also visible in the work of Yves Congar, whence it influenced the conception of the Church at Vatican Council II.

In fact, however, what is usually associated with the term "Gallicanism" is not episcopal, but political Gallicanism, a system that

[45] Costigan, "Bossuet and the Consensus of the Church," 660.

[46] Ibid., 667.

[47] Congar, *L'Église,* 401.

ceded most ecclesial authority to the state. During the reign of Louis XIV Catholicism was the established state Church of France, Protestantism was not tolerated, and there was a danger that the king would create a schismatic national church, as Henry VIII had done in England.[48] In 1789, on the eve of the Revolution, the king still controlled the appointments of bishops and abbots in the French church. Many of the monastic appointments were sinecures, given out as courtly favors, with the result that many monasteries were effectively secularized: monks owned property and lived off the income of the monastic lands like secular landlords. Again, the bishops were appointed from the nobility, and many behaved like noble lords. Thus, a clerical oligarchy, beholden to the king but not to the pope, ruled the church in France.[49] The Civil Constitution of the Clergy, passed by the Constituent Assembly of the Revolution in 1790, enforced control of the clergy by the revolutionary state. Clergy were to be regulated and paid by the state (which had expropriated church property). In December 1790, the clergy were made to swear an oath of loyalty to the state, the laws, the king, and to the revolutionary constitution. Both the civil constitution and the oath of loyalty were outgrowths of the political Gallicanism of the *Ancien Regime,* in which the state had effectively controlled the church. State control of the church continued under Napoleon's regime—who went so far as to hold captive Pope Pius VII from 1809–1814—and under the restored Bourbon kings. It was this aspect of state control of the church which infuriated the enemies of Gallicanism, which energized the French ultramontane movement, and which led to the definition of papal infallibility at Vatican I.

A similar movement, Febronianism, existed in Germany, in which episcopal authority was exalted, and control of the church was largely in the hands of prince-bishops.

Deism and the Enlightenment

Historically, Deism began in seventeenth-century England as a rationalist simplification of Christianity. Lord Herbert of Cherbury, often called the father of English Deism, reduced religion to five points, held by most subsequent Deists. (1) There is one God, (2) who ought to be

[48] See *HC:VI,* 57–70.
[49] *HC:VII,* 12–18.

worshiped, (3) virtue and piety are the chief parts of worship, (4) persons should repent for sin, (5) God rewards good and punishes evil in this life and the next.[50] Though Deism varied greatly among its practitioners, Deists generally rejected miracles and other forms of supernatural intervention, including the Incarnation and Resurrection, and often revelation itself. God could be known as the creator from nature and by reason; this God was the true God sought by all religions. Deism became, in the eighteenth and nineteenth centuries, a creed held by many philosophically-minded persons in various countries; typical exponents were Voltaire and Thomas Jefferson. Voltaire believed in a creator God, whose majesty was evident in the cosmos. But his God did not intervene in nature, perform miracles, become incarnate in Jesus of Nazareth, or answer prayer. The world was guided by the natural laws God had created, but God did not thereafter become involved.

This philosophical Deism, a belief in an extrinsic, absentee God who observes the world but is not immanent or active in it, has become widespread since the eighteenth century, particularly among scientists. The universe described by modern science, after all, largely proceeds according to its own laws without the need of divine direction or intervention; one may posit a God who created the universe and its laws, but thereafter everything, including the emergence of life and humanity, could be accounted for by the operation of natural laws alone. This extrinsic notion of God has infected even many Christians. According to Bede Griffiths, Hindu children, when asked where God is, point to their hearts; Christian children, asked the same question, point to the sky.[51] This, needless to say, has undermined the credibility of the Church's sacramental vision of the universe, which depends on God, Christ, and the Spirit being immanent, present, and acting in and through material reality. Effectively, it represents a loss of a participatory notion of ontological hierarchy: God remains, and nature remains, but there is little continuity and mediation between them. Deism then appears to be an outgrowth of Ockhamism: like the Ockhamist God, the Deist God is extrinsic to the world; unlike the all-controlling God of Ockham (or Calvin and Luther), the Deist God does not actively control the course of the world.

[50] E.C. Mossner, "Deism," *The Encyclopedia of Philosophy* vol. 2 (New York: Macmillan, 1967) 327–328.

[51] *The Cosmic Revelation* (Springfield, Ill.: Templegate, 1983) 24.

This same effect flowed from the Enlightenment. According to Carl Becker, the principal characteristic of the Enlightenment was a secular outlook on reality:

> The basic idea underlying all the tendencies of the Enlightenment was the conviction that all human understanding is capable, by its own power and without any recourse to super-natural assistance, of comprehending the system of the world and that this new way of understanding the world will lead to a new way of mastering it.[52]

The Enlightenment varied from country to country. In France, its main spokesmen, the *philosophes* (e.g., Voltaire, Denis Diderot), were fiercely anticlerical, because of the authoritarian character of French state-catholicism. The German Enlightenment was more moderate. But Immanuel Kant's critique of metaphysical knowledge led to a God who could be known only through nature and the dictates of conscience. Enlightenment thinkers inculcated a respect for religious toleration, the natural rights of persons, freedom, and equality. But their skepticism towards tradition undermined traditional religious faith and the credibility of ecclesial hierarchy. The God of the Enlightenment thinkers, many of whom were Deists, was a God of reason and morality who was on the margins of the world. In place of God's saving presence in the sacraments, the Enlightenment placed its faith in science, the perfectibility of humankind, and secular progress. Traditional religion, and especially the sacramental hierarchy, were challenged by Enlightenment thinkers like Voltaire as "priestcraft": the epitome of superstition, obscurantism, and tyranny.

Summary

It is assumed in Catholic circles that the post-Tridentine Church was the continuation of the medieval Church, and in essential features it was. But in the medieval Church, both Catholic and Protestant elements existed in tension; in the Tridentine Church the Protestant elements were eliminated; Catholics emphasized whatever was non-Protestant, and vice-versa. Thus in the Tridentine Church there was much less allowable

[52] "Enlightenment," *Encyclopedia of the Social Sciences,* 5:547; see also Peter Gay, *The Enlightenment: An Interpretation. The Rise of Modern Paganism* (New York: Random House, Vintage, 1966).

diversity of opinion concerning the papacy, Mary, clerical marriage, the role of the bishops, lay authority, and so on. In the medieval church, a strong undercurrent of conciliarism existed, even among the cardinals; in the Tridentine Church conciliarism survived only in France and Germany. No ecumenical council was held for three hundred years. There was much less diversity in theology, and less openness to natural science. What Nicholas of Cusa could hold in the fifteenth century, Galileo could not hold in the seventeenth. The Tridentine Church was less corrupt than the medieval, but more authoritarian, more clerical, more papal, more narrowly Roman, except in France and Germany where Roman authority was mitigated by lay rulers. Yves Congar wrote in 1961:

> The Catholic Church since the sixteenth century has put into practice a genuine 'mystique' of authority in which the influence of the Society of Jesus has doubtless played a part. This 'mystique' may be characterized as the notion of a complete identification of God's will with the institutional form of authority. In the latter, it is God himself whose voice we hear and heed. The fairly wide margin which the Middle Ages still left for the subordinate's appraisal is for all practical purposes, reduced almost to nothing. The Pope is the Visible Christ.[53]

Against the onslaught of Enlightenment secularism, the Church developed a siege mentality. Most modern ideas came to the Church from outside, cloaked in the guise of anti-clerical and anti-Catholic Liberalism, and were at first resisted, for example, the separation of Church and state, liberty of conscience, freedom of religion, universal human rights, the antislavery movement, and so on. This cost the Catholic Church intellectual credibility. But, on the other hand, to her undying credit, in the face of militant secularism and humanism, the Church refused to be secularized, and clung to her sense of the transcendent, her sacramental worldview, mysticism, saints, belief in grace, miracles, apostolic succession, and intuition of a hierarchy of being.

[53] "The Historical Development of Authority," *Problems of Authority*, J.M. Todd, ed., 145.

Chapter 9

Vatican I and Vatican II

The emphasis of the Tridentine Church on papal authority culminated in the definition of papal infallibility at Vatican Council I. Vatican II, however, set this definition in the context of episcopal collegiality. Both of these councils are crucial for an understanding of the Catholic notion of hierarchy.

Ultramontanism

Ultramontanism was a movement to centralize Catholic authority and power in the papacy.[1] Though its roots go back to the seventeenth century, when Ultramontanes opposed the control of Louis XIV over the Church, it expanded from 1815 on, especially in France. The anarchy of the French Revolution, the subservience of the Church to the state in France and Austria, the captivity of Pope Pius VII by Napoleon (1809–1814) and that pope's heroic resistance to the emperor's coercion, the political instability of Europe, and the advance of liberal secularism, all contributed to the desire for an international leader to unify the Church and make it independent of the control of nationalist political factions and secular movements. In 1799 a Camaldolese monk, Mauro Capellari, later Pope Gregory XVI (1831–1846) published *Il Trionfo della*

[1] For a study of Ultramontane ecclesiology, see R. Costigan, *Rohrbacher and the Ecclesiology of Ultramontanism* (Rome: Universita Gregoriana, 1980) passim.

Santa Sede e della Chiesa (The Triumph of the Holy See and the Church) which argued that the Church was infallible because it derived from the pope, its chief and its foundation, who was himself infallible.[2] After Capellari became pope, this book was republished, and greatly influenced the lower clergy.

An early apologist was Joseph de Maistre, a layman, whose book *Du Pape* (1819) became a charter of Ultramontanism. De Maistre identified papal infallibility with sovereign (political) power. "*Infallibility* in the spiritual order, and *sovereignty* in the temporal order, are two words perfectly synonymous. The one and the other express this high power which rules all, from which all other [powers] are derived; which governs and is not governed, which judges and is not judged."[3] Only a sovereign, absolute monarch, de Maistre thought, could unify and govern the Church and give it independence from the secular control of kings and princes. Ecumenical councils could not do this, since they only met intermittently.[4] They were no more than the parliament or estates-general of Christianity assembled under the authority of the sovereign pope.[5]

De Maistre's argument was political, not theological. He based his case on the need to unify the Church and on the need for religious order in society: "Remember often this chain of reasonings: no public morality nor national character without religion, no European religion without Christianity, no Christianity without Catholicism, no Catholicism without the Pope, no Pope without the supremacy that belongs to him."[6] The strength of his work was its polemical attack on the servitude of the French Church under Gallicanism, and the case for ecclesial independence under a papal monarchy. But it was weak in its grasp of history and its analysis of scripture, and did not ground papal authority either in the college of bishops or in the *jus divinum* (for which reason *Du Pape* was received coolly in Rome). The papacy, for de Maistre, was a matter of political necessity but not divine right. Like Capellari, de Maistre reduced the Church to the pope, from whom the Church flowed, but had no ecclesiology of the episcopate, the laity, the

[2] Congar, *L'Église*, 414.

[3] *Du Pape* (Paris: Beaucé-Rusand, 1819) 2.

[4] Ibid., 16–19.

[5] Ibid., 20.

[6] Written in a letter in *Oeuvres complètes*, vol. 12 (Lyons: Vitte et Perussel, 1884–1886) 427–428, cited in Costigan, *Rohrbacher*, 24.

sacraments, or the mystical body. Congar remarks: "Thus begins the career of a theory of authority, in fact of the monarchial authority of the pope, without a true ecclesiology."[7]

The most influential French apologist for Ultramontanism was Félicité Lamennais (1782–1854). He scathingly attacked the subservience of the French "court bishops," and pressed for the liberty and reformation of the Church under a papal monarchy. Influenced by de Maistre, he argued that only a free, independent Church could heal the dissolution of society. The dream of Lamennais was "one single society, but vast as the world, one single law, one single head, but all peoples ruled by that law, and all powers submitted to that head."[8] For a society to exist, it must be submitted to sovereign power. For the divine society which is the Church, that power was the papacy, instituted by Jesus Christ. "If then Jesus Christ established the monarchial regime in the Church, if the pope is sovereign in it, to attack his authority, to limit his power, is to destroy the Church; it is to substitute a human government, an arbitrary government, for the one it has received from Jesus Christ."[9]

Both Lamennais and de Maistre had romantic, overly idealistic views of the papacy as the guardian of religion and civilization, and as the source of Catholicism. As a young man, Lamennais had been moved by the spectacle of Pius VII in prison heroically withstanding Napoleon, while the French bishops capitulated to the state ministries. He thus joined an Ultramontanist idealization of the pope to a romantic passion for liberty. In various writings he advocated the liberty of the Church from national control, separation of Church and state, freedom of the press, freedom of education, freedom of conscience and religion, equal rights, universal suffrage, and democracy. This is what he called "catholicizing liberalism," and so he became the father of Catholic liberalism. But his dreams were crushed by Gregory XVI's encyclical *Mirari vos* (1832), which denounced liberalism, rejected the separation of Church and state, liberty of conscience and of the press, and demanded unqualified submission to the encyclical. A disillusioned Lamennais eventually left the Roman Church, concluding that

[7] *L'Église*, 416.

[8] Charles Boutard, cited in Costigan, *Rohrbacher*, 67.

[9] *De la religion considérée dans ses rapports avec l'ordere politique et civil*, in *Oeuvres Complètes*, vol. 7 (Paris: Paul Daubrée et Cailleux, 1836–1837) 125, cited in Costigan, *Rohrbacher*, 62.

the hierarchy was against liberty after all. Nonetheless, the movement that he had inspired continued after him.

Thus in part Ultramontane ecclesiology was politically driven; its major exponents, de Maistre and Lamennais, argued that a universal sovereign was necessary to ensure the liberty of the Church and to preserve Christian society. Emotionally and popularly, Ultramontanism was part of the current of Romanticism then sweeping Europe, which exalted hero figures as saviors. Other factors were also important in the eventual triumph of Ultramontanism, which in fact originated not in the hierarchy, but among the rank and file of the Church. Lower middle class clergy resented the autocratic rule of bishops, most of whom were nobility, and supported Ultramontanism as a way of liberating themselves from oppressive episcopal authority. On the popular level, the emergence of a personal devotion to the pope, especially Pius IX, an immensely popular pontiff, greatly furthered Ultramontanism. In the hands of polemical journalists such as Louis Veuillot, this adulation of the pope reached absurd, even idolatrous extremes, as when Veuillot printed hymns or portions of the breviary in which the name of the pope, "Pius," was substituted for the name of God, "Deus."[10] The Roman Jesuit journal *La Civiltà cattolica,* wrote: "When the pope thinks, it is God who is thinking in him."[11] W.G. Ward, leader of the extreme wing of the English Ultramontanes, held that every doctrinal pronouncement of the pope was "infallibly directed by the Holy Ghost," and characterized bulls such as *Quanta Cura* (1864) as "the word of God," thereby putting the pope's words on a par with scripture.[12] Ultramontanist proponents tended to think that they alone were Catholics, and that Gallicans and others were little better than Protestants. As late as 1912 Umberto Begnini, professor of ecclesiastical history in Rome, could write in the *Catholic Encyclopedia* that Ultramontanism and Catholicism were the same thing, and that "those who combat Ultramontanism are in fact combatting Catholicism."[13] This kind of self-righteousness was characteristic of Ultramontanists throughout and after Vatican I.

Ultramontanism was theologically derived from Neo-Scholasticism, especially the ecclesiologies of Aquinas and Bellarmine, and was

[10] Examples are given in C. Butler, *The Vatican Council* (London: Longmans, Green & Co., 1930) 76–77.

[11] Ibid.

[12] Ibid., 73–74.

[13] *Catholic Encyclopedia,* XV, 125.

poorly grounded in either church history or scripture. Congar states that Ultramontane ecclesiology in France had as its major sources Italian treatises written in the late 1700s against Gallicanism.[14] The most influential Ultramontane historian in France was René-Françoise Rohrbacher, whose 29-volume history of the Church interpreted both scriptures and church history with the intent of proving the monarchy of the papacy. His history displaced Gallican histories in French seminaries in the 1840s. Rohrbacher argued that Jesus had conferred monarchial powers on Peter. This was his interpretation of the "Thou art Peter" passage in Matthew 16:18-19. Peter's faith, conferred by Christ, was the rock on which the Church was built; the keys given to him symbolized universal authority: "Everything is submitted to those keys, everything, kings and peoples, shepherds and flocks."[15]

The authority given to Peter was immediate, not mediated by the Church or the bishops, and was absolutely sovereign: "Rohrbacher portrays Peter as exercising to the full all the powers and functions of the Supreme Pontiff, just as they are found exercised by later popes."[16] He argues that Peter founded not only the see of Rome, but also the see of Antioch, and, through his disciple Mark, the see of Alexandria. Therefore he could state that "no church was founded in all of Italy, in Gaul, Africa, Sicily and in the surrounding islands except by those whom the apostles St. Peter or his successors had made bishop."[17] Thus the Church itself derived from Peter and his successors the popes, who inherited his plenary powers. The Church had become the spiritual empire of Christ: "All the great material empires of the ancient world are supplanted and utterly transcended by this new spiritual one, which is presided over by the Vicar of Christ, the Roman Pontiff."[18] According to Rohrbacher, the popes had regenerated civilization after the fall of Rome; they had defended liberty among the peoples against secular tyrants, especially the Germanic emperors; they had been patrons of science and the arts, and promoters of enlightenment and creativity.[19]

[14] "L'ecclésiologie de la Révolution française au Concile du Vatican sous la signe de l'affirmation de l'authorité," in M. Nédoncelle et al., *L'Ecclésiologie au XIX siècle* (Paris: Cerf, 1960) 91.

[15] Cited in Costigan, *Rohrbacher,* 158.

[16] Ibid., 163.

[17] Ibid., 164.

[18] Ibid., 182.

[19] Ibid., 196–203.

In a long study of Rohrbacher, Richard Costigan admits that his history is driven by the "ideology of papal primacy."[20] Yet this Ultramontane ideology, politically motivated and weak both historically and theologically, triumphed during the nineteenth century and culminated in Vatican Council I.

Vatican Council I

In addition to the Ultramontane movement, political events led to Vatican Council I. Pope Pius IX (1846–1878) had begun his papacy by giving the papal states a semi-democratic form of government. But in 1848 revolution broke out in Rome, and under Garibaldi and Mazzini a short-lived Roman Republic was created, with the pope exiled in Southern Italy. When Pius was reinstalled on the papal throne by the French (1850), he was hardened against liberalism, which he equated with anarchy and persecution of the Church. Somewhat later, a liberal government under Camillo Cavour in the northern Italian state of Piedmont abolished many religious orders there, confiscated their property, abolished clerical immunity in civil courts, and took over education from the Church. In 1860 the Piedmontese invaded and annexed the papal states, leaving the pope with only the city of Rome and its environs. Pius responded by condemning most forms of liberalism in the encyclical *Quanta Cura* and the appended *Syllabus of Errors* (1864). In addition, he formed the intention of summoning an ecumenical council to combat the evils of the times, mainly liberal political movements and secular and rationalist philosophies.

The council convened December 8, 1869, with about seven hundred bishops (and almost no laypersons) present, of whom thirty-five percent were Italians.[21] Almost immediately, an ideological divide formed between Ultramontanes and those opposed to liberalism on the one side, who wanted a solemn definition of papal infallibility, and moderate Gallicans, concerned to defend the rights of the episcopate, and liberal Catholics, both of whom opposed a definition of infallibil-

[20] Ibid., 177–203.

[21] The following account follows Roger Aubert, "The Vatican Council," chap. 22 of *History of the Church, vol. VIII: The Church in the Age of Liberalism,* Hubert Jedin, ed. (New York: Crossroad, 1981) 315–334; and Margaret O'Gara, *Triumph in Defeat: Infallibility, Vatican I, and the French Minority Bishops* (Washington, D.C.: The Catholic University of America Press, 1988).

ity. The latter, or minority group, accounted for about ten percent of those present. The council was controlled by the Curia and the Ultramontane group from the beginning. The consultants selected to prepare the conciliar decrees, sixty Romans and thirty-six foreigners, were almost all Ultramontanists and anti-liberals. The agenda was prepared by the pope. The crucial election to the Deputation on Faith, the dogmatic commission that was to deal with papal infallibility, was arranged by Cardinal Manning (an extreme Ultramontanist) so that no member of the minority was on the list of persons to be elected. According to Roger Aubert, this "put an end to the possibility of dialogue between the two opposing positions. . . . From this moment on there were many who began to doubt the freedom of the council."[22]

Initial discussions concerned the draft of the schema on faith, which opposed the errors of modern rationalism. After revisions, this was approved unanimously and issued as the Dogmatic Constitution on the Catholic Faith, *Dei Filius*. Significantly, it was issued in the name of the pope, "with the approval of the sacred council," as if the council had only an advisory function.[23]

Originally, the topic of papal infallibility was not included in the agenda of the council. But the Ultramontane majority successfully petitioned to have it added. Because time was short, this group also petitioned to have papal infallibility considered immediately, without first discussing the schema on the Church. This was opposed by the council presidents, for fear of alienating the minority bishops, but approved by Pius IX. Seventy-one minority bishops protested, arguing that the nature of the Church should be considered first, because consideration of papal infallibility apart from the Church would lead to distortion. But they were resigned in advance to defeat: "We have been taught by an experience sufficient, and more than sufficient—that, far from entreaties of this kind being respected, they have up to this point been regarded as not even worthy of a response."[24] Their petition was denied by the pope. Indeed, from the point of view of the minority, who viewed the papal office as proceeding from the Church, to discuss papal infallibility apart from its setting in the Church was backwards and misleading, but from the point of view of the Ultramontanes, who saw the Church as proceeding from the pope, it made sense.

[22] "The Vatican Council," 322.

[23] Tanner, vol. II, 804.

[24] O'Gara, *Triumph in Defeat*, 5.

The initial schema of the document on infallibility, *Pastor aeternus,* seemed to uphold a separate, personal infallibility for the pope, apart from the Church—just what the minority feared and what the extreme Ultramontanes like Manning and Pius IX himself wanted. But as a result of discussions and modifications of the text, due to the concerns of the minority, a more moderate text emerged. On July 11, 1870, Bishop Gasser gave a long speech in which he explained the Deputation's rationale for the text (this speech is still critical for understanding the meaning of the final text). Nonetheless, the initial vote on this text was 451 *placet* [it pleases]; 88 *non placet,* and 62 *placet juxta modum.* Because of the size of the opposition, a group of minority bishops pleaded with Pius IX to make some concessions so the minority could vote for the schema. Pius refused, and instead the Deputation added the words "ex sese, non ex consensu ecclesiam," indicating that infallible papal statements were infallible "in themselves, and not from the consent of the church." The final vote was held on the schema so modified on July 18, amid a terrible thunderstorm, but some seventy bishops of the minority, rather than voting against the schema, had already left the council. In their absence the final vote was 533 *placet,* 2 *non placet.* On July 19 war was declared between France and Prussia, making it difficult for the council to continue, and in October Pius suspended the council indefinitely.

The final document, the Dogmatic Constitution on the Church of Christ, *Pastor aeternus,* contains two critical affirmations, one affirming the pope's absolute jurisdiction (chaps. 1–3), the other stating his infallibility (chap. 4). The critical passages are as follows:

> [Chapter 1] We teach . . . according to the gospel evidence, a primacy of jurisdiction over the whole church of God was immediately and directly promised to the blessed apostle Peter and conferred on him by Christ the Lord . . . [they then cite Matt 16:16-19]. Therefore, if anyone says that . . . it was a primacy of honor only and not one of true and proper jurisdiction . . . let him be anathema. (*DS* 3053, 3055)
>
> [Chapter 2] Therefore whoever succeeds to the chair of Peter obtains, by the institution of Christ himself, the primacy of Peter over the whole church. . . . In consequence of being joined, as members to head, with that [the Roman] see, from which the rights of sacred communion flow to all, they will grow together into the structure of a single body. (*DS* 3057)
>
> [Chapter 3] We teach and declare that, by divine ordinance, the Roman church possess a pre-eminence of ordinary power over every

> other church, and that this jurisdictional power of the Roman pontiff is both episcopal and immediate. Both the clergy and the faithful . . . are bound to submit to this power by the duty of hierarchical subordination and true obedience . . . . This power of the supreme pontiff by no means detracts from that ordinary and immediate power of episcopal jurisdiction, by which the bishops, who have succeeded to the place of the apostles by appointment of the Holy spirit, tend to govern individually the particular flocks which have been assigned to them. . . . This power of theirs is asserted, supported and defended by the supreme and universal pastor. . . . So, then, if anyone says that the Roman pontiff has merely an office of supervision and guidance, and not the full and supreme power of jurisdiction over the whole church. . . or that he has only the principal part, but not the absolute fullness of this supreme power; or that this power of his is not ordinary and immediate both over all and each of the churches and over all and each of the pastors and faithful: let him be anathema. (*DS* 3059–3064)

> [Chapter 4] We teach and define as divinely revealed dogma that when the Roman pontiff speaks *ex cathedra,* that is, when in the exercise of his office as shepherd and teacher of all Christians, in virtue of his supreme apostolic authority, he defines a doctrine concerning faith or morals to be held by the whole church, he possesses, by the divine assistance promised to him in blessed Peter, that infallibility which the divine Redeemer willed his church to enjoy in defining doctrines concerning faith and morals. Therefore, such definitions of the Roman pontiff are of themselves, and not by consent of the church *(ex sese, non autem ex consensu ecclesiae),* irreformable. (*DS* 3074)[25]

In these definitions Ultramontane theology and command hierarchy are regnant. Dom Cuthbert Butler wrote in 1930: "The upshot of the Council was to identify the Ultramontanism of the Roman theological schools, as formulated by Bellarmine, with Catholicism, Gallicanism being ruled out."[26] From the definitions, it appears that the juridical structure of the Church derives from Christ, who passed the fullness of power onto Peter, whence it is passed onto the pope and thence to the bishops. This seems to have been the received opinion after Vatican I. As late as 1964, James McCue, writing in *Theological Studies,* stated: "We tend to think of the Church as deriving from the papacy as from

[25] ET from Tanner, vol. II, 812–816.

[26] *The Vatican Council,* vol. 1, 39.

a unique source: Christ creates the pope, the pope creates the bishops, the bishops create the congregations."[27] In this interpretation Peter is given a separate, personal fullness of authority, which is then communicated to the bishops and the Church; so also with infallibility.

This is how Orthodox and Protestant interpreters have read these definitions, with the consequence that they have been judged heretical by both groups. Emmanuel Lanne writes:

> There is no doubt that the primacy of Rome is the principal obstacle standing in the way of a reconstituted unity with the Orthodox Churches. . . . There are in fact very many Orthodox, including those best disposed towards the Roman Catholic Church, who would regard the two definitions of 1870 as *heresy in the strict sense of the term.* That is to say, they regard them as a serious innovation in matters concerning the faith, in contradiction to revelation, and in particular to the general teaching of the fathers.[28]

The authors of *Papal Primacy and the Universal Church* (Lutherans and Catholics in Dialogue, vol. V), write regarding the authority of the bishop of Rome:

> His jurisdiction over the universal church is in the words of Vatican I, "supreme," "full," "ordinary," and "immediate." This authority is not subject to any higher human jurisdiction and no pope is absolutely bound by the decisions of his predecessors. This view of the exercise of papal power has been vehemently repudiated by Lutherans and viewed by them as leading to intolerable ecclesiastical tyranny.[29]

The Vatican I definitions raise a number of problems. In the first place there is the question: "In what sense was Vatican I an Ecumenical Council?" "Ecumenical" means "universal." The first seven councils have been deemed ecumenical by Protestants, Orthodox, and Catholics, since they have been received by the whole Church (though sometimes this reception took a long period). But Vatican I has not been received by the whole Christian Church. Even in the Western Church,

[27] "The Roman Primacy in the Second Century and the Problem of Development," *TS*, vol. 25 (1964) 162–163.

[28] "The Papacy and the Reformation: To What Extent is Roman Primacy Unacceptable to the Eastern Churches?" *Concilium*, vol. 4, no. 7 (April, 1971) 62. Italics in original.

[29] *PPATUC*, p. 13.

seventy minority bishops walked out rather than sign *Pastor aeternus*. It is true that these bishops eventually, under pressure, accepted the document, but according to Margaret O'Gara's *Triumph in Defeat*, the French minority bishops only accepted it because they were able to interpret it as *not* demanding a belief in a separate, personal infallibility of the pope. Of course, in the Ultramontane view, which followed Bellarmine, schismatics such as the Orthodox and Protestants were not part of the (visible) Church; therefore their dissent from the definitions was irrelevant. (They were not even represented at the council.) As late as 1943, Pope Pius XII wrote in the encyclical *Mystici Corporis* that schism separated one from the Body of the Church (*DS* 3803). But Vatican II indicated that the Church of Christ, though it "subsists" in the Roman Catholic Church, is not identical with it (*LG* #8), and that all Christians are united with Christ through baptism and with Catholic Christians through the Holy Spirit (*LG* #15). If, then, the Orthodox and Protestants are members of the Christian Church but they reject the definitions of *Pastor aeternus* as heretical, it is hard to see how those definitions can be called ecumenical in the same sense that those of the first seven ecumenical councils are. Furthermore, the minority bishops complained persistently that the council was not free, and it seems that real dialogue was inhibited, as Roger Aubert admits (above p. 227). In particular, the notorious phrase "ex sese, non ex consensu ecclesiae" was added only a day or two before the final vote, and scarcely discussed at all; rather, it was imposed by the majority (including the pope) on the minority. This impugns the claim of the council to be ecumenical, for, as we have seen, ecumenical councils have achieved their status as ecumenical precisely because they were understood to represent a consensus of bishops and the faithful, not just a majority. In the light of these objections, it is questionable whether Vatican Council I can be considered ecumenical to the same degree as are the first four ecumenical councils, a point which Harry McSorley also makes.[30]

[30] "The only way in which one can maintain that most of the medieval 'general' councils, as well as those of Trent and Vatican I, are 'ecumenical' in the same sense as the first four councils, which have been almost universally received by Christians, is to suppose that the separated churches of the East and later churches of the Reformation are simply not part of the universal church or the body of the faithful, or that reception by these churches is not required for a council to be ecumenical." "Some Forgotten Truths about the Petrine Ministry," in *Journal of Ecumenical Studies*, vol. 11, no. 2 (Spring, 1974) 234–235.

Another problem is the apparent assertion that Peter was granted a personal, absolute jurisdiction (or infallibility), separate from the Church, which was then communicated to the bishops. In the light of recent scholarship it is hard to see how this is credible. I have argued in chapter 3 that Peter's primacy is a collegial primacy exercised as a charism of leadership within, not over, the college of apostles. Peter seems to be the spokesman and facilitator of the consensus, but he is not shown as exercising an absolute jurisdiction. In the most momentous decision made by the early Church, the decision to include uncircumcised Gentiles, it is James, the leader of the mother Church in Jerusalem, not Peter, who renders the final decision. Again, while the bishops of Rome did exercise jurisdiction within Roman patriarchate, and while individual churches did appeal to Rome when it was convenient for them, the bishops of Rome did not exercise any such jurisdiction in either North Africa or the East, especially in the ecumenical councils, as deVries has shown (chap. 5). The Ultramontane thesis that the Church *derives* from the pope, as from a source, is historically false and is not defended today by patristic scholars. Yet this idea seems to underlie the definitions of *Pastor aeternus.*

There is, however, a more moderate interpretation of *Pastor aeternus* which has become widespread among Catholic theologians since Vatican Council II. Let us consider the definition on infallibility first.

The Vatican I documents say that the infallibility exercised by the pope is the infallibility "which the Redeemer willed his church to enjoy in defining doctrine." Furthermore, the charism exercised by the pope in an infallible decision is *not* revelation or inspiration, from which he might define a new doctrine; it is to expound the deposit of faith transmitted by the apostles and preserved by the Church in scripture and tradition. Thus it would seem that this infallibility is not a personal, separate infallibility, but the infallibility vested in the whole Church which assists the pope "in the exercise of his office as shepherd and teacher of all Christians." When speaking infallibly, the pope speaks the mind of the whole Church. It is true that the documents say that papal definitions are infallible "ex sese, non ex consensu ecclesiae," "of themselves, not from the consent of the church." But the discussions held at the time of the council indicate that what was intended to be excluded by this phrase was the necessity of a subsequent, formal ratification by the bishops of a papal definition to make it infallible. The fourth article of the Gallican declaration of 1682 had stipulated that no papal definition could be regarded as infallible until it had received the consent of all the bishops—and it was this stipulation that was rejected by the addition of the *ex sese* phrase. What Vatican I rejected then, was the "consensus" of the Church understood in its Gallican sense as "subsequent ratification," not consensus meaning the "mind of the Church" (an idea which is better rendered by the Latin *sensu*).[31]

A number of speeches made by majority leaders during the deliberations on *Pastor aeternus* indicate that it was not the intent of the majority to separate the infallibility of the pope from that of the Church. Msgr. Pie, in explaining the first official draft of the decree, emphasized that the pope's infallibility was wedded to that of the Church: the head, he said, cannot separate itself from the body.[32] The final official explanation for the Deputation of Faith was delivered by Bishop Gasser, two days before the final vote. He stated:

> Finally, we do not separate the Pope (or rather we separate him as little as possible) from the *consensus* of the Church, provided that that *consensus* is not laid down as a condition [of infallibility], whether antecedent or subsequent. We are not able to separate the Pope from the *consent* of the Church because the Church can never be lacking this *consensus*. For since we believe that the Pope is infallible through divine assistance, by that very fact we also believe that the definitions will not lack the assent of the Church; [this is] because it could not come about that the body of the bishops would be separated from its head, and because the universal Church cannot fail.[33]

When asked if the definition of papal infallibility would render future ecumenical councils unnecessary, Gasser replied: "they will be as necessary in the future as in the past . . . . The most solemn judgment of the Church in matters of faith and morals is, and always will be, the judgment of an Ecumenical Council, in which the pope pronounces judgment, the bishops of the Catholic world sitting and judging along with him."[34] Finally, Margaret O'Gara argues that it was precisely because the French minority bishops were able in good conscience to interpret the definitions as *not* defining a personal, separate infallibility of the pope, that they eventually agreed to support *Pastor aeternus*.[35]

[31] See Thomas A. Caffrey, S.J., "Consensus and Infallibility: The Mind of Vatican I," in *The Downside Review*, vol. 88, no. 291 (April, 1970) 112.

[32] Ibid., 108–111.

[33] ET ibid., 121; Mansi, 52, 1213–1214.

[34] Mansi, vol. 52, col. 1211; ET in Butler, vol. 2, 134–135.

[35] *Triumph in Defeat*, 194–255.

It goes without saying, of course, that the pope is limited in his exercise of infallibility. The Swiss bishops, in a pastoral letter explaining infallibility, explained it thus: "He [the pope] is bound by and limited to the divine revelation, and to the truths the revelation contains; he is bound and limited by the divine law and by the constitution of the Church; lastly, he is bound by that doctrine, divinely revealed, which affirms that alongside the ecclesiastical hierarchy there is the power of temporal magistrates, invested in their own domain with a full sovereignty."[36] Pius IX congratulated the Swiss bishops on this explanation of infallibility. Thus infallibility as defined by Vatican I is far more restricted than the relatively unlimited papal infallibility defended by Prieras and Cajetan in their dialogues with Luther (chap. 7).

Probably the best indication that papal infallibility is really an expression of the infallibility vested in the whole Church is the way the popes have actually exercised the prerogative of infallibility. Two *ex cathedra* definitions in particular are universally regarded as infallible: the definition of the Immaculate Conception by Pius IX in 1854, and the definition of Mary's Assumption by Pius XII in 1950. Neither definition was issued by an ecumenical council. But in each case the popes stated that it was their intention to give solemn expression to the beliefs of their brother bishops. They therefore polled all the bishops, and instructed them to consult the faithful, to ascertain what actually was the faith of the Church. Only when they were satisfied that all, or virtually all, the bishops and the faithful held the beliefs to be defined, did they go ahead and promulgate the definitions.[37] (However, these definitions are also open to the charge that they do not reflect the beliefs of Protestants or Orthodox.)

All this being said, however, it must be admitted that the language chosen by the fathers of the council, especially the *ex sese* phrase, begs to be misunderstood as defining a separate, personal infallibility. This

[36] Cited in Francis Dvornik, *The Ecumenical Councils* (New York: Hawthorne Books, 1961) 105.

[37] J. Robert Dionne surveys the evidence for the consent of bishops, theologians, and faithful to the two definitions. In the case of the Immaculate Conception, it was 90 percent or more; in the case of the Assumption, which had been celebrated as a feast in the Eastern and Western churches for centuries, consent was about 96 percent. Most dissent focused on the untimeliness of the definitions and on their ecumenical implications, not on their content. *The Papacy and the Church* (New York: Philosophical Library, 1987) 303–336. He notes that "in the end the doctrine of the Assumption was defined primarily because of the *sensus fidelium*"(336).

came about because of a lack of genuine dialogue with the minority bishops, whose advice, if heeded, would certainly have resulted in a more modest formula.

Can this same type of interpretation be applied to the passages on jurisdiction (chaps. 1–3 of *Pastor aeternus*)? The language of Vatican I seems to indicate that the jurisdiction of Peter and his successors is prior to and superior to that of the Church or the other bishops. But the explanations given during deliberation emphasize that the head is not separate from the body. If so, then the jurisdiction exercised by Peter and the popes need not be interpreted as a separate, personal jurisdiction *over* the Church. This seems to be the interpretation of Vatican II, which repeats some of the language of Vatican I, but sets it in a quite different context. On jurisdictional power it says, "For in virtue of his office, that is, as Vicar of Christ and pastor of the whole Church, the Roman Pontiff has full, supreme, and universal power over the Church. And he can always exercise this power freely" (*LG* #22). This formulation seems to indicate that the power exercised by the pope is a power that comes to him in virtue of his office as supreme pastor; in other words, it is a jurisdictional power exercised within and in conjunction with the Church itself, not separate from it or over it.

Nonetheless, the language used by Vatican I scarcely conveys this, and until Vatican II a "maximalist" Ultramontane and Roman interpretation of papal jurisdiction prevailed. Catechisms presented the pope as an absolute monarch over the Church with the bishops as his deputies, and priests also learned this in seminaries.[38]

Vatican I was essentially an incomplete council. It was not able to discuss and issue its intended decree on the Church. Thus it failed to discuss the place of the bishops in the Church and their relation with the pope. The pope, it said, exercises immediate and ordinary power over the Church, but so does each bishop in his diocese: "The power of the supreme pontiff by no means detracts from that ordinary and immediate power of episcopal jurisdiction by which the bishops, who have succeeded to the place of the apostles by appointment of the Holy Spirit, tend to govern individually the particular flocks which have been assigned to them" (*DS* 3061).

Vatican I then allows for concurrent and overlapping jurisdiction in each diocese, but does not clarify how the jurisdictions relate one to

[38] J.-M. R. Tillard, *The Bishop of Rome* (Wilmington: Michael Glazier, 1983) 29–34.

another. Moreover, it never treated the problem, commonly discussed by medieval theologians, of a heretical or schismatic pope, or of an infirm or mentally ill pope. There is in fact no provision in canon law for dealing with such a contingency. The great failure of the council then was its failure to locate the powers of the papacy within the context of the larger Church—the bishops and the faithful—and to protect against possible abuse of papal power. Vatican II addressed the first of these problems, but not the second.

Between the Councils

After Vatican I, as a result of the definitions on jurisdiction and infallibility, unilateral, monarchial papal decisions became the rule, for example, in the condemnation of Modernism. The popes did not normally collaborate with the bishops in their teaching or governance of the Church. Bishops were expected to communicate the pope's decisions to their flocks, and often tended to be monarchic, "little popes" in their own dioceses. Gallicanism and Febronianism had been defeated, and there was no countervailing authority of emperor, kings, or princes to balance that of the triumphant papacy in the Church.

And yet between the councils there was a startling renewal in theology. John Henry Newman's work on the importance of the laity in the formation of the mind of the Church and on the development of doctrine, was important. So was the work of patristic scholars like Yves Congar, who helped recover the sense of the Church in ancient times. Dialogue with the Orthodox and with Protestants was critical; on the eve of Vatican Council II, John XXIII established the Secretariat for Christian Unity, and considered that the unity of Christians was one of the important goals of the council. The revival of biblical and liturgical studies in Catholicism in the early twentieth century were especially important in shaping the vision of Vatican II.

As a result of theologians questioning papal positions, the ordinary papal teaching on several important points was changed at Vatican II, as J. Robert Dionne has made clear.[39] Let us consider two such areas.

The teaching of Pius IX and Leo XIII on the relation of Church and state was that the state had a duty to protect and promote Catholicism as the official state religion. In the *Syllabus of Errors* (No. 55) Pius IX

[39] *The Papacy and the Church*, passim.

had condemned the opinion that "The Church from the state and the state from the Church is to be separated" (*DS* 2955).[40] Leo XIII in his encyclical *Immortale Dei* (1885) held that it was the duty of the state to worship God . . . according to the Catholic religion, and that there *must* exist a connection *(colligatio)* between the Church and the state similar to the union of the soul and body (*DS* 3168).[41] But as a result of the work of theologians between the councils, especially John Courtney Murray, S.J. (who was for a time silenced by the Holy See for his theological writings), and as a result of the debate of bishops during the council itself, this teaching was changed at Vatican II:

> If . . . special legal recognition is given in the constitutional order of society to one religious body, it is at the same time imperative that the right of all citizens and religious bodies to religious freedom should be recognized and made effective in practice. (Declaration on Religious Freedom #6)

Similarly, the *Syllabus of Errors,* number 15, states that it is an error to say that a person may "embrace and practice that religion which by the light of reason he [she] thinks is true" (*DS* 2915). But Vatican II's Declaration on Religious Freedom states:

> This Vatican Synod declares that the human person has a right to religious freedom. This freedom means that all men are to be immune from coercion on the part of individuals or of social groups and of any human power, in such wise that in matters religious no one is to be forced to act in a manner contrary to his own beliefs. (#2)

Dionne thinks that these changes are in fact reversals of previous papal teaching.[42] I think it is possible to argue that they are developments.

[40] This teaching seems to continue the teaching of Lateran Council IV (1215) that the state had a duty to enforce the Catholic religion: "We excommunicate and anathematize every heresy raising itself up against this holy, orthodox, and catholic faith . . . . Let secular authorities . . . be advised and urged and if necessary compelled by ecclesiastical censure . . . to take publicly an oath . . . that they will seek, in so far as they can, to exterminate *(exterminare)* from the lands subject to their jurisdiction all heretics designated by the church in good faith." Tanner, vol. 1, 233. Tanner translates *exterminare* as "expel"; I have substituted "exterminate" following the translation given in B. Tierney, *Origins of Papal Infallibility: 1150–1350* (Leiden: E.J. Brill, 1972) 277.

[41] Dionne, *The Papacy and the Church,* 132–133.

[42] Ibid., 145–194.

But it is clear that they represent major changes, and that these changes occurred because the bishops at Vatican II were influenced by the teachings of theologians, as well as by their own pastoral experience, and that therefore the final formulation of these doctrines (as given at Vatican II) came about as a result *not* of unilateral papal proclamations, but of dialogue between theologians and the magisterium.

A final example concerns the membership of non-Catholics in the Church. Pius XI wrote in *Mortalium animos* (1928) as follows:

> Since the Mystical Body of Christ, that is to say, the [Roman Catholic] Church, is like the physical body, a unity, a compact thing joined together, it would be false and foolish to say that Christ's Mystical Body could be composed of separated and scattered members. Whoever therefore is not united with it is not a member of it nor does he communicate with its Head Who is Christ.[43]

Similarly, Pius XII wrote in *Mystici Corporis* (1943)

> Actually only those are to be included as members of the Church who have been baptized and profess the true faith, and who have not been so unfortunate as to separate themselves from the unity of the Body, or been excluded by legitimate authority for grave faults committed. . . . For not every sin, however grave it may be, is such as of its own nature to sever a man from the Body of Church, as does schism or heresy or apostasy. (*DS* 3802, 3803)[44]

Both Pius XI and Pius XII seem in these passages to identify the Mystical Body of Christ with the Roman Catholic Church. But this, as theologians pointed out, raised a problem with the theology of baptism, for the Catholic had always held that Protestant and Orthodox baptisms were valid, and hence incorporated the baptized into the Church. Vatican II declared that the Church of Christ "subsists" *(subsistere)* in the [Roman] Catholic Church, but is not identical with it (*LG* #8). Thus Vatican II modified previous papal magisterial teaching. As Dionne makes clear by an exhaustive study of the documents, this modification occurred because of the work of theologians, whose critical reception of the papal teachings resulted in a more adequate for-

[43] *Mortalium animos* in *AAS* 20 (1928) 5–16, ET from Dionne, *The Papacy and the Church,* 195.

[44] ET in *The Papal Encyclicals, 1939–1958,* Claudia Carlen, ed. (Wilmington, N.C.: McGrath Publishing Co., 1981) 41.

mulation of the teaching.[45] Thus he cites 1 Cor 12:21: "the Head [cannot say] to the feet, 'I have no need of you.'"

Dionne reaches the conclusion that doctrine develops through the interplay of authoritative papal pronouncements and the reception of those pronouncements by the rest of the Church, especially the theologians, whose reception consists not just in passive obedience but in an active exercise of the *sensus fidelium*.[46] He notes that reception can be understood in two ways: as the reception of papal magisterial pronouncements by the Church, and conversely as reception by the pope of movements within the Church. This latter has not been denied by the magisterium: the Marian dogmas are examples of the popes promulgating as doctrine what began as a lay pietistic movement in the Church. What the magisterium has hitherto denied, Dionne notes, is that "the teaching of the ordinary papal magisterium has sometimes had to be modified and/or reversed because of the modalities of its reception."[47] This recalls the statement of II Constantinople, cited above (chap. 5) that the truth cannot be made clear except through debate in common. Without such constructive debate, Vatican II would have simply repeated the teachings of Vatican I and of previous popes.

Vatican Council II

The council originated in the thought of Pope John XXIII, who attributed the idea to an inspiration of the Holy Spirit. He saw the mission of the council as teaching the ancient doctrine in a more effective and updated way to the modern age. As he declared in his opening speech, "The substance of the ancient doctrine of the deposit of faith is one thing, and the way in which it is presented is another."[48] Hence his watchword for the spirit of the council was *aggiornamiento*—"updating." Before convening the council, he inquired of the cardinals, the bishops, the Curia, heads of religious orders, Catholic universities and ecclesiastical faculties, what questions should be studied by the council.[49] Thus the issues considered truly reflected the concerns of the worldwide Church. Present at the council were the world's bishops,

[45] Dionne, *The Papacy and the Church*, 195, 236, 260–282.
[46] Ibid., 353.
[47] Ibid., 362.
[48] *The Documents of Vatican II*, Walter Abbott, ed. (New York: Guild Press, 1966) 715.
[49] Ibid., 707–708.

abbots, theological experts (so-called *periti*), heads of religious congregations, and Jewish, Protestant, and Orthodox observers (who could speak but not vote). The council itself met in four sessions from 1962–1965, during which the bishops and theological experts had ample time to get to know one another, pray together, and discuss issues together—an essential process for discerning the will of the Spirit and developing consensus.

To facilitate discussion, initial proposals called "schemata" (singular: "schema") on seventy topics were drawn up by preparatory commissions largely staffed by Curial officials under the headship of Cardinal Ottaviani, director of the Holy Office (the former Inquisition).[50] Not surprisingly, these reflected the monarchial and Neo-Scholastic theology of Vatican I. The actual drafting and presentation of the documents to be discussed was to be in the hands of ten commissions, each with a specific area of competence (theology, liturgy, etc.). Therefore control of these commissions meant control of the discussion. The first order of conciliar business was to elect members to these commissions. The Curia circulated a list of candidates favorable to its own positions. But the bishops elected their own slate of candidates. In this way, the membership of the ten commissions was balanced between the progressive majority and the Curial minority. This contrasts with Vatican I, where the Ultramontanes maneuvered to screen out all progressive candidates from the conciliar commissions, thus ensuring in advance that the council would not reflect the views of the Gallican minority.

The Vatican II bishops also rejected the initial Curial schemas on Revelation and the Church as too juridical, clerical, and Neo-Scholastic, and demanded that new drafts be presented. Thus control of the council passed from the Curia to the bishops themselves, and the final documents reflected the mind of the bishops, not just the mind of the Curia or the pope. Vatican II, then, was a truly participatory council. Views pro and con on all issues were thoroughly discussed, and the bishops, to their great credit, did not manipulate the discussions. The final documents represent not majority positions, but are as close to consensus as is practically possible. This is reflected in

[50] See Alberigo, Giuseppe, and Komonchak, Joseph, *History of Vatican II,* vol. I (Maryknoll: N.Y.: Orbis, and Leuven: Peeters, 1995) 227–318, 405–429; Thomas Bokenkotter, *A Concise History of the Catholic Church* (Revised ed.) (New York: Doubleday, Image Books, 1977, 1979) 411ff.; and *Commentary on the Documents of Vatican II,* Herbert Vorgrimler, ed. (New York: Herder and Herder, 1967) vol. 1.

the final votes on the documents, which typically passed with about a 99 percent majority of the approximately twenty-four hundred voting members present. I would maintain that Vatican II is one of the best examples of participatory hierarchy in action in church history. It was not perfect, of course: lay persons were present, but did not vote; non-Catholic observers were present but did not vote; women's voices were largely unheard. But given the monarchial history of the Church for the previous four hundred years, it represented a signal advance.

With respect to hierarchy, the most important document of Vatican Council II was the Dogmatic Constitution on the Church, *Lumen gentium.* This magnificent document, which expresses the heart of Vatican II's ecclesiology, begins by considering the Church[51] as a *Mystery.* This term derives from the biblical Greek *mysterion* (cf. Eph 1:9), and was used by the Greek fathers (e.g., Clement of Alexandria) to mean the "representation of sacred things through perceptible signs," i.e., sacrament.[52] Like the sacraments, like the incarnation, the Church unites two dimensions, the spiritual and the material into a single reality, a mystery which cannot be fully expressed conceptually, sociologically, or juridically, but is best expressed sacramentally. The whole mission of the Church as sacrament is to bring human beings into intimate union with God and to participation in God's divine life (*LG* #1, 2). Vatican II, then, reverses a trend going back to the Middle Ages, especially prominent in *Pastor aeternus* of Vatican I, which saw the Church primarily in terms of juridical authority and power. Rather, it returns to the patristic conception of the Church in which juridical authority flowed from sacramental consecration and was not separated from it.

Lumen gentium also approaches the Church from a predominantly biblical standpoint, and applies a variety of biblical images to the Church. The most prominent of these is the Church as the "People of God" (*LG,* chap. 2), an image derived from the Old Testament, where Israel is understood as the Holy People of God, and from 1 Peter 2:9: "But you are a chosen race, a royal priesthood, a holy nation, God's own people." "People of God" in this usage does not mean just the

[51] "Church" in *Lumen gentium* means the "Church of Christ" and therefore includes all who are united with Christ through baptism and the Holy Spirit. This "Church" "subsists" in the Roman Catholic Church, but it is not restricted to it (*LG* #8).

[52] Michael Lawler, *Symbol and Sacrament: a Contemporary Sacramental Theology* (New York: Paulist Press, 1987) 30; see Lawler's discussion of the relation between *mysterion* and sacrament, 29–34.

laity, but the entire Church, clerical, lay, and those in religious orders. It contrasts with the Vatican I tendency to derive the Church from the pope or equate it with the hierarchy. At the same time it does not mean that the Church is a democracy or that "the people are the Church." For the Church is the *holy* people of God, those people who have been or are being sanctified by the Spirit. Furthermore, the "People of God" includes the hierarchy, which is also willed by the Spirit—a point *Lumen gentium* emphasizes (chap. 3). What the image "People of God" does is recover the patristic notion of the Church as a communion of the faithful, a *communio.* Unlike the Ultramontane view, which saw the Church as proceeding from the pope, the "People of God" points to the Church as proceeding from the community of the faithful, unified in the Holy Spirit, under the headship of Christ (*LG* #9, 13). In a commentary on *Lumen gentium,* Aloys Grillmeier writes "One of the achievements of the council was the rediscovery of the universal church as the sum and communion of the local churches . . . and the rediscovery of the universal church in the local church."[53]

Another significant affirmation of *Lumen gentium* is its theology of the episcopate (*LG,* chap. 3). Following Peter Lombard, the Scholastic theologians, such as Aquinas, taught that the episcopate was not an order, nor was episcopal consecration a sacrament.[54] Hence Aquinas among others saw the bishops as deriving their juridical authority from the pope, not from Christ through their episcopal consecration. After the Council of Trent, the sacramentality of episcopal consecration came to be generally recognized, but episcopal authority was still thought of in juridical terms: the bishop, it was thought, had additional powers beyond those of the priest: he could ordain priests, for example. *Lumen gentium* affirms that the whole college of bishops is the successor to the college of apostles, and that this was by divine institution (*LG* #20). The college of bishops is divinely willed and instituted; it did not arise merely from human custom or convenience. In being ordained a bishop, one is united to the community one represents, to the college of bishops, and to its head, the bishop of Rome.

Vatican II teaches that the episcopacy is the fullness of the sacrament of orders (*LG* #21). The power and authority of the bishop de-

[53] Aloys Grillmeier, Commentary on *Lumen gentium,* chap. 2, in *Commentary on the Documents of Vatican II,* H. Vorgrimler, ed., vol. 1, 167.

[54] Seamus Ryan, "Vatican II: the Rediscovery of the Episcopate," in *The Irish Theological Quarterly,* vol. 33 (July, 1966) 209ff.

rives from his consecration, and cannot be exercised apart from the college: "Episcopal consecration, together with the office of sanctifying, also confers the offices of teaching and governing. (These, however, of their very nature, can be exercised only in hierarchical communion with the head and members of the college.)" (*LG* #21). Thus, as Seamus Ryan points out, Vatican II unites the authority of sacramental consecration and juridical authority into a single hierarchical authority, flowing from the sacrament of orders. This was a recovery of patristic thought and practice, and a reversal of the medieval practice of separating sacramental authority from juridical authority (which the medievals claimed came from the pope). Ryan writes: "The bringing together of these two elements—the *sacramental* and *juridical* dimensions of the episcopal office—was the most significant contribution of the Council towards an integral theology of the episcopate."[55]

In what does the fullness of ordination consist? In the past it has been argued that the bishop had more powers—*potestas* than the priest. But this makes the fullness of ordination too juridical and too individualistic: in fact, according to *Lumen gentium,* the bishop can only exercise his episcopal authority when in communion with the head and members of the college. Greek Orthodox theologian John Zizioulas argues: "Because of the relational nature of ordination, no ordained person realizes his *ordo* in himself but in his community. Thus if he is isolated from the community he ceases to be an ordained person (no anathematized or excommunicated minister can be regarded as a minister)."[56] Susan Wood therefore argues that the fullness of orders consists in the bishop's union with and incorporation into the episcopal college through his consecration, in which (and only in which) union he succeeds to the grace and authority of the apostles.[57] She notes, citing Zizioulas, "a bishop succeeds the apostles not as an individual but as head of his community."[58] In his community, the bishop represents Christ, and is the center of unity, but he also represents the community before Christ, as when he offers the sacrifice of the Mass in the name of the community. Furthermore, he represents his local community in the college of bishops, and hence in the universal

[55] Ibid., 219.

[56] *Being as Communion* (Crestwood, N.Y.: St. Vladimir's Seminary Press, 1985) 233–234.

[57] "The Sacramentality of Episcopal Consecration," *TS* 51 (1990) 485.

[58] Ibid., 488.

Church; there he bears witness to the practices and traditions of his community, which may differ from those of other communities. *Lumen gentium* states that "each individual bishop represents his own Church, but all of them together in union with the pope represent the entire Church." (*LG* #23). Again, the Holy Spirit does not just speak to the community through its bishop; it may also speak to the bishop through the community. For this reason, Cyprian made it his practice not to make decisions without consulting the presbyters of the community (see chap. 5). Similarly, Saint Benedict established the practice of chapter meetings, since "the Lord often reveals the best course to a younger monk."[59]

Lumen gentium also deals with the vexing question of papal authority. First, it sets the discussion of papal authority in the context of the episcopate: the pope exercises his power as head of the college of bishops, not unilaterally. Following Vatican I it affirms that "in virtue of his office, that is, as Vicar of Christ and Pastor of the whole Church, the Roman Pontiff has full, supreme, and universal power over the Church. And he can always exercise this power freely." (*LG* #22). Further, "The Roman Pontiff . . . is the perpetual and visible source and foundation of unity of the bishops and of the multitude of the faithful." It likewise affirms papal infallibility in terms drawn from Vatican I. But the Document on the Church also affirms that the *bishops* possess supreme power in the Church: "Together with its head, the Roman Pontiff, and never without this head, the episcopal order is the subject of supreme and full power over the universal Church." (*LG* #22). Note that this juridical power does not proceed from the pope (as the Ultramontanes thought); it proceeds from Christ, through episcopal consecration. Like the pope, the bishops are also vicars of Christ: "Bishops govern the particular churches entrusted to them as the vicars and ambassadors of Christ" (*LG* #27). Thus there seem to be two subjects of supreme power in the Church: the pope, and the bishops, acting in concert with the pope. But, as Karl Rahner argues in a commentary on *Lumen gentium,* the pope, when exercising supreme power, always acts as *head of the college,* not as a private person. Hence there is really only one possessor of supreme power in the Church, the pope united with the college of bishops; but this "head" can exercise its

[59] *The Rule of St. Benedict* (Garden City, N.Y.: Doubleday, Image Books, 1975) 51, cited in chap. 6, above.

power in two ways: through the pope acting alone (but as the head of the college), or through the entire college united with its head.[60]

It is a commonplace that Vatican II completed Vatican I, which was interrupted before it had a chance to formulate a document on the episcopate and the whole Church. *Lumen gentium* fulfilled this task. But in so doing, as J-M. R. Tillard argues, it provided a new interpretation of Vatican I, by complementing the latter's "papalist" theology with a theology of the episcopate and of the local church. Thus it is not just the pope who is the head of the Church, it is the pope united with the episcopal college; it is not just the pope who is the Vicar of Christ, it is both the pope and the bishops. The Church is not just built on the rock of Peter, it is established on both the apostles *and* Peter (*LG* #19), and proceeds both from the bishops *and* Peter's successor. Where Vatican I sees the Church as proceeding from its head, the pope, Vatican II, while maintaining that the pope is the source of unity, sees the universal Church as the communion of local churches, each of which is the true Church of Christ: "A diocese . . . loyal to its pastor and formed by him into one community in the Holy Spirit through the Gospel and the Eucharist . . . constitutes one particular church in which the one, holy, catholic and apostolic Church of Christ is truly present and active" (*CD* #11). In particular, it is the celebration of the one Eucharist that knits the local church together:

> In any community existing around an altar, under the sacred ministry of the bishop, there is manifested a symbol of that charity and unity of the Mystical Body without which there can be no salvation. In these communities . . . Christ is present. By virtue of Him the one, holy, catholic, and apostolic church gathers together. For "the partaking of the Body and Blood of Christ does nothing other than transform us into that which we consume." (*LG* #26)

Finally, *Lumen gentium* has an important section on the laity in the Church. The laity are the largest part of the People of God, incorporated by baptism into the Body of Christ. Gathered together in their local church, with their bishop, and united by a common Eucharist, they are the Church of Christ: "This Church of Christ is truly present in all legitimate local congregations of the faithful which, united with their pastors, are themselves called churches in the New Testament" (*LG*

[60] *Commentary on the Documents of Vatican II*, vol. 1, 202–204.

#26). The laity share in "the priestly, prophetic, and kingly functions of Christ" (*LG* #31). In a very important passage, *Lumen gentium* states that the laity not only share in Christ's prophetic office, but in the inerrancy of the Spirit: "The holy people of God shares also in Christ's prophetic office. . . . The body of the faithful as a whole, anointed as they are by the Holy One (cf. John 2:20, 27), cannot err in matter of belief. Thanks to a supernatural sense of faith which characterizes the People as a whole, it manifests this unerring quality when, 'from the bishops down to the last member of the laity,' it shows universal agreement in matters of faith and morals" (*LG* #12). Though Vatican II does not say so explicitly, this passage would seem to be grounds for holding that the Spirit, as it moves among the laity, may originate insights or practices that are then discerned by the hierarchy and proclaimed to the universal Church. This was exactly what happened with the two Marian doctrines: a belief in Mary's immaculate conception and assumption grew up among the faithful and was eventually proclaimed as doctrine. Similarly, the canon of scripture was influenced by usage in the churches by the People of God, and even some of the passages of scripture (the hymn in the Prologue in John 1, and the hymn incorporated into Philippians 2) reflect beliefs that grew among the people.

This in turn affects Vatican II's teaching on infallibility. Briefly, the pope can issue infallible definitions, but his infallibility is that of the Church itself; it is the Church's infallible teaching which the pope proclaims, not his own (*LG* #25). But such an infallible teaching would have to be based on the sense of faith of the faithful, according to the passage cited above. Therefore, *Lumen gentium* states that "to the resultant definitions the assent of the Church can never be wanting" (#25). If such assent were wanting, one would have to conclude that the definition did not in fact express the mind of the whole Church, and was therefore not infallible (see chap. 12).

We have seen that two traditions of ecclesiology run side by side through the history of the Western Church. One is the conciliar tradition, which is based on the early councils, and is expressed in an exaggerated form at Constance, which saw the ecumenical council as supreme *over* the pope. The other tradition, reaching back to Popes Damasus, Leo the Great, and proclaimed by Gregory VII and the medieval popes, and later by the Ultramontanes, is that the pope has supreme jurisdiction *over* the Church, including any council. In its extreme form, this tradition even claims that the Church itself derived from Peter, and hence from the pope. What Vatican II has done is to unite these two traditions as complementary, in the process purging each of extreme formulations. For Vatican II it is both the college of bishops and the pope, acting in concert, that possess supreme teaching and governing authority in the Church. But their decisions and proclamations also should be aligned with the sense of the faithful. This seemingly unwieldy arrangement has no parallel in secular politics or sociology. It can easily happen (and has) that one or the other partner would achieve practical dominance over the other. Nevertheless, I think this is the ideal to be striven for. In the last three chapters, I explore how this ideal can be understood in relation to ontological hierarchy, sociological hierarchy, and ecclesial hierarchy.

Post-Vatican II

It must be admitted that the reforms inaugurated by Vatican II were but a beginning; much remains unfinished. This is especially obvious in the context of the ecumenical movement. The relation between the power of the bishops and that of the pope was not spelled out or made clear at Vatican II, and is subject to more than one interpretation. A serious lack was the failure of the council to set any limits to papal power, or to deal with the perennial question of how the Church is to respond to a heretical, schismatic, infirm, or mentally ill pope. Rahner, in his commentary, thinks that no juridical safeguard is appropriate, that Catholics will just have to trust that the Holy Spirit will protect the Church from abuse of papal power.[61] I believe that this is inadequate, and that juridical safeguards against papal (and episcopal) autocracy are needed in the Church. Again, Vatican II made no substantial changes in the juridical structure of the Church, so that in practice its progressive theology of collegiality, laity, and local church can be simply ignored by the pope and the Curia. Finally, it is not clear if or how the laity share in the governance of the Church. Though the documents speak of the laity sharing in Christ's prophetic and kingly office, the main thrust of the documents sees the laity as instruments of the hierarchy: their call is to put the teachings of the hierarchy into action in the world.

Thirty years after the council, the results of its vision have been mixed. There have been great changes in the liturgy, in ecumenical

[61] Ibid., 203.

relations, in the participation of the laity in liturgy and theology, in dialogue with the secular world, including the sciences. There has also been a marked secularization of attitude in the Church, and a commensurate loss of devotions and the sacramental sense, not intended by the Council. In the area of hierarchy, there has been progress towards a participatory structure especially at the local level. Priests now routinely administer the parish in conjunction with parish councils and lay administrators. Conferences of regional and national bishops now occur annually, and national bishops' conferences have initiated important teachings in their own right (e.g., on the economy and war and peace). In 1965 Pope Paul VI established a Synod of Bishops to give advice to the pope.

But the deeper problem of papal absolutism has changed little in practice. Virtually all bishops continue to be appointed unilaterally by the pope and the Curia, a point criticized by Archbishop John Quinn in his Campion Hall address. He notes that the appointment of bishops by the pope is a recent innovation: "Until roughly 1800, Rome's intervention in the appointment of bishops in dioceses outside the Papal States was rare. Until 1829, it was the policy of the Holy See to leave the appointment of bishops to the local church where possible. At the death of Pope Leo XII in 1829, there were 646 diocesan bishops in the Latin Church. Of this number, excluding those in the Papal States, only twenty-four were directly appointed by Rome."[62]

Now, however, as Quinn explains, the decisive voice in the selection of a bishop is not that of the local episcopate, still less that of the people: "The real decisions are made at other levels: the [papal] nuncio, the Congregation of Bishops, the secretariat of State."[63] The Bishops' Synod, which ought to assist the pope in governing the Church, has done little more than approve papal opinions. The 1969 extraordinary synod on collegiality, for example, issued no reports of its own, but simply approved three reports that were read to it.[64] The question of artificial contraception Paul VI reserved for his own decision, rather than allowing the council to decide it. Everyone knows the result. Paul's decision to prohibit artificial contraception went against

[62] "The Exercise of the Primacy: Facing the Cost of Christian Unity," *Commonweal* (July 12, 1996) 17.

[63] Ibid.

[64] *Vatican Council II: More Post-Conciliar Documents,* Austin Flannery, ed. (Northport, N.Y.: Costello Publishing Co., 1982) xvii.

the advice of his own commission which had been charged with studying the question, a commission made up of bishops, theologians, and laity. By a vote of fifty-four to four this commission recommended changing the teaching to allow artificial contraception for serious reasons, a change they saw as a development, not a reversal, of previous teaching.[65] Catholic laity in the United States and Europe have by a vast majority decided to follow their own consciences and ignore the pope's teaching in this area. The birth-control decision is a good example of decision by command hierarchy. Had the pope allowed the bishops and theologians to discuss the question, as had been the rule at Vatican II, thus allowing a participatory and collegial decision, the result would certainly have been more satisfactory, in all probability along the lines of the majority report of the birth control commission.

During the pontificate of John Paul II a chorus of voices have been raised claiming that the pope and the Curia are becoming excessively authoritarian. The Cologne Declaration of 1989, signed by one hundred and sixty-three European theologians, accused Rome of "robbing" the local churches of their autonomy, of "autocratic methods" in episcopal appointments which overrode traditional local prerogatives, of demanding "blind obedience," and of "violating the principle of subsidiarity in the church."[66] Bishops also have complained. Bishop Raymond Lucker of New Ulm, Minnesota, is quoted in *The New Yorker* as follows: "There is a mind-set in Rome holding that change is wrong and frightening, that to raise questions is in itself a challenge to the authority of the pope. . . . For those in power in Rome, the Church is not 'the People of God.' . . . It is an imperial monarchy that must maintain absolute control."[67] And Archbishop John Quinn states that "bishops and episcopal conferences feel that such grave questions as contraception, the ordination of women, general absolution, and the celibacy of the clergy are closed to discussion." He specifically criticizes the Curia, which, he says, often sees itself "as subordinate to the pope but superior to the College of Bishops."[68]

Evidence of this can be seen in the treatment of regional episcopal synods which came into being after Vatican II as attempts to foster

[65] See "Majority Papal Commission Report," *The Catholic Case for Contraception,* Daniel Callahan, ed. (New York: Macmillan, 1969) 149–173.

[66] *Origins* (March 2, 1989) 633–634.

[67] *The New Yorker* (July 22, 1991) 52.

[68] "The Exercise of the Primacy," 13.

collegiality and subsidiarity. Recently such synods have been controlled by Rome in a less-than-collegial fashion. At the 1990 synod on the formation of priests, the issue of the restriction of the priesthood to celibate males was removed from the agenda, and discussion of it was prohibited by order of the Vatican.[69] The same paralysis has affected American episcopal conference attempts to deal with the priest shortage and the ordination of women, since "Rome has declared the question of alternatives to male celibate priests a closed question."[70] The 1992 CELAM IV conference of Latin American bishops was heavily controlled by Rome, so that discussion of this critical question was again suffocated.[71] Finally, the recent papal statement rejecting the ordination of women was made with almost no participation of bishops, theologians, laity, or women. Thus, although there is far more participation at the local level after Vatican II, this is not true of Rome itself, which remains captive to the monarchial ideology that the pope makes the decisions, and the unity of the Church consists in obedience to those decisions.

The next three chapters will attempt a systematic exposition of participatory ecclesial hierarchy, following the direction of Vatican II.

[69] Peter Hebblethwaite, "Brazilian bishops 'true to form' at world synod," in *National Catholic Reporter* (October 19, 1990) 9.

[70] Msgr. William H. Shannon, "Are There Any More Priests Out There?" in *America* (October 12, 1991) 241.

[71] See Gary MacEoin, "Rome tries, fails to recolonize Latin church," in *National Catholic Reporter* (November 13, 1992) 10–11; Thomas Stahel, "A Tale of Two Cities: Rome and Santo Domingo," in *America* (November 28, 1992) 419.

Chapter 10

Ontological Hierarchy: The Mystical Body of Christ

He is the image of the invisible God, the firstborn of all creation; for in him all things in heaven and on earth were created . . . all things have been created through him and for him. He himself is before all things, and in him all things hold together. He is the head of the body, the church; he is the beginning, the firstborn from the dead, so that he might come to have first place in everything. For in him all the fullness of God was pleased to dwell, and through him God was pleased to reconcile to himself all things, whether on earth or in heaven, by making peace through the blood of his cross. Col 1:15-20

In this admittedly dense chapter, I will advance six related theses: (1) In ontology, as in society, integration and unity are only possible through hierarchy. Diversity on lower levels of being is integrated, but not reduced to uniformity, by higher levels of being. The epigraph above expresses this idea. (2) Ancient, medieval, and Renaissance notions of hierarchy of being were based on the insight that there are higher levels of being, and that higher states of being are mediated to lower states through sacramental participation. This idea is opposed by the modern secular ontology of reductionism and separation, which, deriving from modern natural science, reduces all being to one level: the material, and hence to fragmented, separate atoms or individuals. (3) The idea of a hierarchy of being has been distorted through much of Christian history by the notion of monarchial rule and dominance. This notion led to an idea of God as extrinsic and marginal to the universe, and hence to modern secularism. (4) The central part of the chapter will present a model of participatory ontological hierarchy which incorporates modern scientific ideas of hierarchy. This hierarchy of being ascends from the impersonal to the personal, to the superpersonal (the Trinity). (5) The Christian doctrine of the Trinity expresses a conception of ontological hierarchy that is relational, participatory, communal, and consensual rather than dominative. The *kenosis* (self-emptying) of the second person of the Trinity, the Son, in becoming incarnate (Phil 2:6-11) is the opposite of dominance: it is self-sacrificing love, intended to bring about participation. *Pace* Catherine LaCugna, however, I argue that the doctrine of the Trinity is not anti-hierarchical, but expresses a hierarchy of participation and communion. (6) The simile of the Church as the body of Christ, though in the past distorted by notions of dominance, properly interpreted also supports the idea of a participatory and communal hierarchy.

The notion of a hierarchy of being, or ontological hierarchy, is rooted in the experience of the sacred. Mircea Eliade explains: "for the man of all premodern societies, the *sacred* is equivalent to *power*, and, in the last analysis, to *reality*. The sacred is saturated with *being*. Sacred power means reality and at the same time enduringness and efficacity. The polarity sacred-profane is often expressed as an opposition between *real* and *unreal* or pseudoreal."[1] What is opposed to the sacred is the profane, that which is desacralized, transitory, perishing, inefficacious. This is the ordinary, everyday world of modernity: "The *completely* profane world, the wholly desacralized cosmos, is a recent discovery in the history of the human spirit . . . Desacralization pervades the entire experience of the nonreligious man of modern societies."[2] (Anyone who doubts this should try explaining the meaning of "sacred" or "holy" to a class of college students.) Sacred reality, then, is *more real* than profane reality; it is being to a higher degree. This notion of a hierarchy of being is absolutely fundamental to ancient, medieval, and Renaissance Christianity. The Gospel of John, for example, is structured around a series of contrasts between ordinary, perishable reality and eternal reality given by Jesus and the Spirit. Thus ordinary biological life is contrasted with eternal life, birth from the flesh with the birth from the Spirit (John 3:6); ordinary water with living water (John 4:11); natural bread with the bread of life (John 6:35), and so on. The same

[1] *The Sacred and the Profane* (New York: Harcourt, Brace, & World, 1959) 12.

[2] Ibid.

contrasts appear in Paul's letters between flesh and Spirit (e.g., Galatians 5, Romans 8). And this same notion underlies the difference between natural life, which perishes and which cannot endure the full vision of God, and resurrected life, which never perishes but lives in God's presence. Indeed, the resurrection is only possible in a higher state of being, as Paul struggles to make clear in 1 Corinthians 15.

In premodern societies the sacred is experienced as manifested through natural forms and objects. Natural things, such as trees and stones, can participate in and make present the power and reality of the sacred. Space can be made sacred so it becomes different from the formless profane space outside it. Time also can be made sacred, and so different from ordinary time.[3] This idea, that ordinary things can participate in and make present the reality of the sacred, and hence mediate higher states of being, underlies the Christian idea of the sacraments. Sacraments participate in and mediate the sacred to persons, and persons to the sacred. In most forms of Christianity, they are essential means through which the Church brings persons into participation in the life of God.

Sacraments are also important in the hierarchical structure of the Church. The ultimate authority in the Church is, of course, the Lord Jesus Christ, the head of all creation and of the Church. On this belief Christianity is based: "if you confess with your lips that Jesus is Lord and believe in your heart that God raised him from the dead, you will be saved" (Rom 10:9). But after Jesus' death the question is: how is the authority of Christ mediated to the Church? Disagreement on this point lies at the heart of divisions between Christians. For churches in the episcopal tradition, the bishops participate in the grace and authority of Christ to sanctify, teach, and govern: that is their special charism and the foundation of their authority. Thus hierarchy and authority in the Church are based on ontological hierarchy and the law of participation, without which the bishops are simply elected leaders who may be removed at the pleasure of the congregation. Other figures in Christian history also owed their authority to participation in a higher ontological reality: prophets, but also kings. Down to modern times kings were understood to derive their authority from God and Christ. Thus the king's authority was to an extent an authority of virtue, rooted in the sacred. This helped legitimize the king, and unify society.

[3] Ibid., 20–113.

Thus ancient and medieval religion and society were based on an ontology of participation and communion in a higher reality. But during the seventeenth century, this ontology was replaced by an ontology of reductionism and separation, based on the idea that God was extrinsic to the creation (Ockhamism, Deism), that creation was governed by its own mechanical laws, and that the ultimate constituents of the created world were individual, separate atoms of matter that were connected with each other only through mechanical laws (Newtonian science). The elimination of substantial forms was a crucial move of early modern science. (For Aristotle and Aquinas, substantial form was an intrinsic, holistic, organizing principle which made any entity to be what it was: a whole with an essential nature and a purpose, rather than a mere collection of parts.) Newton wrote: "the moderns, rejecting substantial forms and occult qualities, have endeavored to subject the phenomena of nature to the laws of mathematics . . ."[4] But substantial forms were the unifying principles of bodies; without them, bodies were no more than the sum of their constituent atoms. The loss of the idea of substantial forms as unifying principles, and the reduction of matter to separate atoms, led to the displacement of an organismic view of reality by an atomistic view of reality, based on an ontology of separateness and individuality. As noted in chapter 7, the theological roots of this came from Ockhamism.

Ultimately, this philosophical shift transformed modern society. Enlightenment social thought saw individuals as prior to society: society was created by individuals in a "state of nature" voluntarily ceding some of their rights to form a "social contract." Individual freedom became the supreme good of modern societies. Mind became separated from matter, the observer from the observed object, organisms from their environment, fact from value, science from religion, and human beings from God. The idea of a continuity of being based on participation faded from memory, to be replaced by an ontological hierarchy based on command and force: God was extrinsic to the world, and governed through will, not participation in being. Gradually this Deistic God became more and more remote from everyday life until, like the Cheshire cat, only the grin remained. In the process, the natural world came to be understood as desacralized, self-sufficient,

[4] Preface to the First Edition of *Principia Mathematica,* ET in *Mathematical Principles of Natural Philosophy,* Great Books of the Western World, vol. 34 (Chicago: Encyclopedia Brittanica, Inc., 1952) 1.

governed by its own autonomous laws, which were discoverable by science.[5]

The atomistic and reductionistic view of nature, which gradually triumphed in one branch of science after another, replaced a sacred world with a profane and secular world, in which being had been reduced to one level: the material. Even human persons now are said to be no more than the sum of their molecules, genes, and neurons. As Nobel Laureate and biochemist Jacques Monod puts it: "Living Beings are chemical machines."[6] Biologist Francis Crick agrees: "The Astonishing Hypothesis is that 'You,' your joys and your sorrows, your memories and your ambitions, your sense of personal identity and free will, are in fact no more than the behavior of a vast assembly of nerve cells and their associated molecules."[7] Philosopher Huston Smith notes: "Itself occupying no more than a single ontological plane, science challenged by implication the notion that other planes exist. As its challenge was not effectively met, it swept the field and gave the modern world its soul."[8] Thus, in a kind of dialectical progression, the elevation of God to a position of extrinsic dominance over the world led to the detachment and marginalization of God from the world, and ultimately to an autonomous secular world, in which all being is reduced to one level: what might be called ontological egalitarianism. This supports the argument of previous chapters, that a hierarchy of dominance and egalitarianism are two sides of the same coin, since both have identical concepts of hierarchy.

This has created a profound loss of transcendence, and widespread alienation. The deep need for purpose, love, and belonging that human beings feel seems to find no home in a universe of dead matter, governed by blind, mechanical causes. This was poignantly expressed almost a century ago by Bertrand Russell:

> That Man is the product of causes which had no prevision of the end they were achieving; that his origin, his growth, his hopes and fears,

[5] On the movement from an organismic to a mechanistic understanding of the universe, see Carolyn Merchant, *The Death of Nature* (San Francisco: Harper & Row, 1980), and Morris Berman, *The Reenchantment of the World* (New York: Bantam, 1984).

[6] *Chance and Necessity* (New York: Knopf, 1971), 45.

[7] *The Astonishing Hypothesis: the Scientific Search for the Soul* (New York: Charles Scribner's Sons, 1994) 3.

[8] Huston Smith, *Forgotten Truth* (New York: Harper, 1976) 6.

> his loves and beliefs, are but the outcome of accidental collocations of atoms; that no fire, no heroism, no intensity of thought and feeling, can preserve an individual life beyond the grave; that all the labors of the ages, all devotion, all the inspiration, all the noonday brightness of human genius, are destined to extinction in the vast death of the solar system, and that the whole temple of Man's achievement must inevitably be buried beneath the debris of a universe in ruins—all these things, if not quite beyond dispute, are yet so nearly certain, that no philosophy which rejects them can hope to stand.[9]

Jacques Monod echoed these thoughts in 1971: "The ancient covenant is in pieces; man knows at last that he is alone in the universe's unfeeling immensity, out of which he emerged only by chance."[10]

In these passages we see the results of a tragic ontological egalitarianism; all being has been reduced to matter, and humans cannot ultimately rise above the common fate of the material universe, which is decay and death. This view, of course, represents a massive challenge to the Church, whose whole *raison d'être* is to bring persons into an eternal sharing of the very life of God. If there is no level of being above that of matter, then the Church and its Gospel are based on an illusion. Thus a retrieval of a credible notion of an ontological hierarchy of participation is important if one is to preserve a sacramental view of reality and avoid the Scylla of a divine tyrant and the Charybdis of secularism.

Before proceeding, it may be best to consider briefly a frequent objection. Many persons after Kant hold that we cannot know anything about being or metaphysics, at least through reason. This is a complex problem, which can only be treated briefly here. I follow Norris Clarke in holding that every individual existent, insofar as it exists at all, makes its presence known to other beings by its activity.[11] Every proton, atom, molecule, creates a tiny field (gravitational, electromagnetic, etc.) which communicates its being and nature to other beings around it. Though we cannot know the nature of things directly, we can know the nature of things through their activity. We know the nature of a proton by measuring its mass, its electric charge, etc.; each such mea-

[9] "A Free Man's Worship," (December 1903), reprinted in *Mysticism and Logic* (Great Britain, 1917; Garden City, N.Y.: Doubleday, Anchor paperback, no date) 45.

[10] *Chance and Necessity*, 180.

[11] Norris Clarke, "Action as the Self Revelation of Being," *Explorations in Metaphysics* (Notre Dame: University of Notre Dame Press, 1994) 45–64.

surement measures the activity of the proton. And this is true of any being in the universe. Now, no one person can have comprehensive knowledge of another entity or even of oneself. Only God has that. All human knowledge is perspectival, that is, our knowledge is limited by our historical situation, our brain capacity, gender, temperament, etc. To use a simile, knowledge is like the view of a mountain: no person can have a comprehensive view, but each can have a partial view, limited by one's perspective. Scientists, therefore, use the idea of models. A model is an approximation of the reality it seeks to describe, from a certain limited perspective. Every model is limited. But some models are more true than others. The model of the earth as round, though not entirely accurate (the earth bulges slightly at the equator), is closer to the truth than the model of the earth as flat. Usually more than one model is needed to get a close-to-complete picture; subatomic particles must be described by both particle and wave models; the best description of their behavior is mathematical. There are differing models for gravity. And there are differing models of metaphysical reality: one may use Aristotelian terminology, another personalist terminology, another Buddhist terminology, and so on. Within this range of models some may be more accurate than others. Thus we can have real, though approximate, knowledge of the nature of beings, not just of their appearances. This epistemology is known as critical realism.

Hierarchy of Being: Traditional Views

Aquinas' view of the hierarchy of being was discussed in chapter 6. That view, influenced both by Neoplatonism and Aristotelianism, described an ascending degree of powers and activity as one moved up the scale of being from mineral to plant to animal to human. The hierarchy was inclusive: Higher entities contained all the powers of lower creatures, but additional powers besides. Plants, for example, had the power of nutrition; animals, the powers of nutrition, locomotion, and sensing; humans, the powers of nutrition, locomotion, sensing, and reason. The addition of higher powers did not suppress lower powers, but included them in a higher synthesis. Aquinas also held that all the diverse grades of being were necessary for the fullness of the created order (*ST* I, q. 47, a. 1). Even though rocks and plants were lower in the scale of being than angels, a universe containing rocks, plants, animals, humans, and angels was better than one containing just angels, because the diverse grades of beings expressed the whole range of God's goodness better than any single creature or type of creature could. Thomas was not consistent in this idea, however, for he also thought that lower creatures existed to serve the needs of higher creatures: "in the order of the universe, lower beings realize their last end chiefly by their subordination to higher beings. . . . Imperfect beings serve the needs of more noble beings: plants draw their nutriment from the earth, animals feed on plants, and these in turn serve man's needs."[12] The whole universe is ordained to the good of God, as an army is ordained to victory, and the internal order of the universe follows from this; the parts of the universe are ordained to the good of the whole, since in general the good of the parts is subordinated to the good of the whole (*SCG* III, 64, 10). What is lacking here is an emphasis that the parts, while existing to serve the whole, are also *good in themselves* and have their own *raison d'être.* While Aquinas does say that the reason God created so many diverse things is to manifest the full range of the divine goodness, since one class of things could not express the full range of the divine goodness, he does not seem to take the next step and argue that therefore all lower beings are good in themselves, irrespective of whether they serve the needs of higher beings. Thus he can write: "In a certain sense, therefore, we may say that the whole of corporeal nature exists for man, inasmuch as he is a rational animal."[13] This logic leads him to declare that there will be no plants, animals, or other "mixed bodies" in the resurrected creation, since these will not be needed to satisfy the needs of the resurrected body. The four elements, however, will remain (having been cleansed by the final conflagration), since they are necessary even for the resurrected body.[14] In all this he shows the influence of Neoplatonism, in which the fullness of good existed in the supreme One, and overflowed into creatures below, becoming attenuated as it descended into the material world.

The strength of the traditional conception of the hierarchy of being was that it provided a framework in which all of creation was unified by its relation to God—hierarchy made unity possible. The beauty and lawful design of creatures and creation pointed to God as the common creator: "The heavens are telling the glory of God; and the firmament proclaims his handiwork" (Ps 19:1). This was a *participatory hierarchy*—

[12] *Compendium of Theology,* #148, Vollert's translation, 167.

[13] Ibid.

[14] Ibid., #170, 190–191.

creatures participated, according to the capacity of their natures, in the being of God. There was no unbridgeable gulf between God and an orphaned creation; the beauty of the creation was a reflection of God's beauty; its design a reflection of God's wisdom; its goodness a reflection of God's goodness. It is true that, in traditional Jewish and Christian thought, creatures (even angels) do not share in God's essence; they are not little fragments of God. Rather creation proceeds from God's will. Yet there is in the traditional view a real sense of participation in a continuous scale of being, from the mushrooms to the angels, from the dregs of the universe to God. In this view every being had its assigned place and reason for being in the hierarchy; the cosmos was in a real sense, a home. One does not detect in medieval thought, for example in Aquinas, Bonaventure, Dante, or Chaucer, the deep alienation and pessimism so characteristic of modern thought (though these do appear after the Black Death). Though earthly life might be seen as a "vale of tears," yet in the end, in the words of Julian of Norwich, "All shall be well, and all manner of things shall be well."

The weaknesses of this traditional scheme are also evident. First, there was a tendency to undervalue the material world, and beings lower in the hierarchy, which existed to serve higher beings. Matter, in the Platonic, Aristotelian, and Thomistic traditions, is pure potency and passivity; all real activity is contained in the form which unites with the matter. Thus matter of itself adds nothing positive to form except individuation. It is also the form which is the object of knowledge; matter itself cannot be directly known. Thus in these traditions, there is little influence of matter on form, or of the parts of a complex being on the whole. This is apparent in the thought of Aquinas (see chap. 6). What was of interest to ancient and medieval thinkers was the form, not matter, and the perfected state of beings at the top of the ontological hierarchy—the blessed, the angels, and God—in whom the deficiencies of matter had the least influence. Thus interest in the workings of the material world—the focus of modern science—was comparatively limited in late antiquity and the Middle Ages. The tendency was to see the material world as little more than a scaffold from which to ascend to the heavenly realms.

A corollary to this was that the people most closely associated with matter, peasants, trade persons, and women, were at the bottom of the social hierarchy, while intellectuals, whose work was with knowledge of forms, were at the top. Typically medieval chroniclers "persisted in regarding the nobility as the foremost of social forces and attributed a very exaggerated importance to it, undervaluing altogether the social significance of the lower classes."[15] The parallel between this conception of ontological hierarchy and the dominant medieval conception of ecclesial hierarchy, especially as found in Aquinas and Bonaventure, is obvious (see chap. 6). All juridical authority flows from the top (the pope) down; there is no complementary bottom-up influence from the laity, priests, or even bishops. Second, the emphasis on vertical ascent and the relation of all things to God obscured the importance of horizontal interrelationship among entities. Beings were analyzed as composites of form and matter, substance and accidents, but the notion of relationality as an essential aspect of being was comparatively undeveloped. The whole scheme of Aquinas' *Summa Theologiae*—the coming forth of beings from God and their return to God through Christ—underlines the medieval interest in relation to God, but also its comparative disinterest in exploring the interrelationships of beings with one another. Third, there was little realization of the importance of history in these traditions. The notion of ontological hierarchy was developmental, in that persons were understood as growing towards the perfection that would come in the resurrection—such development was the whole point of the Christian life. But there was no commensurate idea of development taking place in history. Any idea of progress, or development through history, seemed to be absent. The study of history did not revive until the time of the Renaissance.

The whole traditional framework of ontological hierarchy, resting as it did on Neoplatonism (and to a lesser extent on Aristotelianism), was largely discredited by the scientific revolution, the Enlightenment, and the Reformation. The crucial philosophical change which underlay this was the rise of Ockhamism (chap. 7), which denied a participatory hierarchy of being, and substituted a hierarchy based on will and power. Luther swept away medieval ladder imagery and notions of a hierarchy of being and substituted a hierarchy of will: Christians were saved not by grace understood as a participation in God's being, but by faithful trusting in God's promises, and by grace understood as a divine boon (chap. 7). Early modern science, for its part, rejecting the Aristotelian categories of substantial form, focused instead on what could be weighed and measured, i.e., matter, and in time produced a worldview which is almost the exact reverse of that of the Middle Ages.

[15] J. Huizinga, *The Waning of the Middle Ages* (New York: Doubleday, Anchor Books, 1949, 1954) 57.

However, a way to a retrieval of an authentic notion of ontological hierarchy has opened up in natural science itself, which has come to understand the world as a succession of hierarchy of levels. This provides a foundation upon which to build a renewed idea of ontological hierarchy.

A Scientific Model of Hierarchy

As noted in the introduction, in recent decades a new notion of hierarchy has been emerging in the natural sciences. Authors such as Michael Polanyi, Marjorie Grene, Paul Weiss, Ian Barbour, Arthur Peacocke, David Layzer, Stanley Salthe, and others, argue that nature is composed of a hierarchy of levels of increasing complexity and more inclusive wholes.[16] Thus quarks are organized into atoms, atoms into molecules, molecules into macromolecules (e.g., DNA), macromolecules into cellular organelles (e.g., the mitochondria), organelles into cells, cells into tissues and organs, organs into (animal) bodies, animals into societies, societies into ecosystems. Each level includes and builds on all lower levels. But each level is distinct, and must be described by concepts and theories which are not reducible to nor derivable from lower level concepts and theories. For example, biological concepts such as fitness, adaption, organ, and sexuality cannot be defined or explained in chemical or molecular terms. Furthermore, new and unforeseeable properties and characteristics emerge at each level. Life is not a property of simple molecules, but is a property of cells; self-consciousness is not a property of molecules or cells, but is a property of humans, the most complex organized molecular systems known.

Again, while it is obvious that in complex systems the parts influence the whole, the whole system (in various ways, depending on the system) also influences the parts. Thus ecosystems influence populations, populations influence individuals, individual bodies regulate the

[16] See the following: Michael Polanyi, "Life's Irreducible Structure," *Knowing and Being* (Chicago: University of Chicago Press, 1969) 225–239; Marjorie Grene, "Hierarchies in Biology," *American Scientist,* 1987, 504–510; Paul Weiss, "The Living System: Determinism Stratified," *Beyond Reductionism: the Alpbach Symposium,* Arthur Koestler & J.R. Smythies, eds. (Boston: Beacon, 1969) 3–55; Ian Barbour, *Religion in an Age of Science* (San Francisco, Harper, 1990) 165–171; Arthur Peacocke, *Theology for a Scientific Age* (Minneapolis: Fortress, 1993) 213–254; David Layzer, *Cosmogenesis* (New York: Oxford, 1990); Stanley Salthe, *Evolving Hierarchical Systems* (New York: Columbia University Press, 1985).

organs and the molecules which constitute them, and so on. Yet the activities of higher levels do not interfere with the processes on a lower level; rather, they build on them, but also act to limit and organize them. Natural selection at the level of an animal population limits which individuals survive, and thence regulates the composition of the population, without interfering with the laws by which individual animals procreate and flourish. Again in a living system (e.g., a cell or a body), of the almost infinite possible chemical interactions which can take place, only a very small selection are being realized at any one time, which selection directly correlates with the task being performed by the whole. Somehow then the molecular and cellular processes of the living system seem to be selected and regulated by the whole system.[17] Even atoms and molecules, which are clearly built up of more elementary parts, are now understood to be integral wholes. As Ian Barbour writes, "The atom must be viewed as a total vibratory system; the electron is more like a state of the system than a separate individual entity."[18]

This notion of the whole influencing and organizing the parts can also be seen in the interaction of the mind and the body. Roger Sperry (a psychobiologist and Nobel laureate) among others has argued that mental and spiritual forces are emergent properties of brain processes which causally determine the patterns of neuronal firing in the brain, and hence control behavior. Thus it follows that "not only in the brain, but throughout nature the more highly evolved 'macro' properties of all things exert downward control over the lower 'micro' properties of the components."[19] There is then a two-way interaction between parts and wholes at all levels throughout nature.

Thus we have a model of an inclusive hierarchy of wholes and parts under dual or reciprocal control. Arthur Koestler has coined the term "holon" to describe this situation. (I refer the reader to the introduction and the explanation and figure given there.)[20] Holons are parts within

[17] See Weiss, 8–9. Whether or not there are holistic causes, similar to what Aristotle and Aquinas called substantial forms, is accepted as a possibility by only a minority of scientists. For the evidence of holistic, formal causes in nature, see my article: "Aquinas' Concept of Substantial Form and Modern Science," *International Philosophical Quarterly* (Fall, 1996).

[18] Barbour, *Religion in an Age of Science*, 167.

[19] Roger Sperry, "The New Mentalist Paradigm and Ultimate Concern," *Perspectives in Biology and Medicine*, Spring 1986, 416–417.

[20] Arthur Koestler, "Beyond Atomism and Holism—the Concept of the Holon," *Beyond Reductionism*, 192–227.

greater wholes, but are themselves wholes with respect to their constituent parts. As a part, a holon influences the whole of which it is a part; as a whole, it constrains and organizes its own constituent sub-holons.

A classic example of a holon is a cell within the body. The cell is influenced by its constituent parts, most obviously by the DNA which controls its development. But the whole cell also seems to organize, constrain, and control the activities of its constituent parts.[21] Thus the information encoded in the DNA must be read by messenger RNA, and translated into the formation of new proteins. But which proteins are to be created in any situation? Not all are being created at once. New proteins are built up as they are needed by the whole cell, to repair the cell wall, or an internal organelle, or repel an invader. It is the state of the whole cell that "decides" which section of the DNA shall be read and which proteins synthesized. There is a two-way influence, then, of part to whole and whole to part. The cell, then, is an active whole with respect to its parts. But within the body the cell's activity is controlled by the needs of the whole body. Human tissue cells, for example, will grow in tissue cultures, but randomly and without direction. Within the body their growth is controlled by the whole organism, except in cancers, where the control mechanism has broken down. (Cancer here is the exception which proves the rule. The unregulated growth characteristic of cancerous cells is clearly abnormal, and demonstrates that normally there is an overall regulation to the growth and development of cells by the whole body. The mechanism of this regulation is not yet fully known.) Now each cell of a body contains, in its DNA, a map or template of the organization of the whole organism. But within the body, each cell expresses only a tiny portion of the whole DNA code: nerve cells activate the portions controlling the development and activity of nerve cells, muscle cells the portion governing muscle cells, and so on. *No single cell expresses the whole coded activity of the DNA.* The whole code of the DNA can be expressed only through the totality of the cells of the body.[22] Thus every cell is a

[21] See Brian Goodwin, "Developing Organisms as Self-Organizing Fields," *Mathematical Essays on Growth and the Emergence of Form,* Peter Antonelli, ed. (Edmonton: The University of Alberta Press, 1985) 185–199; idem, "Toward a Science of Qualities," *New Metaphysical Foundations of Modern Science,* Willis Harmon and Jane Clark, eds. (Sausalito: Institute of Noetic Sciences, 1994) 215–250.

[22] In fact, much of the DNA code does not seem to be expressed at all, and seems to be redundant or superfluous in the operation of the organism.

holon, and each cell has a contribution to make to the harmonious functioning of the total organism.

Now the model of hierarchy just described has several interlocking characteristics. It is (1) integrative, inclusive, and participatory; (2) subsidiary; (3) dual or reciprocally controlled; (4) developmental. I will comment on these in order. (1) The model brings out the manner in which diverse parts are integrated into a single whole (or system) capable of concerted and unified action; it is through the organizing activity of higher levels on lower levels. Individual parts (e.g., cells) participate in the organizing activity of a larger whole, and hence are integrated or unified, while retaining their characteristic structures and activities; they are not dissolved into the larger whole. Further, each part is important to the completeness of the whole, since each part expresses a unique activity that contributes to the functioning of the whole. But (2) the model also highlights the subsidiarity in that it is composed of subsidiary units, or holons, which themselves act as subwholes, and to a large degree have their own autonomy of action and function. Thus the integrating holistic cause in an organism such as the human body does not therefore separately control each one of the trillions of cells and molecules which make up the body; rather, that integrating control is exercised stepwise through a hierarchy of subsidiary holons. The heart, for example, controls the activity of the muscles of which it is constituted, even to an extent if it is outside the body, *in vitro*. Each holon, therefore, has what might be called *semi-autonomy*. And this is typical of subsidiary systems generally. Again (3) in this model, control flows from the whole to the constituent parts but also from the parts to the whole. There is therefore dual control, acting through subsidiary units or holons. (4) This model is also not static, but developmental, in that the integrating holistic cause is always *teleological*. It guides the overall morphogenetic development of an organism from embryo to adult, and operates to direct the organism to a goal, such as mature flourishing and reproduction. Thus we have a model of holons within holons within holons, or, to vary the language, systems within systems within systems, all structured hierarchically, and all having semi-autonomy. An entire series of nested holons is called a holarchy (see chap. 1). In science, the upper limit of this holarchy is the society of human persons, the earth's ecosystem, or perhaps the physical universe, depending on how the holarchy is described.

Virtually everything in nature is a holon. And all of nature can be looked at as a holarchy composed of increasingly more inclusive, complex, yet integrated holons (though the nature of the integration depends on the nature of the system). Below I will suggest that this natural holarchy can be extended into the spiritual dimension as well, where it culminates in the most inclusive, complex, and integrated whole of all: the Mystical Body of Christ.

A Participatory Model of Ontological Hierarchy

The traditional hierarchy of being and the recent scientific model, though they may seem to be speaking of disparate realities, and using different terminology, actually complement each other. The former focuses on spirit, but undervalues matter, the latter focuses on matter, but undervalues the role of spirit. By putting the two together within a common framework, a model of ontological hierarchy can be created which combines the strengths of each conception, avoids the weaknesses, and carries contemporary credibility.

There are similarities between the traditional hierarchy of being and the modern scientific hierarchy of nature. The Aristotelian and Thomistic notion of hierarchy associated certain powers or capacities with each ontological level: existence with the mineral level, life and growth with the plant level, sensing with the animal level, and so on. Further, the powers of higher levels included but augmented those of lower levels. Similarly, the scientific model sees various properties emerging at successively higher levels of complexity and organization: life and growth emerge at the cellular level; movement at the multicellular level, sensation at the animal level, consciousness at the level of higher animals, reason and self-awareness at the human level. Both the traditional and the modern envision lower powers, capacities, and properties as retained and subsumed by higher levels of complexity; higher properties typically include, and do not suppress, lower ones. Similarly, more complex levels and processes do not interfere with the functioning and operation of lower processes but presume them; if the laws and operations of lower operations did not remain intact, the higher levels of complexity could not occur. Thus the laws of physics are presumed in chemical systems; and the laws of chemistry in biological systems. But higher levels do limit and order the operations of lower levels. For example, a free electron can have either of two states of spin. But once incorporated into an atomic orbital with another electron, the electron is constrained to assume only one state of spin, and its companion electron in the orbital must have the opposite spin (this is known as the Pauli exclusion principle). Again, glucose, used as sugar in many higher forms of life, can in its free state have either a left- or right-handed form; but in all living cells, only right-handed (dextrorotary) glucose occurs. Both the traditional and the modern notions of hierarchy emphasize that hierarchical systems are integrative and inclusive.

There are, however, differences between the traditional and the modern conception. In the traditional understanding, there were discontinuities between levels of being: mineral and plant, plant and animal, animal and human. The modern understanding, influenced by the theory of evolution, sees unbroken continuity between levels. The traditional notion of hierarchy in nature was not subsidiary; influence flowed from the form to matter, and the whole to parts, but not vice versa. There was no clear notion of subsidiary forms or holons. Aquinas held that each organism was composed of prime matter and the substantial form; there were no intermediate, subsidiary forms.[23] Finally, the traditional concept of ontological hierarchy had little room for history or evolution.

A major difference is that in scientific notions of the hierarchy in nature, the emergence of higher properties is closely tied to the increase in integrated complexity of a material system. Therefore the upper limit of complexity is usually seen to be human society, or the biosphere on earth—both complex systems, exhibiting much greater internal differentiation, more holons, and a higher degree of integration than, say, a star or a galaxy. (In a galaxy, the constituent holons would be stars; in a star, the constituent holons would be atoms.) Few scientists, however, would envision the hierarchy as extending to include *non-material* entities such as disembodied souls, the blessed in heaven, angels, or God. If heavenly existence represents a higher state of being than that of earthly life, can we extend the hierarchy of being into non-material realms? To do this, we have to get behind the divorce between "matter" and "spirit" and see them in a framework in which they can be united. The metaphysics of Aquinas, as interpreted and modified by Norris Clarke, offers such a framework. Aquinas' concepts are difficult, and his language dated and technical; my account here will be, because of space, only a brief summary of some points of his metaphysics.

[23] I discuss this at length in "Aquinas' Concept of Substantial Form and Modern Science."

Aquinas begins with the insight that being or existence is not a static, brute fact (as it tends to be in modern philosophy), but an activity. He uses the Latin infinitive *esse* for "to be," but in English his sense is best conveyed by thinking of exist-ing or be-ing as gerunds, like "running." The act of being or existing is the most basic activity of all entities—it is that active presence by which any entity, from an atom to a person, communicates its own existence to other beings. Now for Aquinas, the fullness of being is God, and in God we can see what the fullness of Being is really like. It is co-terminous with the fullness of personhood, life, love, power, beauty, consciousness, self-awareness, understanding, integration, and inter-relationship; each of these is simply an aspect of being *(esse)*. Aquinas' idea is that all these aspects of *esse* exist in their fullness and are united in God, who is *Esse*, Being itself. God is Being by essence, whereas all creatures possess existence as a gift from God; in technical Thomist language, they possess being by "participation," a term deriving ultimately from Plato (Greek: *methexis*). The idea is that being exists in God fully and infinitely, but in creatures only partially and in a limited, qualified manner. God cannot not exist; whereas the existence of creatures is not necessary but contingent; creatures do not possess existence in themselves (as God does); they are brought into existence and maintained in existence by God. Thus *esse* in creatures (including angels) differs radically from God's *Esse*. Creatures are brought into existence and held in being by God's will; God's essence, on the other hand, *is* to exist. This is also true for members of the Trinity—the Son and the Spirit, who are said to proceed from the Father's being and essence, not from his will, as creatures do.

Aquinas also draws a distinction between the essence or nature of a creature and its act of existing *(esse)*. The essence of a creature is its nature, *what* it is. The essence of a hydrogen atom is an atom with one proton and one electron in an orbital around the proton. We can imagine the essences of entities which may not exist. Physics was able to describe possible trans-uranium elements which did not exist in nature (e.g., Plutonium), and actually create these in the laboratory; it has done the same with many subatomic particles. Modern synthetic chemistry is constantly creating new compounds, which do not exist in nature, though their essential nature can be calculated and described before they are created in the laboratory. In actually existing entities, essence and *esse* are distinct but cannot be separated (to do so would destroy the creature). According to Clarke's interpretation of

Aquinas, the essence of a creature limits how much of *esse,* and the quality of *esse,* that entity can receive or manifest.[24] Bearing in mind that *esse* is not simply raw existence—the "being there" of a stone—but is also consciousness, activity, interrelationship, freedom, and so on, we do not expect that a hydrogen atom would exhibit the same degree of being as a person. A hydrogen atom, it is true, lasts longer than the physical human body (though not longer than the personal soul), but does not exhibit a high degree of intrinsic activity: it is largely passive, at the mercy of external forces. Mature persons, however, exhibit a high degree of intrinsic activity, generating their own internal purpose, and carrying this out in activity, shaping their environment accordingly. Persons also have a higher degree of freedom, consciousness, interrelationality, and self-awareness than the simple atom. That is because the essence or nature of a person is capable of expressing more of being, and a higher quality of *esse,* than the essence of a simple atom or compound. Using the language of participation, we can say that the human person *participates* more fully in the being of God than does an atom or chemical, always bearing in mind that participation does not mean that creatures are fragments or pieces of God—which would be pantheism. (It is better to think of them as reflections of God.) But some creatures reflect a more comprehensive image of God, and others less, depending on their essence. In Christian theology, it is Jesus the Christ who is the most perfect reflection of God, in whom being, actuality, consciousness, relationality (love), freedom, are at their maximum. So high was the incarnate Lord in the scale of Being that he could not be held by death.

Now in this conception of an array of creatures, each species exhibiting a different degree of participation in and expression of ultimate being, we have a framework that is capable of encompassing an ontological hierarchy which ranges from the simplest creatures, such as quarks or subatomic particles, to the most lofty beings, such as persons, angels and even God (though God is not 'a' being, but Being itself). In this framework there is no gulf between matter and spirit; matter is only a more limited state of being, with less intrinsic relationality, consciousness, self-awareness, than spirit. Matter might be seen as spirit in a very limited form, "solidified" spirit, a suggestion

[24] "The Limitation of Act by Potency in St. Thomas: Aristotelianism or Neoplatonism?" in *Explorations in Metaphysics* (Notre Dame: University of Notre Dame Press, 1994) 65–88.

made by Karl Rahner.[25] As material beings become more complex, the essential qualities of spirit, such as activity, consciousness, freedom, self-awareness, and personal relations, become more pronounced.

Let us consider activity as an example. Activity in this sense means that a being possesses within itself its own principle of self-determination and action, in contrast with passivity, which means that the being is affected by external forces. The activity of an atom or mineral is minimal; it consists in its simple act of existence, in its being what it is, and communicating this being to others. In the case of a hydrogen atom, this would involve affecting the gravitation field around it, and affecting adjacent atoms through electrochemical bonding. Mainly, however, simple atoms, chemical compounds, and minerals are passive, shaped by external forces. Plants exhibit a greater degree of internal activity: they exist, but they also grow and reproduce, and affect their environment, for example by transforming carbon dioxide into plant material and oxygen. Animals exist, grow, and reproduce, but also have the powers of sensing and movement. Typically, they affect their environment more and are less passive than plants. Human beings exist, grow, sense, move, and reproduce, but also can reason and respond to God. The degree of their internal activity is greater than that on other earthly beings: they have a great effect on their environment (often detrimentally), they are not so passive as animals or plants, and they can cooperate with God in their own eternal salvation and in that of others. Thus the activity of humans can have eternal consequences. The activity of angels is greater still; though they do not grow, sense, or reproduce, their powers of activity and knowledge, not limited by a body, greatly exceed those of humans. Finally, the activity of God is unlimited and infinite: God creates the universe from nothing and sustains it in existence at each moment, while knowing the activity of its every atom, and the thoughts and intentions of every human. Thus there is a progression of degrees of activity, and a reduction of passivity, as one moves up the hierarchy of being.

The point of union between matter and spirit is found in human persons, who are by essence composed of both. But the human person is not, for Aquinas (as it is for Descartes) a soul "in" a body. The soul is the form of the body, the holistic cause which organizes all the matter and holons of the body into a unity, and guides the maturation and development of the body. But the soul, being essentially spiritual, also has the capacity to exist without the body. While in the body its functions

[25] *Hominisation* (New York: Herder and Herder, 1965, German original, 1958) 53–61.

require the body's organs (e.g., the brain to think), and are limited by the limitations of the natural body (e.g., the capacity of brain to think or to remember). Eventually the aging of the body (due to buildup of detritus in cells, etc.) exceeds the soul's ability to integrate the bodily elements, and the body dies.

Human beings in their earthly life, however, do not in Christian thought represent the summit of the scale of human being. In the state of the fall human nature is disintegrated, so that the passions are opposed to the reason, and the body subject to disintegration and decay. In the resurrection, however, humans will possess a glorified, imperishable body. This is the point of Paul's discourse on the resurrection where he contrasts celestial bodies with terrestrial bodies (1 Cor 15:40) and the physical *(psychikos)* body with the spiritual *(pneumatikos)* body (1 Cor 15:44), and states that "flesh and blood cannot inherit the kingdom of God" (1 Cor 15:50). But, as Aquinas explains it, the body will be glorified because of the soul's closeness to God. For Aquinas, the soul is the form of the body—that which makes the body a unity. Because sin has separated the soul from the power of God, the soul cannot forever keep the body intact; eventually it disintegrates. But in heaven the sinless person will be completely united with God, and the soul itself will be informed by God's glory; that glory will overflow the soul, and glorify the body (*ST* III, q. 83, a. 1). The resurrection, then, will be due to an integration of the person with God, which will in turn result in a full integration of reason and will, soul and body, so that the body will be transformed and enjoy a deathless state of being. Resurrected persons, then, are more fully integrated than persons in the earthly state, and are higher in the scale of being: their activity, life, freedom, consciousness, and personal relations vastly exceed those still in the viatory state. Beyond humans are the angels, who are usually thought of as simple, but a better image might be that they are beings possessed of great powers, yet total integration: their mind is not opposed by their will, nor by the "bodies," if indeed they are material creatures at all. (Saint Bonaventure thought angels had a kind of materiality; Saint Thomas disagreed.) Unlike a human being, an angel can sum up and express his/her whole being in a single act. (I pass over the difficult case of the fallen angels, who have been reduced to a fraction of their former being.) Finally, beyond the angels is God, who again is usually thought of as perfectly simple. But in God exists the "ideas" and knowledge of all created beings and all history, yet these are so totally integrated that God is one, integrated and unified to an infinitely greater degree than any creature can be.

Thus one can argue that there is a progression of *integrated diversity and complexity* as one moves up the scale of being. The most elementary entities, such as quarks or subatomic particles, have the fewest internal parts, and the least complexity. Above these are the plants, animals, and humans, each of which is successively more complex, and hence requires a greater degree of integration. (The human brain is by far the most complex material organism in the known universe.) But spiritually, most human beings are not well integrated in this life; those in heaven are more integrated: their whole being is surrendered to and integrated by the love of God. Finally, angels, it can be argued, are more perfectly integrated still, and God most of all.

A similar progression can be seen in relationality or communion, an area not well developed in Aquinas, but developed by Norris Clarke, who argues that substance and relationality or communion are two equally primordial aspects of being: "To be is to be substance in relation,"[26] and "To be . . . is to be in communion."[27] Simple particles exist in relation to other particles: almost all are bound into atoms. But the relations are simple, not complex and multileveled. More complex organisms are built up of atoms made up of simple particles in interrelationship. But these atoms are built into larger organic molecules, and hence exist in interrelationship with other atoms; the organic molecules are themselves arrayed into complex relationships within cells; the cells are interrelated so as to form tissues, the tissues, organs, the organs, an integrated animal. At the human level interrelationship becomes not only material, but also spiritual: a communion of persons united in love. But this communion, in the state of earthly pilgrimage (the viatory state), is sadly damaged by alienation, hatred, conflict, and so on. The blessed in heaven enjoy a far more perfected communion, since they participate as fully as possible in the life of God and in each others' lives, through Christ and the Spirit. Above the created order, but penetrating it, exists the Trinity, a communion of persons in total interrelationship, to such a degree that the persons wholly interpenetrate one another in *perichoresis*. Thus, we find that being, as it becomes more complete and full, becomes more personal and communal. In its fullest, being is persons in communion.[28]

[26] "To Be Is to Be Substance in Relation," *Explorations in Metaphysics*, 102–122.

[27] *Person and Being* (Milwaukee: Marquette University Press, 1993) 82.

[28] See *Person and Being* for a luminous account of the being as persons in communion.

Parallel to the hierarchy of relationship is an increasing degree of self-determination, self-possession, and self consciousness in beings. Simple minerals have a minimal degree of self-determination. Plants have more, animals more still. In persons, having free will and self consciousness, self determination becomes greater, and self possession takes on the aspect of self-awareness. But persons in this life almost never achieve full self-possession; there remain unconscious and instinctual drives poorly integrated into the psyche, and only partly under the control of the will. Persons in heaven are more fully self-possessed and self determined, as are angels. And the "persons" of the Trinity enjoy total self-possession, yet are in total communion with each other. Thus, as Clarke shows, both the in-itself and for-others aspects of beings, being as self-possessedness, and being as communion, increase together as one moves up the scale of being.[29] If we define person as a center of intelligence, free will, and self awareness, then the scale of being moves from impersonal, to personal (humans, angels) to superpersonal (the Trinity).

Finally, there is progression of value and goodness as one ascends the scale of being. Existence itself is the basic good; it is good that something exists rather than nothing. The existence of an atom, a compound, a mineral, is good. But the existence of living matter is an additional good: life is a perfection added to the mere existence of matter. Again, the existence of consciousness, which emerges in the higher animals, adds a further good. The existence of human spiritual consciousness, which has the capacity to be self-aware, and also to be aware of others, to empathize and love, and to know and love God, is a further added good. Some persons may deny this, and claim that rather than suffering, it would better to be like the animals, without foresight, worry, anxiety, etc. But very few persons, even if intensely unhappy, would consent to surrender their self-awareness, for example by a brain operation such as a lobotomy, and be reduced to the level of consciousness of an animal. There is something good about consciousness and awareness in themselves, which transcend suffering. This is also true of higher levels of awareness, such as those experienced in mysticism, which outweigh much suffering. As Paul writes: "I consider that the sufferings of this present time are not worth comparing with the glory about to be revealed to us" [Rom 8:18]. The awareness and love

[29] Ibid., 42–82.

achieved by those in the full presence of God is like mystical experience, the state is a good onto itself, which far outweighs the suffering entailed in reaching it—like the experience of having ascended a mountain. Conversely, the state of those in hell involves not so much physical suffering, as a drastic shrinkage of consciousness. At the summit of this scale of goodness is the Triune God. Now in this scale, higher goods do not annul lower goods, nor are they achieved by suppressing lower goods. The operations of atoms, chemicals, and minerals are not vitiated by being included in a plant, animal, or human; in a certain sense those operations are ennobled, since they support a higher level of operation. This is even true of the blessed in heaven; the exalted state of the soul in its relationship with God will eventually entail the resurrection and perfection of the body, so that the good of the body will be included in the good of the whole person.

Thus the fact that there is a progression of perfection and good as one ascends the scale of being does not mean that lower beings have no value in themselves, or that they exist only to serve higher beings. If, as Aquinas affirms, the full extent of God's goodness (and wisdom, beauty, power, majesty, since these are all aspects of God's being commensurate with God's goodness) can only be expressed in the whole array of beings found in creation (*ST* 1, q. 47, a. 1), and if every species expresses some unique facet of God's beauty and being, then every species possesses its own good, its own *raison d'être.* The creation would be a poorer expression of the beauty and majesty of God if it consisted only of humanity and whatever is needed for human sustenance. Each species is in fact a *holon* in the ontological hierarchy; a sub-whole with its own integrity and purpose, which is also a part of a larger whole.

A similar argument can be made for the role of matter in creation. Matter does more than just serve as a receptacle for form, as in Neoplatonism; it has a positive role, making each individual distinct and separate from other individuals, even in the same species. Thus matter adds diversity within a species, as well as allowing a diversity of species to exist. This diversity is also essential to the full expression of the goodness and beauty of creation, and necessary if creation is to reflect the fullness of God's glory.

Finally, the creation does not exist in a vertical ontological hierarchy alone; it also develops through history. According to the theory of evolution, higher species develop through the complexification of matter, which occurs through the passage of time. One may attribute this to the "self-organizing" properties of matter (as biologists commonly do), but from a theological perspective, it can be seen as Christ gradually drawing the creation into higher levels of complexity, being, and spirit, through a process of internal self-transcendence, a perspective beautifully articulated in the work of Teilhard de Chardin. Thus the ontological hierarchy, at least as it is expressed in the material creation, does not appear all at once, but across aeons of time. This points to the important fact of development through history, something not recognized by the ancients or medievals.

The model of ontological hierarchy sketched out above, then, draws from both the traditional and modern conceptions of hierarchy. Like the medieval notion, it envisions an ontological hierarchy stretching from the lowest beings to the highest, bridging the realms of matter and spirit. Like the medieval notion, it is based on participation in being, recognizes the causal role of spirit in the hierarchy, and the action of higher levels of being in unifying lower levels. But like the modern, it allows for the importance of material complexification, for the influence of matter on the nature of an organism, for the subsidiary character of species and lower beings, for the ontological importance of lower creatures in themselves, for a holarchy of increasing complexity and integration, and for evolution through history. In this model causal influence flows both from the top down—God creates and guides the world, but also from the bottom up—material factors do influence the character of lower beings. I agree with John Polkinghorne and others that the laws of matter have to a degree their own God-given autonomy, and are not directly controlled by God's will (though God does hold them in being). That lower beings influence higher (as well as vice-versa) can be seen in the Christian affirmation that God responds to prayer (as do the angels and saints, in the belief of many denominations). Following modern ecology, I would see a mutual interdependence of beings at all levels of the ontological chain, both horizontally in their interrelations within a given ontological level, and vertically, in their interrelations across ontological levels. These interrelationships are explored by modern ecology, which, however, limits interrelationships to the material world. But in Catholic belief this would extend to the angels, and the blessed as well, who are involved with aiding those on earth, while those on earth can pray for and aid those in purgatory.

The Trinity

The Trinity is the culmination and fulfillment of ontological hierarchy, the very fullness of being. Christian doctrine of the Trinity states that the triune God exists as three divine persons, or *hypostases,* who share one substance *(ousia),* one essence, and one being. The distinction between person, (hypostasis) and substance which is central to this definition goes back to the Cappadocian fathers, Saints Basil, Gregory of Nyssa, and Gregory of Naziansus.[30] The fact that the three share the same divine substance makes them ontologically equal; what distinguishes them is their origins and mutual relations. The Father is uncaused and ungenerated *(agenetos),* and is the cause and source of both the Son and the Spirit, who, however, proceed from the essence of the Father, —and therefore share his essence—not from his will, as creatures do. The Son is "begotten," i.e., proceeds from the Father's essence, not "created." The Son is in fact the "Only Begotten" (*monogenys,* John 1:18). The Spirit, according to Gregory of Nyssa, proceeds from or out of the Father *through* the Son, the Son acting as an intermediary.[31] This became the accepted teaching in the Eastern Church. For Gregory, the Son is never without the Spirit nor the Spirit without the Son. The model of the Trinity in the West, which was based on the thought of Saint Augustine, differed slightly from that in the East. According to Augustine, the Spirit proceeds both from the Father and from the Son, since it is the Spirit of both of them. The acceptance of this model in the West eventually led to the insertion of the *filioque* into the Western Creed. In the understanding of both the East and West, however, the three divine persons exist in a relation in which each of the three persons is wholly immanent in and penetrates the others: a mystical communion. The East expresses this by the term *perichoresis,* the West by *circumincession,* both terms signifying mutual indwelling (cf. John 14:10: "I am in the Father and the Father is in me").

The relatedness and integration of the three persons, then, is greater than that possible in any natural entity (atom, chemical compound, crystal, or organism), in which the parts are formed together into a unity, but do not interpenetrate each other. The unity of natural entities is friable, and can always be broken; whereas that of the Trinity cannot. Similarly, the relatedness between two natural beings, or within any creature in nature, can always be dissolved; the interrelatedness of the Trinity can-

[30] See Gregory of Nyssa, "On the Difference between *ousia* and *hypostasis," Documents in Early Christian Thought,* Maurice Wiles and Mark Santer, eds. (Cambridge: Cambridge University Press, 1975) 31–35.

[31] See the account in J.N.D. Kelly, *Early Christian Doctrines,* rev. edition (San Francisco: Harper & Row, 1960, 1978) 263–269.

not. Again, the life of the Trinity is eternal and self-subsistent; the life of creatures is always given from without and contingent. The consciousness, knowledge, understanding of creatures (even angels) is limited; that of the Triune God is not. Lastly, the self-giving love *(agape)* of creatures is limited, that of the Trinity is not.

Thus, the Trinity represents the maximum perfection of Being in all its manifold aspects, including personhood, love, and communion. Its activity, relatedness, integration, and life surpasses the activity, relatedness, integration, and life of any creature(s); it is the summit of ontological hierarchy, which includes and incorporates in itself all the perfections found to lesser degrees in created beings. They in fact participate by degrees in the perfections of the Trinity, which remains undiminished, inexhaustible in its fecundity. The Trinity does not dominate lesser beings. It is the ultimate whole, which holds all holons in being and integrates them into a coherent, lawful universe. Its hierarchy represents a hierarchy of fullness, inclusion, and participation, not dominance. This is powerfully expressed in the Christian understanding of the *kenosis* (self emptying) of the Son in becoming incarnate. Since persons could not come to God (because of sin), God came to them in their own likeness, to draw them into participation in the divine life. This is expressed in Philippians 2:6-7: "Christ Jesus, who, though he was in the form of God, did not regard equality with God as something to be exploited, but emptied himself, taking the form of a slave, being born in human likeness."

The mutuality of the Trinity is meant to be a model for human mutuality: "that they may all be one. As you, Father, are in me and I am in you, may they also be in us . . . I in them and you in me, that they may become completely one" (John 17:21, 23). This, then, is the model for Christian communion: a community united by the indwelling of the Spirit, made possible by the incarnation, Jesus' death, resurrection.

Now several scholars have argued that the doctrine of the Trinity is incompatible with what we have called "Imperial theology": that because there is one God, or one Christ, there must therefore be one supreme earthly ruler who reigns as God or Christ's Vicar: one emperor or one pope to whom all are subject and owe obedience. The classic statement of this incompatibility was by Eric Peterson,[32] but it has been restated recently by both Jürgen Moltmann and Catherine LaCugna. Moltmann (a Protestant) writes:

[32] *Der Monotheismus als politisches Problem* (Leipzig: Jakob Hegner, 1935).

> Monarchial monotheism justifies the church as hierarchy, as sacred dominion. The doctrine of the trinity constitutes the church as 'a community free of dominion.' The trinitarian principle replaces the principle of power by the principle of concord. Authority and obedience are replaced by dialogue, consensus and harmony . . . The hierarchy which preserves and enforces unity is replaced by the brotherhood and sisterhood of the community of Christ. The presbyterial and synodal church order and the leadership based on brotherly advice are the forms of organization that best correspond to the doctrine of the social trinity.[33]

LaCugna carries this thesis even further. She argues that trinitarian doctrine has been distorted after the Cappadocian fathers by a separation of the economic Trinity—the way the Trinity is revealed to us in history—from the immanent or theological Trinity—the way the triune God is in Godself. She argues that traditional speculation, for example by Aquinas and Gregory Palamas, tended to be confined to the relationality within the immanent Trinity, but was not applied to the economic Trinity. Rather, the economic Trinity was reduced to the monarchial model, since, it was argued, from outside God appeared to be One, and this oneness became the model and justification for one monarchial ruler, whether emperor or pope. LaCugna argues, however, that the immanent Trinity is really a community of equals, and this should be the model for the Church also.

> Both Eastern and Western ethical traditions have lost sight of the revolutionary theological and political implications of what was worked out in the doctrine of the Trinity. It is incongruous that the pattern of subordination between persons, having been painstakingly excised from the relationship between God and Christ, would have been transferred *by both East and West* to the relationship between God and creature, and projected onto relationships in the created order: God is over the world, male is over female, rational being is over inanimate. . . . The *arche* of God, understood from within a properly trinitarian theology, excludes every kind of subordination among persons. . . . A reconceived doctrine of the Trinity affirms what Jesus Christ reveals: that love and communion among persons is the truth of existence. . . . *Therefore any theological justification for a hierarchy among persons also vitiates the truth of our salvation through Christ.*[34]

[33] *The Trinity and the Kingdom* (San Francisco: Harper, 1981) 202.
[34] *God for Us* (San Francisco: Harper, 1991) 399–400, emphasis in original.

In both these authors we see the term "hierarchy" used as the equivalent of dominance. Moltmann at least admits that some form of leadership is required in the Church. He is correct in his estimate that a synodal Church order best corresponds to the doctrine of the social Trinity, though a synodal Church order requires the primacy of one person to function.

LaCugna's analysis is hampered because she has no middle term between hierarchy as domination and absolute equality. The notion of a participatory hierarchy never seems to have occurred to her. She thus gives us a distorted interpretation of the trinitarian doctrine and tradition.

To begin with, she agrees with Karl Rahner's widely accepted thesis that the economic Trinity is the immanent Trinity, and that the two should not be disjoined. That is, we can only understand what the Trinity is in itself from its revelation to us through Christ and the Spirit in salvation history. She writes: "Finally, *it is impossible to think of the divine persons in an entirely abstract way* disconnected from their presence in salvation history because it is only through the Son and the Spirit that the unknowable God (Father) who dwells in light inaccessible is revealed to us."[35] But she admits that the biblical, creedal, and liturgical evidence points to a "strong doctrine of the monarchy of the Father."[36] Indeed, it seems that the biblical evidence is overwhelming that Jesus saw the Father as "greater" than he: he explicitly affirms this in the Fourth Gospel: "The Father is greater than I" (John 14:28). Elsewhere he says that he and the Father are one (John 17:11), that the Father is in him, and he in the Father (John 17:21). But Jesus never says that he and the Father are equal! Indeed, his choice of the title "Father," in the context of the ancient world, would have carried a strong connotation of hierarchy. Jesus constantly speaks of doing his Father's will, of being sent by the Father, of the work his Father has given him, and so on. His entire ministry is conducted in obedience to the Father's will—this is especially clear in the Lord's Prayer—"thy will be done," and in his prayer in Gethsemane—"Not as I will, but as thou wilt" (Matt 26:39, RSV). But of course his relation with the Father was not a hierarchy of domination, but of participation: obedience to the Father is the condition of participating in the Father's glory and kingdom—this is the whole lesson Jesus came to teach.

[35] Ibid., 70.
[36] Ibid., 69.

LaCugna argues that the Cappadocian interpretation of the Trinity, which saw the Father, Son, and Spirit as equal in substance, essence, and being, meant that there could be no hierarchical *relations* between them: "the primacy of the Father is incompatible with the idea that Father, Son, and Spirit share a common *ousia*."[37] This is her own assertion, but it was not the understanding of the fathers or of the tradition. The Father was understood to be *greater* than the Son, because he was the source and cause of the Son's being. Thus Gregory of Naziansus wrote: "We admit that in respect of being the cause the father is greater than the Son. . . ." He goes on to argue that the Arians make the mistake of thinking that because the Father is greater than the Son in respect to being *Cause*, therefore it follows that the Father is greater than the Son in *being*. This Gregory denies: "For while we assign this word greater to His Nature viewed as a Cause, they infer it of His Nature viewed in itself."[38] LaCugna, reversing the Arian position, mistakenly assumes that ontological equality must imply relational equality. But it did not for Gregory of Naziansus, nor, apparently, for the writer of the Fourth Gospel, who saw the *Logos* as one with the Father, but Jesus as subordinate to the Father. LaCugna might argue that the subordination applies only to the Son as sent, i.e., only in respect to his mission, but not to his eternal procession from and relation with the Father. Yet she cannot so argue and at the same time assert that the economic Trinity is the immanent Trinity, and that we only know the immanent Trinity through the economic Trinity. Indeed, she criticizes Augustine rather severely for making a distinction between the mission and the procession, "which had the effect of defunctionalizing the Trinity by minimizing the relationship between the divine persons and the economy of redemption."[39] In the end, LaCugna's argument fails because she cannot conceive of hierarchy except as domination, and assumes without warrant that ontological equality must entail relational equality. And in insisting that we must understand the immanent Trinity through the lens of the economic Trinity, she leaves herself exposed to a strong counterargument. If the immanent Trinity is to be understood through the economic Trinity, and if (as she admits) the biblical evidence is that the economic Trinity was subordinationist, then it follows that the immanent Trinity

[37] Ibid., 71.

[38] "The Third Theological Oration: On the Son," XV, in *NPNF*, Second Series, vol. 7, 306.

[39] *God for Us*, 101.

is subordinationist also, at least in some respect. But just as there can be a hierarchy of relations between two persons who nevertheless are equal in respect to their nature, essence, and substance, so also can there be hierarchical relations within the Trinity while there is a commonality of substance and being among the persons.

I agree with LaCugna and Moltmann that the doctrine of the Trinity is incompatible with a divine monarchy and ecclesial hierarchy *understood as domination.* But it is *not* incompatible with an ecclesial hierarchy of participation; in fact, it serves as its exemplar and model. Within the Trinity there is total communion and participation of the persons in each other, yet there remains a hierarchy of *relationships:* the Father is greater than the Son, and presumably of the Spirit also, since the Father is the source and cause of the Spirit as of the Son. This is a model for the Church as hierarchical communion.

Also in its relation with persons and the world, the Trinity is a model for the Church. For the Son, in order to become incarnate, emptied himself and takes the form of a slave, in order to draw all persons into a sharing of his life and his Father's life, through the Holy Spirit. But his self-emptying does not mean he forgoes his authority. As Jesus of Nazareth, he teaches with a divine authority—he changes the law of Moses on divorce, for example, a law which had been given (in the eyes of the Jews) by God, and which could be changed by God alone. He forgives sins, to the astonishment of the Jews, who realize only God can forgive sins. The transfiguration shows forth his divinity. Lastly, he prophesies that he will appear as the eschatological judge (Matt 25:31-46), separating the saved from the damned. But in his earthly incarnation as Jesus of Nazareth, his authority is exercised as an authority of virtue: moral example, teaching, and service, never as an authority of force or domination. And this also is to be a model for the Church (cf. chap. 12).

The Body of Christ

The life and presence of God is mediated to the whole created order through Christ and the Spirit, as the passage from Colossians given in the epigraph states. Through Christ God is reconciling all things to himself. A similar passage in Ephesians states: "For he [God the Father] has made known to us in all wisdom and insight the mystery of his will, according to his good pleasure that he set forth in Christ as a plan for the fullness of time, to gather up all things in him, things in heaven and things on earth" (Eph 1:9-10).

Christ, then, through whom the world was created, is also the one who will integrate it in a cosmic reconciliation to which all history is tending. This reconciliation has already begun in Christ, but will not be fully accomplished until the *parousia* and the resurrection. This means that the ontological hierarchy described above is in its present state fractured and imperfect; human beings are not in full participation and communion with Christ and the Trinity, nor, if we can believe Romans 8, is the creation, which itself awaits a transformation: "The creation itself will be set free from its bondage to decay and will obtain the freedom of the glory of the children of God" (Rom 8:21). Thus the hierarchy of being is not static, but is developing towards a fullness and perfection which it will obtain in the *parousia* and the resurrection.

This final state, which we might call the mystical or cosmic body of Christ, will be the consummation of hierarchical communion for all creatures in Christ. Communion through love will be at its most complete, but so will diversity, for as beings are elevated in being through resurrection, they gain in self-possession and in communion.

A fruitful way of thinking of this is the model of holarchy sketched above. Each being in the eschaton will be a holon, within larger wholes, and ultimately within the whole of the mystical body of Christ. Hierarchy here will not be domination, but integration into a greater whole in which the individual entities become transcendent by participating (to the extent of the capacity given by their essence) in the life of a greater whole. Norris Clarke notes that the fullness of personhood is only possible through self-transcendence. The human self is so constituted that it is fulfilled, not by remaining in itself, separate but equal to other selves, but through a self-emptying, a *kenosis,* through which it receives participation in a greater whole, the life of the Trinity. This pattern of transcendence is identical to that of the Trinity itself and to the *kenosis* of the Son in becoming incarnate. Such self-transcendence and integration into a greater whole is only possible through ontological hierarchy.

The visible center and instrument in history for this movement towards the fullness of communion is the body of Christ, the Church, in which this process is sacramentally effected and fulfilled. The mission of the Church is to be a catalyst, a light, a sign and sacrament of the hierarchical communion offered by Christ to the world (*LG* #1). In the end, after the resurrection, the visible institutional Church will be unnecessary, precisely because every creature (except those in hell) will be united into the mystical Body of Christ.

Pius XII, in his encyclical *Mystici Corporis* (1943), identified the mystical body of Christ with the Roman Catholic Church, and also stated that Christ governs the Church through the pope, who is the sole Vicar of Christ.[40] But this is a distortion of the full meaning of the body of Christ. The mystical body of Christ is not confined to Roman Catholicism, or even to Christianity; Christ can work to bring persons into communion with himself outside of Christianity, as *Lumen gentium* (#16) clearly states. But the fact that Christ can work outside the Christian Church does not make the Church irrelevant. It remains the single most powerful sign and source of Christ's salvation in history, and the place where the communion with Christ is accomplished most fully.

Conclusion

The model of participatory hierarchy sketched above is an alternative to a hierarchy of domination, in which God is viewed as a cosmic autocrat who is obeyed out of fear, and to an ontological egalitarianism, which places humans on the same level as the rest of creation, "alone in the universe's unfeeling immensity" as Jacques Monod puts it. Such ontological solitude and divorce from a greater continuum of being seems to me to be at the root of most of the nihilism, anxiety, loneliness, and despair that is so prevalent in modern art, literature, and life. A loss of a hierarchy of being can also result in pantheism, which leaves little room for spiritual self-transcendence. A participatory ontological hierarchy, on the other hand, locates persons in a great continuum of being, and opens the possibility of spiritual self-transcendence into a communion of love with God and other persons. It also can ground a real hierarchy of goods and values, in which higher goods do not suppress lower goods, but include them while augmenting them.

A participatory hierarchy of being also holds out a solution to the perennial problem of unity and diversity, the one and the many. Each creature, from atoms to angels, is in fact a holon: a whole having its own integrity and purpose, yet generating a network of relationships by its activity, and so existing within larger wholes, both horizontally,

[40] *Mystici Corporis Christi,* 1, 40, 44; ET in Claudia Carlen, ed., *The Papal Encyclicals, 1939–1958* (Wilmington, N.C.: McGrath Publishing Co., 1981) 37–45.

within the community of beings on its own ontological level, and vertically, within the continuum of being which culminates in the mystical body of Christ and the Trinity. As Aquinas notes, only the full diversity of beings is capable of manifesting the fullness of goodness, beauty, and being that exists in the blessed Trinity. Such a diversity of beings would have to include human persons since in its most perfect, being is personal, or, as Norris Clarke notes, interpersonal. Thus every being is in some sense a partial reflection of God, and shows forth some aspect of God's beauty, and so is important to the whole. Yet the whole array of created beings is united in a great continuum which culminates in God. No part of what is good in this vast array will be lost: this is the meaning of the resurrection. Heaven is not an empty theater of pure spirits; it is, as C.S. Lewis reminds us, a state of *matter* as well as a state of spirit; it is spirit and matter reconciled into a "new heaven *and* a new earth" (Rev 21:1), in which both human spirits and bodies will be transformed, along with a transfigured creation. In this state the activity of beings at every level of the hierarchy will be brought to perfection. Matter itself will be brought to a state of perfection it does not now possess. The ultimate principle of integration for this resurrected community of beings is the cosmic Christ, who reconciles all things in heaven and earth.

In chapter 12 I will argue that the diversity, integration, and holarchical structure of the mystical Body of Christ should be expressed in the visible Body of Christ, which is the communion of the Christian Church. Chapter 11 will consider the implications of participatory hierarchy for the visible social structure of the Church, especially the Roman Catholic Church.

Chapter 11

The Church as a Society

The Church, drawing its source of life from the risen Christ and the Spirit, exists in the world as a society (*LG* #8). Vatican II notes that the social structure of the Church is meant to serve the Spirit of Christ in its work of building up the body: "For just as the assumed nature serves the divine Word as a living instrument of salvation inseparably joined with him, in a similar way the social structure of the Church (*socialis compago ecclesiae*) serves the Spirit of Christ who vivifies the Church towards the growth of the body" (*LG* #8).[1] The question to be explored in this chapter is: what kind of social structure of the Church best serves the Spirit of Christ in building up the body?

There are many types of societies, and even many definitions of society. The "best" social order therefore will depend on the type and purpose of the society. One order might be appropriate for a group of friends, another for a military unit, another for a school, another for a business, and so on. Now the purpose of the Church is to bring about the union of human beings with God and with one another through Christ: "By her relationship with Christ, the Church is a kind of sacrament or sign of intimate union with God, and of the unity of all mankind. She is also an instrument for the achievement of such union and unity" (*LG* #1). Thus the social structure of the Church ought to be such as to bring about a unity between God and human beings and also to foster a real unity among persons. Indeed, the Church in herself is to be a sign of this double unity. In the previous chapters we encountered

[1] ET from Tanner, vol. II, 854.

two models of Church unity: the monarchial model of unity, derived from submission to a single head, and the conciliar model, based on the consensus of a plurality of authorities. In this chapter I will argue for a model of participatory hierarchy, which is close to the conciliar model, though it incorporates the first model's emphasis on a primacy.

The Monarchial Model of Unity

As we have seen, this model has a long history in the Church. Ignatius of Antioch held that the unity of the local church was founded on submission to the bishop. Eusebius of Caesarea claimed that the unity of the universal Church was secured by submission to the one emperor: just as there was one Lord of heaven, so there was one lord on earth. These same arguments were made by the popes of the Middle Ages, and by Aquinas: the pope is the one Vicar of Christ on earth. Just as Christ is the head of the invisible Church, so the pope is the head of the visible Church. The bishops in this model draw their juridical power (though not their sacramental authority) from the pope. Robert Bellarmine continued the monarchist tradition: the true Church was those who professed the Christian faith, were in communion through the sacraments, and submitted to the rule of the legitimate pastors, especially the pope. Vatican I centralized church authority even more: though the pope, in issuing an infallible proclamation, is morally obliged to seek the consent of the bishops, he is not legally obliged to do so. Vatican II, though it returned to a more collegial notion of the Church, did not change the *juridical* structure of the Church. Today, at the level of the universal Catholic Church, virtually all the power is centralized in the papacy. The pope appoints the bishops, oversees their activities, and can remove them from a diocese. He or his appointees control the agendas for regional and national episcopal conferences. Only the pope can summon an ecumenical council. He can issue binding interpretations of doctrine and practice, as John Paul II did in the case of women's ordination. No ecclesial authority can overturn the judgment of the pope, and there is no canonical procedure for the removal from office of a tyrannical, insane, or heretical pope. In practice the pope receives advice from members of the papal Curia (who are appointed by the pope), from bishops, and others. But he is not bound to follow this advice, and can decide against the majority opinion, as Paul VI did in his decision on artificial contraception, when he opposed the advice of 93 percent of his own advisory commission.

In actual practice, there is greater participation at the level of the local church, where the bishop receives advice from priests and the priests' senate, from lay deaneries, from the pastoral council, and so on. But, again, the laity and the priests have no juridical authority against that of the bishop. Nor, for that matter, do other bishops: The National Council of Catholic Bishops might be able to argue with and persuade an errant bishop, but they have no juridical authority to discipline him; only the pope or his representatives do. Finally, at the level of the parish, the priest usually works in cooperation with the parish council, the parish trustees, and committees of the parish. But ultimate authority over the parish is still vested with the priest and the bishop. Increasingly, however, as the priest shortage worsens, priests and bishops may have no choice but to work in cooperation with parish administrators who are laity or members of religious orders, since there are not enough priests to administer all the parishes.

How well does a monarchial social and political structure serve the Spirit of Christ in building up the Church? It cannot be denied that in the past this model of hierarchy produced a tightly disciplined Church with a strong Catholic identity. Particularly in the nineteenth century, during the long papacy of Pius IX, and in the first half of the twentieth century, the Catholic Church appeared populous, powerful, and successful. Membership in religious orders and the priesthood was very high. At enormous sacrifice, immigrant Catholics in the United States built monumental churches, and an impressive Catholic school system. Catholic missions flourished, especially in Africa. Among many in the Church there was a strong commitment to the sacraments and a sense of the transcendent and the sacred, expressed in various devotions, such as the adoration of the Eucharist. Persons raised in the Church developed a marked sense of Catholic identity, often retained even if they left the Church (James Joyce's novella *The Dead* could only have been written by someone with a Catholic sense of the unity of the living and the dead).

On the other hand, the defects of the pre-Vatican II Church are well known. We have seen above that the excessive emphasis on papal authority led to the estrangement of both the Orthodox and the Protestants, thereby fracturing the body of Christ into competing denominations. Papal authoritarianism, unchecked by countervailing power, led to the tyranny of the Roman Inquisition, and oppression within the Church. The same factor led to the Galileo case and the alienation of the Church from natural science and from modern currents of thought:

loyalty to the pope and the institution outweighed free intellectual inquiry. The suppression of Modernism by Pius X in 1907 exacerbated this, and led to a period of intellectual sterility in the Church, especially in Italy.[2]

The close cooperation of the Catholic Church with the ruling elite in places like Latin America led to its support of dictatorial regimes, while its teaching of obedience to authority helped perpetuate these regimes in power. The Church was controlled by a clerical caste, subject to no accountability except to its own superiors, while the laity's duty was obedience. The clergy were the "teaching church," while the laity were the "learning church." (The first theological graduate facility opened to laity in America was Marquette, in 1967.) Most laity were uneducated immigrants; before 1950 Catholicism in America and elsewhere was largely a Church of ethnic enclaves. Laity were not officially encouraged to read the Bible until 1943. The laity tended to be passive in their religion, and were often satisfied with minimum external observance. One thinks of whole countries (Italy, Mexico, much of Latin America) where few men attend church. The role of women in the Church was limited to family or religious orders. Nominal Catholicism seemed to be compatible with widespread corruption in many Catholic countries (e.g., Italy, Brazil, the Philippines). As late as 1964 Thomas Merton complained that too often the laity felt that the life of Christian perfection was meant only for priests and religious, whereas the laity could be satisfied with avoiding serious sin.[3] The Church was excessively focused on external observance and was legalistic: it was deemed a mortal sin to intentionally eat meat on Fridays, to miss Sunday Mass, or to practice artificial contraception. (This recalls the complaint of the first Protestant Reformers that the medieval Church laid heavy, legalistic burdens on the faithful, from which Luther freed them.) Finally, the Church was exclusivistic: there was not much dialogue with other Christian denominations, or with

[2] "Many of the Church's most brilliant thinkers were silenced or driven out of theology. . . . Catholic seminaries remained medieval ghettos until the middle of the twentieth century. . . . The Modernist crisis was a catastrophe for the church. It led to an intellectual sterility that still weighs heavily on its life and caused a cultural lag most apparent in Italy itself, where the long arm of the Curia made the repression most severe. . . . Rome in the twentieth century became a byword for intellectual sterility." Bokenkotter, *A Concise History of the Catholic Church*, 366–367.

[3] *Life and Holiness* (Garden City, N.Y.: Doubleday, Image Books, 1963) 13–14.

the secular world, until Vatican II. I recall being told by a young monk at Harvard, about 1960, that "we have the truth, and don't need to look further."

The monarchial social structure of the Church then did not serve the spirit of Christ all that well in building up the Body. To be sure, there were successes, but also striking deficiencies. It led to ruptures in the Body, to clericalism, legalism, and in many cases to nominal, merely external observance. Essentially, the Church was unified as much by authoritarian hierarchy as by the Spirit. But the foundation for this authoritarianism were traditions which could not stand critical and historical scrutiny. Once they were challenged by emerging biblical, liturgical, and historical studies, by dialogue with non-Catholics, and by Catholic laity who moved out of the ethnic neighborhoods into pluralistic suburbs and professional careers, the Church had to change. Cardinal Suenens states: "Today one thing is certain: the era of absolute monarchy is over, and authority must be exercised within a new sociological context."[4] I do not believe that the Catholic Church can return to the monarchial model of past centuries without an enormous loss of credibility and relevance, and ultimately, without a loss of its catholicity.

Modern political history supports the contention that a monarchial model of hierarchy is not viable as a social structure whose purpose is to foster participation and unity. All modern Western polities have rejected absolute monarchy as a viable political model, and have embraced some system of representative government and division of powers in the government as a way of guarding against tyranny. Those countries which have not adopted such checks and balances (e.g., the Soviet Union, North Korea, China) have experienced vicious tyrannies. The experience of the sixteenth and seventeenth centuries showed that the doctrine of the divine right of kings was inadequate as a political philosophy, and it has almost no defenders today. One could not simply depend on the Holy Spirit to curb the appetite for power of a Louis XIV; political checks and balances were needed to prevent tyranny and abuse of power, as Montesquieu argued in *The Spirit of the Laws.* Similarly, the Church should not depend on the Holy Spirit to prevent abuse of power by the papacy, which also claims to rule by divine right; checks and balances are needed as well.

[4] *Coresponsibility in the Church* (New York: Herder and Herder, 1968) 100.

Finally, sociological studies also show that command and control methods of hierarchy result in resentment, passive resistance, and apathy. This is discussed below.

Egalitarian Models of Ecclesial Social Structure

There are almost no fully egalitarian models of ecclesial social structure in church history. The best examples are probably Quaker meetings, in which any member, prompted by the inner voice, can stand and address the meeting. But even most Quaker groups have regular clergy, and therefore some kind of leadership. Furthermore, the Quakers have failed to preserve a great deal of Christian tradition: they have no doctrine, no sacraments, nor do they emphasize scripture. The Quaker movement is very small, and dwindling. Given all this, it is hard to see how it could serve as a model for the universal Christian Church, though its pacifist witness is of value to the larger Church.

An interesting sociological study of egalitarian organizations was performed by Katherine Newman.[5] Her study focused on California workers' collectives committed to egalitarian social organization. Three of these were businesses, four were service collectives (e.g., alternative schools, child care centers), five were information collectives (offering information on such topics as rape prevention, employment, or mental health). There were no leaders in these collectives; each member had an equal vote, and decisions were made in frequent group meetings. Over time, all but two of these collectives developed core leadership hierarchies. This was due to the pressure of securing funding through grants, and the development of full-time salaried versus part-time workers. The two collectives which did not develop hierarchies were both businesses, whose income was sufficient to prevent their having to apply for external funding. Newman's conclusion was that the development of hierarchies was not due to internal dynamics but to involvement and competition with external hierarchically run organizations (usually to secure funding).

This has an interesting parallel in church history, in that the strongly hierarchical structure of the Western Church was developed in part in

[5] "Incipient Bureaucracy: The Development of Hierarchies in Egalitarian Organizations," *Hierarchy and Society: Anthropological Perspectives on Bureaucracy*, Gerald Britain and Ronald Cohen, eds. (Philadelphia: Institute for the Study of Human Issues, 1980) 143–163.

competition with the hierarchy of lay nobles and rulers. But it does suggest that egalitarian organizations are not stable or enduring, and cannot flourish in competition with hierarchically-structured competitors. Further, these workers' collectives were small groups, not international organizations comprised of millions of persons. Given the limitations of egalitarian organizations, the organization of the universal Church of Christ in a strictly egalitarian fashion, in which each member had a vote on all major decisions, does not seem to be a practical possibility.

A Participatory Model of Social Hierarchy

A participatory social hierarchy is one in which members have a high degree of participation. This includes participation in decision making, without which participation in other aspects of the society will likely be curtailed. There is a large body of literature concerning the importance of participation in organizations. Much of this has been authored by sociologists and concerns management in modern corporations. But significant contributions have also been made by recent popes: Pius IX, Pius XII, John XXIII, and John Paul II.

Now it might be objected: what has this to do with the Church? The Church is of divine institution and cannot be treated as a merely secular organization. It is true that the Church cannot be treated as merely a secular organization; as the body of Christ, it has a divine aspect, which grounds its hierarchy. But it is also a human organization, and is subject to the same social dynamics as other large organizations. If authoritarian methods alienate and dispirit workers in corporations, they will alienate and dispirit members in the Church; if participatory methods empower and motivate workers, and result in worker identification with organizational goals, the same will be true of the Church. In applying the lessons of sociology and participatory management to the Church, I am *not* arguing that the Church should be considered merely as a secular society, or "run like a business." It should be run like a church. But if the aim of the Church is to bring members into a personal relationship with Jesus and a participation in the life of the Trinity, then it cannot afford to embrace a social hierarchy that alienates its members, or reduces them to passivity and apathy. Its social hierarchy must be consonant with its purpose, and with the participatory ontological hierarchy through which it is constituted. How a participatory social hierarchy should be structured we can learn from sociology. This topic will be developed in the following paragraphs, which focus on four points: participation, subsidiarity, conflict and dissent, and authority.

Management methods that emphasize worker and employee *participation* have grown rapidly in North America in the last twenty years, mostly with business organizations, but with other types of organizations as well. Benjamin Tregoe and Peter Tobia write: "The old command-and-control model that once was the organizing principle of our military and industrial orders has gone the way of the three martini lunch. The new paradigm emphasizes decentralization, flexibility, and influence more than power, and participation more than one-man or elite rule."[6] Worker participation involves complex organizational structures, which differ according to the purpose and situation of a given organization. Nevertheless, there are certain constant features.[7] Worker participation entails giving groups of workers more freedom and responsibility to do a given task according to their own pace and using their own methods. Worker groups or teams may be given responsibility for ordering supplies, setting schedules, organizing their own work group, electing their supervisor, and even hiring new members of the work team. In many cases, "self-managed teams are structured to operate almost as small, independent business units."[8] This typically results in greater worker productivity and satisfaction. Michael Naughton writes: "With work teams in place, GM's Pontiac division has seen a 12% improvement in production and a better cooperative attitude between labor and management. Management has realized that a lack of responsibility among workers breeds apathy."[9]

Participatory management necessitates general rather than close supervision, i.e., supervisors set general goals and objectives rather than give specific directions. Worker responsibility in turn requires that workers be kept well-informed of all relevant data, including organizational purposes and goals, and where their work group fits into the organizational process. It also necessitates worker involvement in decisions that affect their area of work. Communication is therefore

[6] "Strategy and the New American Organization," *Industry Week* (August 6, 1990) 28.

[7] The following is drawn principally from Rensis Likert, *New Patterns of Management* (New York: McGraw-Hill, 1961).

[8] Joseph Boyett and Henry Conn, *Workplace 2000: The Revolution Reshaping American Business* (New York: Penguin, a Dutton book, 1991) 239.

[9] "Participation in the Organization: An Ethical Analysis from the Papal Social Tradition," *Journal of Business Ethics* 14 (1995) 930.

necessary both from the top down, but also from the workers upward to supervisors and upper levels of the organizational hierarchy. Failure of upward communication will result in the workers' feeling that they have no influence, will undermine their sense of responsibility, and will deprive the organization of possibly important insights. Needless to say, repressive supervision suffocates upward communication, as does an atmosphere of distrust, fear, or hostility; effective communication requires an atmosphere of trust and an attitude of cooperation and support from supervisors.

All this requires specially trained and sensitive leadership. Rensis Likert writes:

> Although the leader has full responsibility, he does not try to make all the decisions. He develops his group into a unity which, with his participation, makes better decisions than he can make alone . . . Through group decision-making each member feels fully identified with each decision and highly motivated to execute it fully. The overall performance of the group, as a consequence, is even better than the excellent quality of the decisions. . . . Although the leader accepts the responsibility associated with his role . . . he seeks to minimize the influence of his hierarchical position. He is aware that trying to get results by "pulling rank" effects adversely the effectiveness of his group and his relationship with it. . . . The leader strengthens the group and group processes by seeing that all problems *which involve the group* are dealt with by the group.[10]

Joseph Boyett and Henry Conn agree:

> Leaders direct and control, but their direction tends more toward defining end purposes and their control leans more toward empowering people and holding them responsible for their own means to those ends. . . . They possess and exercise skills to resolve conflict and balance the interests of multiple constituencies to build consensus. . . . The leader of the future American business will trust his or her subordinates and reject the possibility that the organization can be successful as a result of command and control. Obtaining employee commitment will be seen as the only option for securing future success. The leader of the future will push responsibility and accountability down to the lowest ranks of the organization. He or she will rely upon people at every level to do the right thing as they understand it.[11]

[10] Likert, *New Patterns of Management,* 170, emphasis in original.
[11] *Workplace 2000,* 145, 146, 156.

It is important to note that participatory management is *never* egalitarian; leadership to facilitate participation is essential. "The data show the great importance of the quality of leadership. For every criterion, such as productivity, absence, attitudes, and promotability of the supervisor, the same basic patterns of supervision yielded the best results."[12]

All forms of participatory management attempt to include workers and employees in the decision-making process; many strive towards consensus decision making, though not all decisions can be so made. For example, when worker-groups hire a new member, the decision is typically made by consensus.[13] Consensus decision making has the advantage that all members identify with the decision, and work to support it. This in turn fosters identification with the goals of the organization, and higher worker productivity.[14]

An interesting study is reported by Likert.[15] The study covered five hundred clerical employees in four identical divisions. In two of the divisions, participatory methods of management were introduced. Supervisors were trained in group leadership; groups at each level of the hierarchy were given greater freedom in decisions and in implementing the work; subordinates were involved in decisions related to work. Simultaneously, the remaining two divisions were organized on a more "hierarchical" and authoritarian basis; decisions were made high up in the hierarchy with no subordinate input, and simply enforced by supervisors. The work force was cut by 25 percent and standard times for work operations were computed and enforced. After one year, production had increased in the latter divisions by 25 percent, and in the participatory divisions (which did not have any work force layoff) by 20 percent. However,

> Although both programs achieved increases in productivity, they yielded significantly different results in other aspects. The productivity increases in the hierarchically controlled program were accompanied by shifts in an *adverse* direction in such factors as loyalty, attitudes, interest, and involvement in work. Just the opposite was

[12] Ibid., 25.

[13] *Workplace 2000*, 251.

[14] See Jack J. Holder, Jr., "Decision Making by Consensus," *Business Horizons* (April, 1972) 47–54, reprinted in James Gibson, John Ivancevich, and James Donnelly, Jr., *Readings in Organizations* (Dallas: Business Publication, Inc., 1973) 173–185.

[15] *New Patterns of Management*, 62–69.

> true in the participatory program. For example, when more general supervision and increased participation were provided, the employee's feeling of responsibility to see that the work got done increased. Observations showed that when the supervisor was away, the employees kept on working. In the hierarchically controlled program, however, the feeling of responsibility decreased and when the supervisor was absent the work tended to stop.[16]

Likert thinks there is "every reason to believe that had the clerical experiment been continued for another year or two, productivity and quality of work would have continued to increase in the participative program, while in the hierarchically controlled program productivity and work would have declined as a result of the hostility, resentment, and turnover evoked by the program."[17]

To implement participation of employees in any large organization, it is essential that the organization be composed of human-sized intermediate or subsidiary groups. In most corporations the primary group is the work group, composed of four to twelve employees. This group is part of a larger group, which is part of a larger group, and so on, to as many levels as exist in the organizational hierarchy. Typically the supervisor of a lower level group is a subordinate member of a higher level group; in this way, lower groups are linked to higher level groups in a continuous chain. Likert provides a figure which schematizes this arrangement:

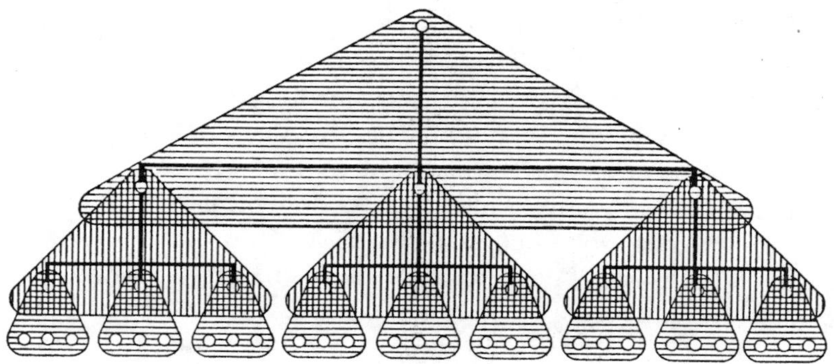

The overlapping group form of organization. Work groups vary in size as circumstances require although shown here as consisting of four persons.[18]

[16] Ibid., 65.
[17] Ibid., 69.
[18] Ibid., 105.

This arrangement parallels the type of hierarchy we have already encountered in previous chapters. Using that terminology, each subsidiary group can be seen as a holon, and the whole organization as a holarchy (the organization itself is of course a part of other, larger social wholes, and is so a holon itself). Note the importance in Likert's scheme of both upward and downward communication, to link the various levels and holon groups into an organizational whole. A failure in either type of communication will result in the subgroup being cut off from the rest of the organization. It is thus important that lower level supervisors represent and voice the opinions of their groups in higher level groups; failure to do this is a failure in effective supervision. Likert writes:

> To function effectively, a supervisor must have sufficient influence with his own superior to be able to affect the superior's decisions. Subordinates expect their supervisors to be able to exercise an influence upward in dealing with problems on the job and in handling problems which affect them and their well being. . . . When a supervisor cannot exert sufficient upward influence in the hierarchy to handle these problems constructively, an unfavorable reaction to the supervisor and to the organization is likely to occur.[19]

Likert also distinguishes between "man-to-man" *[sic]* organization, and a group pattern of organization.[20] In the former, decisions are made at the top, and vice-presidents meet with the president individually to report on their own departments. Group meetings are held to share information, but not to make decisions. The consequence is that individual vice-presidents lobby the president so as to obtain decisions favorable to themselves or their department, but not necessarily favorable to the whole corporation. This pits one department against others, and leads to factionalism, conniving, secrecy, etc. Major problems are not raised at group meetings, but individually with the president in the hope of obtaining a decision favorable to just one department. Upward communication is filtered through individual vice-presidents, who may distort it to serve their own interests. In the group system of operation, by contrast, problems are discussed and decisions made in group meetings. This makes it difficult for any one department to force a decision beneficial to it but detrimental to the whole organization. Decisions are made based on information and

[19] Ibid., 113.
[20] Ibid., 106–113.

contributions from all departments and are more likely to benefit the whole organization rather than one subgroup. Upward communication is more effective, since if important information is withheld or distorted by one party, it will be corrected by another.

While most sociological and managerial studies of participatory management stress increases in productivity gained through participatory methods, papal teaching on this subject emphasizes the benefit to the workers themselves: participation fosters the human dignity of workers and their full development as persons.[21] Thus Pope Pius XI (1922–1939) argued that partnership contracts (in which the worker is a kind of partner in the organization) be preferred over wage contracts (in which labor is exchanged for wages).

> We consider it more advisable, however, in the present condition of human society that, so far as possible, the work-contract be somewhat modified by a partnership-contract, as is already being done in various ways and with no small advantage to workers and owners. Workers and the employees thus become sharers in ownership or management or participate in some fashion in the profits received.[22]

Pope John XXIII emphasized that worker participation was necessary for the full development of the human person: "There is . . . an innate need in human nature requiring that men engaged in productive activity have an opportunity to assume responsibility and to perfect themselves by their effort."[23] Workers should have an active role in the operation of the organization in which they are involved. The organization "must not treat those employees who spend their days in service with the firm as though they were mere cogs in the machinery, denying them any opportunity of expressing their wishes or bringing their experience to bear on the work in hand, and keeping them entirely passive in regard to decisions that regulate their activity."[24] The managers of an organization must maintain a unity of direction and purpose lest the firm fall into anarchy, but do not have the right to keep workers passive and inactive. The pope further maintained that

[21] My information in this section is drawn from Michael J. Naughton, "Participation in the Organization," 923–935.

[22] *Quadragesimo anno*, 65, ET from Michael Walsh and Brian Davies, *Proclaiming Justice and Peace* (Mystic, Conn.: Twenty-Third Publications, 1991) 59.

[23] *Mater et Magistra*, 82 (Glen Rock, N.J.: Paulist Press, 1961) 32.

[24] Ibid., 92, ET in *Proclaiming Justice and Peace*, Walsh and Davies, eds., 98.

as workers became more educated, they would want "to assume greater responsibility in their own sphere of employment."[25]

John Paul II, in his encyclicals *Laborem exercens* and *Centesimus annus* develops the idea that human work is a collaboration or co-creation with God which participates with God's ongoing work of creation. Work is a "sharing of the activity of the Creator" in bringing the creation to the perfection of the kingdom of God.[26] The creativity of each person reflects God's own creativity, and should be expressed in the workplace. Ultimately, human work contributes not only to earthly progress, but also to the "development of the kingdom of God."[27]

John Paul analyzes participation as composed of a dialectic of two attitudes or activities: solidarity and opposition. Solidarity exhibits a person's willingness to identify with and work for the common good of an organization or community. This involves the understanding that one's own individual good is realized in the fulfillment of the larger common good. But working for the common good may also involve opposition to particular ways in which the organization, or members of it, strive to fulfill the common good. Such opposition should be constructive, not destructive; its ultimate aim is to improve the common good; it is therefore conducted within the framework of solidarity.[28]

Papal teachings on participation are complemented by their teaching on the principle of *subsidiarity.* This principle was stated by both Pius XI and John XXIII and has been affirmed by succeeding popes. John XXIII writes, quoting Pius XI:

> It is a fundamental principle of social philosophy . . . that one should not withdraw from individuals and commit to the community what they can accomplish by their own enterprise and industry. So, too, it is an injustice and at the same time a grave evil and a disturbance of right order, to transfer to the larger and higher collectivity functions which can be performed and provided for by lesser and subordinate bodies. Inasmuch as every social activity should, by its very nature, prove a help to members of the body social, it should never destroy or absorb them.[29]

[25] Ibid., #96, p. 98.

[26] *Laborem exercens,* 25 (Boston: St. Paul Editions, 1981) 57–59.

[27] Ibid., #27, p. 64.

[28] See Karol Wojtyla, *The Acting Person* (Dordrecht: D. Reidel, 1979; Polish original, *Osoba i Czyn,* Cracow, 1969) 280–287.

[29] *Mater et Magistra,* 53, citing *Quadragesimo Anno,* 79 (New York: Paulist Press, 1961, 1962) 23–24.

The principle of subsidiarity was formulated primarily to prevent the state from absorbing or encroaching on the work of subsidiary communities. Thus it states that the federal government should not do what the state can do; the state should not do what the county can do; the county should not take over the work of the city or village, nor the village of the neighborhood, nor the neighborhood of the family. The purpose of larger social units is to aid and empower the lower, not do their work for them, except in those rare cases where the lower, subsidiary social unit is dysfunctional (e.g., a dysfunctional family).

Papal and episcopal teaching encourages the maintenance of small scale organizations. Pius XII stated "Small and medium-sized holdings in agriculture, in the arts and crafts, in commerce and industry, should be safeguarded and fostered. Such enterprises should join together in mutual aid societies in order that the services and benefits of large-scale enterprises will be available to them. So far as these larger enterprises are concerned, work agreements should in some way be modified by partnership agreements."[30] In the same vein, the United States bishops have consistently deplored the absorption of small family farms by larger farms, and the absorption of small businesses by larger.[31]

Respect for the principle of subsidiarity is an integral part of the common good. It is a characteristic of totalitarianism that a centralized power structure attempts to eliminate all subsidiary social groups that might provide opposition and to control individuals directly. The elimination of viable subsidiary communities is likewise a characteristic of modern mass societies, which tend to be composed of atomized individuals. Such individuals are isolated from any community in which the common good can be actuated, and typically will pursue individual interests at the expense of the common good. John XXIII explains the importance of subsidiary communities to the common good:

> This [the common good] comprises the sum total of those conditions of social living, whereby men are enabled more fully and more readily to achieve their own perfection. Hence we regard it as necessary that the various intermediary bodies . . . be ruled by their own laws and as the common good itself progresses, pursue this objective in a spirit of sincere concord among themselves. Nor is it less necessary

[30] Radio broadcast, September 1, 1944, *AAS* XXXVI (1944) 254, cited in *Mater et Magistra*, 84 (Glen Rock, N.J.: Paulist Press, 1961) 32.

[31] See "Strangers and Guests," A Regional Catholic Bishops' Statement on Land Issues (Sioux Falls, S.D.: Heartland Project, 1980).

> that the above mentioned groups present the form and substance of a true community. This they will do, only if individual members are considered and treated as persons, and encouraged to participate in the affairs of the group.[32]

The great importance of mediating structures has been emphasized by Peter Berger and Richard John Neuhaus. Intermediate social structures (e.g., family, neighborhood, church, work-group) allow individuals to achieve participation, meaning, fulfillment, and personal identity in human-sized communities, rather than becoming individual atoms lost in a vast collectivity. The values of the common good are mediated to individuals through such intermediary social structures (e.g., families), and individuals can in turn through them influence the life and values of larger society, just as individual workers can influence the policy of the larger organization through worker groups. Berger and Neuhaus write:

> Without institutionally reliable processes of mediation, the political order becomes detached from the values and realities of individual life. Deprived of its moral foundation, the political order is "delegitimated." When that happens, the political order must be secured by coercion rather than by consent. And when that happens, democracy disappears.[33]

In terms of hierarchy, subsidiarity means that authority is not concentrated in a single center, whether person or institution; it is spread out across a plurality of agents who exercise various degrees of authority. The authority of those governing small communities (a family or village) is limited by the authority of those governing the larger community or communities (the state, the nation). But conversely, the authority of those governing the largest communities is also limited by those governing the subsidiary communities. The President of the United States cannot override the authority of a governor, or mayor, a corporate CEO, or a local police officer; he may persuade them, but not coerce them. Thus government in a society composed of healthy subsidiary communities must, as Berger and Neuhaus note, be secured by consent, not by coercion, as in totalitarian systems.

[32] *Mater et Magistra*, 65 (Glen Rock, N.J.: Paulist Press, 1961) 27.

[33] *To Empower People: The Role of Mediating Structures in Public Policy* (Washington, D.C.: American Enterprise Institute for Public Policy Research, 1977) 3.

Finally, the principle of subsidiarity ensures the possibility of real participation by individuals in social and political activity (just as subsidiary work groups ensure the possibility of participation by workers in the governance of the corporation). Without such intermediary structures, most individuals are lost in the crowd, and have no forum in which to make their voices heard. A crowd, or a mass, is typically governed by a few demagogues or tyrants at the top, and those lower down are reduced to passivity and obedience.

The model of a society based on subsidiary social communities parallels the holarchy composed of holons that we have encountered in biological and ontological hierarchy. In the language of holarchy, each subsidiary community, such as a family, a church, a neighborhood, a work group, is a holon, a limited whole composed of subsidiary wholes (individuals) and a part of larger wholes. Each social holon has its own structure of limited authority, which is a part of larger authority structures, but which also has its own partial autonomy over against the encroachment of such larger authority structures.

In the Christian Church, the smallest holon might be "two or three gathered together in my name." A Christian family would certainly be an elementary holon, transmitting the faith of the universal Church to its children. Larger holons might include parishes, dioceses or regional units, national divisions or churches, and the worldwide denomination. In an ecumenically reunited Church, each denomination would probably be a holon, replete with its own governing structure, which would nevertheless be in some fashion incorporated into the governance of the universal Church. The universal Church should be open to influence by smaller holons, and they in turn should be open to the influence of the universal Church. And while the universal Church is made up of local churches, certain characteristics of the Church, such as catholicity, are found more fully in the universal Church (see chap. 12).

The advantage of a holarchical model of Church structure is that it preserves both genuine diversity and unity. In this model, local churches cannot be seen as mere appendages of the universal Church. But neither can the universal Church be merely a loose affiliation of local churches.

A third point to be considered (after participation and subsidiarity) in the discussion of a participatory social hierarchy is the question of *conflict and dissent*. The usual problem with organic models of society has been that they suppress conflict and dissent in the name of a putative organic unity. This has certainly been a problem in Catholicism, which in the name of the unity of the Body of Christ has for centuries suffocated dissent and conflict, even to the point of overriding the principle of subsidiarity.[34] An interesting contribution to this problem comes from the pen of Cardinal Karol Wojtyla (now Pope John Paul II). Wojtyla argues that participation entails both solidarity and constructive opposition, that is, opposition maintained out of concern for the common good. "More precisely, in order for opposition to be constructive, the structure, and beyond it the system of communities of a given society must be such as to allow the opposition that emerges from the soil of solidarity not only to *express* itself within the framework of the given community, but also to *operate* for its benefit."[35] Wojtyla thinks that the dialectical tension between solidarity and opposition is a permanent feature of the common good, notions of which should never lead to the stifling of opposition. Rather, what must occur is dialogue: "The principle of dialogue allows us to select and bring to light what in controversial situations is right and true, and helps to eliminate any partial, preconceived or subjective views or trends."[36]

Margaret O'Brien Steinfels, editor of *Commonweal,* makes the same point in her article "Dissent and Communion," in which she discusses the role of dissent in the Church. In her view, "a true understanding of communion implies dissent, and real dissent demands communion."[37] A church in which dissent was impossible would be a totalitarian church in which the status quo never changed because it could not be questioned. In fact, however, Vatican II modified several traditional teachings of the Church. Pius IX had taught that Catholicism should be the officially sanctioned religion of the state; Vatican II declared that there should be freedom of religion, and that conscience should be free. Vatican II similarly changed the traditional teaching on the salvation of non-Christians, and the status of non-Christian religions.[38] These developments in Catholic teaching occurred because of dissent

[34] Thomas O'Meara, "The Raid on the Dominicans: the Repression of 1954," *America* (February 5, 1994) 8ff.

[35] Karol Wojtyla, *The Acting Person,* 286–287. Wojtyla thinks this analysis of participation applies to all human communities (hence presumably to the Church): "Our concern is therefore with the *genuinely personalistic structure of human existence in a community,* that is, in every community that man belongs to," 282, emphasis in original.

[36] Ibid., 287.

[37] *Commonweal* (November 18, 1994) 10, emphasis in original.

[38] For a thorough discussion of these changes, including extensive citation of texts, see J. Robert Dionne, *The Papacy and the Church* (New York: Philosophical Library, 1987) 83–284.

by some theologians from the traditional teaching. John Courtney Murray, S.J., was silenced for a number of years for his teaching that the Church should be separated from the state, but his position was eventually vindicated at Vatican II, where he was the principal architect of the council's Declaration on Religious Freedom. Yves Congar and Henri de Lubac were also silenced, though their teachings, too, were vindicated at Vatican II.

But, if dissent is essential to the Church as communion, it also entails real solidarity with and loyalty to the Church. As Steinfels puts it: "real dissent demands communion."[39] All of the above named theologians, when silenced by the Church, accepted the authority of the magisterium and abided by its decision, until the magisterium itself recognized the merit of their positions (Congar and de Lubac were eventually named cardinals). Constructive dissent works within the communion of the Church, and attempts to enrich that communion with its insights. Destructive dissent, on the other hand, destroys communion, and so undermines its own authority. Steinfels writes: "There is a danger today of established dissent, dissent as a way of life, dissent as the primary stance some take towards the church. . . . There is something we might want to call dissent of the heart—a state in which one's own spirit stands pridefully apart from the community."[40] Of course the line between constructive and destructive dissent may be difficult to judge in some cases, but that does not impugn the validity of the distinction. Another way of framing the contrast might be to distinguish between dissent directed at core beliefs (e.g., the divinity of Jesus) and dissent directed against peripheral beliefs (e.g., priestly celibacy).

In biblical terms, constructive dissent is prophetic; the dissent of the prophet against the misuse of institutional authority, the sinfulness of the elite or the people, always comes from a concern that the society or Church be brought back to their true mission. Any society, including the Church, needs prophets just as much as it needs institutional leaders; there is a dialectical tension between the two, like the tension between solidarity and opposition described by Karol Wojtyla. There is always the danger that institutional authority will be abused, or that a society will become hardened in sin; but likewise

[39] Ibid., 11.

[40] Ibid.

there is the danger that those prophesying change will fall into destructive opposition and attempt to destroy the society which nourished them.

There is a final point to be considered, and that is the nature of *authority* in a participatory social hierarchy. I have, above, distinguished between an authority of force and an authority of virtue, where virtue means excellence in any practice or activity. This typology clashes with the traditional sociological analysis of authority which comes from Max Weber, whose classifications, though widely criticized, still provide the starting point for most sociological discussions of this topic. Thus it may be well to clarify the relation between my typology and Weber's. Weber distinguished three ideal types of *Herrschaft,* variously translated as "authority," "imperative control," or "domination": traditional, charismatic, and legal-rational. These differ in the source of their justification, or legitimation. Traditional authority is that exercised by traditional leaders, patriarchs, or sacred figures. Its source of legitimacy is simply custom or tradition. Charismatic authority derives from the personal charisma of a leader or hero. "This is the 'charismatic' domination [*herrschaft*], as exercised by the prophet or—in the field of politics—by the elected warlord, the plebiscitarian ruler, the great demagogue, or the political party leader."[41] Finally, there is legal-rational authority, that is "domination by virtue of 'legality,' by virtue of the belief in the validity of legal statute and functional 'competence' based on rationally created rules. . . . This is the domination exercised by the modern 'servant of state.'"[42]

Weber's classifications were put forth as ideal types which would likely overlap in any given instance. Nevertheless, his classifications seem open to several criticisms. First, they are not logically distinct. The authority due to tradition and that due to law would seem to be two aspects of one type of authority. Typically traditional authorities ground their authority in some form of law, even if only an oral law, while the authority of the legal bureaucrat is sanctioned by tradition. Second, Weber's categories do not seem to easily encompass authority which is based on expertise, that is, an authority of virtue, the authority of an expert, a guide, a teacher, a guru. Such authority is not exactly charismatic authority for it is not based on personal charisma

[41] Max Weber, "Politics as a Vocation," *From Max Weber: Essays in Sociology,* H.H. Gerth and C. Wright Mills, eds. (New York: Oxford, 1946) 79.

[42] Ibid.

but on acquired competence. But it is also not necessarily legal-rational authority, which is grounded in law, rational rules, or bureaucracy. Third, I would maintain that traditional authority, such as that of priests, is usually based on an authority of virtue. Traditional authority figures possess their authority not just from habit, but because people continue to believe that they have a certain power or virtue that is effective. A Hmong shaman has authority because the Hmong people believe she has power to cure illness; if they lose that belief, as they are with their exposure to Western medicine, the authority of the shaman vanishes, however strongly vested in tradition. The same is true of priests, patriarchs, and so on. As for legal-rational authority, this is based either on force or the threat of force, or on the belief that the person in authority has a certain competence or expertise. Thus authority can be analyzed in terms of a dialectical continuum: on the one hand, an authority of force, on the other an authority of virtue. Most types of authority can be located somewhere between these two pure types.

What kind of authority do we find in a participatory hierarchy? It seems to differ from traditional authority structures in two respects. First, in participatory hierarchy, authority is not centralized in one or a few figures, but is spread out. We have seen above that a participatory organization will have a subsidiary structure, which means authority is spread across many subsidiary leaders, as well as one or more overall leaders. But even within any subsidiary unit, authority is diffused. If decisions are made by consensus, then the authority for the final decision is shared by the entire group. This is true, for example, in cases where subsidiary work groups or teams do their own hiring. It is also true in cases where a given work team has most of the expertise relating to its task of production; its expertise will give it authority in its own area, and in a participatory structure it will be involved in management decisions affecting its area of work. Second, authority in a traditional "command and control" hierarchy is typically based, in the last analysis, on force. But in a participatory hierarchy, authority is exercised through persuasion. Leadership is necessary, but the leader is one who can bring the group into a consensus consistent with the purpose of the organization. Force may be necessary in some extreme instances (e.g., a worker may have to be fired), but this is not the typical mode of operation of participatory authority. If leaders lead by persuasion rather than by fear and the threat of force, their authority is likely to be closer to an authority of virtue than an authority of force. The best persuader (other things being equal) will be one who embodies the virtues to be inculcated.

Participatory Social Hierarchy and the Church

How well does the model of participatory social hierarchy sketched above fit the contemporary Catholic Church? In some parishes there is considerable participation by members: decisions are typically made jointly by the priest, staff, and parish council (which is made up of elected parishioners). Though priests are not elected, bishops usually make an effort to appoint a priest who will fit the parish. At the regional and national level, the United States bishops have consulted widely with laity before issuing their pastoral letters, for instance, the letter on the economy. Margaret O'Brien Steinfels, however, remarks that European bishops were distinctly uneasy with the consultative methods of the United States bishops.[43] But there is little participation on decisions that affect the universal Church. Such decisions, for example those concerning clerical celibacy or the ordination of women are usually made by the pope alone (though he may consult with the Curia), in what Likert has termed the "man to man" decision process, rather than the "group process," resulting in scheming, lobbying, and attempts by factions to influence the decision of the pope. The Vatican has prohibited discussion of clerical celibacy or women's ordination by national bishops' conferences. The extraordinary bishops' synods, supposedly called for the purpose of advising the pope, have had little discernible effect on papal decisions. Recently, after the United States bishops had approved an inclusive-language lectionary for the nation's Catholic parishes and had received tentative approval from Rome, the Vatican reversed its position and prohibited this lectionary. Thus regional and national bishops cannot even make decisions concerning the use of their own native language. This is a flagrant violation of the principle of subsidiarity, which would be judged by the Church to be a serious sin if it occurred in the social order. And this is only one example among many. The Cologne declaration lists a whole host of grievances against Rome, for example, that bishops have been imposed on dioceses in violation of the traditional and canonical rights of the local churches to participate in the decision, a violation of the principle of subsidiarity.[44]

43 "Dissent and Communion," 13.

44 "The Cologne Declaration," *Origins* 18:38 (March 2, 1989) 633–634.

Oddly enough, the principle of subsidiarity has never been clearly applied by Rome to the Church itself, though there has been talk of doing so.[45] Nor has the Vatican admitted that the papal teachings on worker participation in the organization should be applied to the participation of workers or members of the Church. The argument seems to be that the Church has a different principle of hierarchy and authority than secular society; the authority of the pope and bishops is based on divine commission, not on any kind of representation, and so the principles that apply to secular society do not apply to the church. In response to this, it is important to note a few points.

First, the fundamental theological reason for respecting subsidiarity in the decision-making process of the Church is that the Spirit does not guide the Church through the pope and the Curia alone, but through the bishops and the faithful as well. The Document on Divine Revelation *(Dei Verbum)* states that the growth in understanding of the tradition occurs through "the contemplation and study made by believers" and through the bishops (#8). And, as noted in chapter 5, the Second Council of Constantinople averred that the truth can only be made clear by debate in common. It is true that decision-making in the Church is not identical with that in a secular society or corporation; ecclesial decision-making requires a process of discerning the will of the Spirit. But for this discernment to be effective, it is essential that subsidiary units be allowed to participate in the decision process. This is why St. Benedict insisted that the abbot consult the whole community on all important matters, since "the Lord often reveals the best course to a younger monk."[46] This is also why the ancient councils strove to achieve consensus and not just a majority decision, since consensus was held to represent the will of the Spirit.

Second, the principle of subsidiarity is based on *justice:* the claim of the popes has been that it is a grave injustice for a higher social unit to

[45] Pius XII recommended in 1946 that the principle of subsidiarity be applied to society as well as to the Church (*Acta Apostolica Sedis* 38 [1946] 144–146). But this has not been put into practice. Again, the preface to the 1983 Code of Canon Law, Latin edition, recommends that subsidiarity be applied to the Church (*Codex Iuris Canonici* [Vatican City: Libreria Editrice Vaticicana, 1983] Preface, xxii, n. 5). And the 1985 Extraordinary Synod of Bishops' *Final Report* recommends studying "whether the principle of subsidiarity . . . can be applied to the church . . ." *Origins* 15:27 (December 19, 1985) 44. Archbishop John Quinn also encourages the application of subsidiarity to the Church. "The Exercise of the Primacy," *Commonweal* (July 18, 1996) 18.

[46] *The Rule of St. Benedict* (Garden City, N.Y.: Doubleday, Image, 1975) 51.

take over the work of a lower social unit. This would seem to apply irrespective of whether or not the bishops and the pope hold their authority from Christ—in fact, it should apply even more to an institution whose mission is to be a sign of Christ, and hence of Christ's justice, in the world. Exactly the same could be said for worker participation; if it is an injustice, and disrespectful of human dignity, to deny workers participation in secular organizations, how much worse is it to deny them participation in an organization which is to be a sign of justice to the world? The American bishops admitted this is their 1986 letter Economic Justice for All: *"All the moral principles that govern the just operation of any economic endeavor apply to the church and its agencies and institutions; indeed the Church should be exemplary."*[47]

A third point is this. The churches which are growing, even in secular environments (e.g., the United States), are those that have participatory structures and elicit a high degree of participation from their members. These are typically evangelical churches, including Protestant churches (e.g., Assemblies of God), the Jehovah's Witnesses, and the Mormons. These groups differ greatly among themselves with respect to their theology. What they share in common is a participatory social structure. Typically they are small, are locally and democratically run, and have a high degree of commitment among their members. In my community (Cottage Grove, Minnesota), the local Jehovah's Witness Kingdom Hall was erected by the whole congregation in three days (over a weekend). Evangelical groups are noted for the high degree of enthusiasm they generate among their members. This is reflected in the contributions made, which are much higher than those in an average Catholic parish. Andrew Greeley has noted that Protestant contributions generally are about twice that of Catholic contributions, and has concluded that the difference is due to alienation of Catholic parishioners from the Church, an alienation caused by resentment against the hierarchy.[48]

I concur in this conclusion. Though Catholic decline can be explained in part by secularism and by other factors, probably the single most important factor is the authoritarian, command hierarchy enforced by Rome (and by some bishops). This has resulted in Rome stonewalling on the question of clerical celibacy and women's ordina-

[47] *The Catholic Challenge to the American Economy,* Chapter V, section 3, Thomas Gannon, ed. (New York: Macmillan, 1987) appendix; emphasis in original.

[48] Andrew Greeley, "Where have all the contributions gone? And why?" *National Catholic Reporter* (November 11, 1988) 17–19.

tion at a time when the Church, especially in Latin America, desperately needs more priests. It has alienated Catholics in the United States, France, Belgium, Germany (where one and one-half million recently signed a petition asking for election of bishops and more freedom in the Church), and even Poland and Ireland. It has alienated large numbers of women in the Church, (who are often teaching young Catholics), especially women in religious orders. Patricia Wittberg, in a study of the decline of Catholic religious orders, notes that the leaders of American women's congregations were radicalized by the authoritarian methods of the Sacred Congregation of Religious, the Curial group that oversees religious orders. "The SCR routinely refused to answer LCWR's [Leadership Conference of Women Religious] repeated requests to be represented on Vatican commissions that dealt with their lives. The pope, too, refused to meet with them. The SCR also repeatedly attempted to insert statements about obedience to the pope in the sisters' new constitutions whether or not such explicit obedience had been a part of the orders' tradition."[49] In fact, churches that emphasize member participation are growing; churches that do not are dying. This generalization applies not only to Catholicism, but to the state-affiliated Protestant churches of Europe (e.g., Sweden, Germany), which perhaps even more than Roman Catholicism have been governed by top-down methods. In such churches as the Lutheran Church in Sweden, the Church of England, and the Lutheran Church in Germany, nominal membership is high, but actual participation is extremely low; typically less than 10 or even 5 percent on a given Sunday.

Nevertheless, the case for participatory hierarchy should not be made primarily by sociological arguments. The Church is not just a society in the world; it is a divinely constituted institution, whose hierarchical structure flows from its ontological structure. Thus the traditional justification for hierarchy has been theological, not sociological, and it is that argument that we now must consider.

[49] Patricia Wittberg, *The Rise and Decline of Catholic Religious Orders* (Albany: SUNY Press, 1994) 261. She also reports the following occurrence concerning a 1982 joint assembly of LCWR and CMSM: "The planners of the assembly's liturgy had asked ten of the participants—five men and five women—to assist in the distribution of communion. As these persons approached the altar, the presiding Vatican officials publicly rebuffed the five women and refused to allow them to assist their male counterparts. 'Many LCWR members, until then supportive but not especially devoted to the women's issue, date their awakening to that event'" (261).

Chapter 12

The Church as Communion: That All May Be One

> *It is the Holy Spirit, dwelling in those who believe . . . who brings about that marvelous communion of the faithful and joins them so intimately in Christ that He is the principle of the Church's unity. . . .*
> *In order to establish this Holy Church of His everywhere in the world until the end of time, Christ entrusted to the College of the Twelve the task of teaching, ruling, and sanctifying. . . .*
> *It is through the faithful preaching of the gospel by the apostles and their successors—the bishops with Peter's successor at their head—through their administration of the sacraments, and their loving exercise of authority, that Jesus Christ wishes His people to increase under the influence of the Holy Spirit. Thereby too He perfects His people's fellowship in unity.* (Vatican II: Decree on Ecumenism, #2)

> *"The Church as communion is a sacrament for the salvation of the world."* World Synod of Catholic Bishops, Final Report, 1985.[1]

The "Final Report" of the 1985 world Synod of Catholic Bishops states: "The ecclesiology of communion is the central and fundamental idea of the council's [Vatican II] documents."[2] By communion the bishops mean primarily the communion of the faithful with God

[1] "The Final Report" of the 1985 World Synod of Catholic Bishops, Part II, D, 1; *Origins* 15:27 (December 19, 1985) 44.

[2] Ibid., Part II, C, 1, 43.

through Jesus Christ in the sacraments. Through the Eucharist, the faithful are built up into communion in the body of Christ, the Church (1 Cor 10:16). Thus communion with God and communion of the faithful in community complement each other, and both are made possible by participation in a greater whole: the divine Trinity. Communion also means that the one Church "exists in and through" particular local churches (*LG* #23), which are not uniform but pluriform, each of them inculturating the universal Church according to its own local characteristics and distinctive charisms.[3] The bishops note the importance of the college of bishops and its head, the pope, in preserving communion, but also state that "because the church is a communion there must be participation and co-responsibility at all of her levels."[4] Finally, they note that there is a real, though imperfect communion existing between the Roman Catholic Church and other Christian Churches.

Building on the bishops' ideas, we might advance a four-fold notion of communion.[5] The first aspect entails ontological communion with the Trinity, expressed in the sacraments, liturgy, mysticism, and life of the Church. This aspect, which might be called *transcendent communion,* constitutes the very being of the Church, whose whole mission is to draw humanity into communion with God the Father through Jesus the Christ and the Holy Spirit. A second aspect is communion of the universal Church with particular, local expressions of the Spirit, working through subsidiary holons: individuals, local and regional congregations, religious orders, and so on. Though the divine Trinity is a unity, when incarnated in the life of the Church it is expressed through a multiplicity of local forms and charisms. We have seen (chap. 4) that the New Testament Church was composed of a number of diverse churches in communion, and that the diversity of these churches allowed for a fuller expression of the Spirit than any single church could have. Communion does not mean a uniformity which dissolves the particular charism of a local body, but an integrated diversity of particular holons, be they individuals, small groups, congregations or dioceses. This might be called *local or particular communion,* whose preservation ensures that the insights, born of the Spirit, which come to expression in individuals

[3] Ibid., Part II, C, 2; 43.

[4] Ibid., Part II, C, 6; 44.

[5] This notion borrows heavily from the concept of "catholicity" developed by Avery Dulles in his masterful work, *The Catholicity of the Church* (Oxford: Clarendon Press, 1985).

or local congregations not be stifled by those superintending the universal Church, but be ratified and proclaimed by them. Examples of this in Catholicism are the different rites; the differing styles, theologies, and charisms of the various religious orders; and the great diversity of local parishes in a diocese. Third, it is necessary that the Church be in communion with the revelation handed on from Christ, expressed in the apostolic teachings, and passed on in authentic tradition. This might be called *communion in time.* But not all things in the tradition are from the Spirit. Rather, the tradition needs to be reappraised with the developing understanding which comes to the Church from the Spirit. As *Dei Verbum* notes in a beautiful and important passage (*DV* #8):

> This tradition which comes from the apostles develops in the Church with the help of the Holy Spirit. For there is a growth in the understanding of the realities and the words which have been handed down. This happens through the contemplation and study made by believers . . . and through the preaching of those who have received through episcopal succession the sure gift of truth. For as the centuries succeed one another, the Church constantly moves forward toward the fullness of divine truth until the words of God reach their complete fulfillment in her.

Communion in time, then, should include fidelity to the ongoing guidance of the Spirit. If communion in time meant simply repeating the unchanged formulas of the past, and handing on a statically conceived "deposit of faith," the Church would fail in its mission of growing to understand the fullness of divine truth. Communion in time must therefore include an aspect of *development.* And this development, according to *Dei Verbum,* owes something to the "contemplation and study made by believers" (including theologians) and the *sensus fidelium,* as well as to the bishops. Essential too in this progress is the preservation of prophecy for the edification of the whole Church. The fourth aspect of communion might be called *horizontal communion:* that is, communion among all the local churches across geographical regions. This would include communion among various Christian denominations. Also, it would include communion, or partial communion, with all those expressions of truth which might appear outside of the Christian Church, whether in non-Christian religions, or in secular movements. For the mission of the Church is to gather up and express the whole Truth of the Spirit, in all its pluriformity and multiplicity, whether that occurs within or without Christian ecclesial boundaries.

The unifying principle of the Church as communion is the Holy Spirit. But the visible governing structure charged with holding the various aspects in balance is the college of bishops united with the bishop of Rome, who exercises primacy within the college. Without such a structure, the tendency is for the Church to fall apart into a scattering of local churches. But for this structure to work there must be a balance between the bishops, who each represent a particular local church, and the primate, who facilitates consensus. If the primate becomes too powerful, forcing the bishops into subservience, or if the bishops become too powerful and the primate too weak, the structure cannot adequately accomplish its task of integration.

This fourfold concept of communion approximately corresponds with the four marks of the Church given in the Creed: the Church is "one, holy, catholic, and apostolic." The integration of the universal Church with local churches corresponds to the 'oneness' of the Church; what I have called transcendent communion corresponds to 'holiness'; continuity with the apostolic tradition with 'apostolicity'; and horizontal communion with 'catholicity'.

This idea of communion, then, involves a dynamic tension and integration between contrasting elements: institutional and charismatic, hierarchical and lay, sacramental and prophetic, conservative and progressive, transcendent and earthly. The reconciliation of these diversities is a perennial challenge for every Christian and generation of Christians, and for every local, national, or universal Church. What threatens communion is excessive emphasis on one aspect at the expense of others. This is the essence of heresy. It is also implied in the meaning of the Hebrew and Greek words translated as "sin," which literally mean "to miss the mark,"—(as an archer shooting wide of a target).[6]

If the Church is to be a sign and sacrament of the communion of God and humanity, and of human beings with each other (cf. *LG* #1), then it must express this multivalent, dynamic notion of communion in its ecclesial and hierarchial structure. If it does not, it will violate and contradict its own nature and mission. Yet the fact that communion is multivalent means that there are many ways in which the Church, or a church, can deform or betray communion. It could become secularized and fail to express the transcendent communion with the Trinity. Conversely, it could emphasize the transcendent yet

[6] "Sin," in John McKenzie, S.J., *Dictionary of the Bible* (New York: Macmillan, 1965) 817.

suffocate the aspect of local self expression. It could fail in its mission to hand on the essential teachings of the apostles. Conversely, it could become fixated on past apostolic teachings and never develop in its understanding of those teachings. Such archaism is a perennial temptation of religions. One thinks of the Sadducees in Second Temple Judaism as well as of Christian sects which seem to be frozen at some point in Church history. Finally, an individual church can turn inward, isolating itself from other churches and become a sect, thus violating horizontal communion. This contradicts the catholicity of the Church: its obligation to remain in communion with the fullness of Christ and the Spirit in all the multiplicity of their local expressions.

Given this idea of communion, the Christian Church today seems an imperfect, broken, manifestation of communion; it is as much a sign of disunity and fragmentation as it is a sacramental sign of the unity of God and humanity. In my opinion no contemporary denomination or confession presently expresses in itself all aspects of the fullness of communion. Rather, each denomination or confession emphasizes some aspects and typically minimizes those emphasized by other denominations. The Roman Catholic Church has for centuries claimed to be "The Church," which retained the fullness of catholicity, while other churches were seen as imperfect. In the light of the biblical and historical research presented in earlier chapters, it is hard to see how this claim can be maintained. While it may be true that the Roman Church retains implicitly or potentially all the elements of communion, these are not all equally expressed, especially at the universal level. The subsidiary structure of the Church, the active participation of the laity and the local church in ecclesial governance, the *sensus fidelium,* the prophecy and charismatic gifts, have all been subordinated to a monarchial interpretation of the Petrine primacy. Above all, this monarchial interpretation has deformed the primacy itself, so that instead of being a rock of unity (Matt 16:18) it has become, in the eyes of others, a stumbling stone, a scandal (Matt 16:23) which causes division in the Church.

If this analysis is correct, it follows that the surest way the Christian Church can recover the fullness of communion is through ecumenical reunion. Each of the major denominational groupings possesses some aspects of communion necessary for fullness and lacks others. Given the natural tendency to define oneself by stressing what one's competitors lack, it seems unlikely that any of the denominations can recover the fullness of communion alone without the cooperation of the others. In a sense, the body of Christ is like a body in which each part is growing in isolation from the others. Ecumenical reunion, guided by the Spirit, which integrates the whole, is essential to restore the health and fullness of the body.

Implications for the Roman Catholic Church

I will not attempt to sketch here an abstract blueprint for an ecumenically reunited Church; to do so would be premature and presumptuous: such a reunited Church can only emerge through prayer, collective discernment, dialogue of all parties, and an attempt to reach some consensus. Certainly I would hold that an ecumenical "great Church" should incorporate the principles enunciated in this book: participatory hierarchy at all levels, a subsidiary, holarchical structure, a college of bishops and a pope, and preservation of the four aspects of communion discussed above. I also hold for the necessity of a Petrine primacy to ensure unity within the college of bishops, and hence within the Church. The attempt to eliminate hierarchical structures for an egalitarian or "democratic" Church seems to me to be a prescription for fragmentation and anarchy. Any ecumenically reunited Church would have to be constellated around some kind of hierarchy.

What then ought to be the role of the Roman Church in fostering ecumenical reunion? *The greatest gift that the Roman church can give to the ecumenical movement is to reform itself,* so that it might become a model of participatory hierarchy and a sacramental sign of unity. Certainly the ecumenical movement can make great advances apart from the Roman Church. But ultimately, if my analysis is correct, the charisms of the Roman Church, especially the Petrine primacy, will be important for a fully united Church. But if that primacy is locked into a monarchial command hierarchy, it will be unacceptable to other denominations and hence impotent to contribute to ecumenical unity. In this context, John Paul II's concern, expressed in *Ut unum sint*—"to find a way of exercising the primacy which, while in no way renouncing what is essential to its mission, is nonetheless open to a new situation"[7]—is extremely important, and may prove to be the key which unlocks the door to ecumenical reunion. In the remainder of this chapter, then, I will consider how the Roman Church might reform itself so as to contribute to ecumenical unity.

[7] *Ut unum sint* (Boston: Pauline Books and Media, no date given) n. 95, 102.

The fundamental theological principle upon which reform ought to be based is this: the Spirit is given to the whole People of God (*LG* #12) and hence works in the Church both through the laity and the hierarchy, that is, it teaches both from the bottom up and from the top down or, to shift the metaphor, from the center to the periphery and from the periphery to the center. Cardinal Suenens has written: "The Church, in asking the faithful to accept their full and prophetic coresponsibility in the world, knows well that the Holy Spirit is at work to accomplish in and through them his great designs."[8] It is true, as John Paul II writes, that the mission of the bishop of Rome and the College of Bishops consists in 'keeping watch' *(episkopein)*, over the apostolic faith.[9] But this mission of *episkopein* (which is guided by the Spirit) needs to be balanced by a discernment of the prophetic and developmental guidance of the Spirit, especially as it acts through the *sensus fidelium.*

Thus the *Ecclesia docens* (the teaching Church) is also the *Ecclesia discens* (the learning Church), and vice versa. As well as bestowing and conserving the apostolic deposit of faith, the Spirit guides the Church in its growth in understanding of the revelation as it progresses towards the fullness of truth. Each of these points is implied in the passage from *Dei Verbum* cited above (p. 313), which states that both the contemplation and study of believers and the preaching of the bishops contribute to the developing understanding of the tradition, under the guidance of the Spirit. Finally, the Spirit also works in communions outside the purlieus of the Visible Church. In short, it works through each of the aspects of Communion explained above.

The error of those who want to deny any hierarchy to the Church is to assume that the Spirit works mainly through the laity rather than the ordained clergy. In this view, the will of the democratic majority should be imposed on the whole Church. The opposite error is to assume that the Spirit works only through the clerical hierarchy and/or the pope, Christ's sole vicar on earth.

Yet every Christian, by virtue of baptism and confirmation, participates in the Spirit. The theology of the mystical body, sanctioned in *Mystici Corporis,* emphasizes this. What is not mentioned in *Mystici Corporis* is that the laity may also participate in the *prophetic and teaching*

[8] Leon-Joseph, Cardinal Suenens, *Coresponsibility in the Church* (New York: Herder and Herder, 1968) 206.

[9] *Ut unum sint,* 101.

gifts of the Spirit. This is brought out in 1 Corinthians 12: In the church there are apostles, prophets, teachers, forms of leadership, and not all these gifts are reserved to the clerical hierarchy. But if the Spirit teaches through many agents and voices, as the doctrine of the *sensus fidelium* also states (chap. 5) then the best process for discerning the mind of the Spirit is one which respects the participation of all relevant parties—a conciliar, consensual form of discernment and decision making. We have seen this at work in the Hebrew scriptures, in Acts 15, the decision of the early Church to incorporate Gentiles, in the early councils of the Church and at Vatican II. St. Benedict required in his Rule that the abbot consult the whole community on all important matters "since the Lord often reveals the best course to a younger monk."[10] Popes Pius IX and Pius XII consulted the bishops, and directed the bishops to consult the faithful, in order to ascertain whether the beliefs in the Immaculate Conception and the Assumption were in fact held by almost all the faithful before they proclaimed them as dogmas. Conversely, the failure to respect fully this consensual process has repeatedly led to schisms (at Chalcedon, chap. 5; with the Orthodox, chap. 6; with the Protestants, chap. 7). Establishment of consensus involves unforced dialogue, the voicing of dissent, conflict, and the testing of time. Consensus of course does not mean agreement on every detail, but agreement on essentials and acceptance of diversity in inessentials. The achievement of consensus involves reception among the faithful, a process which involves conflict and takes time.[11] The formula of Nicaea was not universally accepted for decades in the early Church.

This process is well described in an essay entitled "Obedience" by Herbert McCabe, O.P., of the English Dominicans. McCabe cites the Dominican Master general, Vincent de Couesnongle:

> The fundamental law of democracy is *majority* rule, but it is not the same with us, in spite of our frequent voting. Our law is *unanimous* rule . . . the prior should not look for a quick vote, but should try to have the question threshed out so that everyone has his say; and a common debate will lead to agreement which is as near unanimous as possible.[12]

[10] *The Rule of St. Benedict* (Garden City, N.Y.: Doubleday, Image Books, 1975) 51.

[11] For an overview of recent thought on reception and the *sensus fidelium,* with bibliography, see Gaillardetz, *Teaching with Authority,* 227–254.

[12] From *Confidence for the Future* (Dublin: Dominican Publications, 1982) cited in Herbert McCabe, O.P., *God Matters* (London: Geoffrey Chapman, 1987) 229.

> For our tradition, an obedient house is one which has got as near as possible to the *truth,* in which there is general agreement about what is to be done so that the will of the superior hardly enters into it. The job of the superior is not to make her or his *will* prevail, it is to play the central role in an educational process by which the good for the house becomes clear to everyone, including her. Our motto, remember, is *Veritas* . . . .
>
> Obedience, then, for us, is displayed in the community united in agreement about how the gospel is to be preached, and the centre of that unity is the Prior or Prioress. He or she is only acting as Prior to the extent that a common mind grows up around her/him. Without this there is no true obedience and no true authority.[13]

Obedience is therefore incumbent on the Prior as well as the monks:

> A Prior who sets himself outside the common mind of the community . . . is failing in obedience as much as any other member might do. . . . Since for us obedience means solidarity with the community, the Prior is only prior as representing the community. I do not mean simply that he is *elected,* but that as Prior he *speaks for* the community as a whole.[14]

According to McCabe, this is the real meaning of the traditional Dominican title for the prior: *Primus inter pares* (First among equals). Christ was obedient to the Father yet was the equal of the Father. Similarly, obedience to the community is a sharing in the relationship of the father and the Son. Such participation is the ultimate root of obedience.[15] This is similar to what we have seen in Acts 15 and in the ecumenical councils. Obedience is obedience to the will of the Spirit as expressed through the consensus of the body.

In a large and diverse Church the reality will be more complicated than in a single religious community. Here unity will require a second principle: that of holarchy. In fact, every complex, composite body in nature is a holarchy. I have argued above that holarchical construction is a universal principle, though the nature of the wholes, parts, and their interrelation varies according to the system. The universality of this principle in the created order suggests that it is a permanent structure of being and hence corresponds to the will of the Creator. Even the

[13] Ibid., 230.
[14] Ibid., 232.
[15] Ibid., 233.

Trinity is a kind of holarchy, though a unique kind. Thus holarchy is no mere analogy, but a model for unity in diversity.

Applied to the institutional Church, the basic holon is the parish; the next larger holon is the diocese, then the regional or national grouping of bishops, then the universal Church. At each level the principle that the Spirit works from the center to the periphery and vice versa should be respected. This should be expressed in ecclesial structures that allow input from the center but also from the periphery. Thus the parishioners should have some say in the selection of priests, along with the local bishop. Bishops should be selected by a joint action of the local clergy and parish representatives, as well as by the other bishops of the region and the representative of the international church—by tradition the bishop of Rome. The same pattern should be followed at the national and international levels.

Clearly such a decision-making process will involve conflict and dissent. But constructive dissent (though not destructive dissent—see chap. 11) can contribute to the discernment of truth. Here let us recall the words of Karol Wojtyla, cited in the last chapter: "for opposition to be constructive, the structure . . . of a given society must be such as to allow the opposition that emerges from within the soil of solidarity not only to *express* itself within the framework of a given community, but also to *operate* for its benefit."[16] Thus dissent should not be suppressed, but allowed to be voiced.

From this emerges a model of unity, obedience, and authority. The unity to be sought is not a command unity, which tends to produce uniformity (but also rebellion and schism), or an egalitarian unity, which also tends to produce uniformity (to be different is to be unequal, so differences are leveled out). It is not a democratic unity, in which the majority imposes its will on a minority. The unity of the Church, insofar as possible, ought to be based on participation and a consensus in core matters which allows for diversity in non-essential matters. Holarchy allows for subsidiary units to express a religion in many different forms and rites, so that such a unity need not be uniformity but reconciled diversity. Such a holarchy will have different hierarchical roles, corresponding to the different levels of holons.

Obedience, as McCabe makes clear, should be filial not servile, and is owed to the will of the Spirit as it is manifested through the consen-

[16] Karol Wojtyla, *The Acting Person*, 286–287, emphasis in original.

sus of the whole Church. Where there is no consensus, obedience should not be imposed, except to protect core beliefs fundamental to integrity of the Church. Thus I would hold that the Catholic magisterium (the bishops and the pope, acting in concert, not just the pope alone) have the right and duty to discipline theologians and others who publicly dissent from the fundamentals of the Christian faith (e.g., by denying the divinity of Christ). But neither obedience nor suppression of discussion should be imposed in areas which are not at the core of the faith and where no consensus has formed, for example the question of clerical celibacy or the ordination of women.

The authority growing from a community in consensus corresponds to an authority of virtue: the authority of the hierarch is rooted in the consensus of the community which he (she) represents. In the Church such a consensus should also represent the will of the Spirit, so that authority would be grounded in that of the Spirit itself. Such an authority is strong and persuasive; authoritative, not authoritarian. On the other hand, an authority of force or command which opposes the will of the community (or of a large part of it) risks suffocating the voice of the Spirit and thus destroying its own credibility. For once any religious authority (priest, bishop, or pope) is perceived as acting out of a concern to maintain power, rather than out of an expression of the Spirit, its credibility and ability to lead collapses: it is perceived as authoritarian but not authoritative. The loss of papal authority in the wake of *Humani vitae* may be an example of this.

What does this mean concretely for the Roman Catholic Church? At the parish level, it means active participation on the part of parishioners. In many parishes, this is already a reality, even at the level of governance. The local pastor often governs with the aid of a parish council. Some input should be granted parishioners (or their representatives, such as the parish council) in the selection of priests, but ultimate authority should rest with the local bishop. At the diocesan level, it is extremely important that the local church have a voice in the selection of its bishops. This is probably the most important structural change that needs to be made in the Roman Church. Walter Kasper has proposed that bishops be appointed by a "joint act of the relevant local church, the fellow bishops in the district . . . and the universal church i.e. the Pope as the head of the College of Bishops."[17] If the individual churches are

[17] "The Church as Communio." *New Blackfriars* (May, 1993) 242.

holons united in a *communio* the best way to represent this institutionally would be an elected episcopacy (which would be a recovery of the practice of the ancient Church). Such bishops would, of course, still be understood as deriving their authority from Christ. An elected episcopacy would restore a parity of authority between the bishops and the pope and move the center of gravity back towards an integrative model of hierarchy. Furthermore, an episcopacy which was not under papal domination would be better able to discern the movement of the Spirit in the Church and the churches. This does not mean that in the case of a maverick bishop the universal Church would be helpless to discipline or remove him. But such an action should take place with the consultation and consent of the other bishops of the Church. The divisive nature of the removal of bishop Gaillot in France was largely due to Rome's acting unilaterally, without consulting or even informing the French episcopate of its action.[18]

Of course, it follows from what has been said above that the authority of the bishop in his diocese ought also to be exercised in a participatory fashion. Authoritarian bishops are no better than authoritarian popes. But in many dioceses, at least in the United States, structures such as pastoral councils, deaneries, priests' senates, etc., are already in place to facilitate a participatory exercise of episcopal authority. And the United States bishops have consulted extensively with the laity before issuing pastoral letters. Further, the election of bishops by the local Church would also diminish the possibility of an abuse of episcopal power.

The real challenge to the Roman Catholic Church is to implement a participatory model of papal authority—as John Paul writes, to find a way of exercising the primacy which is open to a new situation. At present there is a very serious polarization in Roman Catholicism over this issue, with no resolution in sight. Three models of papal authority seem to be vying for assent in the church.

First is the command model, in which the pope is seen as a divinely guided lawgiver and interpreter, who speaks the word of Christ to the flock, whose duty is to obey. In this idea the pope is the sole Vicar of Christ on earth and the ultimate authority in the Church, beholden to no one, not even an ecumenical council. (This is paralleled in

[18] See Steven Englund, "L'Affaire Gaillot," *Commonweal* (October 6, 1995) 12–18. Englund points out that there were many reasons to dismiss Gaillot, but the Vatican's failure to act in concert with the French episcopacy exacerbated the scandal.

Islam by the Shia idea of a divinely guided Imam, represented by the Ayatollahs in Iran. It is paralleled in politics by the theory of the divine right of kings.) This model is based on a narrow reading of Vatican I, which did grant the pope supreme jurisdiction in the Church. It is largely enshrined in canon law: *juridically,* there is no appeal from the decision of a legitimate pope, even if that decision is made autocratically, against the will of the episcopate and the laity. This model allows the Church no protection from tyranny. Though many conservative Catholics believe that God will never allow the papacy to become tyrannical or to fall into error, this has in fact already happened. Popes have been condemned as heretical (Honorius), have been deposed, and have condemned each other (during the Great Schism); many papal statements have been reversed by later councils (chap. 9), and autocratic rule by popes at the time of the Reformation contributed to the Protestant schism (chap. 7).

In fact, there is little theological justification for this model. Traditionally, popes have appealed to the three major "Petrine" texts (Matt 16:18; Luke 22:32; John 21:17). But these texts do not underwrite a monarchial claim to authority (see chaps. 3 and 4) and have been interpreted in many ways in the tradition. Few biblical scholars would see in them the words of Christ. My contention is that the best way to interpret these texts is through Acts 15, where we see an unambiguous example of Petrine authority in action. And there it is participatory and based on consensus. Even if the Acts account is idealized, it serves as a narrative charter for decision making in the Church.

Historical justification for the papalist model is also very weak. All major decisions in the early Church were made in councils by the principle of unanimity. Ratification by Rome was essential for these decisions to be binding and Rome was seen as the center of orthodox tradition. But Rome did not have jurisdictional authority over other bishops except those in its immediate region. Fundamental was the principle of episcopal collegiality, which was expressed through local and regional synods and ecumenical councils. A command model of the papacy was never accepted by the East, by the North African Church, or by the Visigothic Church in Spain, nor by many bishops in the French church (e.g., Hincmar of Rheims, Bossuet, the Gallican bishops). As Henry Chadwick has noted, Rome saw the Church as a circle, centered on Rome, whereas the East saw it as an ellipse, with two foci. Nonetheless, the East granted (and still grants) the Bishop of Rome a primacy among the patriarchs, and the title *primus inter pares,* "first among equals."[19] Though the papal monarchy did regain control of the Church from lay lords in the early Middle Ages, that historical circumstance does not justify its continuity into the present, when Church and state are largely separate. In the event of state domination of the Church today (as was the case in some Communist countries), the pope acting in concert with the universal college of bishops could exercise more influence than a papal monarch acting alone. Finally, the fact that the papacy was unable to extricate itself from the Great Schism by its own power, and that papal authority had to be reestablished by an ecumenical council (Constance) under the direction of an emperor (Sigismund), is an historical event which undercuts any claim to monarchial papal authority continuing from Peter to the present.

Many of the arguments for a command model of papal authority have depended on false historical assumptions or on forged documents. For example, from the time of Innocent I on Roman bishops erroneously believed that other Western churches had been founded by Rome and therefore fell under Roman authority.[20] The False Decretals "prepared the way for the principle that the deposition of bishops is a right properly belonging to Rome."[21] The principle that "prima sedes a nemine iudicatur" (the first see is judged by no one), though it appears in two letters of Pope Gelasius, actually entered canon law through the Symmachian forgeries.[22] Yet canon law and papal documents have unblushingly continued to repeat these claims and arguments with no acknowledgment of their historically specious origins.

It is true that a narrow reading of Vatican I tends to confirm a command model of papal authority. But most theological commentators have argued above that there are reasons not to interpret Vatican I this way. In addition, the very strong objections of both the Orthodox and the Protestants (who both see the Vatican I definitions of supreme jurisdiction and infallibility as heretical) need to be taken into account. Finally, this interpretation of the papacy has produced schisms and rebellion, a passive, mechanical obedience, and a gradual crumbling of papal authority, and hence ability to unify, within the Roman Church itself.

[19] "The Circle and the Ellipse," in *Jerusalem and Rome: The Problem of Authority in the Early Church,* by Hans von Campenhausen and Henry Chadwick (Philadelphia: Fortress, 1966) 23–35.

[20] Schatz, *Papal Primacy,* 35, 89.

[21] Ibid., 70.

[22] Ibid., 73.

At the other end of the spectrum are those who would reject hierarchy, especially the papacy, in favor of a democratic or egalitarian Church. Carried to extremes, this ideology rejects even the lordship of Christ (see chap. 3). In this ecclesiology, the pope and the bishops would probably be reduced to mere figureheads. But such a model is also inadequate. I have argued in chapter 3 that there was a hierarchy of authority even within the Jesus movement itself. Jesus left apostles as his successors and invested them with a certain authority (chap. 4). From early times the successors to the apostles were understood to be the bishops, though the process of that succession was complex and differed from church to church (chap. 5). Most of the foundational doctrines of Christianity were laid down by councils of bishops, whose teachings were received as authoritative. Within the early Church, Rome was accepted as the center and touchstone of orthodoxy. The bishop of Rome, as the successor of Peter and Paul, was accorded a primacy of honor, and his ruling was often appealed to by distant churches.

The charism of the bishop of Rome, I have argued, is to be a facilitator of consensus and a center of unity among the episcopal college, as Peter was among the apostles. This agrees with the opinion of Orthodox theologian Alexander Schmemann, who argues that primacy is a power for bringing about unity within episcopal synods and within the Church (chap. 5). The danger of an egalitarian Church is that having no unifying authority or center, it would disintegrate into dispersed factional congregations. These, lacking an episcopal link to the apostolic tradition, would be liable to tailor the faith to fit the taste of any particular congregation or group. Such fragmentation has been an ongoing problem with congregational ecclesiologies.

A third model, neither command nor egalitarian, is that of the pope as the head of the college of bishops in which the pope and the bishops are together the subject of primacy, each bishop being a vicar of Christ. John Paul II, at least in some of his writings, appears to endorse this model.

> When the Catholic Church affirms that the office of the Bishop of Rome corresponds to the will of Christ, she does not separate this office from the mission entrusted to the whole body of Bishops, who are also "vicars and ambassadors of Christ." The Bishop of Rome is a member of the "College," and the Bishops are his brothers in the ministry.[23]

[23] *Ut unum sint*, n. 95, p. 102.

This model accords with the scriptural evidence well; in Acts 15 the decision is made by consensus. Luke 22:32 says that Peter should "strengthen your brothers" not "Lord it over your brothers." It accords with the practice of the early Church, in which decisions were made by ecumenical councils, but Roman ratification was considered essential. It agrees with ancient precedents such as Apostolic Canon 34 (see chap. 5), which asserted that the bishops should do nothing without the consent of him who is their head, but neither should the head do anything without the consent of the bishops. Finally, it accords with both the definitions of Vatican I and Vatican II (chap. 9). It allows for an authoritative papacy, which speaks the mind of the Church, but not an authoritarian one. An example of this style of papal authority in our time was John XXIII who initiated Vatican II but allowed the bishops rather than the Curia to control the council, thus allowing genuine dialogue to emerge. His founding of the Secretariat for Promoting Christian Unity gave great impetus to ecumenism. His example of humble service in high office gave non-Catholic Churches a new vision of the possibilities of the papacy as a unifying ecumenical agent.

This model has much better ecumenical possibilities than either of the other two. The command model is unacceptable to non-Roman Churches, as well as to most of the members of the Roman Church; as such, it cannot unify the Church. But the egalitarian model would also be ecumenically fruitless, since it offers no real principle or way of achieving unity. The unique charism which the Roman Church has to offer other ecclesial bodies is the charism of the papacy as a center for unity. A pope who is a mere figurehead would have nothing to offer the ecumenical movement. Only the third model, with its emphasis on hierarchy, participation, and relationship, offers possibility for real ecumenical advance.

How should the pope be selected in a reformed Catholicism? Presently he is elected by the cardinals, who are themselves appointed by the pope, an incestuous arrangement which preserves power in the hands of an elite. Since the pope's proper role is the head of the whole college of bishops, it would make sense for him to be elected by the whole college of bishops. But since he is also the ultimate head of the religious orders, the heads of those orders also should have a vote. And since his office affects the laity as well, they also, through representatives, should have a voice. Such an elective arrangement may be vulnerable to politicking (as all electoral arrangements are), but at least would ensure that those affected by the papal office were the ones empowered to choose the supreme pontiff, according to the ancient principle: "Quod omnes tangit, ab omnibus tractari et approbari debet."

Obstacles to Ecumenical Communion within Roman Catholicism

The greatest obstacle to the realization of the Church as communion is the conception of hierarchy as command. It is this notion which is largely responsible for the polarization now affecting the Catholic Church. One pole, identifying hierarchy with centralized control and command, wishes to *eliminate* hierarchy from the Church. Carried to extremes, this position leads even to the denial of the Lordship of Christ. The other pole, also identifying hierarchy with centralized control, wishes to enforce it. This wing seems committed to the ideology of a divinely guided papal monarchy, which has been for the most part the operative conception of papal authority in Rome since the medieval period. Yet this notion remains a serious obstacle to the realization of the Church as communion.

In his *On the Coming of the Third Millennium,* John Paul II writes as follows: "The approaching end of the second millennium demands of everyone an *examination of conscience* and the promotion of fitting ecumenical initiatives, so that we can celebrate the great Jubilee, if not completely united, *at least much closer to overcoming the divisions of the second millennium."*[24] I applaud this call for an examination of conscience, which applies not only to individuals, but to whole institutions, including the Roman Catholic Church and the Papacy. An examination of conscience by the Church and the papacy is essential if ecumenical reunion is to progress.

John Paul II himself may have begun this process in his remarkable encyclical, *Ut unum sint.* This document is one of the most irenic and ecumenically-minded papal documents in history. John Paul is sincerely concerned for ecumenical reunion. He has laid out a program for ecumenical discussion leading up to the year 2000.[25] He rightly thinks that the mission of the Bishop of Rome "is particularly directed to recalling the need for full communion among Christ's disciples."[26] He has

[24] *Apostolic Letter: Tertio Millennio Adveniente,* ET: *On the Coming of the Third Millennium* (Washington, D.C.: United States Catholic Conference, 1995) 45.

[25] In *On the Coming of the Third Millennium.*

[26] *Ut unum sint,* 15.

offered an apology for those actions of the papacy which contributed to ecclesial divisions.[27] He has made ecumenical reunion a priority of his pontificate. As noted above, he sees the ministry of the Bishop of Rome as exercised in communion with the bishops of the episcopal college. Finally in view of the requests of other Christian Churches, he opens the possibility of "finding a way of exercising the primacy which, while in no way renouncing what is essential to its mission, is nonetheless open to a new situation."[28]

A response to the Pope was given by Archbishop (of San Francisco) John R. Quinn in his address at Campion Hall, Oxford, June 29, 1996. He begins by observing that the only reason to advance new ways of exercising the primacy is if current ways are evaluated as inadequate, especially with respect to ecumenism. He continues:

> Yet it must honestly be acknowledged that many Orthodox and other Christians are hesitant about full communion with the Holy See not so much because they see some doctrinal issues as unsolvable, not because of unfortunate and reprehensible historical events, but precisely because of the way issues are dealt with by the Curia. It also must be said that this is a concern all over the world. Recent events in Switzerland, Austria, Germany, and France, in Brazil, Africa, and the United States are only one indication of how widespread this concern is. The concern has to do with the appointment of bishops, the approval of documents such as *The Catechism of the Catholic Church,* the grave decline of the number of priests and the consequent decline in the availability of Mass for the people, the cognate issues of celibacy of the clergy, the role of episcopal conferences, the role of women and the issue of ordination of women. Two things are involved in these issues: the decision of the Holy See on a specific issue and the way in which these decisions are reached and implemented. For instance, are such decisions imposed without consultation with the episcopate and without appropriate dialogue? Are bishops appointed against an overwhelming objection of people and priests in a given diocese? Where answers to these and other such questions is affirmative there are serious difficulties for Christian unity.[29]

Quinn suggests that the Curia sees itself as subordinate to the pope, but superior to the College of Bishops. He adds: "To the degree that

[27] Ibid., 97.
[28] Ibid., 102.
[29] "The Exercise of the Primacy," in *Commonweal* (July 12, 1996) 14.

this is so . . . it obscures and diminishes both the doctrine and the reality of episcopal collegiality . . . . bishops and episcopal conferences feel that such grave questions as contraception, the ordination of women, general absolution, and the celibacy of the clergy are closed to discussion."[30] For example, the 1992 Celam conference of Latin American bishops in Santo Domingo was not allowed by the Vatican to discuss the question of clerical celibacy, even though the Church in Latin America is suffering from a severe shortage of priests.[31] In this instance, John Paul's actions belie his statement (above) that the office of the papacy is to be exercised in conjunction with other bishops.

Quinn further notes that "it is the constant teaching of the Church that bishops are judges and teachers of the faith"[32] and that the international Synod of Bishops is meant to be an expression of the bishops' teaching office. But this Synod has not lived up to its promise. In reality, it is the pope who chooses the topic for discussion. Hence, "Many bishops feel that issues which they would like to discuss responsibly cannot come up . . . . My point is simply to underline that issues of major concern in the church are not really open to a free and collegial evaluation and discussion by bishops, whose office includes being judges in matters of faith."[33] This violates both Vatican II's understanding of episcopal collegiality, and the ancient practice of the Church, which understood the Holy Spirit to guide the Church not through one person or office alone, but through the consensus of the whole, especially the consensus of the assembled bishops, who are the successors of the apostles. As noted above, this was affirmed by the Second Council of Constantinople, which declared: ". . . it was established as certain that when the disputed question is set out by each side in communal discussions, the light of truth drives out the shadow of lying. The truth cannot be made clear in any other way [than by communal discussion] when there are debates about questions of faith, since everyone requires the assistance of his neighbor."[34]

Archbishop Quinn also discusses the appointment of bishops, which has been largely reserved to Rome.

[30] Ibid., 15.

[31] MacEoin, Gary, "Rome tries, fails to recolonize Latin church," in *National Catholic Reporter* (November 13, 1992) 10–11; Stahel, Thomas. "A Tale of Two Cities: Rome and Santo Domingo," in *America* (November 28, 1992) 419.

[32] Ibid., 16.

[33] "The Exercise of the Primacy," 16.

[34] Emphasis added. Latin text and English translation in Tanner, vol. I, 108.

> It is not uncommon for bishops of a province to discover that no candidate they proposed has been accepted for approval. . . . it may happen that candidates whom bishops do not approve at all may be appointed. . . . Under the existing policy, collegiality in the appointment of bishops consists largely in offering bishops the opportunity to make suggestions. But the real decisions are made at other levels: the nuncio, the Congregation of Bishops, the Secretariat of State.[35]

Yet this policy is of recent origin: "Until roughly 1800, Rome's intervention in the appointment of bishops in dioceses outside the Papal states was rare. Until 1829 it was the policy of the Holy See to leave the appointment of bishops to the local church where possible. At the death of Pope Leo XII in 1829, there were 646 diocesan bishops in the Latin Church. Of this number, excluding those in the Papal States, only twenty four were directly appointed by Rome."[36] Quinn notes that this situation came about by default: in the vacuum of power created by the fall of Napoleon, Rome assumed the prerogative of appointing bishops. But now, he believes, the time has come to change this policy, "so that local churches really have a significant and truly substantive role in the appointment of bishops."[37]

In fact, while the ideology of papal monarchy was forged in medieval times, its implementation has occurred only in modern times. The contemporary Catholic Church is far more centralized than was the medieval or Tridentine Church. This point has been made by Bishop Walter Kasper: "The Catholic Church and the theological community deliberately and decisively countered the modern principle with the principle of authority. In this the modern Church was and is much more authoritarian and uniformist than the Church of the Middle Ages ever was."[38]

Finally, Quinn discusses the importance of subsidiarity in the Church and notes the statement in the 1983 Code of Canon Law: "the

[35] "The Exercise of the Primacy," 17.

[36] Ibid., 17. Klaus Schatz notes: "It seems, however, that a systematic policy for the nomination of bishops in the sense of promoting specific trends and especially in the service of positions taken by the magisterium has only manifested itself in our own time." *Papal Primacy,* 168.

[37] Ibid.

[38] *The Christian Understanding of Freedom and the History of Freedom in the Modern Era: The meeting and Confrontation Between Christianity and the Modern Era in a Postmodern Situation.* 1988 Père Marquette Lecture in Theology (Milwaukee: Marquette Univ. Press, 1988) 20–21.

principle of subsidiarity . . . must all the more be applied in the Church since the office of the bishops and their powers is of divine law." But he also observes that "large segments of the Catholic Church as well as many Orthodox and other Christians do not believe that collegiality and subsidiarity are being practiced in the Catholic Church in a sufficiently meaningful way. The seriousness of our obligation to seek Christian unity sincerely means that this obstacle to unity cannot be overlooked or dismissed as if it were the quirk of malcontents or the scheme of those who want to undermine the papacy."[39]

In light of this, the greatest contribution that Roman Catholicism can make to the ecumenical movement is a thorough examination of its own conscience, especially of its use and understanding of hierarchy and of papal authority. John Paul clearly desires ecumenical reunion. Yet what speaks loudest to other Christians is his actions. No Church will consent to union with Rome if the pope speaks irenically, but *acts* like an absolute monarch. This has been precisely the objection of *both* Orthodox and Protestants against the Catholic Church for centuries. So perceived, the papacy *cannot* function as a unifying center for Christianity, or even for Catholicism. If my argument is right, he can only be effective if he begins practicing a participatory, not monarchial, style of hierarchy.

Conclusion

According to Ephesians 1:9-10, it is God's mysterious will to unite all things in Christ in the fullness of time. This eschatological integration is the goal of the created order, the Kingdom of God, the Mystical Body of Christ. I have suggested in chapter 10 that it is the culmination of a pattern already found all through creation, a holarchy of integrated complexity and diversity which develops through time. In this holarchy, each creature retains its own being, nature, and identity, while nevertheless participating in a greater transcendent whole according to the capacity of its nature.

The mission of the Christian Church is to be a sign and an agent of the integration of all creatures in Christ. This entails both vertical and horizontal communion, as well as communion in time. But if the Church is to be a sacramental sign of the reconciliation of all things in Christ, it

[39] "The Exercise of the Primacy," 18; *Codex Juris Canonici,* Libreria Editrice Vaticana, 1983, Preface, p. xxii, n. 5, Latin text.

must itself be united. Fragmented into competing denominations, it cannot image the integration of the Mystical Body. But also it cannot be artificially united by a command hierarchy which suppresses legitimate diversity. Thus I suggest that it be united according to the principles of participatory hierarchy and holarchy.

In a holarchical ecclesial structure, the local church is a whole in which Christ is truly present. This is also the case in all larger holons, such as regional assemblies, denominations, etc. But though Christ is present in each local assembly, the fullness of Christ cannot be adequately expressed through just one or a few assemblies. One cell, or even one person, is inadequate to fully express all the potential of the human DNA—the human genome (chap. 10). Only an entire human population can fully express all of its variety. Again, Aquinas argues that the goodness of God cannot be fully expressed in any single species (including humanity); therefore God created a great diversity of species and creatures, so that God's goodness might be more fully expressed (*ST* I, q. 47, a. 1). Similarly, only the integrated ensemble of all local churches can adequately express the richness, the fullness, and the catholicity of Christ. For this reason in a reunited Church whole denominations should be treated as holons, so that whatever authentic insight or charism they possess not be lost to the universal Church. Similarly, whatever comes from the Spirit in non-Christian religions should also be gathered up and preserved in a truly universal Church.

I have suggested that in a reunited Church, each holarchical level would have its own appropriate authority structure, patterned after the principles of participative hierarchy (chap. 11). The structure appropriate to the whole, I have argued, is a universal college of bishops joined with the Bishop of Rome, who has a role of primacy within that College. It follows then that it is this college, and particularly the Bishop of Rome, who has a special responsibility for ecumenical reunion. But the Bishop of Rome is not to be separated from his church. Therefore the whole Roman Catholic Church, which has traditionally prized ecclesial unity, has a special responsibility and call to work for ecumenical reunion.

Yet the Roman Catholic Church presently stands at a crossroads. It can move towards a more open, participatory notion of hierarchy or it can revert to a command hierarchy. In view of its dramatic decline in numbers and credibility, the rise of secularism, the polarization between conservatives and liberals, the cries for an egalitarian Church, the demoralization of the clergy, and the turmoil in theology, the temptation is great to try to restore a pre-Vatican II command-style hierarchy. But this would be a terrible mistake. A reversion to a command hierarchy would violate the Church's essential mission of bringing all into participation and communion with the body of Christ. It would stifle the voice of the Spirit and subvert the Spirit's guidance of the Church. Thus the *principal* reason to oppose a command hierarchy is theological. But bad theology, like bad economics, can entail disastrous historical consequences. The likely effect of a restored command hierarchy would be to reduce the (Roman Catholic) Church to the status of a declining, static, reactionary minority, i.e., a sect. Arnold Toynbee, in his magisterial *A Study of History,* writes:

> So far we have identified the component classes into which a disintegrating civilization breaks—the dominant minority, and the internal and external proletariats. We have also seen something of the nature and origin of these classes: the dominant minority is a perversion of a creative minority whose role of leadership it has inherited, and it embarks on a policy of social repression in order to impose by force the authority which it is no longer accorded in virtue of merit; the internal proletariat comprises that majority within a society which has formerly given its allegiance to a creative leadership, but which is now increasingly alienated from its own society by the coercive despotism of its corrupted masters; and the external proletariat is formed of the barbarian communities beyond the frontiers of a civilization who have been drawn into its orbit, but who now find themselves similarly alienated.[40]

Toynbee notes that the dominant minority are "static by definition," and typically frozen in archaism[41]; consequently they fail to make a creative response to changing challenges, and the civilization declines or collapses. Civilizations grow, on the other hand, by making creative responses to ongoing challenges: this is Toynbee's great law of "challenge and response" which he follows through the history of some thirty civilizations.

The rigidity and static nature of the dominant minority is both the cause and a symptom of the decline of a civilization, or a Church. The end of such a decline is sclerosis, and the civilization or Church turns in

[40] *A Study of History,* revised and abridged by Arnold Toynbee and Jane Caplan (Oxford: Oxford University Press, 1972) 224.

[41] Ibid., 86, 282.

on itself and petrifies. It may survive, but as an historical backwater, with no relevance to the ongoing currents of history. This has happened to many religious groups in the past: for example the Sadducees of the Second Temple period, the Monophysites, and others. It is characteristic of sects: Henry Chadwick remarks that it is a "perennial truth that sects remain conservative, while the church moves with the times."[42] Such a trajectory would be disastrous for Catholicism. It would mean that the Catholic Church would fail in its ecumenical mission and in its call to be a sacramental sign of the communion of human beings with each other and with God. In a word, it would lose its catholicity. What is called for is a creative response to the modern challenge. As noted above, both those who would restore a command hierarchy in the Church, and the egalitarians, have the *same concept* of hierarchy. But to equate hierarchy with command is to leave the Church with a Hobbesian choice between egalitarian fragmentation or a unity imposed by extrinsic force. A recovery of hierarchy as integrative, subsidiary, participatory, authoritative but not authoritarian, offers a middle way, one more in consonance with the biblical and patristic notions of governance, with Vatican II, with *communio* ecclesiology, and the catholicity of the Church.

Such a recovery could catalyze a Pentecostal renewal within the Catholic Church. It could rejuvenate the laity, particularly in regions like Latin America, where they have been passive, or in regions like Europe, where they are alienated. As noted above, churches which encourage lay participation are growing; those which do not are dying. Such a laity could find its own voice and representation in the Church through an elected episcopate. An elected episcopate might constellate renewed episcopal synods whose agendas were not controlled by Rome but which were free to articulate the Spirit as it speaks through the diverse perspectives of regional communions. These, in turn, could find their integration (and correction, in cases of regional or nationalistic bias) through ecumenical councils, held perhaps each quarter century.

Finally, a Roman Catholic Church which embraced a participatory model of hierarchy could provide renewed impetus to the flagging ecumenical movement, as John XXIII did, by manifesting a leadership that saw its mission not as one of centralizing authority, but as sharing authority and so healing of the wounds of division.

I leave the last word on this subject to the recently deceased Léon Joseph Cardinal Suenens, one of the great architects of Vatican II, who

[42] "The Circle and the Ellipse," 31.

exemplified in his life and leadership deep sensitivity to the Spirit and to a participatory style of hierarchy. Cardinal Suenens wrote: "The leader is no longer the man who has all the answers but the man who succeeds in creating the environment in which dialogue, research, and constructive criticism are possible and in which the answers emerge by the gradual process of consent. I think that is the future direction of the Church—all parts moving together through, with, and under authority."[43] Such a hierarchy is the only authentic way of integrating the whole Christian Church while preserving its God-given diversity.

[43] Cited in Thomas Bokenkotter, *A Concise History of the Catholic Church*, rev. ed., 428.

Bibliography

Reference works are cited in "Abbreviations" in the front matter.

Adams, Marilyn McCord. *William Ockham.* Notre Dame, Ind.: University of Notre Dame Press, 1987.

Alberigo, Giuseppe, and Komonchak, Joseph A. *History of Vatican II,* vol. I. Maryknoll, N.Y.: Orbis, and Leuven: Peeters, 1995.

Appleby, R. Scott. "Crunch Time for American Catholicism." *The Christian Century* (April 3, 1996) 370–376.

Aquinas, Thomas. *Compendium of Theology.* Cyril Vollert, S.J., trans. ET *Light of Faith.* Manchester, N.H.: Sophia Institute Press, 1994.

———. *Summa Contra Gentiles.* Anton C. Pegis, trans. Notre Dame, Ind.: University of Notre Dame Press, 1975, 1955.

———. *Summa Theologiae.* New York: Blackfriars, McGraw Hill, 1964– .

Ash, James L. Jr. "The Decline of Ecstatic Prophecy in the Early Church." *TS* 37:2 (June, 1976) 227–252.

Aubert, Roger. "The Vatican Council." *History of the Church,* vol. VIII *(The Church in the Age of Liberalism).* Hubert Jedin, ed. New York: Crossroads, 1981, 315–334.

Augustine, St. *Confessions.* Henry Chadwick, trans. Oxford: Oxford University Press, 1992.

Bainton, Roland. *Here I Stand.* New York: Abingdon Press, 1950.

Bangert, William. *A History of the Society of Jesus.* St. Louis: Institute of Jesuit Sources, 1972.

Barraclough, Geoffrey. *The Medieval Papacy.* New York: Norton, 1968.

Barbour, Ian. *Religion in an Age of Science.* San Francisco: Harper, 1990.

Bassett, William. "Subsidiarity, Order, and Freedom in the Church," in James A. Coriden, ed., *The Once and Future Church.* Staten Island, N.Y.: Alba House, 1971, 259–264.

Baus, Karl, and others. *The Imperial Church from Constantine to the Middle Ages. History of the Church.* vol. II. Hubert Jedin and John Dolan, eds. New York: Crossroad, 1980.

Beck, Hans Georg, and others. *From the High Middle Ages to the Eve of the Reformation.* Montreal: Palm Publishers, 1970.

Becker, Carl. "Enlightenment," *Encyclopedia of the Social Sciences,* 5:547.

Benedict, St. *The Rule of St. Benedict.* Garden City, N.Y.: Doubleday, Image Books, 1975.

Berger, Peter. *A Rumor of Angels.* Garden City, N.Y.: Doubleday Anchor, 1969.

Berger, Peter, and Richard John Neuhaus. *To Empower People: The Role of Mediating Structures in Public Policy.* Washington, D.C.: American Enterprise Institute for Public Policy Research, 1977.

Berman, Morris. *The Reenchantment of the World.* New York: Bantam, 1984.

Bertalanffy, Ludwig. *Problems of Life.* New York: J. Wiley & Sons, 1952.

Bévenot, Maurice. "A Bishop is Responsible to God Alone," *Recherches de Science Religieuse* 39 (1951) 397–415.

Birch, Charles. *A Purpose for Everything.* Mystic; Conn.: Twenty Third Publications, 1990.

Blackwell, Richard. *Galileo, Bellarmine, and the Bible.* Notre Dame: University of Notre Dame Press, 1991.

Boadt, Lawrence. *Reading the Old Testament.* Mahwah, N.J.: Paulist Press, 1984.

Boff, Leonardo. *Ecclesiogenesis: the Base Communities Reinvent the Church.* New York: Maryknoll, Orbis Books, 1986.

Bokenkotter, Thomas. *A Concise History of the Catholic Church.* rev. ed. New York: Doubleday, 1977.

Boyett, Joseph, and Henry Conn. *Workplace 2000: The Revolution Reshaping American Business.* New York: Penguin, 1991.

Bradshaw, Paul F. *The Search for the Origins of Christian Worship.* Oxford: Oxford University Press, 1992.

Brown, Raymond E. *The Churches the Apostles Left Behind.* New York: Paulist Press, 1984.

____. *The Critical Meaning of the Bible.* New York: Paulist Press, 1981.

____. *The Death of the Messiah.* New York: Doubleday, 1994.

____. "The *Gospel of Peter* and Canonical Gospel Priority." *New Testament Studies* 33 (1987) 321–343.

____. *An Introduction to New Testament Christology.* N.Y.: Paulist Press, 1994.

____. *The Gospel according to John I–XII.* Garden City, N.Y.: Doubleday, 1966.

____. *New Testament Essays.* Milwaukee, Bruce, 1965.

____. *Priest and Bishop: Biblical Reflections.* New York: Paulist Press, 1970.

Brown, Raymond E., and John P. Meier. *Antioch and Rome: New Testament Cradles of Catholic Christianity.* New York: Paulist Press, 1983.

Brown, Raymond E., Karl P. Donfried, and John Reumann, eds. *Peter in the New Testament.* Minneapolis: Augsburg, 1973.

Bultmann, Rudolph. *Theology of the New Testament.* New York: Charles Scribner's Sons, 1951, 1955.

Burtchaell, James. *From Synagogue to Church.* Cambridge: Cambridge University Press, 1992.

Butler, C. *The Vatican Council.* 2 vols. London: Longmans, Green, & Co., 1930.

Caffrey, Thomas. "Consensus and Infallibility: the Mind of Vatican I," *The Downside Review* 88:291 (April, 1970) 107–131.

Callahan, Daniel, ed. *The Catholic Case for Contraception.* New York: Macmillan, 1969.

Campenhausen, Hans von. *Ecclesiastical Authority and Spiritual Power in the Church of the First Three Centuries.* London: Adam and Charles Black, 1969. German original: *Kirchliches amt und Geistliche Vollmacht,* 1953.

Canon Law Society of Great Britain and Ireland. *The Code of Canon Law in English Translation.* London: Collins, 1983.

Carlen, Claudia, ed. *The Papal Encyclicals, 1939–1958.* Wilmington, N.C.: McGrath Publishing Co., 1981.

Chadwick, Henry. "The Circle and the Ellipse," in Hans von Campenhausen and Henry Chadwick, *Jerusalem and Rome: the Problem of Authority in the Early Church.* Philadelphia: Fortress, 1966, 1959.

____. *The Early Christian Church.* New York: Penguin, 1967.

____. *The Role of the Christian Bishop in Ancient Society.* Berkeley: The Graduate Theological Union and University of California: Center for Hermeneutical Studies, Protocol of the Thirty-Fifth Colloquy, 1980, 1–14.

Childs, Brevard S. *Biblical Theology of the Old and New Testaments.* Minneapolis: Fortress, 1993.

Clarke, Norris. *Explorations in Metaphysics.* Notre Dame, Ind.: Notre Dame Press, 1944.

____. *Person and Being.* Milwaukee: Marquette University Press, 1993.

Congar, Yves. "La collégialité de l'épiscopat et la Primauté de l'évêque de Rome dans l'Histoire." *Angelicum* 47:4 (1970) 403–427.

____. "The Council as an Assembly and the Church as Essentially Conciliar." Herbert Vorgrimler, ed., *One, Holy, Catholic, and Apostolic.* London: Sheed and Ward, 1968.

____. *Lay People in the Church.* Westminster, Md.: Newman Press, 1957.

____. *L'Ecclésiologie du Haut Moyen-Age.* Paris: Cerf, 1968.

____. "L'ecclésiologie de la Révolution française au Concile du Vatican sous la signe de l'affirmation de l'authorité." M. Nédoncelle et al., *L'Ecclésiologie au XIX siècle.* Paris: Cerf, 1960.

____. *L'Église de Saint Augustin à l'époque moderne.* Paris: Cerf, 1970.

____. "The Historical Development of Authority in the Church." *Problems of Authority.* J.M. Todd, ed. London: Darton Longman & Todd, 1962.

____. *The Mystery of the Church.* Baltimore: Helicon Press, 1960.

____. *Power and Poverty in the Church.* Baltimore: Helicon Press, 1964.

____. "La 'Réception' comme réalité ecclésiologique." *Revue des Sciences Philosophiques et Théologiques* 56:3 (July, 1972) 369–403.

____. "Quod omnes tangit, ab omnibus tractari et approbari debet." *Révue historique droit française et étranger* (1958) 210–259.

Congar, Yves, and B.D. Dupuy. *L'Episcopat et L'Église Universelle.* Paris: Editions du Cerf, 1964.

Copleston, F.C. *A History of Philosophy.* Garden City, New York: Doubleday, Image, 1963.

Costigan, Richard F. "Bossuet and the Consensus of the Church." *TS* 56 (December 1995) 652–672.

Costigan, R. *Rohrbacher and the Ecclesiology of Ultramontanism.* Rome: Universita Gregoriana, 1980.

Courtenay, William J. "Nominalism and Late Medieval Religion," *The Pursuit of Holiness in Late Medieval and Renaissance Religion.* C. Trinkhaus and Heiko Oberman, eds. Leiden: E.J. Brill, 1974, 26–59.

Crick, Francis. *The Astonishing Hypothesis: the Scientific Search for the Soul.* New York: Charles Scribner's Sons, 1994.

Crossan, John Dominic. *The Historical Jesus: The Life of a Mediterranean Peasant.* San Francisco: Harper, 1991.

____. *Jesus: A Revolutionary Biography.* San Francisco: Harper, 1994.

Cyprian, St. *The Unity of the Catholic Church.* Maurice Bévenot, S.J., trans. Ancient Christian Writers Series, Westminster, Md.: Newman Press, 1957.

____. *The Letters of St. Cyprian of Carthage.* trans. and annotated by G.W. Clarke. Ancient Christian Writers Series #47. New York: Newman Press, 1989.

____. *Saint Cyprian: Letters.* Rose Bernard Donna, C.S.J., trans. Washington, D.C.: The Catholic University of America Press, 1964.

D'Arcy, M.C., *St. Augustine: His Age, Life, and Thought.* New York: Meridian, 1957.

Declerck, Paul. "'Lex orandi, lex credendi,' sens originel et avatars historiques d'un adage équivoque." *Questions liturgiques* 4 (1978) 193–212.

de Maistre, Joseph. *Du Pape.* Paris: Beaucé-Rusand, 1819.

de Vaux, O.P., Roland, *Ancient Israel,* vol. 2. *Religious Institutions.* New York: McGraw Hill, 1965.

DeVries, William. *Orient et Occident:* Les structures ecclésiales vues dans l'histoire des sept premiers conciles oecuméniques. Paris: Cerf, 1974.

Dickens, A.G. *The Counter Reformation.* New York: Norton, 1968.

Dionne, J. Robert. *The Papacy and the Church.* New York: Philosophical Library, 1987.

Dix, Gregory, ed. *The Treatise on the Apostolic Tradition of St. Hippolytus of Rome.* London: The Alban Press, 1992.

Duffy, Eamon. *The Stripping of the Altars: Traditional Religion in England 1400–1580.* New Haven: Yale University Press, 1992.

Dulles, Avery. *The Catholicity of the Church.* Oxford: Clarendon Press, 1985.

———. *A Church to Believe In.* New York: Crossroad, 1982.

———. *The Craft of Theology: From Symbol to System.* New York: Crossroad, 1992.

———. "The Ignatian Charism and Contemporary Theology," in *America* (April 26, 1997) 14–22.

———. "The Teaching Authority of Bishops' Conferences." *The Reshaping of Catholicism: Current Challenges in the Theology of the Church.* San Francisco: Harper & Row, 1988. 207–226.

Dvornik, Francis. *Byzantium and the Roman Primacy.* New York: Fordham, 1966.

———. *Early Christian and Byzantine Political Philosophy.* Washington, D.C.: Dumbarton Oaks Center for Byzantine Studies, 1966.

———. *The Ecumenical Councils.* New York: Hawthorne Books, 1961.

Ehler, Sidney, and John B. Morrall, eds. *Church and State through the Centuries.* Westminster, Md.: Newman Press, 1954.

Eisler, Riane. *The Chalice and the Blade.* San Francisco: Harper & Row, 1988.

Eliade, Mircea. *The Sacred and the Profane.* New York: Harcourt, Brace, & World, 1959.

Ellis, Peter F. *Matthew: His Mind and His Message.* Collegeville: The Liturgical Press, 1974.

Empie, Paul C., and T. Austin Murphy. *Papal Primacy and the Universal Church.* Minneapolis: Augsburg, 1974.

Englund, Steven. "L'Affaire Gaillot," *Commonweal* (October 6, 1995) 12–18.

Eno, Robert B., S.S. *The Rise of the Papacy.* Wilmington, Del.: Michael Glazier, 1990.

Eusebius. *The History of the Church, from Christ to Constantine.* George Williamson, trans. Minneapolis: Augsburg, 1965; Wilmington, Del.: Michael Glazier, 1980.

Fitzmyer, Joseph. *The Gospel According to Luke I–IX.* Garden City, N.Y.: Doubleday, 1981.

———. *Scripture, the Soul of Theology.* New York: Paulist Press, 1994.

Flannery, Austin, ed. *Vatican Council II: More Post-Conciliar Documents.* Collegeville: The Liturgical Press, 1982.

Florovsky, Georges. *Bible, Church, Tradition: an Eastern Orthodox View.* Belmont, Mass.: Nordland Publishing, 1972.

Franzen, August. "Council of Constance: Present State of the Problem," *Concilium* 7 (September 1965) 17–37.

Gaillardetz, Richard R. *Teaching with Authority: A Theology of the Magisterium in the Church.* Collegeville: The Liturgical Press, 1997.

Gay, Peter. *The Enlightenment: an Interpretation. The Rise of Modern Paganism.* New York: Random House, Vintage, 1966.

Gierke, Otto. *Political Theories of the Middle Ages.* Frederic W. Maitland, trans. Cambridge: Cambridge University Press, 1900; Boston: Beacon Press, 1958.

Giles, E., ed. *Documents Illustrating Papal Authority: A.D. 96–454.* London: SPCK, 1952.

Goodwin, Brian. "Developing Organisms as Self-Organizing Fields," *Mathematical Essays on Growth and the Emergence of Form.* Peter Antonelli, ed. (Edmonton: The University of Alberta Press, 1985) 185–199.

____. "Toward a Science of Qualities," *New Metaphysical Foundations of Modern Science.* Willis Harmon and Jane Clark, eds. Sausalito: Institute of Noetic Sciences, 1994, 215–250.

Granfield, Patrick. "Episcopal Elections in Cyprian: Clerical and Lay, Participation" *TS* 37:1 (March, 1976) 41–52.

____. *The Limits of the Papacy.* New York: Crossroad, 1987.

____. *The Papacy in Transition.* Garden City, New York: Doubleday, 1980.

Greenslade, S.L. *Schism in the Early Church.* London: SCM Press, 1953, 1964.

Grene, Marjorie. "Hierarchies in Biology." *American Scientist,* vol. 75 (1987) 505–510.

Griffiths, Bede. *The Cosmic Revelation: the Hindu Way to God.* Springfield, Ill.: Templegate Publishers, 1983.

Grillmeier, Aloys. Commentary on *Lumen gentium,* chap. 2. *Commentary on the Documents of Vatican II,* vol. 1, H. Vorgrimler, ed., 153–185.

Hardon, John A. "Robert Bellarmine's Conception of the Church," *Studies in Medieval Culture.* John Sommerfeldt, ed. Kalamazoo: The Medieval Institute, Western Michigan University, 1966, 120–127.

Hays, Richard B. "The Corrected Jesus," *First Things* (May, 1994) 43–48.

Hebblethwaite, Peter. "Brazilian Bishops 'True to Form' at World Synod." *National Catholic Reporter* (October 19, 1990) 9.

Hefele, C.J. and H. Leclerq. *Histoire des Conciles, d'apres les documents originaux.* Tome II. Paris: Letouzey et Anē, 1908.

Hendrix, Scott. *Luther and the Papacy: Stages in a Reformation Conflict.* Philadelphia: Fortress, 1981.

Hengel, Martin. *Acts and the History of Earliest Christianity.* Philadelphia: Fortress, 1979.

Hertling, S.J., Ludwig. *Communio. Church and Papacy in Early Christianity.* Chicago: Loyola University Press, 1972.

Hippolytus, St. *The Treatise on the Apostolic Tradition of St. Hippolytus of Rome.* Gregory Dix, ed.; reissued with corrections, preface, and bibliography by Henry Chadwick. London: The Alban Press, 1992.

Holder, Jack J. Jr., "Decision Making by Consensus." *Business Horizons* (April, 1972) 47–54.

Holmberg, Bengt. *Paul and Power.* Philadelphia: Fortress, 1978.

Huizinga, J. *The Waning of the Middle Ages.* New York: Doubleday, Anchor Books, 1954, 1949.

Hussey, J.M. *The Orthodox Church in the Byzantine Empire.* Oxford: Clarendon Press, 1986.

Ignatius Loyola, St. *The Autobiography of St. Ignatius Loyola.* John C. Olin, ed. New York: Harper Torchbooks, 1974.

____. *The Spiritual Exercises of St. Ignatius.* Anthony Mottola, trans. New York: Doubleday, Image Books, 1964.

Iserloh, Erwin, Joseph Glazik, and Hubert Jedin. "Reformation and Counter Reformation." *History of the Church,* vol. V. New York: Crossroad, 1990.

Jedin, Hubert. *A History of the Council of Trent,* vol. I. London: Thomas Nelson and Sons, 1957. German original, 1949.

Jeremias, Joachim. *New Testament Theology.* London: SCM, 1971.

John XXIII, Pope. *Mater et Magistra.* Glen Rock, N.J.: Paulist Press, 1961.

John Paul II, Pope. *Laborem Exercens.* Boston: St. Paul Editions, 1981.

____. Apostolic Letter: *Tertio Millennio Adveniente,* ET: *On the Coming of the Third Millennium.* Washington, D.C.: United States Catholic Conference, 1995.

____. *Ut Unum Sint,* Vatican translation. Boston: Pauline Books and Media, no date given.

Johnson, Luke T. *Decision Making in the Church.* Philadelphia: Fortress, 1983.

____. *The Real Jesus: The Misguided Quest for the Historical Jesus and the Truth of the Traditional Gospels.* San Francisco: Harper, 1996.

Kantorowicz, Ernst H. *The King's Two Bodies: a Study in Medieval Political Theology.* Princeton, N.J.: Princeton University Press, 1957.

Kasper, Walter. *The Christian Understanding of Freedom and the History of Freedom in the Modern Era: the Meeting and Confrontation Between Christianity and the Modern Era in a Postmodern Situation.* Milwaukee: Marquette University Press, 1988.

____. "The Church as Communio." *New Blackfriars* (May, 1993).

____. *Theology and Church.* New York: Crossroad, 1989.

Kelly, J.N.D. *Early Christian Creeds.* London: Longman, 1972.

____. *Early Christian Doctrines,* rev. ed. San Francisco: Harper & Row, 1978, 1960.

Kempf, Friedrich, and others, eds. *The Church in the Age of Feudalism.* New York: Herder & Herder, 1969.

Kesich, Veselin. "The Problem of Peter's Primacy in the New Testament and the Early Church," *St. Vladimir's Seminary Quarterly,* IV: 2–3 (1960) 2–25.

Kidd, B.J. *The Counter Reformation: 1550–1600.* London: Society for Promoting Christian Knowledge, 1933.

Kilmartin, Edward. "Reception in History: an Ecclesiological Phenomenon and its Significance." *Journal of Ecumenical Studies,* 21:1 (Winter, 1984) 34–54.

Koestler, Arthur. *The Sleepwalkers.* New York: Macmillan, 1959.

Koestler, Arthur, and J.R. Smythies, eds. *Beyond Reductionism.* Boston: Beacon Press, 1971.

Küng, Hans. *Structures of the Church.* New York: Thomas A. Nelson & Sons, 1964.

LaCugna, Catherine. *God for Us.* San Francisco: Harper, 1991.

Lane, George. *Christian Spirituality—an Historical Sketch.* Chicago: Loyola University Press, 1984.

Langford, J.J. *Galileo, Science, and the Church.* Ann Arbor: University of Michigan, 1971, 1992.

Lanne, Emmanuel. "The Local Church: its Catholicity and Apostolicity." *One in Christ* VI:3 (1970) 288–313.

____. "The Papacy and the Reformation: To What Extent Is Roman Primacy Unacceptable to the Eastern Churches?" *Concilium* 4:7 (April, 1971) 62–67.

Latourelle, René. *The Miracles of Jesus and the Theology of Miracles.* New York: Paulist Press, 1988.

Lawler, Michael. *Symbol and Sacrament: a Contemporary Sacramental Theology.* New York: Paulist Press, 1987.

Layzer, David. *Cosmogensesis.* New York: Oxford, 1990.

Leclerq, Jean. "Influence and Noninfluence of Dionysius in the Western Middle Ages." *Pseudo-Dionysius: the Complete Works.* New York: Paulist Press, 1987.

Leff, Gordon. *William of Ockham.* Manchester: Manchester University Press, 1975.

____. *The Dissolution of the Medieval Outlook.* New York: Harper, 1976.

Lienhard, Joseph T. *The Bible, the Church, and Authority.* Collegeville: The Liturgical Press, 1995.

Likert, Rensis. *New Patterns of Management.* New York: McGraw-Hill, 1961.

Lortz, Joseph. *The Reformation in Germany.* New York: Herder and Herder, 1968. German original, 1939.

Lovejoy, Arthur. *The Great Chain of Being.* Cambridge: Harvard University Press, 1936, 1964.

MacEoin, Gary. "Rome tries, fails to recolonize Latin church." *National Catholic Reporter* (November 13, 1992) 10–11.

Marot, Hilaire. "The Primacy and the Decentralization of the Early Church," *Concilium* 7:1 (September, 1965) 9–16.

____. "Unitē de l'Église et diversité géographique aux premiers siècles," *L'Épiscopat et L'Église Universelle.* Yves Congar and B.D. Dupuy, eds. Paris: Cerf, 1964, 565–590.

Martimort, Aimé-Georges. *Le Gallicanisme de Bossuet.* Paris: Cerf, Unam Sanctam #24, 1953.

Maximus Confessor. *Maximus Confessor, Selected Writings.* New York: Paulist Press, 1985.

McFague, Sallie. *Models of God.* Philadelphia: Fortress, 1987.

McCue, James. "The Roman Primacy in the Patristic Era: the Beginnings through Nicaea," *Papal Primacy and the Universal Church.* Paul C. Empie and T. Austin Murphy, eds. Minneapolis: Augsburg (1974) 44–72.

McKenzie, John. "Aspects of Old Testament Thought," *NJBC,* 1284–1315.

____. *Dictionary of the Bible.* New York: Macmillan, 1965.

McSorley, Harry. "Some Forgotten Truths about the Petrine Ministry," *Journal of Ecumenical Studies* 11:2 (Spring, 1974) 208–237.

Meier, John. *A Marginal Jew: Rethinking the Historical Jesus.* New York: Doubleday, vol. 1 (1991), vol. 2 (1994).

Mendenhall, G.E. "Covenant," David Noel Freedman, *ABD*, vol. 1.

———. "Covenant Forms in Israelite Tradition." *Biblical Archaeologist*, 17 (1954) 49–76.

Merchant, Carolyn. *The Death of Nature.* San Francisco: Harper & Row, 1980.

Mersch, Émile. *Le Corps Mystique du Christ.* Paris: Desclée de Brouwer, 1936; ET *The Whole Christ.* Milwaukee: Bruce, 1938.

Merton, Thomas. *Life and Holiness.* Garden City, N.Y.: Doubleday, Image, 1963.

Meyendorff, John. *Imperial Unity and Christian Divisions.* Crestwood, N.Y.: St. Vladimir's Seminary Press, 1989.

Meyendorff, John, and others, eds. *The Primacy of Peter.* London: The Faith Press, 1963.

Meyer, Ben. *The Aims of Jesus.* London: SCM Press, 1979.

Meyer, Harding, and Lukas Vischer, eds. *Growth in Agreement: Reported and Agreed Statements of Ecumenical Conversations on a World Level.* New York: Paulist Press; Geneva: World Council of Churches, 1984.

Möhler, Johann Adam. *Die Einheit in der Kirche oder Das Prinzip des Katholizismus.* J.R. Geiselmann, ed. Cologne: J. Hegner, 1956. ET *Unity in the Church.* Washington, D.C.: The Catholic University of America Press, 1996.

Moltmann, Jurgen. *The Trinity and the Kingdom.* San Francisco: Harper, 1981.

Monod, Jacques. *Chance and Necessity.* New York: Knopf, 1971.

Morris, Colin. *The Papal Monarchy: the Western Church from 1050 to 1250.* Oxford: Clarendon, 1989.

Morrison, Karl F. "The Gregorian Reform." *Christian Spirituality: Origins to the Twelfth Century.* Bernard McGinn, John Meyendorff, and Jean Leclercq, eds. New York: Crossroad, 1989.

Morrison, Karl F. *Tradition and Authority in the Western Church: 300–1140.* Princeton, N.J.: Princeton University Press, 1969.

Mossner, E.C. "Deism," *The Encyclopedia of Philosophy.* Vol. 2. New York: Macmillan (1967) 326–336.

Naughton, Michael T. "Participation in the Organization: An Ethical Analysis from the Papal Social Tradition." *Journal of Business Ethics* 14 (1995) 923–935.

Netanyahu, Benzion. *The Origins of the Inquisition in Fifteenth-Century Spain.* New York: Random House, 1995.

Newman, Katherine. "Incipient Bureaucracy: The Development of Hierarchies in Egalitarian Organizations," Gerald Britain and Ronald Cohen, eds. *Hierarchy and Society: Anthropological Perspectives on Bureaucracy.* Philadelphia: Institute for the Study of Human Issues (1980) 143–163.

Newton, Isaac. *Principia Mathematica.* ET, *Mathematical Principles of Natural Philosophy.* Great Books of the Western World, vol. 34. Chicago: Encyclopedia Brittanica, Inc., 1952.

Nicol, Donald. "The Papal Scandal." *The Orthodox Churches and the West.* Oxford: Basil Blackwell (1976) 141–168, 148–149.

Nichols, Terence. "Aquinas' Concept of Substantial Form and Modern Science." *International Philosophical Quarterly* (Fall, 1996).

Nicholson, Ernest W. *God and His People.* Oxford: Clarendon Press, 1986.

Oakley, Francis. *Council over Pope.* New York: Herder and Herder, 1969.

____. *The Western Church in the Later Middle Ages.* Ithaca, N.Y.: Cornell University Press, 1979.

Oberman, Heiko. *Forerunners of the Reformation.* New York: Holt, Rinehart, and Winston, 1966.

____. *The Harvest of Medieval Theology.* Cambridge: Harvard University Press, 1963.

O'Connor, D.W. *Peter in Rome.* New York: Columbia University Press, 1969.

O'Gara, Margaret. *Triumph in Defeat: Infallibility, Vatican I, and the French Minority Bishops.* Washington, D.C.: The Catholic University of America Press, 1988.

Olin, John C. *Catholic Reform from Cardinal Ximenes to the Council of Trent, 1495–1563.* New York: Fordham University Press, 1990.

O'Meara, Thomas. "The Raid on the Dominicans: the Repression of 1954," in *America* (February 5, 1994) 8ff.

Ozment, Stephen. *The Age of Reform.* New Haven: Yale University Press, 1980.

Papadakis, Aristeides. *The Christian East and the Rise of the Papacy.* Crestwood, New York: St. Vladimir's Seminary Press, 1994.

Patrides, C.A. "Hierarchy and Order," *Dictionary of the History of Ideas.* Philip Wiener, ed. vol. II. New York: Charles Scribner's Sons, 1973, 434–449.

Peacocke, Arthur. *Theology for a Scientific Age.* Minneapolis: Fortress, 1993.

Peterson, Eric. *Der Monotheismus als politisches Problem.* Leipzig: Jakob Hegner, 1935.

Pelikan, Jaroslav. *The Emergence of the Christian Tradition (100–600).* Chicago: University of Chicago Press, 1971.

____. "The Odyssey of Dionysian Spirituality," *Pseudo-Dionysius: the Complete Works.* New York: Paulist Press, Classics of Western Spirituality, 1987, 11–24.

____. *The Spirit of Eastern Christendom.* Vol. 2 of *The Christian Tradition: A History of the Development of Doctrine.* Chicago: University of Chicago Press, 1974.

Perrin, Norman. *Jesus and the Language of the Kingdom.* Philadelphia: Fortress, 1971.

Piepkorn, Arthur C. "The Roman Primacy in the Patristic Era: From Nicaea to Leo the Great," *Papal Primacy and the Universal Church.* Paul C. Empie and T. Austin Murphy, eds. Minneapolis: Augsburg, 1974, 73–97.

Pius XI, Pope. *Quadragesimo Anno.* ET from Michael Walsh and Brian Davies, *Proclaiming Justice and Peace.* Mystic, Conn.: Twenty-Third Publications, 1991, 41–80.

Pius XII, Pope. *Mystici Corporis Christi.* ET, Claudia Carlen, ed. *The Papal Encyclicals, 1939–1958.* Wilmington, N.C.: McGrath Publishing Co., 1981.

Polanyi, Michael. *Knowing and Being.* Chicago: University of Chicago Press, 1969.

Pritchard, James, ed. *The Ancient Near East: an Anthology of Texts and Pictures.* Princeton: Princeton University Press, 1958.

Pseudo-Dionysius. *Pseudo-Dionysius: the Complete Works.* New York: Paulist Press, Classics of Western Spirituality, 1987.

Quinn, Jerome D. *The Letter to Titus.* New York: Doubleday, The Anchor Bible, 1988.

Quinn, John R. "The Exercise of the Primacy: Facing the Cost of Christian Unity." *Commonweal* (July 12, 1996) 11–20.

Rahner, Karl. "The Charismatic Element in the Church." *The Dynamic Element in the Church.* New York: Herder & Herder, 1964.

____. *Hominisation.* New York: Herder and Herder, 1965. German original, 1958.

Reumann, John. *The Supper of the Lord.* Philadelphia: Fortress, 1985.

Richardson, Cyril, ed. *Early Christian Fathers.* New York: Macmillan, 1970, 1979.

Ringgren, Helmer. *Israelite Religion.* Philadelphia: Fortress Press, 1966.

Runciman, Steven. *The Eastern Schism.* Oxford: Clarendon, 1955.

Russell, Bertrand. "A Free Man's Worship" (December, 1903). Reprinted in *Mysticism and Logic.* Great Britain: 1917; Garden City, New York: Doubleday, Anchor paperback, no date, 44–54.

Ryan, Seamus. "Vatican II: the Rediscovery of the Episcopate" *The Irish Theological Quarterly,* 33 (July, 1966) 208–241.

Salthe, Stanley. *Evolving Hierarchical Systems.* New York: Columbia University Press, 1985.

Sanders, E.P. *Jesus and Judaism.* Philadelphia: Fortress, 1985.

Schmemann, Alexander. "The Idea of Primacy in Orthodox Ecclesiology." *The Primacy of Peter.* J. Meyendorff and others, eds. Bedfordshire: The Faith Press, 1963, 7–56.

Schroeder, H.J., ed. *The Canons and Decrees of the Council of Trent.* St. Louis, Ill., 1941.

Schweizer, Eduard. *The Lord's Supper According to the New Testament.* Philadelphia: Fortress, 1967.

Sellers, R.V. *The Council of Chalcedon.* London: SPCK, 1961.

Sheldrake, Rupert. *A New Science of Life.* London: Anthony Blond, 1985.

____. *The Presence of the Past.* New York: Vintage, 1988.

Schüssler Fiorenza, Elisabeth. *Jesus: Miriam's Child, Sophia's Prophet.* New York: Continuum, 1994.

____. *In Memory of Her.* New York: Crossroad, 1983.

Shannon, William H. "Are There Any More Priests Out There?" *America* (October 12, 1991) 241.

Smith, Huston. *Forgotten Truth.* New York: Harper & Row, 1976.

Sperry, Roger. "The New Mentalist Paradigm and Ultimate Concern," *Perspectives in Biology and Medicine* (Spring, 1986).

Stahel, Thomas. "A Tale of Two Cities: Rome and Santo Domingo." *America* (November 28, 1992) 419.

Steinfels, Margaret O'Brien. "Dissent and Communion." *Commonweal* (November 18, 1994) 9–15.

Stormon, E.J., *Towards the Healing of Schism: the Sees of Rome and Constantinople.* New York: Paulist Press, 1987.

Suenens, Léon Joseph. *Coresponsibility in the Church.* New York: Herder and Herder, 1968.

Sullivan, Francis. *Magisterium.* Mahwah, N.J.: Paulist Press, 1983.

Sweetser, Thomas. "The Parish: What has Changed, What Remains?" *America* (February 17, 1996) 6–7.

Tappert, Theodore G., ed. *The Book of Concord: the Confessions of the Evangelical Lutheran Church.* Philadelphia: Fortress, 1959.

Theissen, Gerd. *Sociology of Early Palestinian Christianity.* Philadelphia: Fortress, 1978.

Tierney, Brian. "Collegiality in the Middle Ages," *Concilium* 7 (September, 1965).

____. *Foundations of the Conciliar Theory.* Cambridge: Harvard University Press, 1955.

____. *Origins of Papal Infallibility: 1150–1350.* Leiden: E.J. Brill, 1972.

Tillard, J.-M.R. *The Bishop of Rome.* Wilmington, Del.: Michael Glazier, 1983.

____. *Church of Churches.* Collegeville: The Liturgical Press, 1992.

Toynbee, Arnold, and Jane Caplan. *A Study of History.* Oxford: Oxford University Press, 1972.

Tregoe, Benjamin, and Peter Tobia. "Strategy and the New American Organization." *Industry Week* (August 6, 1990) 28–31.

Ullman, Walter. *The Growth of Papal Government in the Middle Ages.* London: Methuen, 1955.

____. "Leo I and the Theme of Papal Primacy." *Journal of Theological Studies* 11 (1960) 25–51.

Verkhovskoy, Serge. "The Highest Authority in the Church." *Saint Vladimir's Seminary Quarterly* IV (1960) 76–88.

Vermes, Geza. *Jesus and the World of Judaism.* Philadelphia: Fortress Press, 1983.

____. *The Religion of Jesus the Jew.* Minneapolis: Fortress, 1993.

Viviano, Benedict T. *The Kingdom of God in History.* Wilmington, Del.: Michael Glazier, 1988.

Vorgrimler, Herbert, ed. *Commentary on the Documents of Vatican II.* 5 vols. New York: Herder and Herder, 1967–1969.

Ware, Timothy. *The Orthodox Church.* New York: Penguin, 1980, 1963.

Weiss, Paul. "The Living System." Koestler and Smythies, 3–55.

Weber, Max. *Economy and Society: an Outline of Interpretive Sociology.* Guenther Roth and Claus Wittich, eds. 3 vols. New York: Bedminster, 1968.

____. "Politics as a Vocation." From *Max Weber: Essays in Sociology.* H.H. Gerth and C. Wright Mills, eds. New York: Oxford, 1946.

Welker, Michael. "Creation: Big Bang or the Work of Seven Days," *Theology Today,* 52:4 (July, 1995) 173–185.

Wilber, Ken. *Sex, Ecology, and Spirituality.* Boston & London: Shambhala, 1995.

Wiles, Maurice, and Mark Santer. *Documents in Early Christian Thought.* Cambridge: Harvard University Press, 1975.

Wittberg, Patricia. *The Rise and Decline of Catholic Religious Orders.* Albany: SUNY Press, 1994.

Wojtyla, Karol. *The Acting Person.* Dordrecht: D. Reidel, 1979; Polish original, *Osoba i Czyn.* Cracow, 1969.

Wood, Susan. "The Sacramentality of Episcopal Consecration," *TS* 51 (1990) 479–496.

Wright, John H., *The Order of the Universe in the Theology of St. Thomas Aquinas.* Rome: Gregorian University, 1957.

Yoder, John H., ed. *The Legacy of Michael Sattler.* Scottsdale, Penn.: Herald Press, 1973.

Young, William, J., ed. *Letters of St. Ignatius of Loyola.* Chicago, 1959.

Yu, Carver T. "The principle of relativity as a conceptual tool in theology." *Science and Theology: Questions at the Interface.* Murray Rae, Hilary Regan, and John Stenhouse, eds. Grand Rapids: William B. Eerdmans, 1994, 180–210.

Zizioulas, John. *Being as Communion.* Crestwood, New York: St. Vladimir's Seminary Press, 1985.